# AN INTRODUCTION TO
# EUROPEAN
# LEGAL HISTORY

BY

## O. F. ROBINSON, T. D. FERGUS and W. M. GORDON
(Department of Legal History, University of Glasgow)

Ross M. Clark

University of Dundee

## PROFESSIONAL BOOKS LIMITED
## 1985

*Published in 1985 by*
*Professional Books Limited,*
*Milton Trading Estate, Abingdon, Oxon.,*
*and printed in Great Britain by*
*Redwood Burn Ltd, Trowbridge*

ISBN:  0-86205-107-X  Hardback
       0-86205-108-8  Paperback

# EUROPEAN LEGAL HISTORY

Contents        i

A: Roman Law and the Roman Empire: Roman Law and the jurists; The
Corpus Iuris Civilis; Vulgar Roman law in the West; Sources of Church
law; The Germanic codes; The Church of Gregory the Great; From the
ancient to the mediaeval world; The Lombards.
B: The Formation of Europe: The early Carolingians and Charlemagne; The
successors of Charlemagne; Education, law and trade; The Empire in
Germany; The Investiture Contest; Eleventh century recovery.

Definition of feudalism; Feudal law and customary law; The personal
bond; Tenure; Delegation of governmental powers; Judicial proceedings;
Feudal society and the rest of society; The formalization of feudalism;
Feudal law and academic law: the literature of feudal law.

The background to the revival of the study of Roman law; The importance
of the Glossators; Approaches to handling the texts; Methods of
teaching; Forms of literature: glosses and apparatus of glosses; The
Accursian Gloss and its influence; Other forms of literature; Legal
education becomes formalized.

The period of transition and the Post-Glossators; The Ultramontani;
Their approach to the texts; The Commentators and their teaching
methods; The literature of the Commentators; Roman law in use by the
Commentators.

The importance of canon law; Canon law in the eleventh century; Gratian

and the Decretists; The Decretals; The Decretalists; The canonists and
the theory of the 'just war'; The local application of canon law; Canon
law procedure; Substantive canon law.

legislation in Germany.

## Acknowledgements

The other two authors owe much to Bill Gordon, who created the course in European Legal History at the University of Glasgow, and who persuaded his sometimes reluctant colleagues that the study of the later history of Roman law was as important as Roman law itself. Olivia took the initiative in finding a publisher for the book in prospect, and has effectively applied her enthusiasm to the arduous task of putting all the contributions into final shape. She appears deservedly as first author.

Among many others who have made comments or criticisms, and especially our students, we owe particular thanks to: J.H. Baker, E. Bund, R.C. van Caenegem, M.T. Clanchy, I.B. Cowan, B. Dietz, A.A.M. Duncan, J. Durkan, R. Feenstra, J. Gaudemet, R.H. Helmholz, F. Hutchison, J.P. Larner, H.L. MacQueen, A.H. Manchester, A.E. Orücü, D.J. Osler, R.E.S. Robinson, D. Sellar, J.A. Clarence Smith, P. Stein, D.M. Walker, C.P. Wormald and J. Wormald. The noble work of Mrs. Simpson, our secretary, must be apparent to the reader and we are most grateful for her skills and patience.

Translations are by the authors, except where otherwise indicated.

# INTRODUCTION

Geographically, European legal history is primarily concerned with those countries of western Europe that share a common legal heritage, based on the mingling of Roman and canon law - the learned law - with feudalism and customary law. It therefore excludes eastern Europe as defined by the one-time supremacy of Islamic rule or of the Orthodox rather than the Catholic Church although there are of course elements common to east and west, such as the influence of Roman law. Again, although Ireland and Scandinavia are part of western Christendom, neither shared fully in the developments in legal thinking and legal practice which had such profound effects on most of the West. Nor did England share fully in them, but her close ties with France and with Scotland make the anomaly of her isolation worth investigating; moreover, through her colonies overseas England in many cases provided the image of Europe to other cultures. The focus, however, will be on the heart of Europe, the Italian peninsula, France and Germany (that is, the German speaking lands of the Holy Roman Empire).

European legal history is more than the histories of the individual legal systems of the modern European states, although one could argue that the very existence of European legal history may be proved from these individual histories. Historical introductions to their own systems, whether written for Austrian or Spanish, French or German or any other continental students, all feature background chapters on Roman law and its reception and on the influence of the canon law, as well as on customary law and feudalism, before they describe the growth of a national system. Then in their turn Humanism, Natural Law and codification exercised a greater or lesser influence on the shape taken by the particular judicial institutions and procedures. For all the countries of the civilian tradition their classification as such is valid because much of their legal history concerns the interpretation and adaptation of the chief monument of Roman law, the _Corpus Iuris Civilis,_ to fit new circumstances, to match local needs, to form new blends of law. This constant re-interpretation only ceased to be central to legal development after the codifications of the eighteenth and nineteenth centuries, which culminated in the German civil code, the BGB, which came into force in 1900, and the Swiss civil code, the ZGB of 1911. This is one reason why our history stops there; the other is that books on modern law tend to give a brief description of events since the First World War as a background to their treatment of current law and existing institutions. Our last chapter is a brief attempt to bridge any gap that might yawn here.

Among lawyers we hope to interest not only legal historians but also those who are interested in comparative institutions and in the history of ideas; the community of background may surprise the English lawyer. It cannot be unprofitable, in the era of the European Communities, to look behind the trivial details of the harmonization of noise levels on powered lawn mowers or of the permitted ingredients in beer, to the common traditions of the member states. Inevitably we deal mainly with judicial institutions, with the sources of law and with the interpretation of law rather than with the rules of substantive law. It would be difficult to give an overall picture by the latter means, and the detail required would be a deterrent to all but the enthusiast. The published work on the history of some of these rules is mentioned in the Further Reading or the Bibliography.

For the historian law is one aspect of society and it is pervasive;

indeed, for the mediaevalist it is unavoidable. Furthermore, although specific rules of law may be technical and seem dry, many great minds in the past have seen society in terms of its legal organization; much philosophy and political theory has only been conceivable in terms of law. While law may often be the means by which a ruling class can safeguard its position, law is also the means by which justice can be achieved, or at least sought; laws may be oppressive, but the absence of the rule of law is more so.

Our stage, then, is western Europe; our time-span extends from the Roman Empire to the German Empire. Our perceptions, our prejudices and our approaches arise from our Scottish standpoint. We have taught European Legal History as a one-year course at the University of Glasgow for more than a decade, and this book is in the first place an attempt to meet the demands of our students. It is a textbook, not a work of original scholarship. There is a need for a general survey and this is, for the English language, a pioneering work. We hope that it will provide a sketch for many, and for some an introduction from which they can proceed to more detailed studies. This is why at the end of every chapter there is Further Reading, which is limited to the English language and to works which are explanatory rather than engaged in scholarly argument. There is also a Select Bibliography to ease the further investigation of any topic. This includes not only standard works of reference but also books in other languages which we have used in our teaching and research. It is obvious that, even with three of us, many areas we have dealt with can be known to us only at second hand through the specialized work of scholars from many countries. We are conscious of our debt.

A subsidiary point arises from the fact that this is a textbook:

style in nomenclature. Since most mediaeval writing was in Latin, people were generally known by the Latin form of their names, but some mediaeval figures are to be identified in the language of the state from which they came, and others are so well known that their name is translated into the relevant modern usage. After much thought we have decided that we shall be inconsistent. Most names are given in their Latin forms and those that are not will be found by cross-reference in the Index. (Perhaps it is as well to point out here that mediaeval persons are normally known by their Christian name.) Where one form is more familiar - Azo - we have used that rather than the more correct Azzo; similarly we have referred to Peter Abelard and Thomas Aquinas. Other names seem to fall naturally into a vernacular: Jacques de Révigny and Pierre de Belleperche rather than Jacobus de Ravaniis and Petrus de Bellapertica. English historians customarily talk about William Longchamps although he would have been known as Guillaume de Longchamps or Guillelmus de Longo Campo. We have therefore translated common names like John or Peter into English, except where familiar usage is very strongly the other way, as with Johannes Andreae. We hope that double entries - or even treble - in the Index will ward off confusion; there is unfortunately no authoritative list of mediaeval jurists, or even of the relatively few we have mentioned in our text. The Bibliography explains the citations we have used for learned journals, etc., in our footnotes and in the Further Reading; works listed in the latter are given in abbreviated form when they occur in footnotes of the relevant chapter, or subsequently.

It would have been impossible within the reasonable constraints of space and cost to provide an adequate number of maps; we therefore strongly recommend the use of a good historical atlas.

Some dates (many approximate) in European legal history

| | | | |
|---|---|---|---|
| St. Augustine | 354-430 | College of Justice | 1532 |
| fall of the West | 455 | Budé, Guillaume | 1467-1540 |
| Lex Romana Visigothorum | 506 | Vitoria, Francisco de | 1483-1546 |
| Corpus Iuris Civilis | 529-34 | Alciatus | 1492-1550 |
| Pope Gregory the Great | 590-604 | Council of Trent | 1545-63 |
| Fuero Juzgo | 681 | Dumoulin, Charles | 1500-66 |
| battle of Poitiers | 732 | Agustín, Antonio | 1516-86 |
| Charlemagne, Emperor | 800-14 | Cujas, Jacques | 1522-90 |
| Alfred of Wessex | 871-99 | Hotman, François | 1524-90 |
| Otto I, Emperor | 936-73 | Craig, Sir Thomas | 1538-1608 |
| Canossa | 1077 | Loysel, Antoine | 1566-1627 |
| Concordat of Worms | 1122 | Grotius | 1583-1645 |
| Irnerius | c1055-1130 | Vinnius | 1588-1657 |
| Gratian's Decretum | 1140 | Carpzov, Benedikt | 1595-1666 |
| Libri Feudorum compiled | c1150 | Hobbes, Thomas | 1588-1679 |
| David I of Scotland | 1124-53 | Pufendorf, Samuel | 1632-94 |
| Henry II of England | 1154-89 | Stair, Lord | 1619-95 |
| Sachsenspiegel | c1220 | Stryk, Samuel | 1640-1710 |
| Azo | 1150-1230 | Voet, Johann | 1647-1713 |
| Liber Extra | 1234 | Thomasius, Christian | 1655-1728 |
| Accursius | 1185-1263 | Heineccius | 1681-1741 |
| Las Siete Partidas | c1265 | Bynkershoek, C. van | 1673-1743 |
| Bracton | d.1268 | Wolff, Christian | 1679-1754 |
| Louis IX of France | 1226-70 | Erskine, John | 1695-1768 |
| Durantis, Speculator | 1237-96 | Pothier, Robert Joseph | 1699-1772 |
| Philippe de Beaumanoir | d.1296 | Blackstone, Sir William | 1723-80 |
| Jacques de Révigny | d. c1296 | ALR (Prussian code) | 1794 |
| Liber Sextus | 1298 | Code Civil | 1804 |
| Pierre de Belleperche | d.1308 | ABGB (Austrian code) | 1811 |
| Regiam Majestatem | c1310 | Bentham, Jeremy | 1748-1832 |
| Cinus de Pistoia | 1270-1336 | Bell, George Joseph | 1770-1843 |
| Consolato del Mare (mostly) | 1343 | Savigny, F.C. von | 1779-1861 |
| Johannes Andreae | d.1348 | Windscheid, B. | 1817-92 |
| Bartolus | 1314-57 | Jhering, Rudolf von | 1818-92 |
| Baldus | 1327-1400 | BGB (German code) | 1900 |
| Reichskammergericht | 1494 | Swiss Code | 1911 |

Chapter I

## THE BACKGROUND

This chapter is essentially introductory. Its main purpose is to indicate the extent of continuity between ancient and mediaeval worlds, particularly in the legal field but also in institutions of government and in the Church. Moreover, the events of these 'Dark Ages' affected deeply the structures and habits we find when we emerge into the enlightenment of the twelfth century, and therefore an attempt must be made to give a brief account of the confused history of these times. Nevertheless, legal history is our concern, and for Europe that really starts around 1050.

### A: Roman Law and the Roman Empire

(i) Roman law and the jurists

In the Roman Republic, which is generally reckoned to have ended in 27 B.C., there were men of the upper classes who specialized not so much in acting on others' behalf in courts of law (as did orators like Cicero) as in giving advice on legal matters. Self-selected by their interest in the law and because this was an acceptable method of taking part in public life, the jurists discussed and, more importantly, wrote about legal problems. Jurists as a class continued to function in the Empire, although gradually the development of the law became integrated into the machinery of government. In the earlier Empire, the Principate, the period of classical law, jurists advised parties to litigation, they advised the lay judges who decided cases on the facts, and they advised the magistrates with jurisdictional competence, such as the Urban Praetor, who laid down the legal issues which went to the trial judges. Legislation in the strict sense, the passing of statutes, by the Republican assemblies and later by the Senate, was a relatively unimportant source of private law; more important were the formal edicts issued by the magistrates, in particular that of the Urban Praetor, which set out the legal remedies available, and of which the contents seem to have been largely dictated by the jurists. Not surprisingly, as the emperors' rôle came clearly to be that of the chief magistrate and as they acquired a jurisdiction both at first instance and on appeal, they too called on the legal expertise of the jurists, and included such men in their councils. Thus the jurists' rôle, although becoming institutionalized, was as important in the Principate as in the Republic. As late as the early third century there were still individual jurists who were experts with identifiable habits of thought and with independence of mind, but all those of whom we know at this period were also functionaries in the imperial administration. The last major jurist, Ulpian, was killed in 223 when holding the office of Praetorian Prefect, the highest office under the Emperor.

Juristic writings included general commentaries and monographs and also some elementary works, but to a great extent their typical form was casuistic, collections of opinions or problems, in which the jurist argued his way to a particular solution. For example: "A number of people were playing at ball, and one of them pushed a small slave-boy who was trying to pick the ball up, and the boy fell and broke his leg. The question was put whether the slave-boy's owner could raise an action under the lex Aquilia [on damage to property] against the man whose push had caused the fall. I gave the opinion that he could not, since the thing seemed to have happened more by mischance than through fault." This particular text (D. 9,2,52,4 Alfenus, Digest book 2) comes from the compilation of juristic writings

2

known as the Digest, published in A.D. 533 on the orders of the Emperor Justinian. Such an approach leaves room for discussing what degree of roughness would take the incident out of the class of simple accident and make it culpable, whether the answer would have been different if the slave-boy had been forbidden to be near, and so on. It was later to provide scope for widespread development to fit very different circumstances.

The third century was a period of economic crisis and political turbulence -- in the first 262 years of the Roman Empire there were some twenty-five emperors, and then in the next 50 years a further twenty-one. This ended the stability and self-assurance which had permitted individual jurists to have an authority of their own without casting any doubt on the reality of imperial power. The Codex Gregorianus and the Codex Hermogenianus, unofficial collections of imperial legislation, presumably reflect their compilers' names, and we also hear of a jurist called Innocentius who worked under Diocletian (284-305), but thereafter, although there must have been individuals who were acknowledged experts, none are on record; they are veiled behind the various offices of the imperial administration. Stability was restored, but at the price of overtly autocratic government. Only under the Emperor Justinian (527-65), the restorer of the ancient law, do we again learn something of the careers of certain major jurists of his time. (And by his time much of the West had fallen, and the Empire was centred on Constantinople, modern Istanbul.)

(ii) The Corpus Iuris Civilis

Justinian was determined to restore the former glory of the Empire by reconquering Africa from the Vandals and Italy from the Ostrogoths, and in particular by recovering the city of Rome, but his work in restoring Rome's legal glories was largely independent of the military ventures. Indeed, the lawyers he employed to compile the Corpus Iuris Civilis, as it came to be called, all came from the Eastern half of the Empire and will have been Greek speakers; nevertheless Justinian clearly saw himself as in the tradition of his imperial predecessors, back to Hadrian and Augustus.

The contents of the Corpus Iuris Civilis are fourfold: the Institutions (or Institutes), expressly issued as an elementary textbook for first year students of law; the Digest, a compilation of edited juristic writings, dating from the very late Republic to the mid third century; the Code, a collection of imperial constitutions, that is, edicts and judicial decisions, from the time of Hadrian (A.D. 117-38) on, although only a handful comes from before Septimius Severus (193-211); and the Novels, which were Justinian's own constitutions subsequent to the publication, in 533-4, of the other three parts - of them there was never an official, definitive collection. The continuing usefulness of the Corpus as a source of law lies not only in its rich store of ideas, but also in its bringing together different views and arguments, showing law as something dynamic, not as mere rules. The jurists frequently cited their predecessors and the Code is arranged chronologically within each title (which deals with a particular topic), so that developing concepts can be traced as the facts in a particular case were distinguished from previous, apparently similar, circumstances. However, on the instructions of Justinian, the compilers edited both the juristic extracts and the imperial constitutions; thus the law preserved in the Corpus is neither the authentic law of the classical period of Roman law, that is, of the Principate, nor a simple statement of the law of Justinian's own day, but a layered amalgam, which ignored many of the immediately post-classical

4

changes.  The _Institutes_, the _Digest_, and the _Code_[1] were officially brought into force in Italy by the Pragmatic Sanction of 554, when Italy rejoined the territories under Justinian's effective control.


(iii) Vulgar Roman law in the West


However, although the _Corpus_ was of authority within Justinian's realm and that of his successors, that is, within the Byzantine state (as we shall know it in the succeeding period), it was not the law that was known to and practised by most Romans in the western half of the Empire.  In A.D. 212 an edict known as the _constitutio Antoniniana_ had extended Roman citizenship to practically all free inhabitants of the Empire.  There is no complete agreement on what its consequences were for the law. Theoretically, the existing principle of personality of law (that the law you use depends on your personal status) should have meant that everyone thereafter used Roman law, that is, the traditional law of the citizens of Rome, but probability and some positive evidence argue against this.  An increase in the use of Roman law, even in the civilized urban centres of the East which had their own legal systems, can be postulated.  In the western part of the Empire, where there was seldom a pre-existing legal system able to withstand Roman law, the latter seems to have become the sole régime, but it was undoubtedly modified by local custom.  In view of the enormous expansion in the number of persons subject to Roman law and of the political upheavals of the third century, there was a widespread desire

----------

1        Conventionally cited as _Inst._, D., and C., followed by number of
         book, of title, and of juristic fragment or law -- and often of
         sentence; hence the opening extract from the _Digest_ is D. 1, 1, 1.

for simplification and certainty.  Men thought it more important to get a decision that could be given effect at once than to seek the ideal solution.  In the late third century therefore elementary legal books were published with this aim in mind; there survive epitomes of the _Institutes_ of Gaius, the _Regulae_ of Ulpian, the _Sententiae_ of Paul (all jurists of the classical period) and then, a little later, in the early fourth century, selections from some of the leading jurists of the past, known as the _Vatican Fragments_ (because found in a MS in the Vatican library) and the _Collatio legum Mosaicarum et Romanarum_ (_Comparison of Mosaic and Roman laws_).  Their acceptance as the working manuals of the courts is one aspect of the vulgarization of law, which also showed itself in such things as, for example, the blurring of the previously clear conceptual distinction between ownership and possession.

The Later Roman Empire, or Dominate, began under the Emperor Constantine a century after the **constitutio Antoniniana**.  Thereafter the only active source of law was imperial legislation; all legal authority, whether making or applying the law, stemmed explicitly from the emperor. In the fifth century, Theodosius II (408-50), emperor in the East, had a project to codify the whole law; as far as juristic work was concerned it came to nothing, but a collection was made of imperial constitutions issued since Constantine, the first Christian emperor.  This was published in 438, in both East and West, as the _Theodosian Code_.  Although there was little of vulgarized substantive law in this Code, it is notable for its stress on status and its relative neglect of contract -- foreshadowing the mediaeval world.  Furthermore, custom was recognized as a source of law, provided that it was not in conflict with reason or with statute.  This meant local custom rather than the **mos maiorum**, the ancestral custom of Rome; it meant, therefore, the usages of the Greek speakers of the East, and the traditions

6

of the recently enfranchised tribesmen, perhaps even of barbarian _foederati_ (allies).

The other new element in the fourth century was the introduction of Christianity as the official religion of the state. The early Church had been localized and predominantly Greek speaking, with its leading centres in the Near East and Asia Minor. Now, despite Constantine's shift of the administrative capital of the Empire away from Rome to his new eastern city of Constantinople, the Church in the West came rapidly to prominence. The foundation of a legal order for the government of the Church can conveniently be dated to 325, to the General Council of Nicaea; the western Church in a sense came of age around 404 by which time, in the _Vulgate_ of St. Jerome, the whole _Bible_ was translated into Latin from the original Hebrew and Greek. The fourth century was crucial in the establishment of a structured organization in the Church which enabled it not only to play a vital rôle in legal history in the distant future, but also to do so in the fifth century when the western provinces were invaded by German tribes from across the frontiers, settled by them, and step by step withdrawn from imperial control. These German peoples were all Christian, although some held views condemned by Rome and Constantinople as heretical, and so they conformed, at least in theory, to the laws of the Church; they also made use of Roman structures, including ecclesiastical ones, in their administration.

(iv) Sources of church law

The sources of authority to which the Church looked at this stage were partly devotional and partly juridical or administrative. In the first group were the _Bible_ itself, other works recording the apostolic tradition,

7

the writings of the Fathers of the Church, and the literature of the early saints and martyrs; to these were to be added the teachings of the Doctors of the Church. (The four great Latin Doctors are Saints Ambrose (c.334-97), Jerome (342-420), Augustine (354-430), and, much later, Gregory (540-604).)

Among the sources of juridical or administrative nature were the conclusions, or canons, of church councils, the decisions of bishops, and on occasion the secular law, at that period Roman law. While all conciliar canons carried weight, the canons of General Councils of the whole Church, also known as Ecumenical Councils, had the greatest authority, as the public expression of the collective mind of the whole Church[2]; these early ones were backed by imperial authority, for the emperors viewed themselves as exercising a quasi-episcopal function. The Council of Nicaea of 325 was the first; its main business was the condemnation of the Arian heresy, which denied the true Godhead of Christ[3]. Second was the Council of Constantinople in 381, which confirmed the Nicene creed as defining the Catholic faith, and also gave the bishop of Constantinople primacy of honour after the bishop of Rome, "because Constantinople is New Rome". The third, the Council of Ephesus in 431, was largely engaged in condemning

-----------

2    General Councils are referred to by the place of their meeting and a
     Roman numeral, e.g. IV Lateran (or Lateran IV) is the fourth held
     in the great basilica of St. John Lateran, cf. Vatican II.

3    The Nicene creed is the product of this Council: "And we believe in
     one Lord Jesus Christ, the only begotten Son of God, born of the
     Father before time began; God from God, light from light, true God
     from true God; begotten not made, one in essence with the Father,
     through whom all things were made."

Nestorius, bishop of Constantinople, for his denial of the single personality of Christ; Nestorius was deposed by Cyril, bishop of Alexandria, with the aid of Celestine, bishop of Rome. The Council of Chalcedon in 451 was the fourth; it was for this Council that one of the earliest collections of ecclesiastical law, the Didascalia (Teachings), was produced in a Latin version. As well as General Councils there were provincial councils, meetings of the bishops and clergy of one Roman province or of a group, for example Gaul; their canons often referred only to events within the province, but some were seen as of universal validity. Diocesan councils, more commonly called synods, were naturally of still less weight, being concerned usually only with local matters.

The decisions of bishops also varied in authority. Of most importance in the Early Church were the five patriarchs, the bishops of Rome (the word Pope is only the late Latin papa or father), Constantinople, Alexandria, Antioch, and Jerusalem; each exercised a superior jurisdiction. In the West, Rome's formal primacy was unchallenged, although while St. Ambrose was bishop of Milan he was the effective leader of Christendom, partly because Milan was then the western imperial capital (Rome's site was strategically unsuitable for countering the 'barbarian' invasions). During the fifth century Rome's primacy of honour became juridical supremacy in the West, a step made easier by the separation of eastern and western halves of the Empire even before the disintegration of the latter. Pope Celestine I (422-32), who had taken part in the deposition of Nestorius, an eastern patriarch, set up the principle of appeals to Rome from the western provinces, and this appellate jurisdiction was confirmed in A.D. 445 by the Emperor Valentian III (Nov. Val. 17). Leo I (440-61), the Great, by his personal character and ability strengthened the position of Rome as the see of St. Peter, the holder of the keys of Heaven and Hell. A year after playing a leading rôle at the Council of Chalcedon, he negotiated with the invading Huns led by Attila, and induced them to withdraw beyond the Danube.  In 455, although he was unable to stop the Vandals occupying Rome, he was able to prevent any serious bloodshed.  The Papacy was not yet exercising direct and active control over the (Western) Church, but Leo could write (in a letter of 10 August, 446) to certain African bishops: "Rome gives the solution to all cases submitted to her; these solutions take the form of judgments, and Rome declares the penalties for the future."  Nevertheless, there was as yet no clear hierarchy among the sources of the Church's law and, furthermore, the Western Empire, while it lasted, provided unquestioned secular jurisdiction in matters other than those of strictly ecclesiastical discipline, as is evidenced by the Theodosian Code -- although a bishop might well be called upon to act as an arbiter.

## (v) The Germanic codes

The Germanic tribes, Ostrogoths, Visigoths, Franks, etc., who came to settle in the territories of the Western Empire were not 'barbarians' in the sense of savages; they admired Roman traditions, and they were Christians.   There were no invasions, in the usual dramatic sense, of Gaul after the defeat of Attila and the Huns in 451, just a steady, if forcible, advance by the Germanic peoples.   Battles and sacks indeed took place in the migratory movements, but no attempt was made to destroy the Empire as such; the German peoples saw it as a necessary institution, in which they had a right to a place.  The murder of Valentinian in 455, which led at once to the sack of Rome by Gaiseric and his Vandals (whence the pejorative use of the name), rather than the death of Romulus Augustulus in 476, is perhaps the best symbol of the downfall of the Empire in the West. It was somewhat unfortunate, from the point of view of smooth relations between Roman and German, that all the original settlers, except the Franks under Clovis, were Arian heretics. But despite a lack of support from the Church, the Germanic peoples were ready to adopt many of the institutions with which they had come into contact, and one which impressed them enormously was the existence of written law. Hence we find appearing a number of legal codes, written in Latin, designed either for Romans living under Germanic rulers or, as in the case of the Edictum Theodorici (Edict of Theodoric), for the Germans as well. The Edictum seems to have been issued around 460 when the Visigoths were settled in south-west Gaul. It is heavily Roman in its content, and seems to have been necessary because of the absence of any clear political authority which could give a definitive legal ruling. It drew from the imperial constitutions of the Codex Gregorianus, the Codex Hermogenianus, and the Theodosian Code, and from the Sententiae of Paul, but the wording is frequently a simplified paraphrase rather than the original; it is a characteristic product of the vulgarized western jurisprudence. Less controversial in its origins is the Code of Euric, published about 475, in which the Visigothic king was clearly assisted by Roman legal experts; it is more likely to be an application of the vulgar law than a statement of Germanic custom as modified by their contacts with the Romans. Nevertheless, it was probably of territorial application, governing all inhabitants of the regions ruled by Euric; the surviving fragments show undoubted Roman influence, but do deal with areas of the law where such influence is most to be expected. Under Euric the Visigoths had extended their kingdom into Spain; save for the area round Narbonne, their settlement in Gaul was brought to an end by the Franks under Clovis in 507. In 506 King Alaric II had produced a code known as his Breviary, or as the Lex Romana Visigothorum; this consisted of a considerably abbreviated version of the Theodosian Code, together with some later imperial constitutions, an abridged and modified version of Gaius' Institutes, and a few further juristic texts. The whole, except for Gaius, was accompanied by an 'interpretation', which usually summarized and sometimes paraphrased the contents and occasionally made references to other works. Alaric's and Euric's codes reflected the Visigothic view of their relations with the Empire.

Other Germanic codes were issued at about this time which also indicate the German view of their settlements as compatible with the Empire. Even by the Roman provincials their new rulers were not seen as purely parasitical; they were often acceptable as bringing about the restoration of order, suppressing brigands or rebuilding bridges. The Code of Gundobad (474-518) of the Burgundians and the Law of the Bavarians are products of the vulgarized Roman law, codes which must have been produced by Romans serving the Germanic kings, although it remains unclear whether their application was territorial or personal. In northern Gaul the customary law of the Frankish settlers (or Salic law, under which name its later versions were known), was much more Germanic, reflecting a purely agricultural society, but from its beginnings it was drafted in Latin. The existence, the authority of the written Roman law influenced even those settlers who never came into direct contact with the Empire. The Franks on the Rhine who had invaded independently of the Salian Franks had their Lex Ribuaria (Law of the Riparian [Franks]) by the seventh century, and Roman law, transmitted through the Visigothic codes, was known to tribesmen in the Alps in the Epitome of St. Gall, and in the lex Alamannorum.

Of all these codes the Visigothic, whether Alaric's or Euric's as revised by Leovigild, were the most influential. The Lex Visigothorum maintained rules of family law and succession based on Germanic custom: for example, marriage brought about a régime of common property where in Roman law property was separate, or an oral will might be made before a judge, with witnesses swearing to its terms, while a Roman will was normally in writing. Other provisions were in accord with vulgar jurisprudence: for example, a widow could be given tutory of her children, and sale was seen not as a consensual but as a real contract, taking effect by the passing of property in the object sold. There were also rules that belonged to the classical law, such as the invalidity of an immoral or illegal transaction, even if correct in form, or the additional liability of a debtor in arrears to pay interest on the principal owed. The western provinces had been accustomed to the Theodosian Code, to elementary law books and epitomes, and to these Germanic codes for fifty or a hundred years before the Pragmatic Sanction of 554. This was why Justinian's 'correct' revival of the sophistication of classical law, well suited to Byzantines trained in theological niceties, fell flat with Romanized barbarian rulers and also with barbarized Roman subjects. After all, even before Justinian, students in the eastern law schools took a four or five year course to master the intricacies of Roman law; Justinian reformed the curriculum and laid down a five year period of study at Constantinople and Beirut (and Rome presumably, after the recovery of Italy) before qualification as advocate or judge in the supreme courts. There was nothing comparable in the barbarian West. Of the new sources of law only the Institutes seem to have been absorbed. The Digest was too difficult, too complex, too sophisticated, in a word -- unsuitable. The Code, although somewhat better attuned to the needs of the time, was nevertheless too lengthy, and it presupposed a political system that had ceased to exist. The Novels, while they were of importance where the Byzantine Empire continued to flourish,

13

until modified or superseded by the legislation of later Byzantine rulers, were mostly very long, and usually in Greek; the _Epitome Juliani_, containing 122 of them in an abridged Latin version, was the edition known in the West. Furthermore, even apart from problems of doctrine, there was already coolness between the Church in the West and the Church in the East, between Pope and Patriarch. Naturally enough the Church in the West continued to be influential in many aspects of administration; in the absence of effective imperial control, the Church, in particular the bishops in their cities, had acquired a greater jurisdictional rôle than that laid down in Justinian's compilation; its judges had already learned to use the _Theodosian Code_. This was the state of affairs when, in 568, the Lombards invaded Italy; the Pragmatic Sanction had never had effect in Spain or Gaul.

(vi) The Church of Gregory the Great

Secular law in the West had thus become fragmented by the sixth century, but the Church continued to function as a supra-national institution. Councils, general, provincial, and diocesan, continued to meet. In Visigothic Spain the king came to conduct the business of his kingdom at provincial councils; they were the places for considering lay affairs as much as ecclesiastical. In sixth century Gaul, as earlier in Visigothic Spain, there were still literate and legally trained laymen, competent to continue the modified practice of traditional Roman administration. This fact and a different, more popular, structure of government, may explain why the business of provincial councils under the Merovingian dynasty -- the descendants of Clovis -- was purely ecclesiastical; there were, however, more than fifty of these councils in

14

the sixth and seventh centuries. Such activity was one reason why, in the early years of the sixth century, Dionysius Exiguus, a Scythian monk working in Rome, made a collection of Apostolic Canons, based generally on the Latin version (the Didascalia) used at the Council of Chalcedon. (He was also the man who fixed the date of the Christian era as beginning 753 years after the founding of Rome.) This collection, in various editions, was to have considerable authority in the West under the name of the Dionysiana. In Spain it was superseded by a collection known as the Hispana, of which the first edition was compiled in 633. This made use of the Dionysiana but also included canons of Gallican (French) and Spanish councils of the sixth century and, in later editions, of the seventh. The Hispana is noteworthy for being arranged systematically, not chronologically. It was perhaps the most influential example of a local collection, but it was one of several, for there was as yet no clear and convincing authority in the whole Church, no efficient hierarchy.

It was also during this period that a new agency arose within the Church; monasticism appeared in a form acceptable to western notions, unlike the various asceticisms of the east. St. Benedict (c.480-547) established on an organized basis his Rule, a way of life that was out of the world but not hostile to it. Manual labour and intellectual work, as well as prayer, were parts of the Rule and so monastic houses could be both self-sufficient farms and centres of teaching and preaching. Monks of the Benedictine obedience, particularly St. Boniface (c.680-754) from Devon, were the principal carriers of Christianity to the rural areas of Europe east of the Rhine and north of the Alps, although Irish monks, such as St. Columban (c.540-614), also played an important part in the mission field.

The last Latin Doctor among the Church Fathers, Gregory the Great (540-604), Pope Gregory I from 590, lived in the transitional period between the Roman and the mediaeval worlds.  In his younger days, before he became a monk, Gregory held the office of Prefect of the City, the chief magistrature of Rome.  Rome was no longer a great city since its desolation in Justinian's wars against the Ostrogoths, but by this time there were few cities at all in the West, and Rome still had the echo of former greatness. Pope Gregory, like Pope Leo before him, was clearly the moral leader of (western) Christendom; like Leo, he negotiated with an invading people, the Lombards, and in the absence of imperial aid his efforts held them back from Rome.  As pope, Gregory was not uninterested in dogma, but the chaos of the Lombard invasion in Italy, the low moral quality of the Frankish royal court and upheavals elsewhere, meant that the enforcement of discipline was of particular interest to him.  A new category of devotional works, frequently of Irish origin, known as Penitentials, became popular. Their weakness was a tendency to codify the Church's procedures concerning sin and penance in a rather mechanical way, so that penance sometimes appeared as payment for sin rather than as an aspect of contrition. Nevertheless, they fitted with the movement for reform, and Gregory reinforced this movement from above:  "I know of no bishop who is not subject to the apostolic see, when a fault has been committed" (Ep. IX, 59 in Migne, P.L.).  He also intervened of his own initiative in cases of oppression and public scandal.  His theological work, heavily indebted to St. Augustine, remained a storehouse for later thinkers; his decretals, that is his judicial decisions and pastoral rulings, remained an important source of guidance to later bishops.  In view of his international influence, it is hardly surprising that papal decretals became an increasingly important source of authority, particularly as no General Councils were held in the West until the twelfth century.  Gregory's energy and perseverance, his benevolence and practicality, his administrative ability and monastic links, provided a programme for the Papacy, a Papacy which was to survive its unhappiest days in the hands of squabbling and self-seeking Roman families to emerge as the mainspring of reform.

## (vii) From the ancient to the mediaeval world

At the end of the sixth century it was not clearly apparent to contemporaries that the ancient world, the Roman world, had ended in the West. The Senate, however attenuated, still met in Rome, where the Empire remained theoretically sovereign, although the Papacy in practice governed central Italy. The Empire, the Byzantine Empire, effectively controlled the Dalmatian coast and the Exarchate of Ravenna in north-eastern Italy, as is evidenced by surviving documents which duly reflect the law of Justinian and his successors. In the Mediterranean area west of Greece, the Byzantines still held Africa round Hippo and Carthage, the coastal area of southern Spain until 624, as well as Sicily and Calabria or southern Italy, and also Corsica and Sardinia. It was not yet certain that the Lombards would not be made to abandon Italy as the Ostrogoths had before them. Frankish Gaul, henceforward more recognizable as France, like the Rhine provinces under the Burgundians, could be viewed as settled by allies, and Catholic allies in the case of the Merovingian Franks. Only the Anglo-Saxon settlement of England, an outpost of Empire where Roman law had probably never been truly absorbed, was outside the circle, and even there Christianity provided a link with the rest of civilized Europe. In Spain the Visigoths in many ways seemed to have made a fruitful union between Roman and Germanic civilization; the ample surviving evidence in the fields of law and theology (they had been officially Catholic since 589) suggests a civilization inferior to none in the world of its time. King Leovigild

King Leovigild (569-86) had revised Euric's Code; using this as a base, King Reccesuinth produced a new code in 654, entitled the Liber Iudiciorum (Book of Judgments), divided into twelve books, sub-divided into titles, with the subject matter arranged systematically. This in its turn was revised by King Ervig and re-issued in 681 as the Forum Iudicum (Province of Judges; Fuero Juzgo in Spanish); in this some subsequent legislation was inserted. Thus in the mid-seventh century Alaric's Breviary ceased to have any force in Spain, although it continued in use in France, especially in the Burgundian region of the south-east, as can be judged from the numerous surviving manuscripts. It was superseded in Spain, it would seem, because it became outdated in detail, not because the system failed; as a statement of law, indeed, it was comparable to the authoritarian edicts of Lombard as well as Roman law. Nevertheless, among the Visigoths there were constitutional elements, specifically the Church, which tried to decree limits to the autonomy of the kings; we find, for example, a decree of VIII Toledo which distinguished between property held by the king in trust for the people by virtue of his office and property pertaining to his family which could be disposed of at his will. The Liber Iudiciorum similarly contained laws which restricted what the king could lawfully take from his subjects, and which repeated the distinction between property held for the people and property at his disposition, but it went further than its Roman model or the Lombard equivalent in holding the king subject to the law. In practice the king's power was great and often unchecked, but the codes were statements of principle as well as handbooks for administrators, and here the influence of the Church in Spain was centuries ahead of European political theory. In other respects, such as the development of the responsibilities of local communities to hand over runaway slaves and to check on unknown incomers, or the formalization of trial by ordeal,

18

Visigothic Spain was simply evolving in a way that other western societies were, unconsciously, to follow. But the Arab conquest of 711 ended the political history and the creative law-making of Visigothic Spain; much survived, and was to re-emerge in the Christian kingdoms of the Reconquista, but its influence then was either internal or in the American colonies. In the Asturias the Basques (rather like Asterix) held out against the Arabs as they had against the Visigoths, but the Arab impetus was really checked only at the Battle of Poitiers in 732, by the Frankish Charles Martel, founder of the Carolingian line. Thus it was under Frankish influence that the new political map of Europe was to take shape, and among the Franks that one may conveniently look to measure the survival of Roman law amidst the growth of the new customary law. Lombard legislation and practice in Italy were significant for the future, but it was the military strength of the Franks which made them and their legal developments particularly important.

## (viii) The Lombards (or Langobardi)

The Lombards were different from the majority of the Germanic peoples who had settled within the Empire before them in that, when they invaded in 568, they appeared to contemporaries more simply as enemies, as an almost abstract force of pure destruction. The forty years of chaotic conquest that followed left them rulers of some two-thirds of the Italian peninsula, and even after the Frankish conquest of Lombard Italy, the institutions of the Lombard kingdom survived in a way that Ostrogothic institutions had not. Lombard institutions survived partly because they had taken advantage of Roman or sub-Roman structures both in central administration and at the level of the cities and dioceses. Despite much bloodshed, the Roman population survived, and continued formally to use Roman law, although this survival is not really evidenced until the eighth century when records become more abundant. The first Lombard code, the Edict of Rothari, issued in 643, shows no sign of Roman influence, other than being written in Latin, and perhaps in its comprehensive nature. Rothari deliberately set out as much Lombard custom as he and his advisers could, but it seems certain that there were Roman functionaries to collect and write down its 388 titles. Its substance was rather like that of the contemporary Anglo-Saxon codes, with the stress on agriculture and matters such as wergild (feud compensation). Daughters had no claim on an estate if there was legitimate male issue, and in general a man could not disinherit his son either by legal act or by granting away his property; any grant of land had to be made in the popular assembly, and such a grant was only possible for men without legitimate sons. Women were in life-long subordination, to the king if there were no suitable male kin, and they could not dispose even of moveable property without their guardian's consent; there was a bride-price as well as a dowry, and the husband also had to make a substantial gift to his wife after the marriage.

The next major Lombard law-giver was King Liutprand (712-44); he extended the rights of succession of women, and also allowed the alienation of land to the Church. Both these changes demonstrate Roman influence, as did Liutprand's circumscription of the use of trial by battle, explaining: "for we are uncertain about God's judgment, and we have heard of many losing their cases in battle unjustly; but on account of the custom of our Lombard people we cannot ban the practice entirely." Specifically Christian influence appears in the ban on marriage between first cousins, which is ascribed to the injunction of the pope, "the head of God's churches and priests throughout the world". Liutprand added 152 titles to the Edict, a further pointer to the primacy of the written law; royal written law was increasingly acquiring supreme authority. Indeed, this 'descending theme of government' (as Ullmann calls it) explains why Lombard law could co-exist with civil and canon law in the eleventh and twelfth centuries when other Germanic codes were ignored. Germanic civil law imperceptibly succeeded in penetrating Italian life; men of Roman descent continued to use the Theodosian Code or, after the Frankish conquest, perhaps the Visigothic version, but they also found it necessary to follow Lombard law when the Roman law made no allowance for new relationships, or for new social, economic, or political structures. Administration continued to centre on the royal court, normally at Pavia, and local government was conducted from the cities, the ancient civitates which included the immediately dependent country area; Lombard duchies and episcopal dioceses normally coincided. Little positive role was played by the people in Lombard government, although witnesses in large numbers might be required in dispute settlements, particularly in cases of reparation. Litigation took the form either of trial by battle, or of oath, taken by the defender and six of his kin, chosen by the pursuer, and five more free men, chosen by these seven. Written evidence was dominant in the spheres of property law and status, which reflected the very high level of literacy in Italy compared with the rest of Western Christendom. Legal change in the Lombard and its successor Frankish kingdom came explicitly from the top of the pyramid, whereas the other Germanic societies mostly illustrated an 'ascending theme of government'. This concept of legislation and jurisdiction as vested in the state, an entity to be succeeded in due course by the cities and communes, was unique in the West to Italy. It is not surprising that it was in the north Italian cities that Roman law was to have its great revival.

Although the Lombards did eventually blend in with the Roman population of Italy, as the dominance of the Latin element in the Italian language bears witness, their pressure on neighbouring but unconquered areas had political effects lasting over a period of at least two centuries. They played a significant part in the transfer of the internal organization of Byzantine and Roman Italy from a theoretically civil government to a military system of defence, to a sort of feudalism; thus we find in Italy, as in France, the warrior class as one of the chief divisions of the free populace. Power and wealth necessarily continued to rest on land-holding; _tribuni_, who were usually major local landowners, ruled a city state and led it in war. These _tribuni_ were nominated by the Byzantine viceroy, the Exarch of Ravenna, but in practice their office was largely hereditary. _Collegia_, corporate bodies in the cities who had performed the functions of local government in the Later Empire, sometimes survived in the towns; at Naples the _curiales_, the hereditary town councillors, became a guild of notaries. Bishops became public functionaries, and took over much of local government; the great estates of the Church gave them influence and resources. Spoleto and Benevento were Lombard duchies, but they were semi-independent from the beginning, and their special status survived the fall of the Lombard kingdom. And the Lombard kingdom fell, in essence, because Lombard ambitions threatened the Papacy, for which the Franks, who at that time had the strongest army in Europe, were ready to fight. Hence, after campaigns in 754-56, King Pippin of the Franks was acknowledged by the Lombards as their overlord. He then granted the administration of the former Exarchate, from which the Byzantine authorities had been driven out in 751, to the Papacy, but it was not until 774 that Charlemagne invaded Italy, captured Pavia, the Lombard capital, and finally made an end of the independent Lombard kingdom. Thus most of Italy was within the new Holy Roman Empire that was founded or recognized on Christmas Day, 800, when Charlemagne was crowned as Emperor by the Pope.

## B: The Formation of Europe

### (ix)  The early Carolingians and Charlemagne

For two hundred years after the death of the Frankish king Clovis in 511 the Merovingian kings personally or through their lieutenants, the mayors of the palaces, fought and murdered each other for the three provinces of Austrasia (N.E. France and the Rhineland), Neustria (north of the Loire and west of the Meuse), and Burgundy (which included the length of the Rhone); the Frankish kingdom nevertheless remained a single realm, aided by the support of the Church.  Then, out of the Austrasian mayors of the palace there emerged a new line; Pippin II of Heristal, already in effective control of Austrasia, subdued the Neustrian Franks and became their mayor of the palace too.  He restored Frankish supremacy over the Alamanni and the Bavarians, among whom he encouraged missionaries, as he also did among the Frisians.  His work nearly failed for, on his death, he divided his realm, as was the Frankish custom, granting it to his young grandsons, but his bastard son Charles seized power and became the first, the eponymous, Carolingian.  Charles' greatest victory was at Poitiers, near Tours, when he defeated the Islamic invaders who had already overrun Spain.  This was perhaps the decisive battle that ensured a Christian Europe, and with his victory he won for himself the name of Martel, the Hammer; however, his counter-attack, in temporary alliance with Liutprand of the Lombards, was ineffective.  On his death in 741 the realm was divided between his two sons, Carloman who took Austrasia and the east, and Pippin (the Short) who took Neustria, Burgundy, and the west; both were still in name mayors of the palace.

On Carloman's retiral to a monastery in 746, Pippin took all, and in 751 he was elected king of the Franks and anointed to that office by St. Boniface and other bishops.  His coronation had a papal blessing; papal support was reinforced in 754 when, at the abbey of St. Denis, Pope Stephen himself anointed Pippin and his two sons and created them patricians of the Romans.  This was a result of Stephen's appeal to Pippin when the Lombards, after conquering Ravenna, threatened Rome.  His appeal to the Franks, rather than to Byzantium, was natural since, in 727, the Papacy had come to a final breach with the Empire in Byzantium[4], although over three centuries were to pass before the schism with the Eastern, the Orthodox, Church became definite.  The first campaign against the Lombards did not settle the matter, and the Pope appealed for help a second time; on this occasion Pippin acted decisively.  A Byzantine request that Ravenna be restored to the Empire was turned down  and, by the Donation of Pippin, the Exarchate was delivered to the government of the Pope[5].  Relations were for the present excellent, but the possibilities of future conflict between spiritual and secular power were there.  Pippin went on to expel the Arabs from those parts of south-western France which they still held and to bring Aquitaine back to submission.  By the time of his death in 768 France reached to the Pyrenees and the Rhine, as well as retaining nominal suzerainty over Bavaria; Pippin also took the first steps that led to the

----------

4    B. Tierney The Crisis of Church and State 1050-1300 (U.S.A. 1964), document no.5.

5    Tierney, no.7.

Carolingian renaissance in the fields of learning and culture.

Charles, better known as Charlemagne (768-814), became sole king of the Franks on the death of his brother Carloman in 771. In 774, after a war with the Lombards, he captured Pavia and put an end to the independent Lombard kingdom. He then journeyed to Rome and confirmed, probably with some modifications, the Donation of Pippin. From this time Charlemagne styled himself 'King of the Franks and of the Lombards and Patrician of the Romans'. Lombardy, subject to increasing Frankish influence, nevertheless retained its separate character, but the Pope and the papal states also found Charlemagne acting as overlord. Benevento, south of the papal states, remained effectively independent; thenceforward the division of Italy into north and south remained unchallenged until the nineteenth century. On his eastern frontier Charlemagne subdued the Saxons, thus extending his Empire to the Baltic and the Elbe, and he strengthened his suzerainty over the duchy of Bavaria, which included modern Austria -- the East March of Bavaria. In the south-west he created the Spanish March on the southern side of the Pyrenees, roughly Andorra to Barcelona; thereafter Catalonia has an identifiable existence on both sides of the Pyrenees. Only in the north, on the Danish frontier, was Charlemagne content with a defensive role. The sole increase in this empire for his successors was Brittany, whose submission was due more to fear of seaborne enemies than to Frankish expansionism.

In secular law Charlemagne ordered the unwritten customary law of various tribes to be written down, and the Salic Law to be edited authoritatively. His own legislative acts, however, took their legal force from the words of the sovereign, of which the writing was merely evidence -- such royal edicts were known as capitularies. In the sphere of canon law Pope Hadrian I presented Charlemagne in 786 with a version of the

Dionysiana, supplemented by various decretals and some canons of Roman synods, which was thereafter known as the Hadriana. In 802 Charlemagne, two years after his coronation as Emperor by the Pope, laid down that the Hadriana was to be followed by the Church in all his dominions; in practice the Hispana or the Vetus Gallica (the pre-Dionysian collection used in Gaul) continued to be used alongside the newer version, as did various Penitentials. In the ecclesiastical field the Carolingian reform movement saw a joint attempt by secular and spiritual authorities to restore clerical, and lay, discipline, and to recover Church property and patronage from secular hands. But as the unity of the first establishment of the Holy Roman Empire crumbled, so did the reform movement. Simony, that is, the buying and selling of ecclesiastical offices, particularly bishoprics[6], continued to be rife; many bishops were little more than feudal nobles in mitres; church benefices remained in lay hands; celibacy of the clergy remained largely an ideal.

(x)  The successors of Charlemagne


The ninth century saw the steady growth of outside threats to the Carolingian Empire from Moslem pirates, Norse Vikings, and Magyar raiders; the impact of this on the movement known as feudalism will be considered in the next chapter. Within the Frankish realm dynastic struggles continued among the heirs of Charlemagne, aggravated by the Frankish custom of joint inheritance, even of kingdoms. A series of accidents made Charles the Fat sole emperor from 884 to his deposition in 887, and the division which then took place turned out to be permanent. Descendants of Charlemagne

----------

6.  e.g. Tierney, no.13.

continued to rule the kingdoms of Germany, France, and Italy, (as it is now convenient to call them), while semi-independent principalities flourished in Burgundy, Provence, and Catalonia (Barcelona and south-west France); the Basques recovered their independence, and the counts of Brittany offered no more than nominal allegiance. Germany was most prone to attack, having a frontier at the North Sea and easy access from the Mediterranean as well as lying open to the Magyars, who burst through the Moravians of Hungary in the early tenth century. Local separatism was also perhaps strongest in Germany, with Saxons, Bavarians, and Slavs all having their particular interests. In France things may have been a little easier. In 911 Charles the Simple ceded the duchy of Normandy to Rollo the Norseman, obtaining an oath of loyalty from him as count of Rouen; the creation of this buffer zone did in fact check Viking incursions into France. Lorraine was already embarked on its long alternation between French and German lordship.

Italy, too, was ravaged by Moslems and Magyars, and in addition there was civil strife, as the nobles fought each other for influence, for the royal title and for the Papacy. The tenth century was the nadir of the Papacy and the episcopate; in Rome we find John XII elected pope at the age of twenty at a time when a priest was supposed to be at least thirty-five years old and, similarly, in the 930s we find a five year old elected as archbishop of Reims to serve the ambitions of his father, the count of Vermandois. In general the Papacy of this period was merely the tool of the factious Roman nobility, with the emperor intervening on occasion, in his own interests. But anarchy and corruption brought reaction. The Cluniacs, a strict monastic order, arose to spearhead the reform movement, and other groups of monks, following severe versions of the Benedictine Rule, helped to foster a spiritual revival.

In the secular sphere matters improved as the Norsemen made more or less permanent conquests at Novgorod and Kiev, and in the eastern districts of England -- the Danelaw --, as well as in Normandy. The Magyars were finally induced to settle in Hungary and their raids were limited, particularly after the decisive victory of the Emperor Otto the Great in 955 at the Lechfeld (just south of Augsburg). The Moslem invaders of the ninth and tenth centuries had, like the Norsemen, come by sea. Their colony at Fréjus was extirpated in 972 after lasting a century and a half in that stronghold; it had been a base from which they commanded the Alpine passes as well as the coastal regions and the sea. A Byzantine-Frankish alliance had repelled them from the Italian mainland, though not from most of Sicily, by early in the tenth century. The Moslems ceased to exist as a serious threat to sea trade after the maritime victories of the increasingly powerful and effective commercial cities of Italy. Important victories were won by the Venetians off Bari in 1002 and by the Pisans off Reggio in 1005; in 1016 Genoa and Pisa united to clear Sardinia, although Sicily was not to be recovered until the Norman reconquest after 1060 -- when the Normans also took over Calabria, the Byzantine province in southern Italy. Thus by the end of the tenth century conditions were such that men began to conduct their arguments and fight their quarrels with law-suits as well as the sword. And the rivalry of Pope and Emperor, to which we shall shortly come, positively encouraged the pursuit of learning, as each side sought for arguments against the other.

After the ninth century the centre of interest in the development of law in Europe turns away from France, where the kingship went into profound eclipse. The Carolingian line there died out in 987, and the Capetian dynasty, named after Hugh Capet, began the slow process of recovery, based on the lands they controlled directly in the Île de France. South of the Loire there remained a different culture, less rebellious than the turbulence of the northern lords, but no more obedient. There were counts of Barcelona, counts of Toulouse, dukes of Gascony, dukes of Aquitaine, kings of Burgundy (which included Provence); all of them were content with effective independence, and so there was relative peace in the Languedoc. In the north the greater vassals often outshone their king, but the support of the bishops, and the fortunate survival of caution and common-sense as Capetian traits, enabled Hugh Capet's great-great-grandson Louis VI (1108-37), the Fat, to create a relatively prosperous and peaceful order, at least within the Ile de France.

In Germany recovery from the tribulations of the ninth and tenth centuries was quicker; there were fewer over-mighty vassals and a more stable society, with a limited degree of popular participation in public affairs. This last quality, however, also meant that there was more separatism, more stress on local or tribal distinctions, in particular between the four main races, Saxons, Bavarians, Swabians, and East Franks or Franconians. Thus the kings, or emperors as they more usually were, ruled a federal rather than a united realm. This particularism also helps to explain why such a diversity of custom survived in Germany -- the Lehnrecht or feudal law, the Stadtrecht or town law, the Hofrecht or peasant law, etc.. But the emperors could rule, rather than merely reign, partly because there remained ample land for them to give away or to grant as benefices, that is, land held in return for service, and partly because of the support of the Church which favoured unity.

In Italy the descendants of Charlemagne continued to rule from the cities, as had the Lombards before them, until the mid-tenth century, when local power passed at much the same time almost everywhere to the city communes. The German-based Emperors continued to exercise a more or less effective overlordship in the north, as well as involving themselves in the affairs of the Papacy.

(xi) Education law, and trade

In the sixth century there had been higher education at Rome;
Justinian had paid professors of grammar, oratory, medicine, and
jurisprudence, but it seems unlikely that any such posts survived. Nor is
there any evidence for a comparable survival at Ravenna where, if anywhere,
one might expect it for, although the city fell to the Lombards in 751, it
was under papal control by 774. One can, however, assume a certain
continuity of administrative and legal skills, and the training to support
them, at the papal curia or court. In and after the seventh century Latin
continued to be taught and used, for it remained the language of the
Church, and the normal language of written documents. What education there
was, in particular the learning of Latin, was mostly centred on the
monasteries, but until perhaps the eleventh century it remained elementary.
The Carolingian renaissance brought into prominence the work of the
Christian writers of the end of the Empire, such as Boëthius (480-524) and
Cassiodorus (c.490-583); also read were the writings of Irish monks, such
as St. Columban (540-615), and of English scholars such as Aldhelm (c.640-
709) or the Venerable Bede (673-735). There was a conscious attempt to
revive the civilized past; there was a school at Charlemagne's palace, and
others were founded, attached to cathedrals or monasteries. The Caroline
minuscule style of handwriting made reading easier; it was used to copy the
works of the Fathers and the heathen classics, which led to their
widespread availability and contributed to a certain unity of culture. For
example, Alcuin (735-804) came from York to be abbot of the monastery of
St. Martin of Tours; he taught extensively and wrote voluminously on

30

grammar, history, and theology. Paul the Deacon (d. c.797), from Lombardy, wrote on grammar and on the History of the Lombards; he referred in passing (H.L. 1,25) to Justinian's "laws of individual magistrates and judges", which presumably means the Digest. Einhardt (c.775-840), a Franconian, modelled his Life of Charlemagne on Suetonius' Lives of the Emperors. Churchmen produced the Forged Capitularies and the False Decretals, including the Donation of Constantine, by which that emperor purportedly handed over to Pope Sylvester considerable secular power. Such forgery was an exercise rather comparable to the putting by Greek and Roman historians of suitable speeches in the mouths of leading characters; it was not falsification in our modern sense, but a description of what might, and indeed what ought, to have happened. These forgeries made use of genuine material in a way that showed their authors to be learned and widely read. However, the military and political turmoil of the later ninth and earlier tenth centuries put learning into abeyance.

This is the intellectual background to the problem of the extent of continuity in the practice of law. Our evidence is plentiful for matters concerning land, for example, charters granting benefices and laying down the counter-obligations of the grantee or vassal, but is much more sparse in the fields where Roman law had been most highly developed. Trade between different countries, regions and cities never entirely disappeared, particularly in Italy; in France, towns such as Marseille, Arles, Narbonne, Bordeaux, Cahors, Orléans, Autun, Laon, Trier and Metz remained trading centres of a sort. But in spite of the considerable increase in coined money during the eighth century and the revival of urban life in the Carolingian peace, the law of contracts unrelated to land remained a special area, an area for the custom of the merchants, as we shall see in a later chapter.

In Visigothic Spain we find that the Roman element in contracts remained strong; for example, although writing was commonly required, it was still required essentially to prove, not to constitute, the contract. Sale, however, was seen as necessarily involving a transfer of title, and the document was the necessary proof that the price had been paid. The Forum Iudicum seems to have remained influential even after the Arab conquests, perhaps because the surviving Christian kingdoms were relatively isolated; it is probable that its use remained open to the Christian subjects of the Arabs. There are in any case many MSS of the Forum surviving from ninth and tenth century Catalonia and León, and also many bequests of copies. Court proceedings often cite specific texts or sometimes merely refer to them; from surviving court records it is clear that procedure followed the norms of the old law. Notaries flourished, and judges seem to have been at least semi-professional, although nothing is known about their training.

In France the Lex Romana Visigothorum was the legal code for the clergy and the Gallo-Romans; in Aquitaine, in particular, people continued to describe themselves as Romans not Franks, but it is hard to tell how far they could avoid resorting to customary law and rules of feudal law as social facts changed around them, and there was no authoritative source to administer the old written law. In the Midi, where feudal institutions were not universal and many smaller landowners survived with only a loose attachment to a greater man, explicit sales of land continued. However, in the Toulouse area, stipulations, warranties against eviction etc., all disappear from legal documents after 980, and the written evidence portrays a feudal society (where traditio, simple physical delivery, can convey an abstract thing like seisin -- which will be further explained in the next chapter). In a group of charters from what is now Belgium those from before 750 are very Roman in form, citing the _Theodosian Code_; gifts are made in accordance with the requirements of C.Th. 8,12,1 (of 316), save for the registration on the court register, which no longer existed; the term 'trado' is used correctly to indicate the physical delivery of property, and not where it should not be; documents recording sales quite properly use the past tense because the writing is evidentiary, although the contract refers to a delivery for a price rather than the pure Roman agreement -- but this is normal vulgar law; warranties against eviction are valid against the world. But in the later group, from the Carolingian period, a sale is delivery by charter for a return, in other words, it is not really a contract at all but a formal grant of land; the same terminology is used for gift and sale, even when the two transactions appear in the one charter; warranties against eviction are only effective against intrusion by the seller or granter or by his family. In another group (from the Dauphiné) consisting of acts in expectation of death the picture is similar. An eighth century will seems in good form, and indeed refers to Justinian's _Code_; during the ninth century gifts pro anima, that is, for the benefit of one's soul, in expectation of death, are often confused with gifts having present effect, which would require physical delivery; by the tenth century the concept of universal succession, of the heir succeeding to most of the rights and duties as well as the physical property of the testator, has disappeared completely, and the will itself has become rare. North of the Loire the will disappeared during the eighth century, and so did the very word 'sale' for transactions concerning land, which were all seen in terms of grant and service; estates were no longer disposable, and tenure had replaced ownership.

It is not entirely clear why the break with Roman traditions should fall where it does; perhaps Merovingian ineffectiveness left the _Lex Romana_ to flourish, while the early Carolingians had a policy of centralization which was inevitably enforced in predominantly Frankish terms, so that when Charlemagne's empire broke up there was a vacuum for feudal institutions to fill. Although such a theory may explain the evidence from the north, it hardly fits with that from Toulouse. There it is more likely to be linked with the lack of an outside or objective set of standards; in the absence of an accepted governmental authority, the family had become the sole 'force sociale'.

(xii) The Empire in Germany

The reign of Henry the Fowler (919-36), duke of Saxony, marks the coming of the new, the post-Carolingian, order; as well as gaining the allegiance, at least nominal, of Thuringia, Swabia, and Bavaria, he recovered Lorraine for Germany, and he also maintained a steady push against the Slavs in the east. His son, Otto I (936-73), the Great, destroyed the Magyar threat at the Lechfeld, and aimed at becoming a new Charlemagne. Since effective power rested on the extent of a lord's private domains rather than his titular territories, the hereditary aspect of feudalism was often in opposition to any efficient centralization. For if a vassal's lands and offices passed to his successor, usually his son, whether or not that successor was suitable from the king's point of view, it was difficult to put into effect any coherent policy. Otto therefore adopted widely the practice of endowing bishops and major abbots with large benefices; ecclesiastical magnates were in general more efficient and more trustworthy than lay ones, and they offered no hereditary threat, since there was real freedom to reappoint on their death.

In 951 at Pavia Otto took the Italian crown, marrying the widow of the previous king; he returned to Italy in 962, and on this occasion achieved his ambition and was crowned Emperor, a title which is thereafter normally linked with the rulers of Germany. He then proceeded to intervene in the affairs of the Papacy, imposing two popes in rapid succession. In northern Italy he strengthened his power as feudal overlord, although his attempts to extend his influence in the south were only moderately successful. Under his successors Calabria was lost to the Saracens; vain attempts were made to get Germans and Italians to mingle in northern Italy; manipulation of the Papacy in the effort to achieve this was frequent. The Italian cities were growing prosperous in the new era of relative peace, and their leading citizens, who were often also the local landowners, resented, both as merchants and as lords, the Ottonian policy of favouring ecclesiastical magnates and not granting hereditary fiefs.

The Emperor Conrad II (1024-39) put more reliance on hereditary vassals, although he wished to restrain the greater magnates; he did not, however, show any understanding of the communal movement in the Italian cities. In 1037, saying "If Italy hungers for law, I will satiate her", he called a diet (or assembly) at Pavia and regulated the position of the lesser fiefs, confirming their hereditary nature. The following year, at Rome, he laid down that within Roman territory Roman law should decide all cases, a decision clearly favouring the territoriality of law, not to say Roman law; it is, however, not quite clear what he understood by 'Roman law'. Conrad's son, Henry III (1039-56), tried to end private wars by the Indulgence of 1043, whereby he and all those he could persuade or command solemnly forgave their enemies and renounced all feuds; this had even less effect than the Church's efforts in the Truce of God and the Peace of God. In Rome itself, however, it was largely Henry's influence which brought about the election of the great reforming pope, Leo IX, which was to have incalculable influence on the role of the Church and on relations between Church and State.


(xiii) The Investiture Contest


Pope Leo IX (1048-54) surrounded himself with a group of reformist cardinals, drawn from all over Europe, of whom the youngest, Hildebrand, was especially fierce in his belief in the supreme dignity of the Papacy and in the need for the complete independence of the Church from secular domination. A number of councils were held[7], and the search for the authentic rules of the Early Church, for the discipline of primitive Christianity before its corruption in the barbarian age, led to the further investigation of ancient writings; it seems likely that it was in the course of this search that the manuscript of the Digest was recognized for what it was.

Hildebrand became Gregory VII (1073-85); his aims were expressed in the so-called Dictatus Papae, or Papal Statements, of 1075[8]. They set out a programme for a re-birth of spiritual guidance, with authority in matters of faith, morals and discipline coming from the Pope alone. In particular, however, Gregory's pontificate was marked by his struggle with the Emperor Henry IV (1056-1106). This is known as the Investiture Contest because the main issue was the lay claim to appoint bishops and to invest them with the ring and pastoral staff which symbolized their office, as well as with their fiefs; at a lower level there was the issue of lay

----------

7    Tierney, nos. 15 and 16.

8    Tierney, no. 26; cf. R.W. Southern, Western Society and the Church in the Middle Ages (Penguin 1970), p.102f.

appointment of priests to parishes. The practice had originated under the Carolingians, partly from the theocratic nature of the power they claimed, partly from ordinary feudal attitudes concerning public office and land-holding, and partly from the need of kings in difficult times to have loyal vassals and capable servants. The practice had "provided a most effective counter to the disintegrative tendencies of early feudalism"[9], but it had also encouraged simony and a tendency for some sees to become hereditary. The reformers rightly saw lay investiture as, even at its best, aimed at serving secular not spiritual purposes but they, as much as emperors and kings, saw a bishopric's "lands, rights, jurisdictions, and duties [as] one indissoluble juridical entity"[10]. The eventual solution lay in distinguishing separate functions, a solution which in essentials was first put forward by Ivo of Chartres (1040-1116), who realized that spiritual office and temporal jurisdiction were conceptually distinct[11].

Henry IV had received help from Gregory VII against a rebellious Saxony, but he now broke with the Pope. He discarded the (unconsecrated) archbishop of Milan whom he had already invested, disregarded the canonical election of one Atto, and invested a fresh nominee of his own with the see, which had become vital for the German control of Lombardy. Gregory issued threats against Henry. Henry called a synod of German bishops at Worms in 1076 and declared Gregory deposed; the Lombard bishops immediately followed suit. Thereupon Gregory, at the Lenten Synod in Rome, deposed the rebellious bishops, granting them a time for repentance, and excommunicated Henry, forbidding him to exercise his royal office. Gregory's estimate of

--------

9   Tierney, p.25.

10   Tierney, p.34f.

11   Tierney, no.40.

his authority was better than Henry's. The German bishops and lay magnates forced Henry to submit by threatening to renounce their allegiance and elect another king; Henry made his submission as a penitent to Gregory at Canossa, a castle of the Countess Matilda of Tuscany. This was an immense surrender to the papal claims to supreme jurisdiction as God's vicar, but the Church needed the support of the secular power as much as the latter needed the support of the Church, and the struggle was not yet over. Pope Paschal II indeed made the radical proposal that the Church should abandon all lands and temporal powers and return to a primitive simplicity, thus logically achieving the total independence from the secular powers that the reformers sought[12]. But this proposal was too startling for Church to swallow or State to understand, and in view of the economy of the time it was probably impossible to separate spiritual office from material property. The English achieved a settlement in 1107, with the king receiving feudal homage for the temporalities of the bishopric, but only following on a canonical election; the Pope would then send the ring and staff. A compromise in similar terms was achieved for the Empire at the Concordat of Worms in 1122. Henry V (1106-25) guaranteed the canonical election of bishops and abbots, and renounced the imperial claim to investiture with ring and staff; Pope Calixtus, for his part, granted the Emperor the right to be present at elections and to intervene if these were disputed. I Lateran of 1123, the ecumenical council called in the year after the settlement, was not only the first General Council for 350 years, it was also the first to be composed solely of clerics and free of direct imperial influence. The canons of this Council aimed at reforming the ministry of the Church, for example, they insisted on the celibacy of the

----------

12    Tierney, no.42, and p.85f.

38

clergy and they also created a stronger juridical structure to enforce these reforms. I Lateran marks the start of the heroic age of the mediaeval Papacy and of canon law.

(xiv) The eleventh century recovery

In the eleventh century there began to take place (most markedly in Italy, despite the internecine strife and the wars brought on by German ambitions) a renaissance, far outdistancing in importance, for the knight or the peasant or the merchant, those of the Carolingian court or of the fifteenth century. There was apparent an economic revival, of which one aspect was the increase in maritime and overland trade, and another the rise, even outside Italy, of the self-governing town. With a surplus in production, the population rose and city life became much more widely possible; this was favourable to education and scholarship, as well as making life pleasanter, with little luxuries available to many more of the population.

In the early eleventh century we find Peter Damian at Ravenna, teaching canon law; he taught its practice on the prohibited degrees of kindred which was explicitly different from the Roman law. At Pavia both Roman law -- mainly from the Lex Romana Visigothorum -- and the customary and feudal law of the Lombard kingdom were being studied and developed by glossing the texts. Lanfranc was teaching there around 1042, and the jurists of Pavia were sufficiently sure of their discipline to be divided into antiqui, who held to the Lex Romana and other ancient sources, and moderni, who dealt with the blend between the Lex Romana and Lombard custom. The Liber Papiensis, or Book of Pavia, contained material going back to the Edict of Rothari of 643; it was arranged chronologically. It

39

was composed, probably in the early years of the eleventh century, with scholastic and practical comment by Walcausus, who was one of the judges of Henry III's imperial court at Verona. The contemporary _Lombarda_ or _Lex Langobarda_ contained much the same material, but arranged systematically in books and titles; it revealed some knowledge of Justinian's _Institutions_ and of an epitomized _Code_ but its main subject was Lombard custom. Around 1070 there was composed the _Expositio ad Librum Papiensem_, or _Commentary on the Book of Pavia_, which cited various Roman jurists and quoted from Justinian's _Novels_ in the edition known as the _Epitome of Julian_, who had been a Byzantine commentator thereon. The _Expositio_ also quoted, although probably not at first hand, from the _Digest_; and it referred to certain rules of the canon law as in force at the time.

Nor was the Lombard capital of Pavia the only Italian city in which law books survived or were produced. From Perugia there is the _Adnotationes Codicum Domini Justiniani_ (_Notes on the Codes of the Lord Justinian_), which probably dates from the seventh and eighth centuries. It was written in what has been described as horrible corrupt Latin, and it seems that this centre of study failed in the bad years. The _Lectio legum brebiter_ [sic] _facta_ (_A Brief Summary of the Laws_) of the ninth century was compiled mainly from the _Ecloga_ (_Choice Selection_) of the Byzantine Emperor Leo III, the Isaurian, which it ascribed to Pope Leo the Great. The _Ecloga_ was a codification based on the _Corpus Iuris Civilis_ but much simplified and containing many subsequent changes in the law, such as the joint exercise by mother as well as father of _patria potestas_ (paternal power), or the treatment, after the death of one spouse, of the property of the married couple as having been a joint estate; it had been in force in Byzantine Italy. The _Lectio_ suppressed the references to the _Digest_ in the _Ecloga_, and it referred to the _Code_ and _Novels_ together as _ex libro_

40

Novelle; it is also contained material from the Edict of Theodoric and from Lombard law. At Pistoia a glossed version of the Code was extant in the tenth century. There is thus no doubt that there survived in Italy the memory, and some knowledge, of Justinian's Code in an epitomized version, and of some of his Novels; the Institutions were also known. It must be remembered that the Byzantines had long held Ravenna and the Exarchate, that they held much of southern Italy (where pockets of Greek speakers survive to this day) until the coming of the Normans in the later eleventh century, and that communications between Rome and Constantinople never quite ceased. All Byzantine legislation descended from Justinian's Corpus, with simplifications and additions. Manuscripts of the codes of Leo III (717-40), of Basil I (867-86) -- the Procheiros Nomos (Manual of Law) --, and of Leo VI, the Wise, -- the Basilica (Imperial Books) --, all survive from Italy, and another code, specifically for the province, the Prochiron legum (Manual of Laws) was composed there, probably in Calabria. The Normans took over the territorial law they found in force in the south, in itself a sign of continuity. Italian charters also frequently reflect this continuous if vulgarized relationship with Justinianic Roman law. Notaries, public scribes, who had become very important in the Later Empire when so many transactions were required to be recorded in due form on the court registers, also survived the intervening centuries, at the papal curia, probably in some of the Italian cities and also at the imperial court. Notaries created by the Pope or the Emperor had authority to draw up public documents, acceptable in themselves as evidence of the transactions they recorded. Their continued use of forms simply because they were old, even if not well understood, was another factor making for continuity. Cartularies or style books were in widespread use, for teaching as well as practice. The profession flourished again in the new

41

age of law.

Universities, let alone law faculties, were not yet institutionalized in the eleventh century. Eager students followed individual teachers of renown; thus Anselm attracted students to Bec and Canterbury in turn. But bishops or princes might encourage scholars by granting them, and even their students, privileges or immunities; guilds of students or of masters were in the making. By the eleventh century a curriculum had been established. The trivium, or the study of grammar (based on fourth and sixth century Latin authorities), of dialectic or logic (based on Aristotle in Boëthius' translation), and of rhetoric (based on Cicero), preceded the quadrivium, which was the study of geometry, arithmetic, astronomy or astrology (no distinction was yet drawn), and music. At certain centres more specialist studies were undertaken; men came to Salerno to study medicine, as they did in the twelfth century to Montpellier, and it was at Bologna that the serious study of the civil law, the Roman law as preserved in the Corpus Iuris Civilis, began. Medicine and law remained advanced studies, as did theology. The canonists had been searching the ancient authorities since at least the beginning of the eleventh century, and making use of what they found; the lawyers in Pavia and elsewhere were jurists reading their authorities critically and developing the law. When men came upon the Digest they knew what it was and, far more important, they had acquired the intellectual expertise to make use of it. The imperial jurists in particular must have welcomed the Corpus as ammunition against the papalists. With sufficient knowledge and adequate patronage available, the stage was now set for an explosive growth of legal studies.

Further Reading:

F.H. Lawson The Roman Law Reader (U.S.A., 1969)

B. Nicholas _Introduction to Roman Law_ (Oxford, 1962, reprinted)

A. Watson _The Law of the Ancient Romans_ (Dallas, 1970)

H.-J. Wolff _Roman Law_ (U.S.A. 1951 repr.)


H. Chadwick _The Early Church_ (Penguin, 1967, repr.)

R. Collins _Early Mediaeval Spain_ (London, 1983)

J.M. Wallace Hadrill _The Barbarian West_, 400–1000 (London, 3rd ed. 1967)

E. James _The Origins of France_ (London, 1982)

R.W. Southern _The Making of the Middle Ages_ (London 1953, repr.)

C. Wickham _Early Mediaeval Italy_ (London, 1981)

Chapter II

## FEUDAL LAW

(i) Definition of feudalism

Feudalism (we are talking in the context of legal developments in Western Europe) is properly the grant of land, or, later, of office, by a king or other great man to a lesser man in return for military support, this land usually being reckoned an adequate economic unit to maintain the required soldiery. From a slightly different viewpoint, and if the initial conditions are varied a little, it is the system by which a lesser man commends himself and his land to a greater, offering military service in return for protection[1]. This is a deliberately narrow definition, but for a book concerned with legal history it seems better to try to isolate the original and essential elements. The concepts, facts and relationships described are deduced for the ninth and tenth centuries, but most of our evidence comes from the twelfth century and later. Indeed, much of the impact of feudal law came in the latter period, but by then it was already mingled with civil law, the learned law. Furthermore, economic arguments connected with feudal institutions are omitted for the sake of concentration on the (equally artificial) legal picture.

The system of commendation by someone already in possession of land arose more naturally from the political, economic and legal framework of the Later Roman Empire; that of original grant was more fitted to the settlements of the various Germanic tribes. Feudalism was a military matter; as the importance of being able in person to fight diminished so

----------

1    For example, Herlihy, documents 10 and 9.

44

feudalism in the narrow sense faded, although feudalistic legal and economic consequences long endured. And militarily it was linked with the central importance of the heavily armed cavalryman, the knight. There has been much discussion about the origin of the knight's rôle: the invention of the stirrup; the example of Berber and other raiders; King Pippin's postponement, in 755, of the mustering of the Frankish army from March to May, with the consequent greater availability of forage; but it is worth remembering that the shift in tactical importance from infantry to cavalry had already taken place in the Later Roman Empire. From the fourth century to the eleventh, although there might well be danger from a neighbour, there was always danger from the migrant, the raider; mobile troops were required, and the frontier armies of the Later Roman Empire -- the garrison troops -- had become second-class soldiers. Military conditions thus explain the central role of the knight and the pre-eminent need for defence, armed and mobile defence. Allied with the near-permanent state of war were the absence of an ordered political society, because a command from the capital would no longer reliably take effect at the frontier, the absence of constant and sure commerce, because a trader was too exposed to military danger, and the absence of civilization, in the sense that the pursuit of inessentials did not enhance life but threatened survival. Although not invariably, and not everywhere in equal degree, the characteristic need was for local self-sufficiency; hence the manorial economy is typical of feudalism, and towns, insofar as they survived, were by their nature non-feudal. This whole military system became most typical among the Carolingian Franks. Before the Carolingians, custom was very strong in the Germanic north, whereas in the south the influence of Roman law survived; this division, which roughly followed the line of the Loire, persisted and later the northern area became known as the pays de droit coutumier or pays de coutumes and the southern as the pays de droit écrit. In France north of the Loire the situation was summed up as 'Nulle terre sans seigneur', but in the south there was 'Nul seigneur sans titre'[2]; nevertheless, the subsequent growth of forces other than feudalism reduced the clarity of the picture.

(ii)  Feudal law and customary law

Feudal law existed in the narrow sense of the law regulating the personal tie between lord and vassal and the tenure by which the vassal held his land of the lord, but it also had to exist as part of the whole legal framework of society, based on Germanic customary rules, usually unwritten, which were already in use when feudalism emerged. Feudalism blended so well with customary law that the two became interwoven or even confused, but they were not so blended originally. Anglo-Saxon law in England is sufficiently well evidenced to illustrate a customary society that was not yet feudal (in the narrow sense), but it did absorb or receive feudalism readily when the Norman Conquest introduced it in the form of knights and castles. The Anglo-Saxons used written law, but it was written in the vernacular and hence comprehensible to lay judges; feudal law operated in a culture where the written language was Latin and therefore inaccessible to the unlearned, and this helps to explain its reliance on its own local custom. Charters, that is documents (later sealed) laying down the terms agreed between lord and tenant[3], were of very great

--------

2   'No land is without its overlord', and 'No man is lord unless he has
    some title'.

3   e.g., Herlihy, no. 23.

46

importance because they gave the beneficiary a tangible symbol of his right and also because, in spite of the theory of an oral customary law, they were written. Feudal law (in the narrow sense) dealt with land and succession to land, with some crimes, and with the knightly classes; there was virtually nothing on commercial contracts or even on moveables. It was also inextricably linked with jurisdiction, because its third highly characteristic feature, besides the personal tie and tenure, was the delegation, or rather dispersal, of governmental functions, such as defence, policing, justice, taxation, and general administration. The procedures by which disputes were settled came in part from the older tradition of life, in which the elders of the tribe defined what was the law and the king enforced sentence, but they were supplemented by the feudal practice of arms, whether in private war -- which was seen as a legitimate way to pursue a claim -- or in trial by battle. Compurgation, the practice by which a man's innocence or the truth of his claim was maintained, not on the basis of any objective evidence, but by summoning sufficient oath-helpers who would swear to his good character, was an element from customary Germanic law; it relied on the expectation that a man and his deeds would be known to his fellows, and seems not unreasonable in a closed society, provided that there was not too great a disparity of power between the parties. Trial by ordeal also had Germanic roots; it was based on the doubtful premise -- doubtful in view of biblical and missionary history -- that God would not allow the innocent to suffer and would therefore reveal the truth through the reaction to the ordeal[4]. But whichever of these three modes of trial was used, the judgment of the court was likely to be enforced by a feudal lord. Another customary element in

----------

4    Compare Liutprand's view on trial by battle, p.20.

47

feudal society was the institution of kingship; the king was certainly a feudal lord, at the apex of the pyramid, but he was more than a feudal lord; in the interest of public order, the Church reinforced his special role in the feudal age by anointing and other rites[5].

(iii)   The personal bond

The basic tie in feudalism was the personal link created between the vassal and his lord.  The vassal promised faithful service, or fealty, to his lord and did homage, a symbolic act of submission, for the fief, normally land, granted to him by the lord[6].  The lord invested his vassal with his fief, granting him the land and rights over it, and giving him lawful possession of it by delivery of seisin or sasine, another symbolic act such as the delivery of a clod of earth from the estate.  This personal tie was bilateral; both sides had duties as well as rights.  The vassal owed his lord whatever good faith required, and, more specifically, aid and counsel (auxilium and consilium).  Knight service was the basic type of aid, but aid might also include garrison duty, or the provision of a substitute in war when the vassal was personally incapacitated (or a sum of money in lieu -- in English terminology called scutage); it included too the payment of certain regulated sums, known as feudal aids or casualties (see below, p.53) and probably the provision of hospitality.  Counsel involved attendance on the lord, usually at the great feasts but also whenever he wanted to show his consequence, and in particular it involved attendance at his court, with the duty to advise there; this obligation

----------

5    Herlihy, no. 30.

6    Herlihy, nos. 11 and 15.

became in the course of time a right. The lord in his turn must protect and maintain his vassal. Protection was by arms or in some other way such as acting as surety (in Normandy later the vassal must also be prepared to stand surety for his lord up to the equivalent of a year's rent, when the lord was sued in court for a personal injury[7]). Maintenance was by gifts, or by the provision of bed and board and other necessities, or, most commonly, by the grant of a fief or benefice[8]. In theory the bond of fealty was supposed to be stronger than any other save a man's allegiance to God; after all, the fealty was enforced by an oath taken in the name of God. However, family ties and expediency operated, naturally enough, and kings strove to persuade their subjects to hold a higher loyalty to them than to their immediate lords[9]. There were, furthermore, circumstances in which a vassal could renounce his allegiance[10] or be released from its normal operation[11]. Nevertheless, the concept of good faith between lord and vassal and, within the feudal classes, of the right of each man to due respect, were factors that could contribute to the amelioration of society. "Between other lords and their vassals, faith ought so to be maintained that neither one of them ought to call for corporal violence or for violent blows against the person of the other party. If any of them should be

----------

7   Summa de legibus 27,6 (Herlihy, no.32); the Summa is a compilation of Norman feudal custom, first put together about the middle of the thirteenth century.

8   Herlihy, no.23.

9   e.g. Summa de legibus, 12,1 and 13,1.

10  Herlihy, no.12, esp. items 77 and 104.

11  e.g., according to the canon lawyers, in the event of an unjust war; v. p.137 ff.

accused of this in court and convicted, he is bound altogether to lose his fief for violating the faith he was obligated to observe. If this act should be discovered in a lord, homage should revert to his superior and dues should not longer be given, excepting what is owed the prince"[12].

(iv)  Tenure

Tenure is the term used to describe the grounds of a continuing possession of land, or of anything that could be equated with land. In a purely feudal society there was no ownership of land, except for the crown -- which itself held under God; every man held of another, knight from lesser lord, lesser lord from magnate, magnate from the king. Tenancy too in the Roman sense of a contract of hiring and leasing gave way, as far as land was concerned, to fiefs, because men had commended themselves and this was the price they had to pay, or because the king had recovered the land and military service alone was of use to him in the face of crisis, or because money to pay a rent was undervalued because one could not eat it or ride it or wear it (although the heritable holding of land in return for the annual payment of a fixed sum of money appeared early in Scottish feudalism). Thus the link between vassalage and fief or benefice became normal, although vassalage remained possible without a benefice, as in the case of household knights, or a benefice might be something other than land, such as the right to hold a market, or to take rabbits and hares in a warren, or to exercise some particular jurisdiction or office. Tenure could cover land granted whether for feudal services or in alms, or even land that had no lord, which is called allodial land (and did not exist in

----------

12  Summa de legibus 13,2-3.

strict feudal theory). Lands granted to the Church were normally held in free alms (frankalmoign), which meant that the saying of Masses and prayers for the grantor and his family was the only return required. Such piety had its disadvantages in that the Church never died, so that reliefs and aids such as wardship and marriage could never be demanded by the lord. Tenure was also the proper term to describe servile and peasant holdings, and those for which military service was rendered but at a level below knight service, such as sergeantries, blench holding (the Scottish grant of land in return for nominal service), etc; these free tenures had many local variations, as did the villein tenures. Feudal tenure, however, the concern of the law of fiefs, meant primarily holding by knight service or some equivalent. There might be many steps in the chain of feudal tenure between king and knight; the king's direct vassals were tenants-in-chief, normally magnates but not always, for we hear of men holding by sergeantry direct from the king. The process of a tenant granting out part of his fief to another is known as subinfeudation, and in this way the feudal pyramid could become enormously complex since, for example, a tenant-in-chief might through a dowry or some such means become the vassal of a mere knight. The only inherent restriction on subinfeudation was that a man must still be able to perform the services due to his lord. Subinfeudation of other than the direct sort brought about the condition of multiple vassalage, in which a man might have done homage to several lords for several estates[13]; problems of fealty obviously arose, and so the personal nature of the feudal tie was weakened in that not every lord, but only the liege lord (the lord to whom a man promised personal allegiance in his homage, and who had the right to the indivisible profits of overlordship —

----------

13    e.g. Herlihy, no.17.


51

that is, arising from personal relationships such as ward or marriage) was able to rely on his vassals.

In the pure, the military, model, land was granted in return for service and if, through death or incapacity, the service was no longer possible the land reverted -- escheated -- to the grantor. This was neither a good way of ensuring loyal service from the vassal, nor an effective method for the lord of maintaining his military power. As early as 877, under the Carolingian emperor Charles II, the Bald, there is evidence for fiefs being treated as heritable[14], although this ruling, the Quierzy capitulary, was not meant to set a precedent. However, it soon became normal to make a patrimonial claim; a man would expect the heirs-male of his body, or at least the eldest of them, to succeed to his lands, with the services attached to them, or even to some office. Primogeniture was a widespread rule because a normal knight's fief would not have the resources to support more than one knight, together with his men-at-arms; trained war horses in particular were very expensive. (Where, later, one does find fractions of a knight's service, this presumably was commuted into money.) The lord's right to recover his grant was given recognition in his right to claim a relief, a sum of money, from the heir before the latter could do homage and enter the fief. In Normandy in the thirteenth century we learn that the relief due on a knight's fief was £15, on a barony £100, 12d an acre on cultivated land, on a mill which was not otherwise part of a fief £3, and so on[15]. With the development of the heritable principle the lord also acquired the right to appoint a guardian, or to act himself as guardian, if the heir were under age; such a guardian

----------

14    Herlihy, no.21.

15    Summa de legibus 32,3-4.

52

was entitled to enjoy the profits of the estate although he must not waste its resources but no relief was then due when the heir came of age. Similarly, when there was no male heir, the lord had the right to select the husband for a female heir, so that the fief she brought her spouse would be held by someone loyal to the lord. These rights are known as wardship, or ward, and marriage.

There were besides three (or four) feudal occasions, which became traditional, when the lord could demand money from his vassal. These were on the knighting of the lord's eldest son, on the marriage of his eldest daughter, and for the ransoming of the lord's person if he were captured in war; in some places an aid was also due to help with the lord's preparations for going on crusade. Feudal aids were normally levied in proportion to the relief due on an estate, and so both in quantity and in frequency the demands a lord might make were restricted, by custom which became law. Restrictions also came to operate on the length of military service which could be required; forty days was normal, and thereafter the vassal must be paid his expenses. Similarly, the lord's right to claim hospitality would be limited to so many nights a year, and the number of followers he could bring with him would be restricted.

Thus in the normal course of things there was security of tenure. Gradually everywhere the lord's right to recover a fief because of some abuse by his tenant became a matter for trial in the lord's court by the vassal's peers; this was laid down at least as early as 1037 in a constitution of the Emperor Conrad II[16], and similarly in thirteenth century Normandy we are told that for a vassal to be deprived of his land and right, he must be convicted in court, "as the custom of Normandy

----------

16   Herlihy, no. 22.

requires"[17]. One form of misuse was the attempt to alienate the fief or some part of it without the lord's permission; the Emperor Frederick Barbarossa, at the Diet of Roncaglia in 1158, reserved the rights of lords in this matter[18]. The lord's permission, however, could normally be obtained for a payment.


(v) Delegation of governmental powers


The third element in feudalism was the dispersal of governmental powers. It is not clear how far this arose by conscious act and how far it was simply found to have happened. Merovingian and Carolingian kings granted immunities, that is freedom from the authority of royal officials, in matters of taxation or jurisdiction[19], particularly to the Church; some magnates may have extorted such privileges from an unwilling king. On the other hand, powers of policing, judging and punishing as concomitants to the control of land may never really have been questioned in an era of crisis, and the potentiores of the Later Roman Empire had begun to exercise such powers, however unlawfully. In England, as we shall see, custom was decided in popular courts which were carefully controlled by the kings and so, after the Norman Conquest, royal justice was able fairly rapidly to supplant feudal justice. In France the resumption of justice by the crown after the tenth century was a slow process; in the Empire it was even slower. In Scotland the establishment of royal power was only achieved over a long period.

----------

17    Summa de legibus 13,4.

18    Herlihy, no.38.

19    Herlihy, nos. 28 and 29.

Some fiefs were known (in Norman feudalism) as 'honours', because they were linked from their origins with public office. In thirteenth century Normandy we are told that it was the duke, by now the French king, who was responsible for justice and peace, and so must search out and punish those who committed crimes of violence and those whose conduct led potentially to breach of the peace. In return for standing as liege lord to all [free] men he must "rule, protect, defend, and treat them according to the rights, customs, and laws of the land"[20]. His feudal justice was still of more significance than royal justice, although the two gradually merged. This merger occurred partly because only the king had powers overtly to make new laws and a professional civil service to put these laws into practice, and partly because "the lord has the right of judgment over all the fiefs which are held from him, whether they are held indirectly or directly"[21].

It is clear that in the high Middle Ages, throughout the area of the Carolingian Empire although not outside it, there was a distinction between the high justice and the low. The high justice gave power to punish with death crimes deserving of that penalty -- although persons caught in the act of, say, highway robbery could be hanged out of hand -- and also, in civil disputes, to have jurisdiction in cases which were to be settled by trial by battle. The low justice covered petty crime, and other feudal and manorial disputes. In most areas the high justice was restricted to princes, counts, and barons, and a simple knight would only exercise the low within his fief. Whether high or low (or undivided as was the case in some areas) justice was essentially territorial, applying to all who lived within a particular fief. The powers to levy and lead troops, to raise

----------

20  Summa de legibus 11 and 12,2.

21  Summa de legibus 27,7.

certain taxes, to control various aspects of administration, were all important, but the power of justice gave a lord physical control over those within his jurisdiction. It was also a source of profit to him, for any fines he imposed went to him, and the parties to any settlement must normally pay him for the judgment.

(vi) Judicial proceedings

The growth of feudal justice may be illustrated from France, where it absorbed most features of the older customary system. In the Merovingian kingdoms the customary form of judicial proceedings, except where the Church or some lord had been granted an immunity, was for the royal official, the count, who was under oath to know and to observe the law, to make a tour of the area of his authority. This area was divided into hundreds, a customary Germanic grouping, and in each hundred the count summoned all free men to his court, the mallus. There the assembly elected law-finders (doomsmen, scabini) to give their verdicts, under the presidency of the count. Their presence was the more essential while law remained personal rather than territorial; there is on record, for example, a case of 918 in the Languedoc when Roman, Salic, and Gothic scabini acted together. Charlemagne reformed this system. In order to ease the burden of attendance, he required the assembly of all free men in each hundred to meet only three times a year, for the consideration of major causes. Minor causes could be dealt with simply by the scabini (échevins) of whom thereafter there were usually seven for each hundred, elected for life, sitting most commonly under the presidency of the count's deputy; they continued to attend the mallus or placita. This was the origin of the distinction between the high and the low justice. However, as effective government crumbled during the civil wars and the invasions of the ninth and tenth centuries, the popular element in the administration of justice diminished. Procedure became feudalized, either because lords took over, with or without a charter, the exercise of jurisdiction, or because the counts turned their tribunals and the land granted for their support into honours, or because the scabini took advantage of their position to strengthen their place in feudal society. By the eleventh century the hundred courts in France had disappeared, and the scabini were normally within the feudal hierarchy, exercising the high or the low justice depending on their status as vassals. In the regions between the Seine and the Loire, high justice continued to be dispensed in general assemblies of the free population, under the presidency of a count or other magnate. The scabini, sometimes appearing as the lord's council, continued to give a collective judgment or declaration of the law; if necessary, enquiry could be made from such assemblies as to what was the law, the custom. Elsewhere north of the Loire, suit of court, the duty and right to attend a particular court, was attached to a particular tenement rather than to the status of free man, although the difference might not be very great in practice. Among the unfree or the very humble, it was normal for a superior to have jurisdiction over his tenants, not merely a knight over his villeins -- seignorial justice --, but even a villein over another villein, if the latter held land from the former; in such cases, jurisdiction would be restricted to the particular tenement, and would need the express permission of the overlord, whereas in the feudal ranks such permission was implicit.

In the German lands, in contrast to France, the law of fiefs (Lehnrecht) remained distinct from the law of the land (Landrecht), and so the feudal courts developed and remained side by side with the older courts, without absorbing them. Further, as in England, the idea that any free man could be a suitor to the king's court helped to keep alive allodial holding, especially in the Swabian Alps and Saxony. However, the scabini (Schöffen) who met under a judge (Richter) who was usually a feudal lord were normally required to hold land of a certain value, and there was also a tendency to regard their office as hereditary. Hence feudal attitudes, if not precisely feudalism, blended there too with customary law.

(vii)  Feudal society and the rest of society

There were, then, other classes in society than the feudal; this is to take a legal approach, viewing feudalism as a particular set of factors in society.  (It is quite possible to look at society as dominated by feudalism and thus feudal throughout, but that would be more a sociological or economic approach.)  In this narrow sense, peasants or unfree tenants generally did not fall within the terms of feudal law.  In feudalism proper there was no nationality, only hierarchy, but particular consequences were modified by local custom.  And local variations considerably affected the distinction between the lesser gentry, the free peasant, and the sergeant. 'Sergeants' is a translation of the Latin term servientes, and they originated from the men, free or servile, who served in person on their lords.  One group sprang from the major offices of a baronial household, the butler, the steward, the seneschal, the marshal; great families were founded by many such royal servants (this was the origin of the royal house of Stewart) and fortunes were made even by the servants of lesser men. Other sergeants were soldiers, granted land to hold by a military tenure not amounting to knight service.  In Germany, in particular, there was even a class of servile sergeants, **ministeriales**, who might achieve knighthood while still remaining unfree, and yet holding their lands by military service.

In some parts of Christendom, virtually all men were free; this was often the case in hill country, where the population was scattered, centred on a crossroads rather than a compact village, and occupied with raising sheep or with growing vines or olives. Where there was plentiful arable land, manors and nuclear villages were common. The usual model is of one manor to one village, but there might be two or more manors in a big village, and it was possible for one knight in his castle to dominate two or more villages.

The manor as an administrative and economic unit predated feudalism, but it adapted perfectly to it. The open-field system as a method of collective farming had customary roots, and the lord's share, the demesne, readily fitted into the scheme. Within the typical manor there would be some free peasants — some rich enough to own a plough team, others not — and more who were not free, but, in either case, the peasant would in many places make an act of homage to his lord for his tenement and be formally invested with it. A free man might hold by base tenure or an unfree man by free tenure, and both free and unfree would have suit of court at the manor, but the free man holding by free tenure might, in theory at least, have access to the king's courts. For free tenure payment would be in money or in kind; tenure for a money payment was described by the _Summa de legibus_[22] as 'voluntary', because it did not result "from the necessity of inheritance". Servile tenure involved week-work -- the labour of a single man -- for perhaps, three days a week. Free tenants as well might in some

----------

22    26,8.

cases be called on for boon-work, for help with the harvest and at any other particularly busy time in the agricultural year. The villein would be subject at his death to the exaction of his best beast as heriot, the equivalent of the feudal relief, for this forfeit gave his sons the right to take over his (unfree) holding; the villein must also pay a tax called merchet if his daughter married outside the manor (this is the basis for the fictional droit de seigneur). The village mill was often the lord's monopoly, as with the Scots thirlage, and so might be the village wine-press or brewery, and even the free peasant might be obliged to use it. The lord could also raise from the unfree a tax called tallage, originally arbitrary, but by the eleventh century usually fixed as to frequency and amount, often in writing, according to the custom of the manor; there might be other levies on special occasions, roughly comparable to the feudal aids. The lord's court would often be presided over, in the lord's absence, by his reeve or bailie; although the suitors spoke to the custom of the manor, trial by their peers was not a common right for those subject to seignorial courts. Such trial was rather more likely in the north, where Germanic customary law had stronger roots, and rather less so in the south, where men more often remembered that Roman magistrates had been the superiors, not the equals, of those whom they had judged.

In the towns, the burgesses had their own courts based on mercantile custom, from which was to develop the law merchant (see chapter VI). They sometimes held their land freely, as allod, or by some customary title, or often from the king or prince by burgage tenure; such tenures could be bought and sold, just like moveable property, without any lord's consent, and such sales could not be revoked by the seller's heirs or relatives. In burgage holding, sisters usually received an equal portion with brothers, and ward went normally to the next of kin, as was the old Germanic custom

60

not dissimilar to Roman practice. Burgesses often put themselves under the direct protection of the king, for example, in London or at St. Andrew's; towns were in general, especially in the south of Europe, unfeudal.

(viii) The formalization of feudalism

It is something of a paradox that one can see the end of feudalism, in the sense of the essentially simple system that has been described, as falling in the twelfth century, yet it is, in a different sense, just at this period that feudalism appears as something of which the men of the time were consciously aware. It is in the twelfth century that lawyers, known as feudists, first appear in the Italian cities and comment on feudal law as a speciality, and that feudal law becomes a written law -- and therefore able to blend with the civil or learned law. By the beginning of the thirteenth century, although private wars had not completely ceased, life in western Europe was reasonably peaceful; the 'heroic' age of feudal warfare had passed. Markets had grown as the population increased now that there was surplus production; towns and trade were flourishing. Feudal holdings were valued at least as much for their financial returns, such as judicial profits, as for their military strength. Kings and princes more commonly employed mercenary troops of soldiers than the feudal levy; such troops were paid from scutage (as a substitute for military service) or even by taxation raised for this particular purpose. Cross-bows and cannon came to devalue the old knightly skills and techniques; thus we find a weakening of the personal tie between lord and vassal. The tendency to centralization on royal power made overt legislation possible; we shall see examples in England, and the same process was at work in France, in Scotland, and in the Empire. Moreover, professional civil services were

61

also developing[23], and their continuity strengthened royal at the expense of feudal justice. At the Fourth Lateran Council in 1215 the clergy were forbidden to take any part in trials by ordeal; although such trials did not at once disappear, their solemnity was much diminished and they began to fall into disuse[24]. Trial by battle also became less frequent, although it still had a long life (the last, and confessedly antiquarian, attempt to use it in England took place in 1818); in the kingdom of Sicily, Frederick II was able to restrict it severely in 1231[25] on the grounds of its irrationality. The 'bad baron' had largely disappeared, although he had been a very real figure[26]. Lords, not yet in legal terms landlords under a contract, preferred other than military forms of service, and money ties were adequate between lord and vassal when there was little likelihood of their having to go into battle side by side. Money fiefs became common in England and France. From the thirteenth century, although feudal rules on property and succession had a long life ahead of them, the most active sphere of feudal thinking was probably in constitutional law.

The court of the king, the prince, and in some cases of the great dukes and counts, as in Normandy and Flanders, always had had a claim to an authority that was more than feudal. It was to such courts that cases concerning allodial estates must come, as also cases defining the boundary between secular and ecclesiastical jurisdiction. These are described as regalian rights; in the same category fell public highways and even markets, which also pertained by their nature to such sovereign courts,

-----------

23   Herlihy, no.45.

24   Herlihy, no.25.

25   Herlihy, no. 26.

26   v. the poem: Raoul of Cambrai, e.g. s.59 (Herlihy, no.31).

although jurisdiction over them was more likely to be granted away or usurped. The growth of the king's royal, insofar as distinguishable from his feudal, court was both to help and be helped by the growth in the knowledge and use of the civil law. It is a phenomenon, in France especially, of the thirteenth century and after; in France it was linked with the increasing political power of the Capetians. In Germany, the rival appeal of the imperial rôle, exercised especially in Italy, often distracted the prince from strengthening his kingly power; for example, the emperor Frederick III did not set foot in his German territories from 1444 to 1471. In Germany there was no network of itinerant justices or permanent representatives of the crown, such as the Angevins developed in England and the Capetians copied as they could. Nevertheless, it was through the crown that eventually, several centuries later than England and France, Germany was to acquire a degree of judicial centralization.

The other thing that strengthened the royal at the expense of the feudal courts was appeal. The concept of appeal linked the customary, sacred, role of the prince with the imperial supremacy of the civil law, in defiance of the feudal attitude that one's immediate lord was one's only natural judge and that to seek redress elsewhere was to weaken the tie of vassalage. But even in feudal custom the denial of justice to one's man was a breach of the duties of lordship. Hence, when a man was denied a hearing, or when false judgment was given, he could properly accuse his lord before that lord's lord. This was in theory an action for redress quite unrelated to the cause which lay behind the miscarriage of justice, but it is hardly surprising that the king's professional advisers turned such procedures into true appeal. The king's counsellors in such matters would be trained in the civil or the canon law, or both, wherein a hierarchy of courts was normal. The process fitted into the feudal

63

pyramid, at the top of which stood the king's court, but it was not itself feudal. It was another step towards the unity of justice within a realm.

(ix)  Feudal law and academic law: the literature of feudal law

Even before the twelfth century and the explosive growth of interest in the civil law, the law of the Corpus Iuris Civilis (to which the next chapter is devoted, and where some of the technical terms used in the next few paragraphs will be more fully explained), legal scholars at Pavia had produced glosses and commentaries on the Liber Papiensis and the Lombarda; that is, they had explained particular words and phrases, and they had drawn out applications relevant to their own day. In the first flowering of the law school at Bologna scholars were interested in the Lombard version of feudal customary law, for it was in force in much of Italy. Charles  (Karolus) de Tocco from Benevento, who taught at Bologna, composed a gloss to the Lombarda which acquired considerable authority in both law schools and courts. But the tendency in the northern Italian cities during the twelfth century was to belittle the Germanic element in Italian law; in Naples and the south a more sustained interest was shown. However, even if the Glossators of Bologna were eager to stress the values of Roman law, they could not long exclude from their studies all aspects of feudal law. Moreover, there was a formal sense in which the modern, that is post-Lombard, developments of the feudal and  customary law described in such works as the Liber Papiensis could not fail to be recognized, for they included the legislation of emperors such as  Charlemagne, Otto the Great, Conrad II, and others, who claimed to be emperors in succession to Justinian.

In the 1150s one Obertus de Orto, a judge of the imperial court at

Milan, and therefore aware of the traditions of the cities, made a collection best known as the Libri Feudorum (Books of the Feus). This was based mainly on imperial legislation in the kingdom of Italy but also included other materials such as decisions from various feudal courts, Lombard custom and some extracts from the writings of the school of Pavia. The story runs that Obertus' son went to study law at Bologna and was astonished to find no attention paid to the legal system to which his father devoted his life. Obertus replied to his son in two letters in which he laid out the basic elements of feudal law; the composition of the Libri was subsequent. Obertus had the weight of actual practice on his side; as was said: "Roman law is of no weak authority, but its force does not extend to overthrowing custom"[27].

Thus there developed among the jurists better known for their work as civilians (or specialists in the civil, the Roman, law) a degree of interest in feudal law (a specialist on which is known as a feudist). Pillius (fl. 1169-1207), a pupil of the great Placentinus, commented on the Libri Feudorum when he was teaching at Modena, and he started on an Apparatus. Towards the middle of the thirteenth century the Bolognese jurist, James de Ardizzone, reorganized the material, with additions into two books; he also wrote a Summa on feudal law. A third version of the collection divided the books into titles, on the model of the Corpus; an authoritative gloss to this, developing Pillius' Apparatus, was produced around 1220 and used by Accursius in his Standard Gloss. It was in this form -- the Vulgate version -- that Hugolinus (d.1234) added the Libri to the final volume of the Corpus which contained Justinian's Novels. Thus the main collection of the sources of feudal law became classed among

-----------

27  Books of the Feus, II,1.

the libri legales, the legal books of the learned law. Thereafter, no longer despised as barbaric, it was studied as though an integral part of the Corpus. The glossed version of this enlarged Corpus was the edition in normal use by practitioners of law until the sixteenth century or even later. Scholars continued to use it until the critical editions of the nineteenth century were published.

Particular interest in the Libri Feudorum continued to be shown in southern Italy but, among other jurists whose main place is in later chapters, Jacques de Révigny (d.1296) commented on them, and James de Belvisio (1270-1335), sometime royal judge and councillor at Naples, later a lecturer at Perugia and Bologna, wrote on them and on the Novels (the Authenticum version). Baldus (c.1320-1400), a noted civilian and canonist (specialist on canon law) of the fourteenth century, wrote on the Libri and on the treaty of the Peace of Constance (1183), at which the emperor had conceded to the communes of northern Italy the use of their local customs. Antonio di Pratovecchio (c.1380-1468), while at Padua, recast the two Libri into six books, and edited their gloss; another teacher at Padua, Giacomo Alvarotto (c.1385-1453), introduced the non-specific use of the term feudal when he wrote a description of the basic and general principles governing the law of the feu or fief in a book entitled De Feudis (Concerning Feus).

While the academic lawyers were thus refining the concepts of feudal law in the universities, those who actually administered such law, whether on their own behalf or on their prince's, were blending into their practice the learning of the civilians. In England, shortly before 1190, a book known as Glanvill, after its supposed author, described the laws and customs of the realm, especially as administered by the royal courts; the main content is feudal and customary, but Glanvill quotes in certain areas from the Institutions of Justinian, and the shape and concept of the book derive from the learned law. (Glanvill was imported into Scotland somewhat later, with appropriate variations, and this version is known as Regiam Majestatem.) Nearly half a century after Glanvill a feudal lord called Eike von Repgow produced a similar work applicable to Saxony, the Sachsenspiegel (Mirror of the Saxons); it too was concerned with local custom, and it too could not have been written had not the study of feudal law become well established in the universities. It was an unofficial compilation, dealing mostly with matters of customary and feudal land law, but it was of great authority and was later adopted in other regions of Germany. We shall return to the influence of these works in later chapters.

The Customs of Beauvaisis, more properly the customs of the county of Clermont in Beauvaisis, were described in the 1280s by Philippe de Beaumanoir[28]. He also was not a jurist but a feudal lord with considerable experience of the administration of justice. The Customs reveal the blend that had come into being even in the pays de droit coutumier (region of customary law) in France north of the Loire, or, rather, they reveal one particular blend made up predominantly of feudal custom with a seasoning of the learned law. In his prologue Beaumanoir made a very significant point; he stated that he was led to write down these customs for their more secure maintenance, for he had observed that they prevailed over the ancient laws (that is, the Roman law) in practice but that, since memories are fallible, what is not written is soon forgotten. This need to put things into writing was one of the ways by which the learned law came to dominate custom, just as in the first reception of Roman law by the Germanic invaders of the Empire the existence of a written law had affected their

----------

28    Herlihy, no.33.

customs and attitudes. Men's memories of an event which happened only days or weeks ago are unreliable; their memory of how their fathers dealt with some matter of moment is likely to be even less reliable, unless fortified by some record. It is the paradox of custom as a basis for law that one then looks to the record, and custom in the true sense ceases to be operative. The rules and attitudes which had grown up around tenure and services and traditional relationships remained the rules which governed these matters but, through writing, they lost flexibility while at the same time becoming open to reforms, such as the moves towards a more rational form of legal procedure.

Beaumanoir limited himself formally to the customs of his region for "we ought to have a better memory of that which we have seen practised and judged since our infancy in our district, rather than in another district of which we have not learned the customs or the usages". He therefore based himself on the judgments made in the county in his own time, and the clear usages and clear customs long followed there. When there was doubt, he looked to judgments made in neighbouring jurisdictions; if those failed him, he then looked to the law common to the entire kingdom of France. This last might involve the law taught in the universities, the civil law, as well as the custom of the king's own court, but the ordering of priority in his sources is clearly feudal. He gave examples of custom and usage, which he distinguished by holding that custom was, within a jurisdiction, something universally observed, while usage was open to challenge. An example of a clear custom was the rule that a person who admitted a debt must pay up within seven days, unless he were of the nobility when he had fifteen days: "This custom is so clear that I have never seen it challenged". Only a usage, although it was widespread, was the rule that peaceful possession for a year and a day gave sasine or seisin, protected possession, although that sasine was still open to challenge on the question of title and right. He described as a second example of usage the peaceful tenure of a piece of property for ten years, in the view and with the knowledge of those who might have wished to prohibit it. This tenure, as long as there was a causa (apparent grounds for title) such as purchase, gift, legacy, forfeit or inheritance, and as long as the property was held from its lord by some rent that was due to him, gave the possessor sasine and full title. Peaceful possession for thirty years, even without a causa, as long as the lord received his dues, gave sasine and full title. These usages were of no effect where the land was held as dowry or for life or as leasehold or as a pledge, for no one could by his mere will change the grounds for his possession[29]. The year-and-a-day rule was indeed one of customary origin — for example, a serf who managed to support himself for so long in a town acquired freedom from his lord --, but the other two usages are taken directly from the rules on acquisition through prescription laid down by Justinian[30]. The civil law is here apparent, but the context remains essentially feudal, as does the principle that no usage which diminished the normal value of an estate for its lord was valid against him unless he received some form of rent or return.

The academic development of feudal law thus came to be normal, normal in practice, normal in the schools, in the twelfth and thirteenth centuries. Men still stressed the importance of custom, partly for the secure feeling that they were following the habits of their ancestors. Yet writing allowed different types of changes to be made, which could accord with new notions of royal power or new demands of commerce. The blend of

----------

29  Nemo sibi ipse causam possessionis mutare potest (D.41,2,3,19).

30  Inst., 2,6pr.; C., 7,39,8 (AD 528).

feudal and customary law with the civil law created its own new custom (which we shall look at in the later chapter on the ius commune) when the same general principles were applied, although still with local variations, throughout western Europe from the fourteenth to the sixteenth century. Even in the seventeenth century the same received ideas and accepted techniques were common practice throughout Europe. As an illustration, Sir Thomas Craig (1538-1608), a Scottish advocate who had studied in France and who became Sheriff of Edinburgh in 1573, produced a major work, entitled Ius Feudale (Feudal Law), around 1603. It was printed in 1655 and there were still sufficient traces of a European common law for it to be used as a textbook in German and Dutch universities. Feudal customary law is one of the major strands in European legal history; it is mildly ironic that its importance was enhanced by its confluence with the learned law.

Further Reading

M. Bloch Feudal Society (2nd ed. London, 1962, repr.)

F.L. Ganshof Feudalism (3rd ed. London, 1964)

D. Herlihy The History of Feudalism (U.S.A., 1970, repr.)

P. Vinogradoff, "Customary Law" in The Legacy of the Middle Ages, ed. C.G.
    Crump and E.F. Jacob (Oxford, 1926)

Chapter III

## THE GLOSSSATORS

(i) The background to the revival of the study of Roman law


The ground was well prepared, but the arrival of the Glossators as a
school of jurists on the European scene may appear as a sudden phenomenon.
Traditionally the school was founded by one Irnerius, a grammarian of
Bologna. The story goes that he turned to the study of law after having
been consulted about the meaning of the word as (a Roman coin of small
value) in the New Testament phrase: "Nonne duo passeres asse venount"
("Are not two sparrows sold for a farthing?"[Matt.10,29]). His researches
led to the discovery of the technical meaning of the term as in the Roman
law of succession, where it is used as the duodecimal unit for dividing an
inheritance up among more than one heir. From this he went on to the study
and teaching of Roman law. Another tradition links him with the Countess
Matilda of Tuscany, who is supposed to have encouraged him to set up a law
school at Bologna. The suggestion that it was anti-imperial must be
mythical since, as teachers (which is what the term 'doctor' means[1]) of the
secular imperial law, the Bolognese civilians tended to support the Empire.
All that can be said with certainty is that the study of Roman law was
revived at Bologna towards the end of the eleventh and at the beginning of
the twelfth centuries, and that Irnerius was an important figure in that
revival. If he was not the first teacher there, for we do hear of a

----------

1   Master was the normal title of the teacher in  arts at a mediaeval
    university, but doctor became the normal term for a  law teacher in
    Italy from the mid twelfth century; usage varied elsewhere.

certain Pepo (Joseph), he was the first to leave any identifiable writings, and he was looked to in succeeding generations as the founder of the school.

As we have seen, the revival of Roman law was due to a number of causes: the superiority of the written law, the increase in leisure and commerce, the growth of towns, the intellectual battles of papalists and imperialists, but the single most significant factor, the _sine qua non_, was the recovery of the full text of the _Corpus Iuris Civilis_, and in particular of the _Digest_. For, while the _Institutes_ and the _Code_ were relatively familiar, the _Digest_ was not known; a Tuscan judgment of 1076 certainly cites it, but without understanding, and a citation from Ravenna in 1084 ascribes to the _Digest_ a text that is in fact from the _Code_. Two manuscripts seem to have appeared in the eleventh century; the one which survives to this day was written in the sixth century in southern Italy and was held at Pisa by the twelfth century. (It is known to us as the Florentine, because in a war between the two cities in 1406 Florence took it as booty and has possessed it ever since.) The other is the supposed ancestor of all the copies made at Bologna; it is known as the _Codex Secundus_. While we do not know precisely when or how they were discovered, it seems in the highest degree likely that it was by canonists engaged in the search for legal ammunition. It is evident that by the beginning of the twelfth century the capacity, the knowledge, and the techniques existed to master the complex and sophisticated Roman sources.

That Bologna became the first centre specifically concerned with Roman law may be partly a matter of chance, perhaps the chance that Irnerius was there and teaching in the school of arts. But Bologna was a crossing point for trade routes between various parts of the north of Italy and the south; it was also near the border between imperial and papal territory. And

Pavia in Lombardy was not very far away and already a centre of study for Lombard law, and the Lombard lawyers had shown some familiarity with Roman sources.

(ii) The importance of the Glossators

It is commonly said that Roman law was revived in the twelfth century -- or sometimes, more accurately, that the study of Roman law was revived then -- but this does not give a wholly correct impression. Certainly there was an enormous upsurge of interest in and study of the texts of Roman law, and particularly of Justinian's compilation, but what influenced the law from this time onwards was not necessarily what Justinian had intended to have effect as Roman law, far less what had been in force as Roman law in the classical period. What was important was the use made of the texts by the scholars who worked on them; this is why the term civil law is often more apt for the mediaeval (and later) handling of the Roman law texts. There was room for creative activity because of the nature of Justinian's compilation, on which both study and teaching were based. As we saw in the first chapter, arguments incorporated in the texts could be brought out and developed, or adapted to new circumstances.

The work of the Glossators is of fundamental importance in the long process of assimilation of elements of Roman law into European legal systems. First, the Glossators mastered the sources of Justinian's law and in particular the _Digest_, the least accessible by reason of its bulk and complexity. In effect, they produced a working edition of the _Corpus_, for the _Standard Gloss_ of Accursius (to which we shall come) was the culmination of their control of the material. Second, they influenced legal practice and administration, for both of which they provided an

73

education that was secular not ecclesiastical.  It is false to suggest that the Glossators had no interest in law in practice; Irnerius himself acted as judicial assessor, and also as an envoy to the Emperor Henry V on the death of Countess Matilda, while in 1118 he was in Rome taking a prominent part in the election of an anti-pope in the  imperial interest.  Among others who played a significant part in public life were Bulgarus, Hugh of the Ravenna Gate (Ugo de Porta Ravennate), Placentinus, Pillius, Hugolinus, James (Jacobus) Balduini, and Hubert of Bobbio (Ubertus Bobiensis), whose work we shall meet in due course.  Third, the Glossators founded a science of law, in the sense of a framework of juridical concepts which made it possible to provide rational legal solutions to conflicts of interests in society in place of solutions based on custom or mere force.  They offered law as a self-conscious structure, an ordering instrument for society, and this on a European scale.

(iii) Approaches to handling the texts

There has been much discussion of how far the Glossators were influenced by the prevailing Scholastic philosophy.  Scholasticism may be described as a system of philosophy which sought to work out by dialectic the rational, harmonious and divine order which was believed to exist in the world and, indeed, in the universe.  The name Scholasticism later became associated with hair-splitting distinctions and forced logic; some nineteenth century scholars therefore attempted to clear the Glossators of any contamination by denying that there was any dependence.  A better appreciation of Scholasticism, concentrating on its intellectually liberating initial effects rather than the somewhat exaggerated weaknesses of its later days, makes it clear that it would be extraordinary if there were no such influence. The Glossators were, after all, men of their time.

One must expect of the Glossators a knowledge of the subjects of the trivium and quadrivium; of these the most relevant to law were dialectic (or logic) and rhetoric. The arts of reasoning and argument are necessarily of some concern to lawyers. The foundations of both were laid in Greece, the most important contributions being the works of Aristotle known collectively as the Organon (tools, i.e. of thought). But only the more elementary part of Aristotle's work, the Old Logic (logica vetus), was known before the mid-twelfth century; the remainder, the New Logic (logica nova), which forms the basis of the specifically Scholastic logic, came into use in the later twelfth and early thirteenth centuries. It can be demonstrated that the Glossators knew and used the Old Logic and rhetorical devices in their work. Irnerius, for example, used logical techniques to explain difficult texts; prefaces to works such as Azo's Summa Codicis follow the rhetoricians' advice on how to capture the reader's attention by tricks of the trade. There is, however, no reliable evidence of the use of the New Logic; it may have been known to the Glossators, but they had settled their techniques by the end of the twelfth century. The more important point is that the whole attitude of the Glossators corresponded to the aims of Scholasticism -- to harmonize and systematize, to use reason to explain and justify an authority which was at the centre of their studies as a guide to the harmonious order which they sought to discover (and, having discovered, to bring about). For the civilians the central authority was the Corpus Iuris Civilis, as the Bible and the Fathers of the Church were for the theologians, and Aristotle for the philosophers. The Corpus was the chief expression of Roman law, and Roman law held this central authority partly because of the idea of the continuity of Roman law under the Holy Roman Empire -- the idea of renovatio imperii was a commonplace by the end of the eleventh century -- and partly because of its place as part of the classical heritage. Certainly there was Scholastic influence, but dependence must not be pressed too hard, for there may have been reciprocal influence; the Glossators' quaestiones disputatae (Questions for discussion) as a form of instruction seem to have been taken as a model by the theologians. In relation to quaestiones there is a significant difference between the lawyers and the philosophers in that the Glossators' aim seems to have been not so much to confute an opponent's line of argument as to present the arguments for decision by a judge. The solutions are not presented as absolutely correct; after giving arguments for and against a solution, they do not simply point out the faults in the other view but rather put forward a view as preferable, although still open to challenge, leaving the decision to someone else.

Moreover, the Corpus Iuris Civilis itself offered encouragement to harmonization and systematization because Justinian had claimed that it was a harmonious whole. There are also examples of the use of dialectic and rhetoric in the Roman texts, and whether they came from the classical jurists themselves or from interpolation by the compilers of the Corpus was not a matter which troubled the Glossators. In fact, the extent to which the Roman jurists used the techniques of rhetoric or were influenced by Greek philosophy is itself much discussed -- again with a frequent tendency to claim independence for the jurists -- but the Glossators simply looked at the texts as they had them. Furthermore, the Glossators clearly assumed that Roman law, as they understood it, was law to be applied. Although they could not fail to notice that not all its institutions, such as the Roman magistracies, were still in existence, and indeed they pointed out what was no longer used in practice, Roman law was discussed as a living system. For example, there is a text (D.9,2,7,4) which says that no action

76

for wrongful damage would lie as a result of a wrestling or boxing match "because the damage is held to have been done in the cause of fame and valour, not wrongdoing"; they applied this to tournaments among knights. This sort of updating was necessary because an important function of the Glossators was to teach the men who were intending a career as administrators, including forensic employment, in the service of princes and also of the Church; even although many ecclesiastics studied only the canon law, Roman law was a necessary subsidiary source.

(iv) Methods of teaching

The name Glossators is given to the jurists of this school because the characteristic product of their work on the texts was the gloss, marginal or interlinear, either in the sense of an explanatory comment on the individual word or phrase or text (i.e., the whole passage), or in the sense of an _apparatus_ (collection) of glosses to a part or the whole of the Corpus. The so-called Great Gloss of Accursius is the most famous and was the most widely used of such apparatus; it was the standard commentary on the text after its completion in the mid thirteenth century, and its success helps to account for the name 'Glossators'. However, that name is somewhat misleading if it suggests that the gloss was their only literary product, and that the sole interest of the school lay in detailed comment on the Roman texts. What is true is that much of the literary production of the Glossators arose from their teaching, and that most forms of literature other than glosses can be traced back to comments made in the course of teaching. Because of this connection between their teaching and their writing it is illuminating to consider their teaching methods before dealing with the literature they produced.

For example, Odofredus (d. 1265) tells us that the lecturer would work his way through a particular section of the Corpus, such as the Institutes or the Old Digest[2], following the order of the texts, which were known as leges (laws); hence the 'legal order' is the order which Justinian's compilers gave to the texts. The first step was to explain how the books and titles fitted together, that is, why one followed the other in the order that they did. In principle he would go on to discuss each text. First he would set out the factual case or cases dealt with. Then he would read the text through and deal with any grammatical or syntactical problems in interpreting it. He would refer to any parallel passages (similia), and also point out any texts which seemed to conflict (contraria). Where there were apparent conflicts he would resolve them, for example, by forming a distinction (distinctio) to show how one text applied in one situation and the other in one which was different in some way. He might even pick out pairs of arguments (brocard(ic)a or brocards) as commonplace examples of the arguments for and against a proposition -- for example, silence means consent: silence is not consent -- as rules to be applied in different contexts[3]. He would also point out any general applications of the text, showing how it could be used as an argument or 'proof' in forensic debate, that is, as authority for a legal proposition. Especially important texts or the principles contained in them would be picked out as noteworthy points (notabilia). At the end the lecturer would often raise questions

----------

2   For the mediaeval division of the Corpus, v. Appendix I.

3   Tacitly allowing something to happen may operate as consent, as when you allow another to stand surety for you, but if someone sells your property your silence is to be interpreted as ignorance of the deed rather than consent to it.

(_quaestiones_) suggested by the text; he might discuss these in the lecture or, as did John (Johannes) Bassianus, master of Azo, at a separate time set apart for such discussion or disputation (often evenings or Saturday mornings). This last proceeding was very important because the questions discussed or disputed were usually points to which no text offered a clear solution, perhaps because they arose from contemporary practice, and the search for a solution allowed constructive use of the material in the _Corpus_. Ideas were taken from their original context and applied in new ways; a very famous example is the application of the phrase "what touches all must be approved by all" (C. 5,59,5,2 -- "quod omnes similiter tangit ab omnibus comprobetur"), originally concerned with the liability of co-tutors, to insist on the need for consent, whether to certain steps in litigation or to taxation or to other matters, by the parties involved.

Of course, not every text was necessarily dealt with in such detail. We hear criticisms of lecturers who pedantically did so, and we have reports of lectures where the students were told to go and read some texts for themselves because they presented no problems. On the other hand, some university statutes required lecturers to deal with all the texts and to omit none. But the approach described was the general scheme, which was still in use with only minor variations as late as the sixteenth century by those who followed the traditional methods.

(v) Forms of literature: glosses and apparatus of glosses

These are the typical product of the activity of the Glossators as teachers. It is often suggested that they began by writing individual glosses and gradually progressed to writing _apparatus_; while it must be true that individual glosses came first, nevertheless _apparatus_ are certainly older than Azo, who the nineteenth century scholar Savigny[4] thought was the first --at the end of the twelfth century -- to write an apparatus. Whether they go back to Irnerius or his immediate followers, the Four Doctors (Bulgarus, Martin Gosia, Hugh of the Ravenna Gate, and Jacobus), as has been suggested, is more doubtful. Development before Azo is perfectly understandable when glosses and apparatus are seen as a product of teaching devoted to a particular part of the Corpus.

Glosses which have survived from the earlier twelfth century reveal types of gloss corresponding to the various stages of discussion or exposition of the texts as described above, with the exception of quaestiones. These last appear as literature only towards the end of the century and seem to have originated as separate writings, in the form of collections recording disputations in which several lines of argument had been deployed. They then appear as explanatory glosses in the form of questions and suggested answers to questions which had not been settled by the texts, along with the other types of gloss. Insofar as they deal with points of difficulty which are not directly raised in the texts they are distinct from solutions (solutiones) of contrary texts.

One can thus identify forms of literature with methods of teaching. There are introductions to titles (introductiones titulorum) which usually appear as glosses to the rubrics -- for Irnerius found the titles within the books which make up the Digest, Code and Institutes already named, as are the individual novels. Introductions define the main concept or terms used in the rubric, and explain the context of the title and the division of the material within it. Sometimes such introductions led onto a more

----------

4    He was very influential in the development of law in Germany during the nineteenth century; v. chapter XVII.

general discussion; for example, the discussion of the rubric to D. 1,1 On justice and law was very fruitful for wide-ranging jurisprudential argument[5]. There are similar introductions to individual texts. The basic explanatory gloss -- naturally the most frequent of all -- may even be fitted into the text, so that it makes sense only if read as a constituent part. For example, D. 7,1,9,4 (a title on usufruct, or liferent) runs: "There is a point closely related to this (huic vicinus) which is usually discussed in relation to the law on accession to land; it has been settled that the usufructuary is entitled to a usufruct of accessions by alluvio [land added by the gradual deposit of soil by a river]"; the gloss Huic vicinus runs: "Closely related to this because other additions to something subject to a usufruct have been dealt with above and similarly are discussed below". Glosses deal both with textual problems, such as variant readings or the explanation of difficult words, and with juristic matters, such as the reasons for decisions or the citation of other relevant material; in this way a thorough system of indexing was established. Many glosses are signed by a letter or symbol (siglum) indicating the author, but this is not a reliable form of ascription because of errors of attribution and because each generation of the jurists built on the work of its predecessors.

Other forms of glosses were less closely attached to individual words or phrases and reach a more abstract level of interpretation, attempting to fit the text into the system of rules as a whole[6]. In early glosses particularly there are lists of parallel and conflicting passages, (similia and contraria) giving cross-references throughout the great bulk of the

----------

5    Appendix I(a) gives an early example.

6    v. Appendix I(b), showing the modification of the Roman rules.

81

Corpus. Parallel passages naturally reinforced the obvious interpretation of the basic text; with a conflicting passages, a solutions would be suggested which sprang from reading the material - whether within the title or even within the whole Corpus as a whole[7]. A special form of conflicting passage, known as authenticae, arose from the effect on the Roman texts of the Novels, including occasionally the legislation of the Holy Roman Emperors, especially in the Code (that is Books 1-9). For example, Auth. Sacramenta puberum provided that when a minor over the age of puberty incurred an obligation fortified by oath it could not be set aside on the grounds of his minority, which conflicted with the possibility of restitutio in integrum offered by the Roman texts. Irnerius was responsible for many authenticae.

Distinctions are found in all types of gloss to explain doubtful or conflicting points, or to provide a guide through these. For example, the term 'will" (voluntas) we find categorized[8]:

Will [= intention]

| sometimes just | sometimes unjust |
|---|---|
| constant | inconstant |
| of permanent effect | not of permanent effect |
| granting to each his due | not granting to each his due |

----------

7   For example, Irnerius pointed out that Justinian claimed authorship of his Code. Yet many of its constitutions were the work of other emperors; Justinian was not the sole author of the texts, although he was of the Code's compilation; v. H. Kantorowicz and W.W. Buckland Studies in the Glossators of the Roman Law (Cambridge, 1938, repr. 1969 with addenda and corrigenda by P. Weimar), p.233.

8   Kantorowicz and Buckland, p. 301.

Will [= testament]

| sometimes last | sometimes not |
|---|---|
| in testamentary form | not |
| concerning a patrimony | concerning a special fund |
| a soldier's | a rustic's |

and so on. At this level a _distinctio_ may seem elementary, but considerable confusion can arise from not first defining one's terms. Used in a general sense distinctions explained whole areas of law, as can be seen in the example, quoted from Irnerius by Roffredus, on the contract of leasing[9].

Noteworthy points were particular or general thoughts or statements, apt for use as arguments in disputations on imagined cases or in solving actual problems of practice. For example, in the text (D. 7,1,9,4) on the usufructuary and alluvial accessions the gloss on 'entitled' stressed the general rule: "Note here that accessions follow the fate of the thing to which they accede", and went on to list other texts illustrating this rule. Such notable matters were often marked out physically in the MSS by pattern of writing or surrounding ornament.

_Quaestiones_ as literature appeared later than other forms of glosses, as we have said; they involve the assembling of several arguments to find a solution. They will be considered in section vii.

_Apparatus_ of glosses as a form of literature are distinct from reports of lectures. (The latter go back to John Bassianus and so are not as early as the earliest _apparatus_.) But only the earliest of them are individual works. Later ones built on earlier ones, the extent of the borrowing depending on the taste and degree of independence in thought of the later

----------

9    Appendix I(c).

writer; some of the best known authors such as Azo and Accursius took over a great deal from previous writers, although they signed the whole apparatus as their own work -- this was partly because the mediaeval mind had a much less severe view of what we would call plagiarism. We know that Azo in his apparatus to D. 50,17 (the last title in the Digest, de regulis iuris -- on maxims of law) derived much from Bulgarus (d.?1166) and from John Bassianus, under whom he had studied, and that Accursius in his turn absorbed the bulk of Azo's work. Further, it is likely that later writers introduced into their apparatus without acknowledgment ideas from earlier jurists, whether these came from lectures or from any sort of gloss.

As glosses were expanded by the introduction of additional material, including previous work, a gradual change in the structure of apparatus becomes apparent. Glosses tended to become more discursive and to include in the one comment elements which had earlier been distinguishable as separate types. All glosses, not just the simple, explanatory ones, came to be attached to words in the text instead of being fitted in beside the passage without a specific link. This made it easier to find the relevant discussions. Azo seems to have been the first to do this in his major apparatus to the Old Digest and the Code, but for long the introductions and the citations of similar and conflicting passages remained separate. Hugolinus brought in the lists of citations, and this style was followed by Accursius, although he more commonly absorbed such lists in other glosses.

There also seem to have been some formal changes in the style of lecturing as time went by which had their effects in the literature. Alexander de Sancto Egidio's reports of Azo's lectures on the Code suggest that explanations of difficult points were introduced at the point where the difficulty arose rather than at the end, as in the older order, but men such as Odofredus or James Balduini kept to the old order throughout the thirteenth century. A definite change occurred with the Commentators, the next main school of civilians, who laid more stress on the problems to be discussed, because they could discuss them on the basis of the existence of the Gloss as a standard commentary. In their handling, the apparatus changed to a comment on the glossed text which dealt with connected extracts rather than individual passages, and concentrated on the more significant texts.

## (vi) The Accursian Gloss and its influence

The Accursian Gloss, also known as the Glossa Ordinaria (Standard Gloss) or simply as 'the Gloss', is a huge compilation of glosses or apparatus of glosses to the whole Corpus Iuris Civilis. It totals nearly 97,000 items, and while the whole Digest (which is roughly one and a half times as long as the Bible) is perhaps one half of the complete mediaeval Corpus, it is significant of its special importance as a fruitful source of law that its glosses make up two thirds of the total number of glosses. Much is still uncertain about the Standard Gloss, including the method and order of its compilation. We know that Accursius was born c.1184, taught from 1221, and died c.1263, aged 78. The composition of the Gloss was probably his life's work. He was young when he first glossed the Institutes, and he later produced a second edition of that apparatus, but there seems to have been no second edition of the apparatus to any other part. There was a gradual accretion of material but it seems mostly, if not entirely, by later hands. It is not easy to detect Accursius' personal contribution, although it is certain that he made some additions of his own as well as selecting from the work of others, such as Azo. Cross-references provide no real guide to the order of composition among or within the individual parts of the Corpus, because of constant revisions. But it is clear that he viewed his work as one single apparatus to the whole Corpus.

The status that Accursius intended for his Gloss is not entirely clear. If from the start he hoped to produce the definitive edition, he did this without imperial backing or any other authorization which could lay down the authentic interpretation of the texts; but then, Gratian's Decretum was equally unofficial. Moreover, he may have been mindful of the Emperor Hadrian's admonition (D.1,2,2,49) that authority stemmed from the intrinsic value of juristic work. He may well have hoped to provide a definitive selection of material, but his principle of collection is not clear because of the scale of the Gloss, the absence of detailed modern study, and our ignorance of the sources available to him.

What is certain is the success of the Gloss in its own time and afterwards. It gained rapid acceptance in Italy as the standard commentary on the Corpus. When produced in the mid thirteenth century, it was accepted as the latest and most complete apparatus; thereafter, as the standard accepted commentary, it was regularly attached to the text for convenience of consultation. The Gloss is sometimes found without the texts, but for centuries it was rare to find the texts without the Gloss. In one sense it is the culmination of the work of the school of Glossators, that is insofar as it relates to the mastering of the content of the Corpus. In another sense one can say it is a sign of decay, in that it was never superseded, but the fact that it was never superseded more truly means that one approach to the texts had been followed up as far as was worthwhile. New lines were opening up.

Its acceptance can be explained not only by its merits as an apparatus of glosses, but also because it fulfilled the twin needs of practice and of legal science. For those concerned in the practice of law the Gloss provided a guide to the sources and their interpretation at a time when the statutes of many Italian city states were imposing liability on judges and legal assessors for fault in the performance of their duties; this was under the podestà constitution by which an outsider was brought in for a limited period as city manager. For legal science, whether as teaching or as scholarship, the Gloss provided a standard commentary as a basis for discussion and development. Development was possible because the texts were not viewed as a static body of material but as giving the solution to some problems and guidance on others. Thus the Glossators were able to develop the transfer of property by constitutum possessorium, that is in the form of a simple declaration by the transferor that he now held on behalf of the recipient.

The Gloss provided an indication of accepted usages, of answers to questions not settled by the texts, of accepted interpretations of the texts, and so on doubtful points the Gloss came to be given authority, although not usually binding authority. But on occasion it was made binding, as in fourteenth century Verona where a statute of 1328 prescribed that the Gloss must be followed failing any higher authority: in the absence of statute or custom the judge must proceed in conformity with the Roman laws and the Standard Gloss of Accursius, as he had approved it. A statute of 1393 modified this by giving force to the Gloss as approved by Dinus (Dino) of Mugello, for Dinus had written a book On conflicting glosses (De glossis contrariis) and had in it indicated his preferences. Dinus is also notable for his possible share in the compilation of the final title (On maxims of law) in the Sext (one of the sources of canon law), and for his great commentary thereon. But in general the authority of the Gloss, not as an independent work but as an interpretation of the texts, grew gradually, even in Italy where it was in immediate use. The Gloss was of support to judges under the podestà constitution, and their reliance on the Gloss gave it further authority. Sometimes the Gloss was too closely followed, and critics held that timid judges even followed the Gloss against the meaning of the actual texts whereas its proper function was as a guide to an understanding of the text. But such abuse sprang from the podestà system, not from the nature of the Gloss.

Apart from its use in helping judges to their decisions, the Gloss was also of practical help when jurists were called upon to give opinions on points of law submitted to them. In this field too, where several glosses put forward several views, the personal opinion of Accursius was of special importance. Where Accursius had not spoken, in principle the best opinion was to be followed; if this was not clear, the most recent interpretation was to be preferred. For although the Gloss of Accursius was the standard commentary, scholarship did not stand still, and men commented on the commentary.

(vii) Other forms of literature

From the various types of gloss there emerged other literary styles which became independent of the gloss form, and the shaping of most of these is also due to the school we call the Glossators -- hence the slightly misleading element in their title. Of these new styles there were some, variously entitled, such as Summae and Casus, Commenta and Tractatus which were essentially explanatory with a tendency towards generalization; many of these writings originated in the introductions to titles which had so often formed a part of the gloss proper. Quaestiones dealt with unresolved problems and had developed from the solution of conflicting texts; collections of Noteworthy Points and of Brocards were published independently of the texts; _Consilia_ (Opinions) stemmed from actual cases, and Formularies also grew from the needs of practice.

Notaries were mentioned in chapter I as one of the factors making for a degree of intellectual continuity. In the new age they received at least some part of their training from the jurists; Accursius is recorded as an examiner of notarial candidates. And the notaries adapted their formularies to conform to Roman law; this is apparent from actual documents and from manuals such as the _Ars Notariatus_ (_Notarial Art_) of Salatiele. So even at quite a humble level of legal practice the influence of the learned law was to be found, as it was also in the style books of feudal law.

_Summae_ or _Summulae_ were comprehensive commentaries on a whole title or group of titles, and then on a section or the whole of the _Corpus_. They were an early form of literature; _summulae_ are known from three of the Four Doctors, from Bulgarus, Martin Gosia (Martinus) and Hugh of the Ravenna Gate. For example, Bulgarus' _Summula_ on ignorance of law and fact was based on one title from the _Digest_ (D.22,6) and one from the _Code_ (C.1,18). _Summae_ of the _Institutes_ served as general introductions to Roman law. _Summae_ of the _Code_ came to be what amounted to text-books; from quite early days, although by definition based on the _Code_, they included material from the other parts of the _Corpus_, incorporated in the order of titles in the _Code_. The last and greatest example in this tradition was the _Summa Codicis_ of Azo, also known as the _Summa Aurea_ (_Golden Survey_)[10]. Like the _Standard Gloss_, this was a work which owed much to Azo's predecessors, but the version he produced came to be widely accepted by practitioners and

----------

10    Appendix I(d).

scholars.  Its status as a  comprehensive practitioners' textbook was shown by the saying: "No-one can go to court without Azo" ("Chi non ha Azo, non vada a palazzo"); at Cremona, and in some other cities, a statute required possession of a copy before a man could be admitted as an advocate.

Casus were collections of problems or illustrative cases, whether as set out in the texts or imaginary; they were treated in the order of the texts.  To explain several such passages which belonged together and to generalize from the problems posed, there developed Commenta, which included explanatory paraphrases of the main texts.  These came to be but little distinguishable from Summulae.  John Bassianus and others wrote in this form on D.50,17, On maxims of law.  The commentary was to give its name to the next major school of jurists[11].

Also springing from Introductions was another general form of literature, the tractatus (treatise).  Treatises dealt with areas of law not confined to any particular title within any part of the Corpus. Martin's work On Dotal Law (De iure dotium) is sometimes called a treatise, but it was really a summula, being based on one title in the Digest and one in the Code; Bulgarus' Civil Procedure (Ordo Iudiciorum) is truly independent.  Procedure was a favourite subject for the authors of Treatises, but other areas were good subjects for systematization.  For example, Pillius wrote On the violent possessor (De violento possessore), collecting together the various remedies against a person who has taken possession of another's property by some kind of force.  This work deals firstly with civil actions -- for theft, robbery, and force and fear -- then with  interdicts,  possessory and other,  then imperial constitutions

-----------

11   For  an  example  from the stage  intermediate between  Glossators and Commentators, v. Appendix I(e).

which concerned forcible invasion or invasion of vacant property, and finally with the remedies of the criminal law. The texts cited are drawn from the _Digest_, the _Code_, the _Institutes_, and the _Novels_, including one constution of the Emperor Frederick Barbarossa, and there is also a reference to Gratian's _Decretum_.

_Quaestiones_ were, as we have said, usually treated independently of the normal lecture or gloss, although they clearly developed from the solution of conflicting passages. Some are little more than such solutions published separately; others are problems which were the subject of further exposition or disputation, arising either from the texts or from practice[12]. There are _quaestiones disputatae_, or moots, and dialogues between doctor and student; and perhaps one should include the _Dissensiones Dominorum_, which dealt with conflicting interpretations, frequently between the strict law view of Bulgarus and the equitable approach of Martin.

The simplest collections of _quaestiones_ are those based on _quare_ -- why? The wider literary type is the _Sic et Non_ (_Yes and No_) made famous by Peter Abelard in the field of theology, and shaping Scholastic philosophy. The aim was the harmonization of the sources, and the method was already to be found in the _Digest_. For example, D.45,1,56,8 runs: "A slave promised to me by Titius is also promised to me, but conditionally, by Seius. If the slave dies after Titius is in arrears with performance but before the fulfilment of the condition, I can sue Titius, and Seius is not liable if the condition is subsequently realized. If I had released Titius from his obligation, Seius would be liable on the realization of the condition. The difference is that on the death of the slave there is no object for which Seius may be liable, but if there was a formal release and the slave

----------

12    Appendix I (f).

91

survived it, then there is." Of the collections which have survived there is one, with twenty-eight examples, which perhaps dates from the Four Doctors, and another with two hundred and nine examples which comes from the school of John Bassianus.

Quaestiones which arose from the separate disputations held after the lectures allowed development of the law by applying the texts to new situations, real or imagined. Similar literature was produced by the theologians and philosophers, but the civilians again found a model in the Roman texts. 'A wild boar fell into a trap set by you for game, and while he was held there I took him out and carried him away; do you think the wild boar I carried away was yours? And if you think he was yours, suppose I had turned him loose into the woods, would he in that case have ceased to be or have remained yours? And, I ask, ought the action which you would have against me, supposing he had ceased to be yours, to be given as an action on analogous facts? The answer given was: Let us see if it makes any difference whether I have set the trap on public or private ground and, if on private land, whether on mine or someone else's, and, if on someone else's, whether with or without leave of the landowner; moreover, whether the boar has stuck so fast in the trap that he cannot get out by himself, or whether by further struggles he would have got loose. Still I think the governing principle to be this, that if he has come into my power he has become mine. But if you had released to his natural liberty a wild boar who had become mine and he had thereby ceased to be mine, then an action ought to be accorded me" (D.41,1,55 - translation based on that of F. de Zulueta); the Gloss raised the further question whether the captor must know of his success. There survive collections of this kind by Azo and others; Hugolinus' collection is somewhat gloomily entitled Insoluble Problems (Insolubilia).

Of the dialogues between doctor and student, the best known of this period (the type was to recur) is the work known as Quaestiones de iuris subtilitatibus (Questions on the subtleties of law). The work is anonymous and has been ascribed to various of the Glossators. The student puts to the teacher the points which he finds puzzling, and these are explained to him[13].

Dissensiones dominorum (Disputes among the masters) were collections revealing the differing opinions held by various Glossators. For example, Bulgarus held that a husband was bound to return a dowry to his father-in-law after the death of his wife even when there were children, but Martin disagreed. The story runs that Bulgarus' wife did indeed die and his father-in-law consulted Martin for his view on the return of the dowry. Martin said, "I say he can keep it, but he holds he ought to give it back". Bulgarus did give it back without argument, rather to Martin's disappointment. In general there was a conflict of jurisprudential principle between these two. Bulgarus was accustomed to hold to the strict law, and to view certainty of what the law was as most desirable for the parties concerned; Martin, more critical of the texts, preferred to strive for justice in the individual case even at the expense of predictability. This tension is ever-present in jurisprudence; later adherents of equity rather than strict law were often called Gosians, after Martin[14].

Collections of Noteworthy Points were important for the growth of systematization and generalization. Some might be very simple, such as the maxim (Inst. 2,1,12) that things belonging to no one became the property of their occupant. Collections of brocards were often similar to the

----------

13  Appendix I (g).

14  Appendix I (h).

Distinctiones of the glosses proper, but in this form they were not tied to the texts.  Pillius produced one such collection, published about 1185, called the Libellus disputatorius (Book on the art of disputation) which was comparable to Abelard's Sic et Non.  It formed a kind of 'concordance of discordant texts', to borrow Gratian's alternative title for his Decretum.  It is made up mostly of general rules, without exegesis, and it is interesting in particular because it is the first book to abandon the legal order.  It is in three parts -- one on presumptions, one on actions, and one on various heads of disputation; it is systematic within the first two, but lacks overall co-ordination.  It did not have the same success as Azo's Summa, which proved easier to use as well as being more comprehensive; Azo also had produced a collection of brocards.

Apart from Formularies, which we have mentioned briefly, there was another form of literature which arose from practice rather than teaching, the collections of Consilia (Opinions).  Some of the problems in Quaestiones seem to have come from actual cases, and there was little intellectual difference between the two types of literature.  Opinions, however, were responses to points of law put to the jurists; therefore they were preserved for practical as well as doctrinal reasons.

Incidentally, they illustrate well the involvement of the Glossators with public life outside the universities.  The Four Doctors at the Diet of Roncaglia in 1158 all declared in favour of the Emperor Frederick Barbarossa, who was in dispute with the Italian cities over the extent of his imperial rights or regalia in such matters as taxation and control of the appointment of magistrates.  However, they were not agreed on the limits of imperial authority, and the story goes that Bulgarus told the Emperor that his title dominus meant that he was men's lord but not their owner.  Another version, variously ascribed to Bulgarus and Martin or to

Azo and Lothar of Cremona, tells how Martin allowed a plenitude of power to the Emperor and as a reward received a horse from him; whence it was said "Bulgarus dixit (a)equum sed Martinus habuit equum" ("Bulgarus said rightly, but Martin got the horse").

Accursius certainly gave opinions,and so did John Bassianus who gave them on points of feudal as well as civil law. Bulgarus, as we have seen, consorted with emperors, and his Treatise on procedure was written at the request of the chancellor of the papal court for use therein. Hugh on at least one occasion was appointed as judge by Frederick Barbarossa. Placentinus favoured the Italian cities against the emperor, and this may partly explain his moves to Mantua and then Montpellier. His best known student, Pillius, practised as an advocate; it may have been his practical experience which led him to comment on feudal law. He also appeared on occasion in the ecclesiastical courts; on behalf of the monks of Canterbury he appeared against their archbishop in 1187 and against King John over a disputed election to the same archbishopric in 1205.

Hugolinus was a judge, and he also acted as Bologna's ambassador to Rome, Florence and Reggio. James Balduini was podestà of Genoa in 1229 and revised the laws of that city; he was also a member of the city council at Bologna. Hubert of Bobbio was consulted on behalf of the mother of Louis IX of France when she was regent; he also wrote a handbook on procedure for advocates. Roffredus of Benevento had a widespread practice at both imperial and papal bars; his treatise on procedure made use of his own pleadings as examples. Not all of these Glossators, of course, published opinions, although one may assume that they and others gave such opinions. Because of the prolific work of the Commentators there are no surviving opinions from jurists before Dinus, but such publication was not alien to their style.

(viii)   Legal education becomes formalized

While some law had been taught at Pavia, the concept of a university law school really begins at Irnerius' Bologna.  He himself does not seem to have taught formally; the only pupils of his that we hear of are the Four Doctors.  His teaching clearly did not stimulate the crowds in the way that that of his contemporary Abelard did in Paris.  But the Four Doctors acknowledged him as their master, and so we get the start of the master-pupil relationships which are still academically significant in many areas. Certainly at least one of the Four Doctors lectured to audiences of students; there is the anecdote of Bulgarus, the day after his marriage to a widow, reading out the text on which he proposed to comment and being greeted by a roar of laughter.  The text began:  "It is no untouched field that we are entering"; it would be good to know if this was deliberate or inadvertent.

During the earlier twelfth century law became established, along with theology and medicine, as a subject for study after the completion of a degree in arts.  By 1158 there was a statute of Bologna which provided that no one might act as judge or legal consultant there without having studied law for five years.  In the same year Frederick Barbarossa issued a constitution -- the authentica Habita, later inserted into the Code after 4,13,5 (in the older editions) -- which gave specific protection to law students away from home, granting them the privilege of having any actions to which they were defenders tried in their university or by the bishop of their university town.  How many there were at Bologna at this date (for there was as yet no other school of law firmly established) is not certain; Odofredus is alleged to have reckoned there were 10,000, but, assuming this is due to an error, even a tenth as many makes a sizeable group.

96

The major names of this period, Vacarius, Roger (Rogerius), Placentinus, John Bassianus, were all described as the pupils of Bulgarus; this may mean that he was seen as the head of the law school, for Roger and Placentinus were Gosians, interested in the development of equity. It was also the period when Roman law was taken abroad by masters, and taught in other cities than Bologna. Vacarius went to England and settled in Oxford; his _Liber Pauperum_ (_The Poor Men's Book_) first appeared in 1149 and was the first to conflate texts from the _Code_ and the _Digest_. Roger probably took the study of Roman law to Montpellier, and this explains why the first _Summa_ on the _Code_, of which he may have been the author, was translated into Provençal around 1170. Known in this guise as _Lo Codi_, it had a long and influential life in southern France. Placentinus taught at Mantua for some years but went, about 1170, to Montpellier, which thus became an important centre of civilian study. John Bassianus stayed in Bologna; he was also a conservative follower of Bulgarus' strict adherence to the plain meaning of the texts. Placentinus' student, Pillius, of Medicina, led a secession to Modena.

Azo, who died in 1220, was a pupil of John Bassianus; Charles de Tocco was a pupil of both John and Placentinus. He gave up teaching at Bologna to become a judge at Salerno, where he glossed the _Lombarda_. James Balduini was a pupil of Azo, but he preferred the Gosian approach; he died in 1235. By this time there were law schools at Mantua, Piacenza, Modena, Parma, Padua, Vercelli -- where Hubert of Bobbio was teaching -- as well as some short lived ventures in other cities. Roman law was also taught at Montpellier, and perhaps at Valence, although it was forbidden at Paris in 1219, and in England in 1234. However, in 1224 Frederick II founded a university or _Studium Generale_ (that is, a foundation for higher education, specifically with various faculties) at Naples, and in 1244 or 1245 Pope

Innocent IV founded another in Rome.  Roffredus may have taught at Naples from its beginning, but he spent the last thirty years of his life in his native Benevento.

Like the other supreme  Glossator -- and his master -- Azo,  Accursius despised places other than Bologna; he and James Balduini dominated the teaching there through the early thirteenth century.  Since 1219 students at Bologna had had to be examined before proceeding to take a degree; this was laid down by Pope Honorius III and enforced through the Archdeacon of Bologna  who actually awarded the degrees.  There are stories of James Balduini and Accursius acting together as examiners, not always kindly; all examinations were oral.  At this period or somewhat later it became established that five years' study was required for a first degree in civil law (four  years  in canon law) and then a  further  three years  for  a doctorate -- which only needed  one  additional year in canon law.  The doctors were paid directly by the students for their teaching.  Student nations, presided over by a Rector, negotiated with the doctors or the local bishop over the curriculum and timetable, and arranged such matters as lodgings and fair rents.

Thus by the mid thirteenth century there existed a standard gloss on the basic texts and a definitive and systematic text-book.  The pattern of education was set.  It was at this point that a historian of the past two centuries appeared in the person of Odofredus, a pupil of James Balduini, who taught at Bologna and wrote commentaries, in the legal order, on both Code and Digest.  Although he was often critical of the conservative tradition enshrined within the Accursian Gloss, he naturally accepted the Gloss as the basis of his work. Later, after it was accepted as a work of authority, not just of scholarship, the maxim ran: "What the Gloss does not acknowledge, the court does not acknowledge either" ("Quidquid non agnoscit

Glossa nec agnoscit curia").

## Further Reading

R.C. van Caenegem "Law in the Medieval World" 49 TvR (1981), 13

C.H. Haskins  The Renaissance of the Twelfth Century (U.S.A., 1927, repr.)

H.D. Hazeltine in Cambridge Mediaeval History, vol.V (C.U.P. 1927), ch.xxi

E. Meynial "Roman Law" in  The Legacy of the Middle Ages (O.U.P., 1926)

J.A. Clarence Smith  Mediaeval Law Teachers and Writers (Ottawa, 1975)

W. Ullmann  Mediaeval Political Thought (Penguin 1965, repr.)

P. Vinogradoff Roman Law in Mediaeval Europe (O.U.P. 1929, repr. )

H. Yntema "Equity in the  Civil Law and the Common law" 15 Am.J.Comp.L.
    (1967),60

Chapter IV

## THE COMMENTATORS

(i) The period of transition and the Post-Glossators

No exact date can be assigned for the completion of the Accursian
Gloss, but it is clear that, by the middle of the thirteenth century, it
was substantially in the form which has come down to us, and in the process
of being accepted as the standard companion to the Corpus Iuris Civilis.
Scholars used to refer, without differentiation, to all the writers who
came after the Gloss, and whose work continued through to the sixteenth
century (when the new school of Humanists appeared) as Post-Glossators,
from the simple fact that their work assumes the existence of the Gloss.
Modern usage, however, distinguishes among these writers, and the name
Post-Glossators has come to be attached particularly to Italian writers of
the later thirteenth century.  The French jurists of the same period are
known as the Ultramontani (men from beyond the mountains) because to an
Italian they came from the far side of the Alps.  The jurists of the
fourteenth century onwards are usually called Commentators, to indicate
that they were not simply the successors of the Glossators but had their
own individuality and a positive contribution to make to legal development.
    In Italy there seems to have been a period of decline, or at least
stagnation, between the peaks reached by the Glossators and the great work
of the Commentators.  The former school laid a foundation for the study of
Roman law; the latter developed the application of Roman law in practical
affairs.  Indeed, the Commentators brought about the reception of Roman
law into the legal systems of the greater part of Western Europe.
    The theory of decline is open to question, because the Post-Glossators

and their works have not been sufficiently studied to permit a well-informed judgment. Nor is it easy to draw a line between late Glossators (such as Odofredus), and early Commentators (such as Dinus of Mugello) on the basis of their method of instruction, for both founded on commentary rather than gloss. It is not that the former were more theoretical and the latter more practical for, as we have seen, the Glossators were often engaged in public affairs and took account of the developing canon law and of feudal customs. Moreover, there is theory as well as practice to be found in such Post-Glossatorial works as William (Guillelmus) Durantis' Speculum Iudiciale (Mirror of Procedure) or Albertus Gandinus' lucidly systematic Tractatus Maleficiorum (Treatise on Crimes); this dealt primarily with evidence and criminal procedure, but in the discussions of substantive law he drew on his own widespread experience as a judge. Again, it is untrue to say that there was excessive reliance on the Gloss in the later thirteenth century. Insofar as there came to be such excessive reliance, it was a later phenomenon; contemporaries or near contemporaries of Accursius, such as Odofredus or Dinus, were quite ready to be critical of him. Scholasticism doubtless encouraged the greater use of dialectic to solve difficulties in the texts, but this use was not new and was, indeed, the best tool available.

What is true is that, for a period at least, Bologna ceased to be the main centre of legal studies and had to recognize other law schools as equals. Odofredus taught at Padua before he went to Bologna; it was to the University of Padua, not Bologna, that the canons of the Council of Vienne were officially communicated and both universities received from Pope Boniface VIII the compilation of papal decretals known as the Sext. Other influential jurists teaching at Padua were Guy of Suzzara (Guido de Suzaria) and James (Jacobus) of Arena; Albertus Gandinus had studied there, although his career was as judge not teacher. Naples was another centre of legal study. Dinus of Mugello seems to have taught there, and King Charles of Anjou, after his conquest of the Kingdom of Naples and Sicily, brought doctors and students from Orléans to help build up the university which he had reformed; James of Arena was teaching there at the end of the century. Reggio, Modena, Pistoia and Siena were probably the most prominent of the other law schools; for example, Guy of Suzzara taught successively at Mantua, Modena, Padua, Bologna, Reggio, and Bologna again.

Common to all these universities, including Bologna, was an intensified interest in the practical application of Roman law, and especially in its adaptation to the problems posed by new situations such as the existence of numerous independent jurisdictions and legal systems. Problems arising from the conflict of laws and from the reception of local laws into the Roman conceptual framework gave rise to new forms of literature. Quaestiones Statutorum (Problems of Local Legislation -- for statute at this period normally carries this meaning) were produced first by Guy of Suzzara and later by James of Arena and Albertus Gandinus. Both Naples and Orléans were situated in kingdoms independent of the Empire which were, compared with the communes of the cities of northern Italy, large and centralized. In Naples the central authority, the crown, was strong, both willing and able to create new law, and also to continue in modified use the old law of the kingdom, the Lombard law. Not surprisingly Naples became famous for the work done there on public law; in the fourteenth century Lucas de Penna's great commentary on the Tres Libri, the last three books of the Code, which were concerned with administrative law was produced there.

Thus in Italy there was a period of transition. The first great work of mastering the sources had been done, and new challenges had to be faced, in particular the development of legal rules from sources other than the Corpus Iuris Civilis. This in turn raised the question of the relationship of these rules to Roman law and to one another.

(ii)   The Ultramontani


It is clear that the Commentators of the fourteenth century onwards, who were predominantly Italians, made much use of the work of the French writers of the later thirteenth century, and particularly the work of the school of Orléans. Of the three writers most commonly cited by the Commentators two, Jacques de Révigny (Jacobus de Ravanis) and Pierre de Belleperche (Petrus de Bella Pertica), taught at Orléans, while the third, Guillaume de Cunh (Guillelmus de Cuneo), taught briefly at Toulouse; he died as bishop of Comminges in 1335. Orléans had a school of Arts (and probably schools of Theology and Canon Law) before 1200, but its school of Civil Law is known no earlier that 1235, when Pope Gregory IX declared that Pope Honorius III's prohibition on the teaching of the civil law at Paris (decreed in 1219 by the bull Super Specula) did not apply in Orléans and, further, affected only those clerics who had the cure of souls. Orléans thus became a seat of legal learning for clerics, who far outnumbered laymen as students in countries other than Italy. The first known professor of civil law there was Guy of Como (Guido de Cumis), who had been a pupil of Hubert of Bobbio and James Balduini; he was teaching at Orléans by 1243 and, following his masters, was inclined to take a critical approach to the Gloss.

While it would be rash to carry the contrast too far, the universities of the northern Italian cities were modern, in the sense that many lay students came there, and to enjoy themselves as well as to qualify themselves for some career; north of the Alps students were almost invariably clerics who could expect to serve kings or princes in the administration of their territories, and to be paid for their services by clerical preferment. Thus Pierre d'Auxonne, one-time doctor at Orléans, went with Eleanor of Provence (bride of the future Edward I) to England in 1265 and became Official of the archbishop of Canterbury; his legacy of his books to the Sorbonne was the foundation of its library. This had the side effect, even more marked among teachers of canon law, of keeping down the average age of active scholars, since promotion usually took them away from their studies. Two Popes (Clement V and John XXII), four cardinals, and several bishops taught civil law at Orléans at some stage in their careers, and other teachers went on to high office in the service of the king of France. Such service required the ability to accept local customs, often vigorously defended, and to blend them with Roman law, rather than simply maintaining the latter's superiority[1]. It also led to the introduction of elements of Roman law into the decisions given by the royal courts, since these were staffed by men trained in the learned law.

A contemporary colleague of Guy of Como at Orléans was Jean de Monchy who taught civil law until 1263 when he went to Rome and acted for the Pope in various matters, including the negotiations over the recognition of Charles of Anjou as King of Naples and Sicily. He was the master of Jacques de Révigny. Jacques acknowledged him as the source of various doctrines which he himself supported, such as the concept of a legal person as a persona repraesentata (a person given reality by the operation of law -- hence the fiction theory of the legal personality of corporations - whereas human beings have legal personality by the operation of nature).

-----------

1     Appendix II(a).

104

Jacques left commentaries on all parts of the <u>Corpus</u>. He taught until about 1280, and died as bishop of Verdun in 1296.

Pierre de Belleperche was the pupil of one Raoul d'Harcourt, who had studied under and later taught beside Jacques. Pierre began to teach at Orléans around 1280 and was there for some fifteen years. He was less original than Jacques but even more influential, perhaps for the very reason that he was less original and could be more readily accepted. After holding various offices he became bishop of Auxerre and, in 1306, Chancellor of France; he died in 1308. His commentary on the <u>Code</u> was heavily used by Cino Sinibuldi of Pistoia (Cinus de Pistorio), the master of Bartolus; Pierre also wrote commentaries on the <u>Institutes</u> and the <u>New Digest</u>, and a collection of <u>Distinctiones</u>. But he was the last of the great names at Orléans; in the fourteenth century the jurists there tended simply to follow Italian doctrine.


(iii) Their approach to the texts


The name <u>Ultramontani</u> was given by the Italians to the French writers, and especially to those of Orléans, not merely as an indication of their geographical position but also with pejorative implication. Many harsh things were said by the Italians about them, for example, that they were airy-fairy philosophers and useless dialecticians, and that their arguments represented fantasy rather than reason. The <u>Ultramontani</u> in their turn criticized the Accursian <u>Gloss</u> with considerable freedom. We find particular glosses described by them as diabolical or obscure and having more need of a gloss than the text itself, or even as being stupid or rubbish. As is very often the case in academic, and indeed other, controversy, there was a degree of exaggeration on both sides. Comments were needed on the Gloss, and a new form of literature much used by the Ultramontani was that of Repetitiones (Studies), which arose from their practice of delivering lectures in greater depth on certain selected texts. The French writers perhaps did not feel as closely bound to the texts as the Italian writers. The north of Italy was undoubtedly part of the Holy Roman Empire, and insofar as Roman law was studied and applied as the law of that empire, the texts had a strong claim to authority. The kings of France for their part resisted claims that France, because a thousand years ago it had been within the Roman Empire, was thereby subject to the jurisdiction of the Holy Roman Emperors. They claimed to be emperors within their own realm, following the partition of Charlemagne's empire; they rejected the suggestion that Roman law should automatically be applied in France -- except in the south, the pays de droit écrit, where it was recognized as custom.

The willingness of the Ultramontani to argue independently of the texts may well owe something to the study of Aristotelian doctrine and to the work of St. Thomas Aquinas. Aquinas reconciled Aristotelian and Christian thought and gave a new importance to the creative role of reason in establishing legal rules where no definite guidance existed from divine or natural law. He thus gave reason a more positive role than had been allowed to it by St. Augustine, whose approach had tended to dominate thinking up to the thirteenth century; St. Augustine had minimized the role of legal rules in society and also the value of human reason in creating rules. But while the Ultramontani were often critical of the Gloss, they by no means rejected it, even in the more original work of Jacques de Révigny, and Guillaume de Cunh often supported the Gloss against Jacques.

The interest of the Ultramontani in practical questions was of special importance to the subsequent development of Roman law and the creation of

106

the _ius_ _commune_. In particular, their work on the conflict of laws was expanded by the Commentators. But Italian writers, such as Gandinus, had also been moving in this direction and were cited by Cinus, even while he was drawing on the work of Pierre de Belleperche as his main source. The Commentators are properly seen as a new school of jurists, but they built on the contributions, Italian as well as French, of the intervening period. Further, the more one investigates particular doctrines, the more one becomes aware of the extent to which the seed of the concept is likely to be found somewhere within the material collected by Accursius.

(iv) The Commentators and their teaching methods

The Commentators have also been called -- in German -- **Konsiliatoren**, i.e. the writers of **consilia** or opinions. While this is a useful name in that it indicates one of the important functions which these jurists performed, and gives due prominence to the immense number of opinions they produced, the term Commentators is just as apt if one looks at the type of literature published. Not surprisingly, they dealt with essentially the same material as the Glossators, that is, the **Corpus Iuris Civilis** in its mediaeval form which included the **Books of the Feus**, but they paid more attention to special legislation, such as that of the Italian city states. Again, it is not surprising that their teaching methods were similar to those of the Glossators. The emphasis was on lectures on a text or texts of the **Corpus** (or other book being read) including the gloss attached, and they published exegetical material based on this teaching. **Lecturae** (Lectures) were indeed often simply reports of actual lectures; it was quite common for these to be produced with the approval of the lecturer, and in these cases the text would probably be revised by the lecturer before publication. Sometimes, however, it is clear that there was no revision, as when the reporter says that he missed something because of the noise made by the students. In other cases what we have may be lecture notes prepared by the lecturer. Where lectures were delivered in more than one year, the version which has survived may contain additions and second thoughts.

The format of the lectures follows the same general pattern as is found among the Glossators. For example, Cinus, commenting on D. 12.1.40, says: "First I shall divide this fragment into its parts and set out the case, and I shall deal with textual questions. In the second place, I shall draw attention to contradictory passages and solve the contradictions. In the third place, I shall formulate certain questions and add the solutions to them. In the fourth and last place, I shall assemble certain arguments useful for this purpose." However, it was increasingly common to find that the regular lectures did not pay equal attention to all texts. The lecturer might even omit comment on some texts altogether, but this was not always allowed. The statutes of the University of Bologna of 1317 laid down that the doctors were not to pass over any decretal or fragment or paragraph. They also continued the system which required the lecturer to cover so much over each fortnight or month, under penalty of a fine --known as the puncta system. But even without any total omission, the concentration on some rather than others led to certain texts being used as the starting point for long treatises. For example, C. 1.1.1 became the normal peg on which to hang discussions of the effect of local legislation and indeed to develop international private law[2].

Where there were differences of opinion or apparent contradictions in

----------

2    Appendix II(b)

the texts, the list of oppositiones became increasingly lengthy as the number of views to be explained and the list of supporters of each grew. When these lists are looked at carefully it becomes apparent that there was some tendency simply to lift the list from a predecessor and to add the latest views, without any weeding out of earlier ones or checking; one finds lists in which people are given as supporters of an opinion which it is certain they did not hold.    Again, the list of questions dealt with tended to grow, whether they were related to interpretation or to doctrine or -- as was increasingly common -- to the actual application of the law. One can see the lecturer's abiding tendency to increase the syllabus for fear of discarding something of value.

In addition to the regular exegesis of the particular part of the Corpus on which the commentary was being given, there were special lectures on particular texts or particular problems; these, similar to the quaestiones sabbatinae, were now called repetitiones.  In published form they were often collected separately from the regular lectures or commentaries, as they dealt much more fully with areas of particular difficulty and, for the same reason, they were given as special lectures.


(v) The literature of the Commentators


Generally the literature of the Commentators can be classified as first, monographs, second, exegetical material, arising out of teaching, and third, decisions and opinions, often arising out of practice; there were also other forms, such as encyclopaedias designed to be a plain man's guide to the law, or other works not of legal science but for practical use.

Monographs were not a new form of literature, but they were

increasingly common, because the basic mastery of the sources had been established, and there was thus more scope for literature which systematized or developed particular topics. Monographs regularly departed from the order of the texts -- the legal order -- which continued to be used in commentaries; the subjects most often dealt with were feudal law, procedure, and questions of the interpretation of local legislation and of the relation between statutes and (Roman) law and, indeed, the ius commune (common law -- the term will be retained in Latin to avoid confusion with the English Common Law). Among the earliest Commentators to write such a work was James of Belvisio (Jacobus de Bellovisu), who produced a treatise on criminal procedure (the Practica Criminalis) as well as commenting on the Books of the Feus and annotating the Gloss on the Old Digest. James started, and ended, his career at Bologna, but he also established between 1308 and 1321 the reputation of the law school at Perugia, where law had been taught since 1296. (Perugia had been a studium generale since 1308.) Other examples of monographs are Bartolus' De alimentis (On Aliment -- or maintenance) and his On presumptions of law.

Much of the exegetical group was in the tradition of the Glossators, for the needs of students did not vary much and, although the Gloss now provided an adequate foundation, the techniques of problem solving must still be learned. So, as well as additiones (additions) to the Gloss, which were an important production of the Naples school but which are not always readily distinguishable from lectures, collections of cases (casus) continued to be made, setting out factual situations extrapolated from the texts.

The typical Commentary that gave the school its name is illustrated by the work of Cinus of Pistoia. He had been a pupil of Dinus when a student at Bologna, where he probably also taught. He was a poet as well as a

110

jurist, and a friend of Dante and Petrarch; he was an imperialist insofar as he sought an authority which could put an end to the constant and frequently bloody party strife endemic in the Italian communes. He began his teaching career at Siena, having been for some ten years active in practice, and moved to Perugia in 1326. There he wrote his great commentary -- Lectura super Codice (Lecture on the Code) -- which continued to be read as well as cited for more than a century. It was not systematic, but followed the legal order of those passages which provoked comment; the explanation of particular terms was taken quite for granted since it assumed knowledge of the Gloss, but otherwise it was closer to an apparatus than a summa. Cinus had heard Pierre de Belleperche on one occasion, when he came to give a visiting lecture in Bologna, and he made enormous -- and acknowledged -- use of Pierre's commentary; he also drew on the works of Dinus and James of Arena. He enjoyed the dialectical approach of the Ultramontani while remaining aware that the pursuit of logic could lead to arguments irrelevant to the actual application of law. At Perugia he was the master of Bartolus.

Bartolus of Sassoferrato took his doctorate at Bologna at the age of twenty, as pupil of James Buttrigar (Jacobus Buttrigarius) and of Rainer of Forli (Ranierus de Forlivio); the former taught the Code and Old Digest, the latter the New Digest and Infortiatum. (James had practised as a notary when delayed by factional political intrigues in gaining his doctorate; he was, however, doctor at Bologna from 1309 until he succumbed to the Black Death in 1348; Rainer later taught at Pisa and then Padua.) All that is known of Bartolus' life between 1334 and 1339 is that during this time he served as judge in Todi and Pisa and engaged in private study; in 1339 he went to teach at Pisa, where he stayed four years, and then moved to Perugia, where he died in 1357 at the age of 43. He produced a monumental

111

Commentary on the whole of the Corpus (filling nine folio printed volumes in some editions) which had an authority in succeeding generations unmatched even by the Gloss -- nemo jurista nisi Bartolista (no jurist unless Bartolist).

Bartolus' Commentary provided the most complete and richest discussion of the sources, a commentary on them which, like the Standard Gloss, was extensively used, frequently corrected, but never replaced as a whole. Bartolus also produced a number of opinions and many monographs. So extensively was he used that he is often treated as the author of doctrines which he had in fact borrowed from others but to which he gave currency by his support. Lectures on his work were established at Padua in 1544 and at Ferrara in 1613; the name Bartolo instantly conjured up for later generations the picture of a lawyer, as in Mozart's The Marriage of Figaro. Something of his approach, both practical and learned, can be seen from his treatment of C. 1,1,1[3], where he dealt with the application of a local statute to a non-citizen, a theme we have already seen handled by Pierre de Belleperche. His scheme was to investigate whether what was treated as punishable by local statute was punishable both under local statute and the ius commune; in that case it would apply to a stranger. If the matter were not punishable under common law, then a distinction should be made according to whether the stranger had stayed in the place long enough to know of the statute; if he had, then again it would apply. If he had not stayed long enough, then, in principle, he would not be punished, but a further distinction was made. If the matter were one which was generally forbidden, then he should be punished; if it were some peculiar provision,

----------

3    A translation by J.A. Clarence Smith is printed in 14 Am.J.Legal History (1970).

then he should not be, unless he happened to know of the statute. Bartolus' scheme was relatively straightforward in application and hence attractive to the practising lawyer who needed a clear and reliable guide; Bartolus also knew the texts and the work of earlier scholars. "Not everyone agreed with all he said, but he could be called their spiritual domicile in the sense that it was from him that they set out on their journey, and to him that at the end of the day they returned. He expressed thoroughly and completely, with a touch as light as it was sure, the law as it had come to be lived, but in the terminology and according to the concepts which Justinian had caused to be written down."[4]

The other main type of literature of this period was the collection of consilia or opinions, and in this field Baldus de Ubaldis, a pupil of Bartolus, was pre-eminent; some 2,500 of his opinions survive. He taught briefly at Bologna and then returned to Perugia, where he spent most of his time until 1390, when he went to Pavia for the remaining ten years of his life. He was much involved in public life as well as teaching; he was a canonist and feudist as well as a civilian. Opinions were particularly required when there was a possible conflict between Roman law and local statute, or where it was not clear how far, if at all, Roman law applied to cases not specifically covered by its provisions. An opinion generally dealt with the whole case put before the jurist who was to give his opinion, but it might be restricted to a single point. The influence of the jurists on the application of the law was enormously important, and opinions continued to have this importance even after the Commentary had declined into practical insignificance, as is evident from the career of, for example, Jason de Mayno, master of Alciatus, who died in 1519.

----------

4    J.A. Clarence Smith, Mediaeval Law Teachers, p.82.

Sometimes the opinion was given to one or other of the parties to the case, but more often it was given to the court itself. That is, a judge who wished to be informed on the law applicable to the case before him, or to some aspect of it, could put the relevant facts to a suitably qualified adviser, such as a doctor of civil law at one of the universities; he might sometimes be encouraged or even required to consult a doctor teaching at the local university. For example, the judge might put the case: a local citizen is suing a man from Paris in my court; have I jurisdiction? The answer might be a simple yes or no, or it might be explained with reference to appropriate texts; on difficult points the explanations became very elaborate. The practice of seeking advice in this way became regular in the thirteenth century, and it was provided for in the statutes of many Italian cities. William Durantis, in his _Speculum Iudiciale_, devoted a special section to the procedure for seeking an opinion, described technically as its requisition. The practice was particularly important in those cities which had a _podestà_ constitution, as previously mentioned, and it was less important in those parts of Italy with a monarchic constitution, such as the kingdom of Naples or the Papal States.

While an opinion had distinct resemblances to a _quaestio_, it differed in that it did not always give much attention to opposing views but rather concentrated on the jurist's view or, as time went by, the views of the many scholars he cited to give weight to his opinion. For the authority of an opinion was persuasive (_probabilis_) rather than binding (_necessaria_), and the degree of authority was more or less persuasive, depending on the reputation of the person giving it. Sometimes opinions came to receive authority as custom if they were regularly followed and accepted but, in principle, an opinion, however buttressed with authorities, could always be refuted by the exercise of reason. Nevertheless, by the fifteenth century there had developed -- at first among the canonists -- a view that the common or generally accepted view was decisive unless it was demonstrably wrong. This is known as the doctrine of the communis opinio (received view). The rules which developed for the finding of the communis opinio bear a distinct resemblance to the rules governing judicial precedent, which is hardly surprising since opinions performed a function very similar to judicial decisions in case-law systems. As with the rules of judicial precedent, someone might reluctantly have to give an opinion with which he himself did not agree, and one finds this explicitly stated; in teaching, such divergence from the communis opinio could at least be argued rationally. To some extent the doctrine stifled original thought, but for the parties to a case it meant greater legal certainty; the problem of such balance is a perpetual one in the workings of the law, just as the citation of authority is itself a characteristic of lawyers' argumentation. The door to change was, however, always left open, in the sense that a contrary opinion might be argued and accepted to produce a new communis opinio.

(vi) Roman law in use by the Commentators

Opinions are found in all areas of law, both private and public. They inevitably covered questions of feudal law, of custom, of local statute and of other local law, but all are seen as adhering to the framework of the civil law. Moreover, as leading teachers were consulted for their opinions, close contact was ensured between the teaching and the practice of the law, which was beneficial for both. Hence it is not surprising that the literature of the Commentators was not confined to works on Roman law. They were increasingly concerned with the relationship between Roman law and other sources of law, as Roman law spread throughout Europe and there was increasing contact between existing legal régimes and the new learning. One of the most important facets of this relationship was the influence of the civil and the canon law in the field of procedure, which we shall look at more closely in the chapter on the ius commune. Another product of this concern was a literature which compared and contrasted Roman law with an existing law, such as Blasius de Morcone's De differentiis inter ius Romanorum et Langobardorum (On the differences between Roman and Lombard Law). Somewhat akin were the writings of the Neapolitan jurists, such as Andrew (Andreas) de Barulo, on the customs of the kingdom, which had been glossed in the thirteenth century. Andrew also produced a commentary on books 10-12 of the Code, although this was superseded by the work of Lucas de Penna; Andrew's Summa on intestate succession traced the history of the law of succession from the Twelve Tables to Justinian, and it took into account feudal claims and the Lombard custom of the widow's quarter. It must be remembered that, in Italy in particular, local statutes were often drawn up because of the existence of the learned law, and it certainly contributed elsewhere towards the increasing use of written law.

The Commentators' reconciliation of the learned law and local law produced what is known as the 'statute theory'. When dealing with actual practice the usual theory adopted was that the local statutes were the primary source and the civil (and sometimes the canon) law was supplementary. For example, Pisa adopted Roman law but retained certain elements of the Lombard codes; at Como in 1281 it was laid down that judgment was to be given: first in accordance with the city's written statutes; failing them, according to the approved customs of the city; and only failing them, according to the learned laws (leges et iura). In the fourteenth century at Casale Monferrato the primary source was again the written statutes of the city; failing them, the civil law (iura romana);

and failing that, good custom. At Dervio, within the jurisdiction of the archbishop of Milan, men were ruled by a threefold law, canon, civil, and municipal. However, interpretation extended the use of Roman law and the range of its application in various ways. The words of the statute were to be applied in the first instance, as far as they were applicable; indeed, the sense of the provision might be applied even if the exact wording was not to the point. It was also possible to apply statutes by analogy, on grounds of equity (*ratio aequitatis*). For example, statutes dealing with succession and giving preference to agnates (a term which by this time meant relationships through males) were applied and extended in order to protect family property. They were not so extended when the result was clearly seen to be unjust, for example, if the result would be to allow an aunt on the father's side to exclude the mother from a child's succession -- for the mother was a cognate.

In spite of this primacy of the statutes, the civil law was the general subsidiary law and it could prevail in various ways. First, statutes might expressly incorporate the Roman law or *ius commune*, and to that extent the Roman law shared the primary authority. Second, statutes might use technical terms or concepts of Roman law, which would almost inevitably be interpreted in the civilian sense, as, for example, when referring to legal capacity or to pupils or minors. It was accepted that statutes were to be interpreted in such a way as to involve the least divergence from the civil law: for example, Dinus, in his *Consilia*, says: "Doubtful words in statutes are brought within the interpretation and understanding they bear in the *ius commune*", and Baldus similarly held that statutes were to be interpreted so that they involved the least correction of the civil law. Even when statutes attempted to restrict this extension by requiring strict interpretation in the sense in which they had been passed, it could often be argued that they required declaratory interpretation in the light of other available sources of law. Thus the giving of opinions by civilian doctors provided a communis opinio which ran far more widely than the particular jurisdictions, and so played a major part in the creation of the ius commune. In Italy the work of the doctors can be seen as a substitute for the court of appeal or legislative authority that made possible the existence of a common law in other countries. The opinions of men like Alexander Tartagni of Imola[5], who himself selected the first four volumes of his Consilia for printing before his death in 1477, or Philip Decio[6], who was also a canonist as well as a civilian, and for three years a judge of the Parlement of Grenoble, might properly be compared with contemporary reports of the decisions of the Lords of Council and Session in Scotland or of King's Bench or Common Pleas in England.

The Commentators were remarkably free in their application of the texts regardless of the original context. For example, from the fact that in Nov. 105 the emperor was referred to as 'living law', it was argued that property could be tranferred by the emperor without any physical delivery but by simple oral grant, because it is possible for a law to transfer property. We have mentioned, in discussing the teaching methods of the Glossators, the famous text: "What touches all alike must be approved by

----------

5   Doctor of civil and canon law at Bologna, and a teacher who kept his lectures for the evenings, since he had a lucrative practice at the bar.

6   Pupil of Jason de Mayno at Pavia, then doctor at Pisa, then at Padua, Pavia, and Valence, before his return to Pisa and final move to Siena, where he died in 1536 or soon after, at something over eighty.

all", which was widely used as an argument for (relative) democracy in Church and State. The Commentators had no hesitation in applying a text to their own times, however anachronistic they knew its real meaning to be, if its use could be fruitful, as in equating an Italian city with a Roman municipium. Similarly, when they derived arguments from texts which had little or no relation to the current facts, they were not ignorantly distorting Roman law to fit their own times but deliberately adopting its principles as a source of ideas. For example, in one of his opinions, Bartolus dealt with a case where a second husband was seeking aliment (or maintenance) for his (second) wife from the children of the first marriage, to whom the property of his first wife had gone. The claim was denied on the basis of D. 13.6.18.2 which, talking about a slave who has been lent, says that the expense of feeding him, etc., falls by natural reason on the person who makes use of him. Conversely, Bartolus argued from texts on dotal expenses that, where a tenant claimed from his landlord the cost of clearing ditches on the land which he had leased, if this was a regular job then the tenant must pay, but if the clearing was something which was necessary only at considerable intervals then the obligation fell on the landlord. In yet another opinion, a stamped notarial document had been destroyed; the question was, need the copy of the document be stamped? Bartolus held that it need not, because it was a matter of good faith that the same thing be not claimed twice -- a principle which applies rather to the law of contract than to stamp duties.

Their use of the texts was partly due to a feeling that it was desirable to have some authority to quote, however reasonable in itself the conclusion. Bartolus once said: "We lawyers blush to speak without reference to an authority", and the story is told that, on occasion, having given his opinion on a case put to him, he would go to a friend who had a

119

better memory to provide him with the relevant texts to justify the opinion. This characteristic, however, is both a strength and a weakness in the lawyers of any age.

By their work the Commentators developed whole new fields of law, and new doctrines to face new situations; for example, they worked out the distinction between dominium directum (superiority) and dominium utile (literally 'extended ownership'; in effect a share of ownership allowing use) to deal with such cases as the feudal superior and vassal both holding in the same land an interest which could be described as a right of ownership (dominium). It was really the Commentators who turned the Roman texts on criminal law into a legal science and who developed a doctrine of criminal responsibility. It was they who produced the concept of international private law, who worked out the detailed rules of romano-canonical procedure based ultimately on the Roman cognitio procedure, who developed commercial law in such areas as negotiable instruments or partnership (as we shall see in the chapter on the Law Merchant), and who introduced doctrines of legal personality for entities other than human beings. With the assistance of the canonists they gave substance to the concept of the rights of a third party to a transaction, and to the law of agency. It was the work of the Commentators that produced the ius commune, and then enabled the reception of Roman law in the countries of Western Europe during the fifteenth and sixteenth centuries, although there is no doubt that the way for that reception was also paved by the canonists and the ecclesiastical courts.

Further Reading:

H.F. Jolowicz "The stone that the builders rejected" 12 Seminar (1954), 34
F.H. Lawson  The Roman Law Reader (U.S.A., 1969), ch. vii

J.A. Clarence Smith "Bartolo on the Conflict of Laws" 14 <u>Am.J.Legal Hist.</u>
(1970), 157; 247

P. Stein "The mutual agency of partners" 33 <u>Tul.L.R.</u> (1959), 595

W. Ullmann   <u>The Mediaeval Idea of Law</u> (London, 1946)

       <u>Jurisprudence in the Middle Ages</u> (London, 1980)

Chapter V

# CANON LAW

(i)  The importance of canon law

Canon law is the law of the Church, that is, of the Western Church before (and particularly of the Roman Catholic Church after) the Reformation.  (Canon in Greek means norm or rule.)  In its developed form canon law can be said to start with Gratian and his Concordia discordantium canonum (Harmonizing of Divergent Texts), which is otherwise known as the Decretum  -- although more properly the Decreta -- and which saw the light of day around 1140.  Gratian's work and that of his successors until the Council of Trent (1545-63) is known as the ius novum (new law), while that which went before is described as the ius antiquum (ancient law); the period from Gratian onwards is the classical age of the canon law.  The Council of Trent marks the de facto acceptance of a divided Christendom, divided that is within  Western Europe, since the schism between eastern Orthodox and western Catholic, after simmering for centuries, had become formal in the eleventh century.  Canon law in the Roman Catholic Church since the Council of Trent is known as the ius novissimum (modern law).  We have looked briefly at the period of ancient law in the Church as part of the formation of Europe; this book is not concerned with modern canon law as such because the latter is itself a continuation of the system of the classical age, and its subsequent influence is most marked in the development of Natural Law theories.

Much of the development of the classical canon law stemmed from the struggle between Papacy and Empire but, despite the political tensions, it must be remembered that from the twelfth to the sixteenth century there was throughout Europe a relatively uniform structure of ecclesiastical courts, administering a fairly regular system, and staffed by men who had undertaken a reasonably common education in canon, and frequently in civil, law. There were local variations; for example, in Spain the Church had a very limited jurisdiction over testamentary succession, whereas in England this jurisdiction was virtually total over moveable property, and in causes dependent on the person ecclesiastical jurisdiction was much wider in Spain than in England, but there was undoubtedly one international system. Moreover, canon law was more than a collection of technical rules; it was a force which shaped all society, lay and cleric alike, so that their membership of society made them members of the Church and subject to the rational ordering of a daily life that was seen sub specie aeternitatis. "The fact that in its details canon law dealt with contingencies and practical necessities rather than with timeless truths must not blind us to the grandeur of its purpose, which is the ordering of those contingencies in a coherent whole."[1]

This universality of legal thinking and practice must have been an important factor in the creation of the ius commune, and in bringing such outlying areas of mediaeval Europe as Scotland within the framework of European legal civilization, but the extent of the influence of this factor remains somewhat unclear. For one thing, princely and feudal jurisdictions were generally administered by clerics but, in exercising that function, they would normally administer the royal or feudal law; for example, William Raleigh, bishop of Winchester, as a royal judge supported the English barons' refusal to recognize legitimation by subsequent marriage, a

----------

1    S. Kuttner -- Harmony from Dissonance (repr. 1980, London, The History of Ideas and Doctrine in the Middle Ages, pp. 1-16 at p.2).

Roman institution which was taken into the canon law by Pope Alexander III. Thus in practice men might follow local custom rather than the learned law in which they had been trained. On the other hand, canon law made use of the Roman law as well as of its own proper sources, which were described in the first chapter. Canon law procedure was based on the _cognitio_ system of procedure of the Later Roman Empire, because that had been the living system when Christianity was adopted as the official religion of the Empire and institutionalized, and because the Roman texts continued to provide the only systematic guidance. Thus it is arguable how far the romano-canonical procedure, which (as we shall see in chapter VII) penetrated to a greater or less extent every country in Europe, is the fruit of civilian or of canonist thinking. The influence of canon law is undeniable, but its very success makes it hard to measure.

(ii) Canon law in the eleventh century

Around A.D. 1012 Burchardt, bishop of Worms, produced a collection of canon law in twenty books, his _Decretum_. He made use of the _Hadriana_, Penitentials, and other sources, some of them secular. He also made use of the _False_ _Decretals_, a Frankish compilation of conciliar canons which, although mostly genuine, had been given a fictitious papal or imperial source for greater authority; they included the so-called Donation of Constantine, purporting to be an early fourth century grant of secular power to the Papacy[2]. Burchardt's _Decretum_ was used both by Pope Leo IX and by his cousin, the Emperor Henry III, but it was not adequate to

----------

2    Tierney, _The_ _Crisis_ _of_ _Church_ _and_ _State_, no.8; cf. nos. 80 and 82; and see Southern, _Western_ _Society_ _and_ _the_ _Church_, p.91f..

satisfy the needs of the reforming party within the Church. It lacked a coherent system and suitably authoritative texts upon those subjects which were the reformers' chief concern: the primacy of Rome as the Apostolic See, authority within the Church to coerce the sinner, the investiture of bishops -- and lesser clergy -- by laymen, simony or trafficking in ecclesiastical appointments, and the validity of the sacraments.

At the end of the eleventh century rather the same failings still affected the works of Ivo of Chartres, who made much use of his predecessor. Ivo had pointed the way to the solution of the Investiture Contest as early as 1097; as a bishop as well as a canonist he was also concerned with the internal discipline of the Church. He wrote three major books: the Tripertitum (or Three-part Book) was a chronological collection from the Fathers, the Popes, and the Councils; his Decretum (to be distinguished from that of Gratian) was based largely on Burchardt, with additions from the Fathers and from Roman law; the Panormia (Conspectus) was a relatively short and systematic work, intended for everyday reference. The three formed a group of discrete items rather than one coherent whole. Nevertheless, Ivo gave sound advice on the interpretation of historical material, and he distinguished principles of eternal validity from the variable elements of legal discipline, such as the particular circumstances of time or place or person. When such work was combined with the Scholastic thought developed by the contemporary Peter Abelard, it was to prove capable of constructing the necessary blend of authority and argument that, in the Concordia discordantium canonum, founded the science of canon law.

The twelfth and thirteenth centuries were dominated, and not only in the field of the continuing tensions between Papacy and Empire, by law and lawyers. Intellectual argument took legal form, and "on the practical level too, in an age of rapidly advancing civilization and expanding economic activity, there was a widespread popular demand for rational and equitable legal procedures. In such circumstances any ruler whose courts could provide fair and enforceable judicial decisions found his status greatly enhanced, and kings who sought to increase their powers came to rely more on the efficiency of their judges and administrators than on the sanctity of their office or the personal devotion of their vassals. Moreover, the study of Roman law provided a very exalted theory of legislative sovereignty, together with a wholly non-papal account of the origins of imperial authority."[3] In the conflict between Emperor and Pope the Donation of Constantine could as well be interpreted to imply that imperial grant was the source of papal jurisdiction as to prove the latter's supremacy. On both sides the lawyers were hard at work. The canonists may have discerned the _Digest_ for what it was, but it was in the light of the work of the Glossators that their scholarship flourished and made of canon law a system comparable to the civil law.

(iii) Gratian and the Decretists

Gratian is a man of whom we know very little -- although Dante placed him in Paradise. Our only certainties are that he was working in Bologna in the 1130s and 1140s, and that he played a significant part in the production of the work which goes under his name. It remains convenient to talk in terms of 'Gratian' rather than of 'the compilers of the _Concordia discordantium canonum_' who are equally invisible in the mists of time. Gratian's work was produced in the same atmosphere as and not long after

----------

3    Tierney, p.97f..

that of Irnerius and it marked the creation of canon law as a science.    It
was also roughly contemporary with the publication around 1150 of Peter
Lombard's _Sententiae_ and thus signalled the separation of canon law and
theology.   Gratian's work was not commissioned, nor did he hold any
significant official position (or surely we would know more of him), but
through its own virtue it became accepted.   Within fifteen years or so the
_Decretum_ was being analysed and extended by the jurists who are known as
the Decretists.       Gratian's ability to synthesize his sources was
rendered effective in the practice of the courts by the existence of a new,
efficient and centralized bureaucracy, based on the reformed and
consolidated Papacy -- and about this we know much.   The most influential
popes of the next hundred years -- Alexander III (1159-81), Innocent III
(1198-1216), Gregory IX (1227-41), Innocent IV (1243-54) - were all
interested in the administration of the law.   "New legal procedures, often
borrowed from Roman law, were adopted in order to facilitate appeals to
Rome and, as the appeals flowed in by thousands from every corner of
Christendom, the necessary apparatus of papal courts, bureaucratic
administrators, and delegate judges was developed to cope with them.   This
great growth of administrative machinery in the twelfth century added flesh
and bone and muscle to Gregory VII's abstract assertions of papal
sovereignty."[4]   It made effective in each country, in each diocese, the
rules of the Church.   These rules dealt with the obligations of her
members, lay and clerical, with the procedures necessary for the
maintenance of worship, with the administration of ecclesiastical
properties and monies, and with matters of doctrine.

Gratian used ordinary Scholastic methods to order his existing

-----------

4    Tierney, p.98.

materials: the canons of the apostles, liturgical and penitential books, conciliar canons from many sources, papal letters and decrees, the works of the Fathers, and some secular jurisprudence. The diversity of his sources can be illustrated from the First Part, Distinctio 12; it draws from a letter of Pope Calixtus I (218-23), the writings of Popes Gregory IV (827-44), Leo IX (1048-54), and Nicholas I (858-67), a letter of St. Jerome (d.410), Justinian's Institutes 1,2,9 (533), C. 8,52(53),1 (224) -- wrongly cited --, three letters of Gregory the Great (590-604), two letters of St. Augustine (d.430), a canon from the Eleventh Council of Toledo (675), and another from the First Council of Braga (561). More typical treatment of a topic might quote more from the Fathers, including biblical commentary, and rather less from any source later than Gregory I. Not all Gratian's sources seem to have been known to him at first hand, and he made very little use of the canons of the General Councils of I Lateran (1123) and II Lateran (1139); the secular references seem largely drawn from the collections of Ivo of Chartres.

The Decretum in its established form is divided into three parts. The first[5] deals with the nature and sources of law, and with ecclesiastical offices and conduct. The second part[6] deals further with clerical behaviour, with procedure and penal law, with church property, with religious orders, with marriage and, in a semi-independent treatise, with penance. The third part[7] deals with the sacraments and with doctrine; it is known as De consecratione (On Consecration) from the opening rubric.

----------

5   Consisting of 101 Distinctiones, each divided into chapters or canons.

6   Consisting of 36 Causae, each divided into quaestiones, which are in turn divided into canons; De poenitencia (On Penance) is C.33,q.3.

7   Consisting of 5 Distinctiones, each divided into chapters.

Gratian applied to each topic the new dialectic. He put the arguments for and against each proposition, using the sources but aiding them with his own comments. Where there were divergent answers he sought to reconcile them by redefining the meaning of the words or by distinguishing the circumstances which governed a particular application of a principle. By linking them together in this way he aimed to give his authorities coherence, but the user must never take any one text in isolation because conflicting views are offered. It is to the overall resolution and conclusion that one must look and, even so, a complete answer is not always given. For example, C.29, q.2 has eight chapters on the problem of whether a free woman can put aside a man she had thought free if, after their marriage, she finds he is of servile status[8]; the conclusion is not very clear.

The _Decretum_ was a little like the _Digest_ in drawing from a range of sometimes conflicting sources; thus it is not surprising that it gave rise to glosses and comments in much the same way. Moreover, since it was already an established principle of canon law that account must be taken of what the parties had understood, of the circumstances of time or place, of the need to balance two apparently contradictory rules in a particular instance, there was clearly room for further elaboration of the sources by the canonists. Very early some additional texts were included in the _Decretum_; these are known as _paleae_, and may come from one Paucapalea who had produced a short _summa_ before 1148. The actual texts were often already part of the common currency of the canonists, and there was in the Papacy a source of authoritative interpretation; thus the Decretists needed to spend somewhat less time on basic glossing and could move rather faster

----------

8    Appendix III.

129

towards systematic development than the Glossators had been able to do with the Digest. Rufinus, later bishop of Assisi and chosen to give the opening address at III Lateran in 1179, taught canon law at Bologna; around 1158 he published a Summa (of some 170,000 words) which was of great influence in Italy and beyond until its supersession by the work of Huguccio. One of Rufinus' pupils, Stephen of Tournai, who was also a pupil of Bulgarus, published a Summa soon after 1160; through him and others canonist learning spread to France. Bologna, however, remained the centre of the new studies; it was where Huguccio, perhaps the greatest of the Decretists, both studied and taught. His Summa, which appeared around 1188, continued to be cited until the fifteenth century; it was the first to make significant use of both Roman law and the decretals. His views on such matters as when a marriage was to be presumed, the force of a bare pact, the importance of causa in contract, shaped decisively those of his successors; he also laid particular stress on the importance of equity and the need to exercise mercy. Then too it was at Bologna around 1213 that the standard gloss for the Decretum was produced by Johannes Teutonicus (John the German); he made considerable use of the work of Laurentius Hispanus (Lawrence the Spaniard), who in his civil law studies had been a pupil of Azo.

(iv) The decretals

Meanwhile a series of efficient popes, imbued with the legal spirit of the age, were providing more material for the canonists. Alexander III summoned III Lateran; he also issued a number of decretals on matters of legal significance, such as those on legitimation through subsequent marriage. Innocent III summoned IV Lateran in 1215 and was thereby responsible for a very large number of canons. Innocent did indeed study at Bologna for a while in his youth, but recent scholarship has shown that neither of these popes was a doctor of canon law, although they were of great importance in its development. The canons of the two General Councils and the various decretals issued subsequently to the publication of the Decretum were at first simply known as canons extra Decretum vagantes (wandering outside the Decretum) but collections of them soon began to be made. The first was that of Bernard of Pavia (Bernardus Papiensis) who, soon after 1190, produced a Breviarium Extravagantium (Brief Account of the Wanderers) which included decretals of Clement III (1187-91) as well as of Alexander III, and also some older material omitted by Gratian; he stressed the legal points by leaving out most of the usual narrative. The Breviarium was arranged in five books, concerned with ecclesiastical jurisdiction, with procedure, with the clergy and chuch property, with marriage, and with sins and their correction. This arrangement became standard in later, official collections. Other collections were made by John of Wales (Johannes Galensis), Peter of Benevento (Petrus Beneventanus), John Teutonicus, and -- probably -- Tancred; these five collections are known as the compilationes antiquae (old collections). Tancred was a pupil in canon law of Lawrence and of John of Wales and, like the former, in civil law of Azo; he became Archdeacon of Bologna and thus the channel through which degrees were granted there. Whether or not he compiled the collection of Honorius III's decretals ascribed to him, he certainly made use of them in his court and in his teaching. He also wrote a monograph on marriage, and an Ordo Judiciarius (Judicial System) on canonical procedure which remained the standard authority for more than fifty years. It was full but also lucid, and it was arranged conveniently, beginning with the persons concerned in an action, then the preparatory acts, then the stages of the process proper, then the judgment, and finally the execution of the judgment.

Although the compilationes antiquae and other less well established collections had all been useful to administrators and teachers, they lacked authority. Gregory IX therefore commissioned Raymond of Peñaforte to produce an official collection. In terms very similar to Justinian's instructions to his compilers, Gregory told Raymond to edit the decretals, removing contradictions and repetitions; apart from citations from Gregory the Great, very little of the material predates Alexander III or III Lateran. The selection was organised in five books on the system of Bernard of Pavia, and divided into titles on the model of Justinian's Code; the titles in turn were divided into chapters, each with its source at its head, and, again like the Code, normally arranged chronologically within each title. These Decretals were published in 1234 by the papal constitution or bull Rex Pacificus (A Peace-bringing King) as the first authorized, official source of canon law. The work (of more than 300,000 words) has always been known as the Liber Extra from the full title Liber Extra-vagantium Decretalium[9].

Later papal decretals were at first known as Novels, in imitation of the Roman sources. Boniface VIII (1294-1303), however, ordered the consolidation of those which were suitable, together with select canons from the General Councils of I Lyon (1245) and II Lyon (1274); in 1298 this was published as the Liber Sextus (Sixth Book) because it followed on the five books of Extra. The title is a mild joke, for the Sext (as it is commonly known -- sometimes thus cited, and sometimes as VIto --) is in

----------

9   It is often cited as X -- for Extra -- followed by the number of book, title, and chapter; e.g. Tierney, no. 79.

fact divided into five books, with the titles matching those of _Extra_; it finishes with a new title _de regulis iuris_ (_On Maxims of Law_), composed on the model of the last title in the _Digest_ and using much of its material. The _Sext_, which is only about a fifth as long as _Extra_, like its predecessor was exclusive, that is, on its publication -- when Boniface sent copies to Bologna, Padua, Orléans, Toulouse, and to the papal university in Rome -- all material not included, apart from the _Decretum_ and _Extra_, was to have no validity.  This did not hold for the next official compilation, the _Clementinae_ (or _Clementines_), named after Clement V (1304-14) who had proposed the publication of a _Liber Septimus_ (_Seventh Book_) to include the canons of the Council of Vienne (1311); they were issued in 1317 by John XXII (1316-34), who had himself studied law at Orléans.  Subsequent collections, the _Extravagantes_ of John XXII, and the _Extravagantes communes_ -- selected decretals from Boniface VIII up to Sixtus IV (1471-84) -, were not official, still less exclusive.  Their authority was only that of the individual chapters or canons, as remained true of the _Decretum_, until in 1582 _the Decretum_, _Extra_, the _Sext_, the _Clementines_, and these _Extravagantes_ were all published together as the _Corpus Iuris Canonici_.  Even then, although this _Corpus_ was as a collection both official and exclusive, it was not to be interpreted as legislative in the manner of a modern code, but as providing authentic texts from which arguments could properly be drawn.

(v) The Decretalists

Decretalist is the term given to those jurists who glossed and commented on the decretals, particularly _Extra_ and the _Sext_. Decretists as such disappeared as the Decretalists incorporated the material of Gratian's

133

book into their work.  Tancred was one of the first to specialize in the study of the decretals, but by the end of the thirteenth century the distinction was otiose, and it is better to talk simply of canonists.

Geoffrey of Trani (Goffredus de Trano), a pupil of Azo and a doctor at Bologna, gave Extra an apparatus around 1240; shortly afterwards he wrote a brief but influential Summa (which was among the sources for the Scottish Regiam Majestatem).  Sinibald of Fieschi, who became Pope Innocent IV, edited his own decretals and produced a commentary on Extra.  Perhaps unsurprisingly, his work was pertinent rather than original, taking account of the other legal traditions of the period.  It continued to be cited; indeed, it was printed, and it remained in print until the end of the sixteenth century.  Extra had a standard gloss by about 1256 at the hands of Bernard of Parma, who drew from Lawrence the Spaniard and Tancred, among others.  Other canonists were busy with Quaestiones and Summae; Notabilia and brocards were also produced.  Perhaps the most famous canonist of his generation was Henry of Susa (d.1271), usually known as Hostiensis (because he became cardinal bishop of Ostia).  He was a pupil of James Balduini in civil law; he taught only briefly, in Paris, but he wrote enormously.  His Summa Aurea (Golden Summary) made use of the civil as well as the canon law -- he seems to have known Azo's Summa Codicis well -- and was important for the process of the formation of the ius commune.  It brought together and systematized the law of the Decretum and of subsequent decretals; it followed the order of the texts, but where he found gaps in the scheme Hostiensis inserted new titles.  He also produced a Lectura, a detailed commentary, on the decretals of Gregory IX and Innocent IV, which laid particular stress both on equity and the need to love the sinner while chastising the sin and on the theological underpinnings of the canon law. The Summa Aurea became definitive and it, like Innocent's commentary, was re-edited even after the Council of Trent.

William Durantis, known as the Speculator from the title of his major work, the Speculum Iudiciale (Mirror of Procedure), was a pupil of Bernard of Parma; he taught canon law at Modena and perhaps also at Bologna. He later became a judge (auditor generalis) at the papal court for a dozen years, hearing appeals from all over Christendom. Innocent IV and Hostiensis had established a theoretical framework for canon law; the Speculator now laid down the principles of its practice so well that editions of his work were produced down to the seventeenth century, and such noted jurists as Johannes Andreae and Baldus commented on it. Although it followed the internal order of Extra, the Speculum was in four parts, dealing with the persons concerned in an action, with procedure in civil causes, with criminal procedure, and in the fourth part providing a formulary. It made much use of the work of Roffredus, Rolandino Passagieri, Tancred, and many others, but the Speculator emphazised the role of the papal court, making use of his own experience there. The Speculum replaced Tancred's Ordo as the standard work on procedure; it was not itself superseded until the age of the modern law.

Many canonists, having made their mark in academic law, went on to administrative careers in Church or State. The Speculator was papal governor of the Romagna for five years, until his death in 1296; a century earlier William of Longchamps had written a treatise on comparative procedure, both civil and canon, which seems to have been intended for the Plantagenet possessions in France, before he became Chancellor to Richard I of England as well as bishop of Ely. Some, however, remained as scholars, frequently combining civil and canon law. Johannes Andreae produced the standard gloss for the Sext in 1303 and for the Clementines in 1326. He also wrote a commentary on the Sext, a substantial book of Problems on the title _de regulis iuris_ which completed the _Sext_, and a commentary on _Extra_ called _Novella_, as well as two not very original monographs on marriage; he died from the Black Death in 1348. Baldus was primarily a civilian, but he left a notable commentary on the decretals, and to add to his accomplishments he was also a feudist of renown.

In the later fourteenth century the university of Bologna was in decline, partly because of local political turbulence, partly because of the rival attractions of other universities which were founded in considerable numbers in that century. The feudist Antonio di Pratovecchio, who was also something of a canonist, taught at Bologna, Padua, Florence and Siena. Nicholas Tedeschi, who is better known as Panormitanus (from Palermo, where he became archbishop; he is sometimes cited as the Sicilian abbot -- _abbas Siculus_) taught only briefly at Bologna before moving to Parma and then to Siena. He left a very influential commentary on _Extra_, numerous opinions, and a collection of leading points in canon law (_Thesaurus singularium in iure canonico decisivorum_). He was also an important figure in the Conciliar Movement, which tried to heal the Great Schism by arguing that the Church's plenitude of power resided in its whole body, as represented by a General Council in which the Pope participated, and stressing that the Pope was a member of the Church rather than its commander. The Great Schism had its origins in 1309, when Pope Clement V had fixed the seat of the Papacy at Avignon (then in the County of Provence, which owed allegiance to the King of Naples) because he was French and wished to evade the worst of Italian factionalism. There it stayed until 1378 when the successive elections of Urban VI and Clement VII, representing the Italian and the French parties, brought scandal to the Church and revealed the deep political differences in Europe. A settlement was finally reached after the Council of Constance (1413-17), a

136

settlement brought about by legalistic compromise and political exhaustion.

(vi) The canonists and the theory of the 'just war'[10]

The moral and practical problem of whether war can be justified is not new. Roman philosophers had developed theories of the just war, and St. Augustine had given lengthy consideration to the problem as posed for Christians. The eleventh century Peace of God and the Truce of God[11] were attempts to modify the consequences of war. The Decretists attempted to define the just war. Rufinus laid down three requirements: the one who proclaimed the war should have due authority -- that is, be a prince, not a mere lord; the adversary must be guilty of something which deserved measures of force; the actual fighters must be suitable and inspired by worthy motives. Stephen of Tournai pointed out that a war might be justified on the grounds both that the attacker was in the right, and that the defender was in the wrong, or on only one of these grounds. A war waged against a guilty party, but from malice, lacked justification in the initiator of the war; in that the defender deserved punishment it was

----------

10 This description of canonist discussion is deeply indebted to F.H. Russell The Just War in the Middle Ages (C.U.P. 1975).

11 Extra, 1,34,1-2; v. Herlihy, Feudalism, no.48; cf. M. Bloch, Feudal Society, p.412f.. The Peace was intended to protect the helpless -- women, children, merchants, travellers, farmers with their animals and tools, and clerics and religious -- at least from direct attack; the Truce tried to impose temporal restrictions on the waging of war, forbidding it, for example, in Christmastide or in the ten weeks of Spring between Septuagesima and the octave of Easter.

unilaterally just, or justified.  The war by Saul on David (I Sam. 19,
23-6) had no ground of justification, because Saul was moved solely by envy
and David (in this case) was undeserving of such persecution.  In theory a
war was possible in which both parties were in the right, as when a war was
declared on false premises, but in general the Decretists insisted that in
a just war one side only had a monopoly of justice.  Huguccio shifted the
focus from the punishment of crime or sin in the wrongdoer to the
maintenance of proper authority; those who avenged their own injuries were
guilty of sin, unless they were acting on judicial authority.  In his
teaching a war of aggression, as distinct from one of self-defence, was
unjustified, as was a war waged with direct clerical participation, or when
the enemy did not deserve something so drastic as the affliction of war.
But a city, unlike an individual, could defend itself on its own authority,
and denial of free passage was held a just cause; this doctrine was applied
to Jerusalem, as a ground to justify the Crusades.  The Emperor was
justified in making war on subjects who rebelled; he also could properly
authorize war to recover lost property which was being withheld.  The
twelfth century canonists stressed the necessity of a superior jurisdiction
to give legitimate authoriy for the prosecution of a war.  Although their
definition of a prince as one entitled to wage war was somewhat self-
referent, it was a limitation  on the local and immediate violence of lords
and knights.

The Decretalists tried to make more systematic the concept of the just
war.  Lawrence the Spaniard provided five criteria by which the justice of
a war could be assessed:  first, the person waging the war must be a
layman; second, the object of the war must be defence of the patria (one's
native country) or the recovery of stolen goods; third, only necessity made
the war just; fourth, the desire to punish was not of itself justificatory;

and, fifth, the war must be waged on princely authority. These five criteria are described as _persona_, _res_, _causa_, _animus_, _auctoritas_ respectively. Teutonicus adopted them; so did Raymond of Peñaforte who pointed out that all five must be met. Raymond also held that anyone, however just his cause, who intentionally exceeded the limit of minimum force should be excommunicated; he taught that this limit was lower in the defence of property than in the defence of the person. Hostiensis used the Roman law texts, amplifying the gospel command, to imply a cognatic relationship between all Christians, a family bond; his view tended to restrict legitimate authority for a just war to the Emperor or the Pope.

A problem linked with the notion of authority was that of obedience: was a subject bound to follow his lord in a war waged out of cupidity? Teutonicus required a vassal to refrain from giving aid to his lord's enemy, lest he render himself guilty of treason -- a Roman concept -- as well as of rupture of the feudal bond; he also prohibited a vassal from obeying his lord's command to commit atrocities[12]. The Speculator took a position helpful to the efficiency of royal power in France and England; where there was a war involving the _patria_, a vassal's allegiance to his king must take precedence over his obligation to his immediate lord. Innocent IV, speaking as canonist rather than as pope, specifically denied to a vassal, who obeyed the summons to fight in an unjust war, the action on mandate to recover his losses in the war from his lord. (Mandate in Roman law was a request by one party that another should do something for him, without payment, but with reimbursement of expenses.) Innocent thus equated the relationship of lord and vassal to that of mandator and mandatary. He reached his conclusion on the Roman ground that no contract

----------

12    Compare the treatment by Jacques de Révigny in Appendix II (a).

could be enforced which had an immoral foundation. The corollary was that a vassal could not be forced to participate in an unjust war, and that any measure his lord took against him to this end would be in itself unjust. However, when a vassal followed his lord in a just war, he would normally be able to recover his expenses by an action on mandate.

The right of capture was another area of warfare given consideration by the canonists. There were considerable difficulties in trying to reconcile the feudal right to exact a ransom, as well as the pagan Roman law which held that prisoners of war were automatically slaves, with the Church's ban on Christians enslaving other Christians. Hence the canonists' treatment concentrated on how property rights were affected by war. Lawrence the Spaniard discussed whether a just party who had recovered his property by means of war could then make a claim before the courts or properly continue the war. Feudal custom allowed the pursuit of both courses, but Lawrence held that the principle of good faith, as expressed in Roman law, forbade the seeking of the same remedy twice; once satisfaction had been received, the just party must seek nothing further.

Innocent IV and Hostiensis systematically linked the limits on violence and on legitimate spoils to the theory of the just war itself, by specifying how property rights and personal status were affected by the various levels of licit violence. Innocent did not make use of Roman public law in his analysis, because that had predicated a centralized single state, but Roman private law was readily adapted to the feudal confusion of public office and private right. The rule that an illegal or immoral act could not ground a lawful obligation could be used to protect the just and penalize the unjust warrior. Innocent understood that it was unrealistic to try to prevent all acts of warfare between feudal lords, and so he stressed not so much the abstract justice of a war as its legally enforceable consequences. The just war, or any licit defence by force, was deemed to constitute an extraordinary legal procedure, to supplement the normal methods for settling disputes; this put some controls on the incidence of violence.

(vii) The local application of canon law

The description of just war theories has illustrated how, in this as in other fields, canon law developed concepts of lawful authority and due obedience, including the duties involved in the former and the rights implied in the latter. Despite some of the larger claims made for papal jurisdiction[13], we find Innocent IV upholding the proper sphere of secular jurisdiction[14], and even maintaining the reality of legitimate government among infidels[15]. The canonists' definitions of spheres of authority were helpful tools in the political theorizing which led to the creation of nation states in Europe[16]. At least until the sixteenth century canon law continued to be very influential in the growth of public law as a science and in practice; some doctrines of Natural Law also owed much to canon law. However, canon law was not only the concern of the Papacy and the doctors, it also dealt with the daily needs of diocesan administration, and it was at this level that most people felt its effects. We shall therefore look at examples of the pastoral application of canon law, using the records of the diocese of Lincoln in the thirteenth and sixteenth centuries for our

----------

13  Tierney, nos. 87 and 88, quoting Hostiensis.

14  Tierney, nos. 84 and 85; cf. no. 57.

15  Tierney, no. 86.

16  cf. Tierney, nos. 89–92; v. generally the works of W. Ullmann.

illustrations[17].

All Christendom was divided into dioceses, and the bishop of each diocese was the judge ordinary, the man with universal jurisdiction in that diocese, except where there was specific reservation to some other court. The bishop was the proper judge in both civil and criminal cases falling to the courts spiritual; from him there might be appeal to the metropolitan (from Lincoln to the archbishop of Canterbury with his Court of Arches) and also appeal either thence or directly to the Pope. Appeals to the Papacy might be heard in Rome or locally by judges delegate, appointed to hear cases on the spot[18]. The Papacy, as well as providing an appellate court, reserved to itself certain great causes, such as claims against bishops, and also dispensations and absolutions of certain types[19]. The Pope like any other bishop, also had the power and the duty to intervene

----------

17    The Rolls and Register of Bishop Oliver Sutton, 1280-99, ed. R.M.T. Hill for the Lincoln Record Society (vol I = L.R.S. 39, 1948; vol II = L.R.S. 43, 1950; vol III = L.R.S. 48, 1954; vol IV = L.R.S. 52, 1958; vol V = L.R.S. 60, 1965; vol VI = L.R.S. 64, 1969), cited as Sutton III,33 etc.; An Episcopal Court Book for the Diocese of Lincoln, 1514-20, ed. M. Bowker, Lincoln Record Society 61, 1967, cited as Court Book. Lincoln was in some ways an unusual diocese, but these examples of its bishop's jurisdiction can safely be taken as typical.

18    Sutton III,33 -- Sutton and the bishops of Winchester and Salisbury were appointed to hear the case of Edmund, Earl of Cornwall, and his wife, Margaret de Clare, in 1290.

19    E.g., dispensation to a cleric to hold more than one benefice, v. Sutton I,105 or Court Book 103; a cleric who fornicated with a nun was sent to Rome to obtain absolution, Sutton IV,40.

where morals or Christian discipline required it[20]; such intervention might be through judges delegate or by a decretal. The Pope did not necessarily hear cases in person, although he might; at Rome there were auditors (auditores) who, between the twelfth and fourteenth centuries, changed from mere assistants into full delegates. They heard cases individually, but each was bound to take advice from his colleagues. From 1331 there were three panels of judges, and from these there developed the court of the Sacred Roman Rota, whose reports survive partially from the sixteenth century. Religious orders (that is, of monks, nuns, and friars) were in general not directly subject to the bishop as ordinary but only, via their Superiors, to the Pope. However, they would owe some duty to the bishop in whose see their house was situated[21], and they would also be subject to him in matters concerning the cure of souls.

Within the diocese the canons of the cathedral chapter to some extent shared the bishop's power, in that they administered the see during a vacancy, came together to elect the new bishop, and acted as his council and as the reservoir from which he drew his senior staff. Subordinate to the bishop were his archdeacons (of whom there were eight in the large diocese of Lincoln). Within his archdeaconry, a grouping of parishes, each had a wide jurisdiction at first instance covering laymen as well as clerics. From the archdeacon and his court appeal lay to the bishop; major causes lay outside his jurisdiction. Rural deans, or deans of

---------

20  We find Bishop Sutton in 1291 forbidding the letting of lodgings in
    Boston to harlots; the local clergy were to see that this was enforced
    -- Sutton III, 112.

21  v. C.R. Cheney, Episcopal Visitation of Monasteries in the Thirteenth
    Century (Manchester U.P., 2nd ed. 1983) for one aspect.

Christianity, had a similar but subordinate function. Also subordinate was the official, the bishop's official or the archdeacon's official, but in either case a delegate whose specific function was jurisdiction, since his superior might be occupied with other aspects of administration. The bishop's official -- the one usually referred to when the term is used without qualification -- normally had legal training. As he was a delegate, appeal from him lay to the metropolitan or directly to Rome (Sext 2,15,3). Vicars general also emerged as members of a bishop's permanent staff, or household; in many dioceses their duties were administrative rather than judicial, or only exercised in the absence of the bishop. Commissaries might be permanent or ad hoc but, although they might well be used for judicial business, this was not their specific function. There were, however, no hard and fast rules; one man, Richard Roston, was official-principal, vicar-general, commissary-general and chancellor to the bishop of Lincoln between 1514 and 1520.

Civil jurisdiction in the spiritual courts covered Church property, including ecclesiastical benefices (that is, tenure of parishes, canonries, bishoprics, etc.), wills and succession, status, marriage, dowry, obligations fortified by oath, and usury; all these were defined as 'spiritual causes' or annexed thereto. Other cases fell to the ecclesiastical courts by reason of the person involved, such as clerics[22], or widows and orphans, or crusaders, or because some aspect of doctrine or morality was involved. This was the theory; in practice there were

----------

22   Benefit of clergy, although subject to local variations, in general
     allowed a cleric, even one in minor orders, to choose as his forum, in
     criminal as well as civil matters, the relevant ecclesiastical court,
     to the exclusion of secular jurisdiction.

local variations -- for example, the differences between Spanish and English ecclesiastical jurisdiction over testamentary succession. In Lincoln in 1294 we find the bishop appointing commissaries to hear a case concerning entitlement to the mortuary dues of the parish of Milcombe; in another parish one of the local gentry had refused to pay his tithes, and he was told to seek absolution or to come before the bishop for judgment[23]. In 1519 Merton College, Oxford, was cited to explain the decayed state of the parish church at Diddington, whose revenues were annexed to the college[24]. The bishop is regularly found discharging executors who have completed their duties, appointing commissaries to try disputes arising out of wills, asking the sheriff to hand over the goods of one who had died intestate to the sequestrator (so that the Church could make fair disposition of his moveable estate), and dealing with maladministration by executors[25]. The bishop informed the secular courts of people's status, and saw that a widow received her dower[26]. Marriage questions lay in the bishop's jurisdiction, whether for confirmation or dissolution[27]. We find, too, Bishop Sutton granting licences to hold in the seasons of Lent or Advent legal proceedings which required the taking of an oath. In 1298 he dispensed one Agnes Cross from a rash vow she had made concerning fasting, and he bade her do some good work instead[28].

----------

23    Sutton IV,182; III,26.

24    Court Book 90.

25    Sutton III,21, III,48, V,20, V,93.

26    Sutton V,20, IV,126.

27    Sutton IV 66; Court Book 10; v. R.H. Helmholz, Marriage Litigation in Mediaeval England (C.U.P. 1974).

28    Sutton III,81, III,169; VI 59.

The criminal jurisdiction of the bishop's court covered crimes against clerics or Church property, against the ministry of the Church -- and this included crimes committed by clerics[29] --, against doctrine (which included heresy, blasphemy and sacrilege, simony, witchcraft, and disobedience) and against morals. In England most criminal jurisdiction seems to have been concerned with fornication and other sexual offences; most of these cases were dealt with in the archdeacon's court. Assault on or brawling with clerics seems to have been quite common; the excommunication imposed on Robert of Bavert for this reason was lifted when he explained that he had not recognized as a cleric the noisy fellow in striped clothes[30]. Heresy is not common in episcopal records, perhaps because it was often dealt with by specially appointed inquisitors; in 1518 the vicar-general heard the case of Elizabeth Sculthorp who had lost her faith and ceased going to church. She was not accused of witchcraft, in spite of her confession that she had betaken herself and all her children to the devil, but was kindly treated[31]. In 1295 we find an unusual offence; two men, recently appointed as canons in the cathedral chapter of Ferns in Ireland, were to be absolved from the excommunication incurred for attending lectures on civil law at the University of Oxford, and other excesses -- they should, of course, have had formal permission[32].

The main penalties imposed were excommunication, greater or lesser,

----------

29  E.g., the man appointed to a cure of souls who had failed to be ordained priest within the year; he was also charged with perjury and forging papal bulls -- Sutton VI,146.

30  Sutton III, 126; cf. II,35; IV,15; V,113, or Court Book 32f.

31  Court Book 84-5 and cf. 33.

32  Sutton V,76.

interdict, which was collective in that it was imposed on a community not an individual, beatings, fines, fasting, and public or private penance. On clerics alone might be imposed degradation from orders -- which would make them susceptible to secular jurisdiction --, deprivation of benefice, suspension from the exercise of office, and also imprisonment for obduracy, although the secular arm gaoled contumacious laymen on the Church's behalf. Excommunication was understood by the canonists as primarily a means to repentance and amendment; while it might well act as a deterrent, any retributive aim was subordinate to the bringing about of submission, to be followed by a suitable penance. Thus excommunication was pronounced against those who poached game in Spalding Priory's or the bishop's parks, until they made reparation; similarly it was pronounced against those who remained unrepentant in their adultery[33]. To give other examples of penalties, when Nigel of Hargrave had sought sanctuary in St. Giles', Oxford, but was dragged out and severely manhandled, the perpetrators of this violation were sentenced to six beatings and to paying his medical expenses, visiting him in prison, and having three masses said. Robert of Grendon was to receive two beatings in the archdeacon's household for striking a cleric's servant in the face over a game of dice. A canon who struck another cleric was to receive five beatings and was suspended from his ministry for six weeks; the chaplain who struck a canon of Stonely Priory was suspended until he should receive a dispensation and for the rest was to fast three Fridays on bread, beer -- drunk then like tea or coffee now --, and vegetable soup, and to pay three shillings to the Priory. John Fuller, a cleric, who shed the blood of another in a churchyard was to stand at the chancel steps on three successive Sundays

----------

33   Sutton IV,78, V,136; III,189.

singing psalms during Mass[34]. The publicity of such penances was quite often mitigated because humility rather than humiliation was the purpose; fines were on occasion imposed instead. Sometimes monetary penalties were intended as reparation, but sometimes they were simply fines, put to a good cause such as the rebuilding of the Fosse Dyke[35].

(viii) Canon law procedure

Procedure in the ecclesiastical courts seems to have had a considerable influence on that of the secular courts, for example, of the Court of Session in Scotland. Canon law built on the cognitio of Roman law, a rational system taking account of documentary evidence and witnesses' relation of events within their knowledge; the feudal courts preferred trial by battle or by ordeal. In the ecclesiastical courts auditors were appointed to act as examining magistrates, and all the proceedings were recorded in writing (Extra 2,19,11), usually by qualified notaries. By the thirteenth century, if not earlier, proceedings normally started with a written libel served with a summons. In the libel the pursuer had to state what he claimed, and on what grounds, and the nature of the action. The defender would normally appear to contest the claim; this stage was called litis contestatio (joinder of issue) as in Justinian's law. The defender could put forward certain pleas in defence (exceptiones). Declinatory (for example, rejecting the jurisdiction of the court) and dilatory (denying that a claim had yet fallen due) defences must

----------

34   Sutton V,1; III,27; VI,144; V,94, cf. Court Book 138; Sutton VI,73, cf. Court Book 32.

35   Court Book, 109, 139.

be pleaded before *litis* *contestatio*; peremptory defences (that is, those defences which would bar an action in perpetuity, such as duress) came afterwards, and would usually be considered together with the matters of fact. After *litis* *contestatio* the pursuer set out his facts, his allegations, in articles or *positiones*; the defender admitted or denied each, and set out his own *positiones*. The judge then investigated or tried the points not admitted by the defender, and found the facts on the evidence. The evidence might amount to full proof, that is, the testimony of two witnesses or a notarized document, or to half proof, that is, of one witness, or a private document, or general report, each of which could be rebutted. This was more reliable than compurgation which, however, was tolerated in many ecclesiastical courts, for, as has been remarked, as long as local reputation was important and social units were small enough, the oaths of neighbours as to a man's character were probably fairly trustworthy. In canonical procedure, after proof of the facts, the judge heard the parties' arguments on points of law, including the legal effect of the facts proved; he then gave his decision. All the proceedings, including the judgment, were put in writing. Appeal was possible on interlocutory matters as well as on the final decision; this gave considerable opportunity for delaying tactics. For this reason summary procedure was introduced; it was authorized and regulated in 1307 (*Clem.* 5,11,2), but it had clearly been practised for quite a while before.

Criminal proceedings began either with accusation by the injured party or someone on his behalf, or with denunciation in the public interest by someone with no personal *locus* *standi*, or through an official investigation by the court where there had been persistent rumour of wrongdoing. By the fifteenth century, inquiry by the court on its own initiative had become the most common start for a criminal action in the courts spiritual. The accused must receive due notice of the charge made against him and of the witnesses who would be called. Once begun, criminal trials in ecclesiastical courts differed little from civil actions.

Roman rules, including rules of evidence and procedure, were used where appropriate. For example, in marriage litigation they were applicable in questions of capacity or consent, or of certain impediments; Roman rules were not, however, used on presumption of marriage[36], and the treatment of divorce was entirely different. Gratian, quoting Pope Nicholas I, expressed the general canonist attitude to Roman law. "The imperial law is not to be used in every ecclesiastical dispute, especially where it conflicts with the rule of the gospels or the canons.... Not that it is to be completely rejected, for example, against heretics and other wicked men." Indeed, "the imperial law is to be used in ecclesiastical matters wherever it is found not to conflict with the sacred canons"[37].

(ix)  Substantive canon law


Canon law was primarily concerned with the administration of the Church and its rules; from consideration of the wider aspects of government within the Church much political theory applicable to the secular world was developed. Some elements of canon law, however, were related to the daily practice of the secular law. For example, canonical doctrine largely ignored the feudal distinction between moveable and immoveable property; the canonist attitude was adopted from the law of Justinian's time and was partly in the interests of the claims of women, who enjoyed inferior rights

----------

36    Cf. D. 23,2,4 with Decretum Grat., C.30, q.5, cc.1-2.

37    Decretum Grat., D.10,1; dictum post C.15, q.3, c.4.

in feudal property.

Canonists naturally wished to maintain the rule of law, and to this end they stressed the importance of the protection of peaceful possession. The _actio spolii_ first appeared around 1180[38]; by this action the victim of any unjustified loss of possession, indeed of any obstacle to the exercise of a right, could claim restitution. The action went beyond the protection of possession given by the interdicts of Roman law, and far beyond the assize of novel disseisin and other feudal remedies, in that it covered any subject of alleged benefit, including moveable property or an office or benefice. All the claimant had to do was to show that he had held this benefit peacefully before the present possessor; the question of right, of title, could be settled afterwards.

Another development that affected secular law in the sphere of possession was the canonists' restriction on the acquisition of title by prescription. In Roman law, initial good faith was required for such acquisition (_usucapio_), as well as a _iusta causa_ (that is, apparent grounds for acquisition of title, such as sale or gift); supervening knowledge that there was a better claimant did not bar acquisition, provided that no challenge was made. The canonists, however, held that the absence of good faith was bad faith, and of its nature sinful, and so an acquisition where there was supervening knowledge of a better claimant was to be equated with theft. From the fifteenth century the requirement of continuous good faith became in many areas a principle of secular as well as of ecclesiastical law; it was received into French and into German law.

Good faith was stressed by the canonists in other ways. It was on the basis of general good faith that agreements, even without oath, were held

----------

38   _Extra_ 2,13,7; cf. _Decretum Grat._, C.3,q.1,c.3; v. le Bras, 350f.

to bind the parties, thus giving a _causa_, a ground of action, before an ecclesiastical court. _Pacta_ _sunt_ _servanda_ (agreements are for keeping) was the canonist ruling, but performance could normally be required only if the first party had done or offered to do his part. A fair amount of argument was needed to reconcile this doctrine with the Roman view that bare pacts might only act as a defence to an action and gave rise to no obligation. Hence there was considerable emphasis on the will, intention, as playing the fundamental part in grounding obligations, or at least contractual obligations. The doctrine of a _causa_ as a requirement for a contract developed from this approach and became part of the _ius_ _commune_. While the adoption of canonist procedure was of particular importance for the _ius_ _commune_, the substance of canon law was influential in other fields, including the law merchant, and also, of course, in later consistorial jurisdiction.


Further Reading:

G. le Bras "Canon law" in The Legacy of the Middle Ages (O.U.P., 1926).

R.H. Helmholz "Excommunication as a legal sanction" 68 ZSS (Kan.) (1982),
     202.

S. Ollivant  The Court of the Official (Stair Society,vol.34, Edinburgh
     1982).

O.F. Robinson "Canon law and marriage" Jur.Rev. (1984), 22.

J.D. Scanlan "The tribunal of the Sacred Roman Rota" Jur.Rev. (1969), 97.

R.W. Southern Western Society and the Church in the Middle Ages (Penguin,
     1970).

B. Tierney The Crisis of Church and State, 1050-1300 (U.S.A., 1964, repr.).

W. Ullmann  The Growth of Papal Government (3rd ed., London, 1970).

          The Church and the Law (London, 1975).

# Chapter VI

## THE LAW MERCHANT

(i)  Problems of defining the Law Merchant


The Law Merchant is comparable to feudal law in that its origins are customary.  As had happened in earlier centuries with kinship or feudal groups, bodies of craftsmen or traders or seafarers formed associations for their own safety.  A few of those in Italy may well go back to the Roman collegia (associations of men such as the bakers or the salt suppliers of Rome) but mostly they were of Germanic origin; a special peace was often granted -- or sold -- to groups of merchants by Carolingian or Anglo-Saxon rulers.  Most of these associations were based on towns which, as we have seen, emerged in the eleventh century as instruments of the economic revival and as the markets which stimulated yet further growth.  Just as feudal law everywhere involved the personal tie between man and lord, tenure, and delegation of govermental powers (but in different localities the means by which these were achieved and the implications varied), so everywhere the needs of trade were physical safety, financial security, and speedy settlement, and again the mechanisms for satisfying these needs varied.  Different customs applied at sea or on land, between the north of Europe and the south, and even between neighbouring cities.

Common institutions were shared; for example, the use of negotiable instruments received general acceptance, but the precise enforceable rules for their use varied in different countries and in different jurisdictions. In some areas there developed a general mercantile jurisdiction; in others only certain classes of person or of transaction had their own courts. Some modern civilian systems, such as the German and the French, have separate commercial codes; others, such as the Italian, no longer do. In the Scots and the English legal systems commercial law is not formally distinct from other areas, but manuals are written and courses taught on mercantile law in modern Britain. Certain transactions are more commonly entered into by merchants, others by consumers, and there may be special provision for commercial cases, or at least some difference in such matters as the standard of proof required to evidence a transaction. Problems raised by trade across national frontiers need special regulation and so do special customs in a commercial community, whether the members of the modern Stock Exchange or the underwriters of Antwerp in the seventeenth century. Such special treatment, however, is not peculiar to merchants even now, and in the mediaeval and early modern world there were many examples of a law which was restricted to a particular group within a body of citizens.

During the Middle Ages it was the international ramifications of trade and manufacturing which significantly marked out mercantile from other branches of law of more local application. Moreover, from the sixteenth century onwards when national systems are clearly developing, the Law Merchant continued readily to cross the boundaries between them and to preserve its international character. Its common feature was community of institutions rather than community of rules; there was no central legislation, no central court, through which uniformity of rules might be achieved. There continued to be a general tendency to follow accepted custom, and to accept foreign customs or authorities as highly persuasive in the decisions of national courts. Also discernible was an inclination to speed and informality of procedure (for example, arbitration), and to reliance on equity and good faith — although it is worth remembering that this meant equity and good faith as understood by merchants, which might

154

involve strict compliance with accepted custom.  It did not just mean fair
play, or a moral philosopher's concept of good faith.

(ii)  Roman elements in the Law Merchant

The interpretation of good faith in terms of conventional practice was
very Roman, and Roman too were some of the widespread specific rules to be
found in the more developed stages of the Law Merchant.  The Romans had
employed many contracts which were available to anyone suing in a Roman
court; they described these as being of the _ius gentium_, the law of peoples
gonerally.  Thus it was possible to make a binding contract of sale or hire
by simple, unwitnessed and informal agreement on the subject matter and the
price; one could enter into any sort of obligation, simple or complex, by
formally putting a question and replying with a promise (in the contract
known as stipulation).  Roman law had no technically distinct mercantile
law but certain institutions, sometimes of Greek or other origin, were
special to mercantile transactions.  It is not clear that there was any
continuity in these institutions between the ancient and the mediaeval
worlds; certainly the Law Merchant came in time to borrow from the learned
law of the _Corpus Iuris Civilis_.  However, continuity is not impossible,
especially as most of these institutions were particularly concerned with
maritime commerce, which had never ceased between the Italian peninsula and
the Byzantine Empire and  was the earliest field for the codification of
custom in the history of the Law Merchant.

To give some examples: the _actio exercitoria_ was an action given
against a ship-owner in respect of contracts entered into by the master of
the ship -- the comparable _actio institoria_ was given against the owner of
a shop or business in respect of contracts entered into by the manager whom

he employed. _Faenus nauticum_ was a loan (at a high rate of interest) made for the purpose of a sea voyage, repayable only if the ship arrived safely. _Receptum nautarum_ was the implied promise of a carrier by sea that he would deliver the goods entrusted to him, unless the goods were lost through circumstances beyond his control such as shipwreck or attack by pirates. The edict _nautae caupones stabularii_ imposed double liability on the master of a ship (or on the keeper of an inn or stable) if goods were lost, damaged or stolen by his employees. The _lex Rhodia_, or Rhodian Sea Law, dealt with general average; it provided that where cargo was jettisoned in order to save a ship and the ship was saved, the loss was to be shared among all those who benefited including the owner of the ship, so that the whole loss did not fall on the party or parties whose cargo had been jettisoned. When the learned law came to be applied to comparable situations in the mediaeval world, reference was made to the Roman texts on these and similar matters.

(iii)  Maritime codes

Even before the economic revival of the eleventh and twelfth centuries there was some long-distance sea-borne trade in luxuries through certain Italian ports, and when the revival came it was centred upon the Mediterranean; in consequence Italian practice influenced all aspects of commerce as trade spread outwards through Europe. (It should be remembered that even when trade became easier in later centuries, transport by water was cheaper and safer than by land right up until the nineteenth century.) Naples, Amalfi and Salerno aroused the admiration of a Saracen compiler of a handbook for merchants in the late tenth century, although Bari, Trani and the other Apulian ports confined themselves primarily to local trade.

156

These cities were in the Byzantine sphere of influence as was Venice, founded among the marshes at the head of the Adriatic by refugees fleeing the Lombards; she was unique among cities in that her two main exports, salt and glass, owed nothing to the cultivation of the land. It was in the eleventh century that Pisa and Genoa developed as maritime powers; in 1016 they united to clear Sardinia of Moslem control, and the Pisans had already won a sea battle against the Moslems in 1005 off Reggio. The Norman conquest of southern Italy and of most of Sicily during the eleventh century provided allies for the two cities. Then the Norman encroachments in the Balkans led to the hard-pressed Byzantine Empire appealing to the West for help against the threatening Turks. In the wake of the ensuing First Crusade markets in the Levant which had hitherto been dominated by Byzantium's allies were opened to Pisa and Genoa. Venice survived the setback, retained a near monopoly of trade with Constantinople, and established colonies at Tyre and Sidon, but she was no longer unrivalled.

Nothing concerning maritime custom survives in written form from before the beginning of the thirteenth century, but clearly the earliest writings available to us were not the first of their kind. From Venice in 1205 came the Capitulare navium (Shipping Rules) which was reissued in a much fuller form in 1255 under the title Statuta et Ordinamenta super Navibus (Statutes and Regulations on Shipping). This code was extremely influential in the other Adriatic ports, although Ancona had her own code of which a late fourteenth century version survives. In Apulia at the very end of the twelfth century two judges independently put into writing the customs of Bari; one was most conscious of the Lombard element, the other of the ius commune of the northern cities but he included some maritime custom. At Trani the maritime code seems to date from the fourteenth century, although ascribed to the eleventh; it is in Italian not Latin

157

which better fits the later date but it doubtless contains older elements. At Amalfi in the kingdom of Naples there was a code of which parts go back at least to the thirteenth century; it has twenty-one chapters in Latin and forty-five in Italian. The customs of the city of Pisa were first written down shortly after the Peace of Constance (1183), and it was in the early thirteenth century that a maritime court (the ordo maris) came into being there with its own proper code; the oldest surviving version of this Breve curiae maris (Manual of the Court of the Sea) dates from 1305. The consuls, or judges, of the ordo maris at first exercised a concurrent jurisdiction with the city's mercantile judges and were subject to appeal; in the fourteenth century they acquired an exclusive and irrevocable jurisdiction in maritime matters, including shipyard contracts. Genoa's sea customs were of great importance in the Levant. It was Genoese and Pisan influence which led to the compilation in Barcelona of a code which was to become the most widely used of all codes of maritime law; it was originally entitled Costumes de la Mar (Customs of the Sea) but is most generally known as the Consolato del Mare (Consulate of the Sea).

The term 'consul' had developed for judges in the cities' courts. Those who exercised a general jurisdiction came often to be replaced by the podestà but the name frequently survived for those who presided over guild or maritime courts. Those, too, who heard the disputes of their fellow guildsmen or fellow countrymen at fairs or in foreign ports were often called consuls. The term has survived into the modern world for persons appointed to represent the maritime and commercial interests of their country in a foreign state; in the Middle Ages they often exercised a general jurisdiction within a quarter of a town reserved to a particular group of foreigners. A consul might also be a national of the state in which the trading post was sited, who acted as host to a particular group.

From Italy the institution spread to France and Spain as well as the Levant. The county of Barcelona and the kingdom of Aragon were the earliest parts of Spain to share in the economic revival; there the commercial courts were controlled by the crown, unlike the communes of Italy but as in France and England. It was by royal ordinance in 1336 that summary procedure was introduced for the Sea Consulate of Valencia; it was a royal charter which in 1401 established the Barcelona consulate not simply as a maritime court but as one exercising general jurisdiction.

The Consulate of the Sea[1] begins with the procedure for the annual election of the judges by the senior members of the marine corporations and the sea guilds. "Such is the custom. Although it has been stated [in the royal charter of 1284] that His Majesty the King or his procurator would designate annually the person who would exercise the office of judge, the elders of the sea guild enjoy this privilege because His Majesty the King and his procurator have never at any time since the inception of this privilege exercised their prerogative"(art.3). "Consuls shall have jurisdiction in all matters relating to lading charges, damage suffered by the cargo once loaded aboard the vessels, wages of sailors, shareholders of vessels, sale of vessels, throwing of cargo overboard, command of vessels entrusted to patrons or sailors, indebtedness of shipowners who took out loans to equip the vessels, obligations of the merchants to shipowners, obligations of shipowners to the merchants, all salvage found on the sea and on the sea shore, outfitting of vessels galleys barques, and all types of agreement which generally refer to the custom of the sea"(art.22). In case of doubt the consuls were to consult the elders of the merchants' and sea guilds; if the advice differed the consuls were to follow that of the

----------

1    Translated by S.S. Jados, (Alabama, 1975).

elders of the sea guild — not because they were forced to seek advice by royal or other provision, but because it was the ancient custom. The substantive provisions are described as the "beneficial customs of marine intercourse which well-informed people, having journeyed throughout the world, imparted to our predecessors who wrote them down in learned volumes, all of them relating to the proper customs to be followed. In the material which follows one can learn in what way a patron of a vessel is obligated to the merchants, the sailors, the passengers, and other persons aboard his vessel; also, what are the responsibilities of merchants, sailors and passengers toward a patron of a large or a small vessel"(art.46). Other provisions cover the initial construction of a vessel and taking shares in that venture (articles 47-54), conditions in which there would be an obligation to aid another vessel in distress (art. 94), general average (arts. 95-99), the employment of a pilot (art. 250), and there is a considerable section on privateering (arts. 298-334).

The Consulate went through many editions; the repetition of various provisions in modified form indicates the accumulation of material, for example, art. 157 deals with desertion by crew members, art. 158 is an amending article, and the matter is also the subject of art. 268. The book was translated from the original Catalan into Latin, French and Italian; the Italian edition of 1519 was to be found all over Europe and was described as "the custom commonly received in all provinces and lands". It inspired or provided a model for other collections of maritime custom in the northern part of Europe. A collection called Jugements de la mer (Judgments of the Sea) or Rôles d'Oléron (Records of Oléron — from near La Rochelle) goes back to the thirteenth or fourteenth century and, in the older parts, contains Gascon custom. Other additions were from Brittany or Normandy, and it was used also in Flanders, the Netherlands and England,

160

where later the **Black Book of the Admiralty** was compiled. It directly provided the bulk of the material for the **Waterrecht** (**Sea Law**) of Damme and then of Wisby (in the Baltic), and in this form was widely used in the Hanseatic towns such as Lübeck and Hamburg and in other northern ports. These substantial and widely accepted codes gradually superseded most narrowly local customs.

In maritime law there were many institutions peculiar to the sea. Some were modifications of the Roman law, such as the rule of general average, or the form of loan called **faenus nauticum**. Sometimes new custom appears to have been influenced by the revived Roman law, for example, the owning of ships in shares or parts, and the rules of liability after a collision where there had been no fault. Similarly bottomry bonds, giving security over a ship to a creditor, seem to have developed from **faenus nauticum**, being payable only if the ship came safely home. Insurance was a growing field of maritime law, and new legal documents appeared such as bills of lading or analogous documents in which the ship's writer or clerk listed the cargo and gave a copy of the **conossement**, as it is called, to the freighter as proof that the goods had been shipped. These and similar practices found so widespread an acceptance as reasonably to be called universal, and the needs of maritime commerce have changed little, although it is doubtful if in a modern container ship there is a legal requirement to carry a cat to deal with the rats (**Consulate**, art. 68).

(iv)  Burgh law and guilds

In tenth century Italy Pavia (as the capital of the Lombard kingdom) was perhaps the only inland city apart from Rome to attract substantial groups of foreign merchants; it had also its own merchant guild, as well as various craft guilds exercising a monopoly in their respective trades. By the start of the thirteenth century Florence had separate guilds for textile importers and finishers and for textile retailers, as well as for bankers and money-lenders. The economic revival in the eleventh century sparked off a tremendous growth of city life in the twelfth; by the early thirteenth century Pisa had grown from some 30 to 114 walled hectares and Bologna from about 23 to around 100. New towns were founded in considerable numbers, for example, some twenty were established in the district of Vercelli alone. The Peace of Constance in effect gave the cities self-government, free from more than the shadow of imperial control. While the classes were certainly distinct, in practice the line of division between lords and merchants was blurred; land was best, but trade was not vulgar. Not surprisingly as the cities began to write down their customs in their statutes they included customs connected with trade.

The major social development of this period in the cities was the emergence of the guilds. While the guilds' first concern was to regulate themselves in the interests of their members, they were also fairly readily adaptable to the public welfare. City statutes therefore regulated the guilds, and thereafter we find guildmasters or consuls acquiring jurisdiction not only in those matters concerning the guilds but also in general commercial affairs. In some cities there was a clear distinction between the courts; for example, in twelfth century Pisa there was a _curia legis_ (court of law) for what was covered by the city's statutes and a _curia usus_ (court of custom) for mercantile cases -- and it was from the latter, as we have seen, that the _ordo maris_ (maritime tribunal) developed. In Genoa on the other hand the consuls were tax collectors, and commercial cases were heard by the city's general court. In principle the guilds were concerned with their own members, and in this context developed written

162

registers of membership, styles for articles of partnership, etc.. However, in the majority of cities the guild courts became, expressly or tacitly, general commercial courts and even where they did not their members were likely to provide the judges when questions of commercial usage came before the regular courts. The same tendencies are observable in northern Europe in, for example, the Dean of Guild courts in Scotland (which survived until 1975, although they lost their mercantile jurisdiction during the eighteenth century).

It has been pointed out[2] that law and rhetoric had a vital role to play in enabling the new intense urban life to survive without political disaster and with adequate structures for the new scale of trade, both local and national, which was necessary. New structures and forms of association needed expert definition and regulation. Judges and notaries formed influential and sizeable professional groups (for example, 120 doctors of both laws and 1500 notaries, compared to 440 butchers, in Milan and its contado in 1288); they often stood closer to the governing class than to the ordinary guilds. The universities studied intensively the civil and the canon law but the legal expertise so gained was applied to political theory and to commercial needs. The law merchant was based on custom and the usages of trade but it was elaborated and refined by the learned lawyers, men who were living and working in the flourishing centres of commerce. Around 1300 the populations of Venice, Milan, Florence and Genoa were probably approaching 100,000 each, with some twenty-two other Italian cities having between 50,000 and 20,000 inhabitants; in northern Europe only Paris and Ghent were clearly over the 50,000 mark and only London, Cologne and Bruges over 20,000. In southern Italy Palermo,

----------

2    Hyde, chapter 3.

Naples and Messina owed their size and prosperity to their foreign connections; Rome suffered as a city from the removal of the Papacy to Avignon. Most cities, however, were primarily centres for the distribution and consumption of relatively local produce; of the inland cities only Florence would have listed banking, long-distance trade and industry as her predominant concerns. We shall look at banking and international trade in due course.

The guilds, to resume, were primarily concerned with their own internal organization, with the interests of the masters in a monopoly -- or near monopoly --, in the control of the standards of the craft and in relations between employers and employees. Their statutes, once their customs were written down, tended to follow the outlines of their city's statutes, at least in Italy. Sometimes one finds a 'reception', as when the goldsmiths of Brescia adopted as their own the statutes of the goldsmiths of Venice. Particularly in the textile industry traders often carried to their export markets the statutes of their native city. It seems likely that in the northern cities of Europe, of which the most flourishing were concerned with long-distance trade, the guilds were to some degree so influenced, although the very growth of towns will have been enough to call forth somewhat similar institutions. For example, in 1120 their feudal lord granted by charter to the burgesses of Freiburg (in the Black Forest) the right to settle disputes among themselves by the customary law of merchants, and in particular by the custom of Cologne.

In France Philip Augustus (1180-1223) granted rights including jurisdiction over the Seine and its banks to the guild of river merchants. In England we find the regulations of the guilds being proclaimed and put into effect in a general commercial court. For example, at the fair court held in March 1332 at Wye in Kent two girdlers of the City of London saw to

164

the reading of King Edward III's confirmation of their statute that no
girdler should garnish girdles of silk, wool, leather or linen with base
metal, and that in each town two men of the craft should be elected to see
that the statute was observed; two men of Wye were duly elected and went on
to discover five makers of girdles in breach of the regulation whose work
was thereupon burned[3].

Burgh law could cover a wide range of concerns, some of them only
loosely linked to commercial life and some of them merely the consequence
of living in a built-up area. In May 1324 at the fair court of St. Ives
(in Huntingdonshire) accusations brought by neighbours included: "that
there is a deficiency of water in the row of William of Hurst; ... that
John Hering senior receives harlots in a house of his; ... that Robert
Woodward obstructs a certain road near the quay; ... that Lawrence Pegg
does not clean his road in Cross Lane to the nuisance [of passers-by]; ...
and that Richard Brewhouse receives the merry-andrews in the midst of the
fair to the disturbance and peril of the merchants."[4] The safe organizing
of trade needed more than credit facilities, and when a fair was being held
the normal concerns of the town must be adjusted to take it into account.

(v) Fair and piepowder courts

The mediaeval law merchant, in the sense of the customary usages of
traders, had roots in the fairs and markets held, although not always at
regular intervals, throughout Europe even in the Dark Ages. Market

----------

3   Selden Society, vol.23, Select Cases concerning the Law Merchant 1270–
    1638, ed. C. Gross (1908, repr.), p.110.

4   Selden Society, vol.23, p.106f.

165

is usually applied to a regular weekly or monthly gathering serving a smallish district, while a fair is usually an annual meeting, although it may be more or less frequent. We know of fairs in Merovingian Paris and elsewhere in France in the eighth and ninth centuries. From the tenth century on there were numerous royal grants of markets with rights of jurisdiction, and the holding of great fairs such as those of Champagne is well evidenced. Such fairs and markets would be under the special peace of the king. Fairs were by no means exclusively a phenomenon of the north, but they were more characteristic of the north as was maritime trade of the Mediterranean lands.

These early fairs had their own informal courts for dealing with trading disputes and for keeping the peace, the sort of courts which in England were later called courts of piepowder, that is, pieds poudrés - referring to the dusty feet of the merchants or pedlars who travelled from fair to fair. The courts sometimes acquired jurisdiction over persons coming to and going from the fair as well as in matters arising during the fair. The right to grant a market or fair was generally recognized as a regalian right -- a right belonging to a prince -- and the authority which this indirectly gave to the fair court favoured the development of a special custom for merchants and its acceptance as legally enforceable; this included such measures as distraint against any fellow citizen of a defaulting party -- the right of reprisal. In time, and the heyday of the fairs of Lyon and Champagne was during the fourteenth and fifteenth centuries, the fairs also became centres for raising capital, for settling obligations and for transferring credit.

Just as fairs were generally accommodated to the feudal law in that their jurisdiction sprang from a prince's grant (as burghs were granted charters by their feudal lords), so in the north especially the judges might be appointed by the prince. From 1174 the judges at Champagne were appointed by royal ordinances, and from them appeal lay to the Grands Jours (Great Sessions) of Troyes and the Parlement of Paris (of which more in the next chapter). Similarly at Lyon the fair court's jurisdiction was in the sixteenth century extended by royal ordinance to make it a general commercial court. In 1655 Lyon succeeded in following Toulouse, Paris, Nantes, Bordeaux, Poitiers and Tours in obtaining merchant judges selected by their fellows; this was roughly the time at which the Champagne fair disappeared after being for centuries an almost permanent institution, moving quarterly from one of four cities to the next. At a much earlier stage of development Florentine consuls had been exercising jurisdiction over their countrymen at the Champagne fair under the somewhat misleading title (for Florence is in Tuscany) of the Captain of the Lombards.

By the thirteenth century the wool and cloth trade in the north had established itself in cities, especially Bruges, Ghent and Liège, and the fair courts were urban in flavour. In Germany it was the towns along the Rhine which played a leading commercial role, Basel, Mainz, Worms and Cologne. Lübeck, Hamburg and Bremen were the leading towns in the north; all were members of the Hanseatic League. Munich had received its charter in the mid twelfth century from Henry the Lion of Saxony and Bavaria in order to encourage trade along the Danube and through the Alpine passes. In Germany generally before the fifteenth century procedure in mercantile courts seems to have been purely oral -- there are no records and no records of records. In Frankfurt we know that commercial procedure started as arbitration with a special summary process, but it soon became the practice to refer to a carefully kept book of precedents. As early as 1508 there was imperial recognition of the merchant judges at Nuremburg, but as the reception of Roman law gathered pace, mixed courts of merchants and

167

jurists became the rule, as at Leipzig by 1682.

English practice is interesting because written records of merely local commercial jurisdictions survive from the thirteenth century. There were special courts in the staple towns through which, for fiscal reasons, the foreign trade in wool and woollen goods was channelled; from them appeal lay to the Chancellor and the King's Council. There were guild courts, but these English ones were largely confined, even in London, to matters affecting their organization, not to settling disputes between individuals. There were also fair courts, where the mayor or the representative of the feudal lord might preside but judgment was given by the merchants or burgesses. Of the central courts, the Court of Admiralty claimed commercial as well as maritime causes, although it lost the former to the common law courts. In England, however, the term law merchant seems to refer as much to a particularly speedy (cases were traditionally heard between successive tides) and summary form of procedure and to special rules of evidence as to any particular body of substantive law. It has indeed been argued that there was no substantive law peculiar to fair and burgh courts, and that mercantile matters could as readily be brought before the common law courts. Any specific reception by the common law courts of a body of peculiarly mercantile law must remain highly problematic but, on the other hand, juries of burgesses and merchants would be likely to come to somewhat different conclusions from those of juries of knights and peasants. For example, when at St. Ives a horse was arrested as a pledge and a third party claimed that the horse was his, in spite of a sworn verdict that the claim was collusive, "the judgment was put into respite until it should be more fully discussed by the merchants. And the merchants of the various communities and others being convoked in full court" held that the third party's payment of earnest to the defender was sufficient according to the law merchant to give him title[5]. The lack of any commercial code in England means furthermore that records of English fair courts are not necessarily a safe guide to other local jurisdictions in Europe, but these records do offer useful illustrations of the peculiarities of mercantile cases and of the special interests of the mercantile community. For example, after the twelfth century English procedure was predicated upon a shire-sized jurisdiction, yet the needs of merchants must lead them into foreign parts. In 1270 at the fair court of St. Ives, Gottschalk of Almaine (that is, of Germany), burgess of King's Lynn, made a complaint against the communities of Ghent, Poperinge, Douai, Ypres and Lille concerning a consignment of wool to be exported from England to Flanders; he was claiming against the communities, rather than against any particular merchant, under the right of reprisal, and the communities claimed that they had charters from the English crown exempting them from reprisal[6]. In 1291 the records of the same court reveal a fairly widely established occupation, that of broker, which included an official responsibility for weights and measures. "Alnagers of canvas ... made oath that they will act honestly in their office, and that they will make honest measurement for both sellers and buyers, and that they will take nothing from the one party or the other whereby any harm may befall or accrue to the buyer or the seller."[7]

At the fair court of Wye of 1332 a pursuer craved execution of a debt found due to him five years previously in the same fair court; jurisdiction here would seem to have lain only to the fair court. However, frequent

----------

5     Selden Society, vol.23, p.44f.

6     Selden Society, vol.23, p.9f.

7     Selden Society, vol.23, p.41.

sittings for the speedy discharge of business among peripatetic disputants are also evidenced. At a fair court at West Malling, in Kent, in November 1364 we have an example of the defender's normal three opportunities to appear being compressed into one day when Alan Dyer of Maidstone claimed £25.10s. from John Stonehill; the parties were to appear at nine o'clock. John made no appearance and so a hearing was called for noon; again he made no appearance, and so the case was put down for the evening session. When John still did not appear all his property at the fair -- which had already been attached in security -- "appraised by credible men at £27.4s.3d.", was left in the custody of the bailiff of the fair until the next fair the following August[8]. At the staple court of Westminster in June 1401 we find Hamond Eliot of London, grocer, being allowed to "have his law single-handed", that is, he was allowed to swear without compurgators, as to the sum owed him by Martin Dyne of Heydon, chapman; such an oath was "according to their usages and customs and according to the law merchant"[9]. On the other hand, sometimes men seem expected to travel with enough companions to warrant their credibility; Gerard of Cologne "did not come sufficiently equipped according to the law merchant" to the fair at St.Ives in 1270, and he was given two days to find the required five oath-helpers for his claim to a consignment of Rhenish wine which lay with a merchant of Lynn[10].

The importance of fairs declined from the late Middle Ages as steadier demand elicited a more evenly distributed supply. The need for special concessions to foreigners, that is, all men not of the immediate locality, diminished as local feudal jurisdictions gave way to central governmental

--------

8    Selden Society, vol.23, p.112.

9    Selden Society, vol.23, p.114.

10   Selden Society, vol.23, p.5.

powers. It was quite a common privilege of fairs that aubaine or _ius_
_albanagii_ -- the right of the feudal lord to any property within his
jurisdiction of a foreigner who died there, regardless of that foreigner's
heirs or of his will -- should not be  enforced against those attending
them; the privilege could be bought by other merchants.   In France the
crown's general claim to aubaine was only abandoned at the Revolution.
Tolls and taxes might occasionally be waived or more frequently be lowered
for a fair; temporary concessions might be made which freed aliens from
customary restrictions on residence or trade.  Nevertheless the decline was
a lingering one; the piepowder court at Eye in Suffolk kept its records
open until 1813, and Bartholomew Fair in London had a court book until its
demise in 1854, although this recorded payments from the stall-holders, not
pleas.

(vi)  The financial organization of mediaeval business


    While in mercantile transactions relating to land-based commerce there
was not the same acceptance of common rules as in maritime affairs,
institutions did develop which received general or outline acceptance.  A
fair number of these related to money, the lubricant of commerce.  Deposit
banks were fairly common  among the northern Italian cities,  and in France
there was at  Cahors an internationally famous centre of deposit banking.
But although the credit arrangements they offered were of great use to
craftsmen and small-scale traders,  such bankers were often restricted in
the scope of their loans by their cities, which wished to protect their own
currency.  Further, simple loans were harder to make profitable when the
Church frowned on usury.  Merchant bankers,  merchants lending and
borrowing money in the furtherance of international trade, were of much

greater significance in the development of commercial credit. They too accepted money on deposit and paid interest to the depositor; they too lent money so deposited at a higher rate of interest, often to prelates and nobles and above all to kings. Loans to princes could be very profitable; between 1290 and 1310 the Frescobaldi Bianchi of Florence lent the English crown at least £122,000 sterling. The Bardi, bankers to Edward III, were even richer, until they failed in 1346, unable to recover credits of more than a million florins from the kings of England and Sicily.

The chief technique, other than the concessions granted by grateful princes, by which such merchant bankers could make their profits was the letter (or bill) of exchange. Money advanced in one currency in one place was repayable at a later date in another currency and in another place; high interest charges could be hidden in a carefully adjusted rate of exchange. Bills of exchange are one form of negotiable instrument; others (some of modern growth) are promissory notes, bank notes, cheques, dividend warrants, bearer bonds, etc.. They are all documents containing an undertaking to pay money, which by mercantile custom do not need to state the grounds of or the consideration for the transaction. They are transferred by mere delivery (with endorsement where applicable) and the new holder in good faith has full title to any benefits or rights of action. By the end of the thirteenth century business by correspondence had become established practice and, for the great Italian firms at least, money had become a commodity.

The firms which dealt in money and in goods -- such as spices and dyestuffs, skins, silk and wool -- were no longer either associations for one voyage or lifelong partnerships based on community of family property. These kinds of partnership did indeed survive, fitting well into the Roman models of the <u>societas</u> <u>unius</u> <u>rei</u> (partnership for a single deal) and

172

societas omnium bonorum (partnership in all property), but it became more common to arrange an association for a term of years, after which profits were distributed in proportion to the shares which members had contributed. This sort of partnership, with joint and unlimited liability for the partners, was known as the compagnia. Although it was not unlike the Roman societas quaestus (partnership for all business matters), it was more concerned with questions arising from relationships with third parties, in effect with agency; Roman law had been primarily concerned with the internal relationship between the partners. Compagnia was not incompatible with the contract of commission, whereby one merchant took care of another's business for a percentage or a fixed fee. In firms like the Bardi or the Peruzzi the family connection remained strong, and hence membership stayed fairly constant at each renewal of the partnership. Partners shared profits proportionately, but investments by outsiders usually drew only a fixed rate of interest; the number of investors increased greatly in the early fourteenth century. Accounting methods improved; double-entry bookkeeping was introduced around the middle of the century. Although the Italian economy collapsed in the later fourteenth century when huge numbers of firms went bankrupt under the pressures of the Black Death, warfare, bad debts and other troubles, the skills acquired were not lost but were taken over by such firms as the Medici of Florence in the fifteenth century and the Fuggers of Augsburg and also the great banking houses of Bruges and Antwerp in the sixteenth.

Since in a compagnia all partners were liable without limit it became necessary to discover who they were, for firms often traded simply under the family name 'and partners'. Originally the books of the firm were held sufficient for giving this information, but it became a normal requirement of city or guild statutes that the names of the partners be registered by

173

public instrument. From the fourteenth century onwards such registers were widely kept by city authorities as part of their public records. Similarly there was need to record powers to act as procurator on the firm's behalf; such agency was by mercantile custom acceptable, but it only slowly penetrated the ordinary courts.

Maritime ventures were not suited to the compagnia because of the higher risks and because each voyage had its natural conclusion in the arrival of the cargo. Money for voyages, or for other single ventures, was usually raised by the commenda. Under this money was lent for the duration of the venture, with the lender or investor incurring no liability to third parties. The lender usually put up the capital and was entitled normally to three-quarters of the profits, but it was a partnership not a loan. This was the source of the societé en commandite of the later civilian systems, in which one class of member has a responsibility limited to the sum contributed and the other class has an unlimited liability for the debts of the society but has sole control of its management. The lender in the commenda however could as readily be a small investor putting money into a great merchant's affairs as a rich capitalist using the labour of others to garner his profits. The risk was on the lender in that if the ship or goods were lost through accident or vis maior he had no claim for the recovery of his money.

Joint stock companies first appeared in fourteenth century Genoa. Public loans had earlier been raised to finance the expansion of Italian cities, with the loans divided into shares of which the owners were registered; these shares were heritable and, indeed, freely negotiable, that is, they could be bought and sold. Genoa raised such a loan in 1346 for the conquest of two Greek islands, and granted to shareholders a dominium utile in the common stock, the conquered lands. The scale of

174

Genoese trading expanded in the fifteenth and sixteenth centuries by such means, although it was not until the era of exploration beyond Europe and colonial expansion that such companies became a feature of mercantile life in northern Europe.

Insurance contracts were important sooner in maritime than in land-based affairs, appearing early in the fourteenth century. They first took the form of a (feigned) interest-free loan to the insurer to be returned unless the ship -- or earlier the cargo -- arrived safely; towards the end of the century they more often took the form of a feigned sale. An interest of some kind in the safe arrival of the ship or cargo was required of the insurer, or underwriter; an insurance which was a mere wager was not enforceable. The ship in which the goods must be carried was likely to be named, and the period during which the insurer was responsible was usually fixed. Risk in the cargo was borne from when the ship set sail to the unloading of the goods, but in the case of the ship itself it normally also covered the first twenty-four hours in port. In early documents unauthorized change of route freed the insurers from risk but by the end of the fourteenth century it was usually only the destination which must not be altered. Reasonably enough, fraud by the ship's master always released the insurers; an opinion of the early fifteenth century runs: "By the common unwritten custom of the country and by the general and tacit understanding of those concluding the contracts there is one exceptional case in which the risk pertains to the insured, to wit, when it is proved that the things were lost of set purpose by the fraud and contrivance of the captain."[11] Other risks might be excluded by clauses of exception, such as general average or action by a specified enemy. The premium was

----------

11    Cited by Mitchell, p.149.

paid in advance, and it was only slowly that the contract became enforceable as such rather than disguised as a sale. As an institution, however, insurance rapidly became common; in 1393 one Genoan notary drew up eighty contracts within three weeks. Legislation, first in southern then in northern Europe, frequently confirmed custom, although in England there was no legislation before the eighteenth century; the London underwriters explicitly adopted 'the custom of Antwerp'.

As well as dealing with money, negotiable instruments, forms of partnership and insurance, mercantile custom also had its own view of the contract of sale and its related agreements. Perhaps the most dramatic new usage introduced by the growth of trade was the rule that the buyer in good faith at a public market - market overt - immediately acquired title to the goods bought. This was at variance with both Roman and Germanic law. In the former the original owner never lost his title if the property had been stolen, and by Germanic law, while the owner could raise an action against someone who stole from him, if he had lent the property to a friend, that friend acquired the right of action for the stolen goods. It might well be hard for a merchant, constantly travelling, to produce the seller from whom he had bought goods, and he was not in a good position to know if the seller actually had the right to sell. It took time for this usage of merchants to be accepted by the ordinary courts, but provided such protection was firmly linked to market or fair it was likely to be agreeable to the feudal lord as another inducement for men to frequent the market from which he profited. The Church's stress on the value of good faith and the importance of supporting agreements, however informal, also worked to protect the merchant, although in general she preferred the interests of the producer to those of trade. In a few areas, in the Netherlands and in certain German sea-ports, all possession in good faith

176

was protected, but for the most part the rule was restricted to the open market, and in this form passed into later law.

Another tendency arising from mercantile custom was to give effect to formless contracts. Roman law had recognized only a limited number of contracts as being created by consent alone, and it had not given effect to nude pacts; Germanic law recognized only formal and real contracts. The Church's insistence on the honouring of any agreement slowly helped the custom enter the law, and it was accepted in fifteenth century France, as it generally had been throughout northern Italy, on the grounds of equity. Nor was it mercantile custom to require grounds to be stated in any document recording an obligation; this applied particularly to negotiable instruments. Writing was nevertheless a normal feature of commercial usage. This was another area in which the influence of notaries was considerable in bringing about standard clauses to meet the standard situations encountered by merchants.

We shall look again at the commercial courts in the context of the states which gave them their powers, at later measures aimed at the harmonization of international trade, and also at the relationship of mercantile to other custom and to the learned law which shaped the ius commune. The law merchant has been aptly compared with public international law. It was "the system of rules actually enforced in the commercial courts and actually observed by merchants in their dealings with one another, just as International Law is the system actually observed by modern states in the relations of state to state. The treaties, the legislation, and the actions of individual states do not necessarily conform to the generally recognized rules of International Law, but they may be and are used as evidence to establish what those rules really are. In the same way, the statute law of mediaeval states, the ordinances of

177

mediaeval kings and the usages of mediaeval law need not conform in any particular case to the commercial regulations generally enforced among mediaeval merchants, but they may be used to establish the general usages of merchants in commercial cases. Both International Law and the Law Merchant are from their very nature vague and uncertain."[12]

----------

12    Mitchell, p.113f.


Further Reading:

J.H. Baker   "The Law Merchant and the Common Law before 1700" 38 C.L.J.
     (1979) 295

R.H. Bautier   The Economic Development of Mediaeval Europe (London, 1971)

W.S. Holdsworth   A History of English Law, Book IV, 60-154

J.K. Hyde   Society and Politics in Mediaeval Italy (London, 1973)

E. Jenks   "The early history of negotiable instruments" 9 L.Q.R.(1893) 70

R.S. Lopez & I.W. Raymond   Mediaeval Trade in the Mediterranean World
     (New York, 1955)

W. Mitchell   Early History of the Law Merchant (C.U.P., 1904, repr.)

R. de Roover   Money, Banking and Credit in Mediaeval Bruges (U.S.A., 1948)

P. Stein   "The mutual agency of partners" 33 Tul.L.R.   (1959) 595

Chapter VII

## IUS COMMUNE

(i)  The definition of ius commune


The ius commune is not a simple concept.  It is indeed the complex
result of the coming together -- in varying proportions from place to place
and time to time -- of local custom with feudal law, Roman law in modified
and elaborated form, canon law and the law merchant.  It is the culmination
or climax of the new growth of law and jurisprudence which started in the
twelfth century renaissance.  It is also the starting point or source from
which developing municipal systems moved on during the sixteenth century
when single legal régimes became dominant as part of the growth of the
nation state.  Ius proprium, the local law of territories and cities, is
the foil to the ius commune in the narrower sense, the blending of the two
learned laws.  It was dominated by custom and feudal usages, and it was
what the ordinary knight or burgess would think of as his law.  But the
advantages of a written law and the steady progress, on political as well
as intellectual grounds, of canon and civilian influence modified the ius
proprium throughout Europe.  It will be considered briefly in the chapters
devoted to Germany, France, Scotland and, of course, England.

In a basic sense Roman and canon law, developed by the mediaéval
jurists as the learned law, were common to the habits of thought and
background knowledge of all educated lawyers in Europe (with the possible
exception of England) from the thirteenth century onwards -- many law
graduates still receive the LL.B. (a degree in both laws, civil and canon).
It was only in this sense that there was a ius commune in Germany between
the collapse of imperial authority in the earlier thirteenth century and

the deliberate and general adoption of romano-canonical procedure in the higher courts in the late fifteenth century. Among the cities of northern Italy, where too there was no effective superior authority to produce any regulated move towards uniformity, the ius commune was close to being the sum of the customs which were common, with relatively minor variations, to all. These customs were permeated by the learned law which was the major cause of their publication in writing as statutes. In France, Spain, and other monarchic states the ius commune means primarily the law common to the whole kingdom and in particular within the royal courts. In this sense ius commune naturally included the learned law, but the learned law blended with royal legislation as well as with customary practices, old and new.

Thus the particular relationship between the learned law and local usage was one aspect of the ius commune. The later mediaeval jurists were well aware of the problems involved. They wrote about 'special' and 'general' custom, and about the weight of private consent; they even attempted to define custom. Since, as we have seen, those who had the task of interpreting custom were trained more often than not in the learned law and understood rational interpretation in the light of the learned law, the more custom was overtly recognized and written down the more susceptible to civilian influence it became. Thus in Italy 'immemorial' custom came to be equated with the longi temporis praescriptio of Justinian's law and set at ten years unchallenged usage. In another definition, influenced by the canonists' as well as the Roman rules of proof, two acts were held to make a custom; for this purpose decisions of a court came to be defined as acts. This was not a true doctrine of precedent, for it was not the decision itself that was persuasive or even binding, but decided cases were seen as proofs of custom -- an attitude which endured in legal practice within France into the middle of this century.

## (ii)   Across the frontiers


Another aspect of the _ius commune_ was the continuity and similarity of certain approaches to law throughout Europe.   The universities of the Middle Ages were international.   "For three hundred years, from 1050 to 1350, ... the whole of educated Europe formed a single undifferentiated cultural unit.   In the lands between Edinburgh and Palermo, Mainz or Lund and Toledo, a man of any city or village might go for education to any school, and become a prelate or an official in any church, court, or university (when these existed) from north to south, from east to west.   It is the age of ... Vacarius of Lombardy, Canterbury, Oxford, and York; ... of Nicholas Brakespear of St. Albans, France, Scandinavia, and Rome (where he became Pope Hadrian IV); of Thomas of Aquina, Cologne, Paris, and Naples. ... On the level of literature and thought there was one stock of words, forms, and thoughts from which all drew and in which all shared on an equality."[1]   Latin was the common language.   The Scholastic techniques of harmonizing contradictions were coupled with the belief that there was a rational and divine order.   The mediaeval doctors played a role in their societies not so different from that of the Roman jurists, although they put much more stress on harmony and system -- in itself a unifying factor. In the law schools there was teaching in canon and civil law, but not in local law, except insofar as it had been received by the learned law. Nevertheless, by the fourteenth century Roman law was only one piece of the cultural baggage of a jurist, although, in its glossed form, it was his professional tool-kit.   The methods learned in the study of the Roman texts were applied in daily practice to a variety of rules, customary, feudal,

----------

1   D. Knowles   The Evolution of Mediaeval Thought (London, 1962), p.80f.

statutory, imperial, royal. The actual rules of Roman law were frequently subsidiary but its principles, and increasingly its procedural characteristics, dominated the primary sources.

Academic literature included works on court procedure. Among the more influential were Roffredus of Benevento's *Libelli iuris civilis et canonici* (*Forms of Summons in Civil and Canon Law*), William Durantis' *Speculum Iudiciale* (*Mirror of Procedure*), and the *Practica aurea* (*Golden Manual of Procedure*) of Petrus Jacobus, which was produced in Montpellier at the beginning of the fourteenth century. The manuals of notarial practice, such as the works of Salatiele and Rolandino de Passagieri, were also linked with the law schools. Notaries were trained in the universities, and shared to some extent in the common culture of the doctors. Imperial and papal notaries knew no frontiers, although others had a more limited sphere of action[2], but the tendency was undoubtedly towards harmonization, whether in the Italian communes or in princes' courts, and particularly in matters of commercial law. And the common approach to procedure survived even when intellectual fashions changed. The Humanists and Natural Lawyers might reject as fustily mediaeval the work of the Glossators and Commentators on substantive law, but until the eighteenth century they took for granted romano-canonical procedure. And despite the canonist sources, this procedure survived in Protestant Europe after the unity of western Christendom dissolved in the Reformation and Counter-Reformation.

There were also certain customs, or certain kinds of custom, which were of their nature transnational. We have already given some consideration to the Law Merchant; there were comparable, and even related, areas of law, such as the widely accepted rules on piracy, the dubious

----------

2    Appendix IV.

status of privateering, the whole business of imposing some mitigating rules on the conduct of war and of providing conventions for the easier making of peace. The work of Alberico Gentili, doctor of civil law at Perugia and later Regius Professor of Civil Law in the University of Oxford, although overshadowed half a century later by the more original work of Grotius, was confessedly in the Bartolist tradition. He discussed the privileges granted to accredited envoys, the freedom of the seas and the limit to which territorial sovereignty extended over adjacent waters, the justification of war, the treatment of persons such as hostages[3] and non-combatants, safe conducts and prize law, and similar matters. His method was not the mediaeval one of elaboration on the Roman texts, but his reasoning was based on civilian and canonist arguments as well as on those of the Humanists and other moderns; his writings were firmly in the tradition of the _ius commune_.

(iii) Italian practices

Feudal jurisdictions faded faster in northern Italy than elsewhere, owing to the greater development of trade and city-based life, but they did not totally disappear. In general, the private jurisdictions of lesser vassals gave way before those of the princes, which had a more public character. Different procedures often subsisted side by side. For example, at Pavia in 1112 the consuls exercised jurisdiction, but trial by battle was held before the local count. In 1181 at Verona a case was

----------

3   Hostages were not prisoners-of-war, but they were unable to make a will, because they were held to come under the Roman rule that a man in enemy hands had no power of testation.

heard in the consuls' court-house by the consuls sitting together with the count and the bishop. In 1225 at Siena, where Roman law was the custom of the city, trial by battle was justified on the grounds that Otto I had made it part of the general law in the tenth century. The Peace of Constance weakened the jurisdiction of the bishops as feudal lords, and the communes generally took over lay jurisdiction within the area of the diocese.

The judges in the eleventh century cities were usually simply the civic magistrates; judicial business only gradually became a specialized activity, but by the thirteenth century a professional judiciary was frequently replacing magistrates with general powers. Sometimes consuls were specifically appointed de placitis (for pleas), but often an outsider was brought in for a term of six or twelve months as podestà. Some men made the podesteria a career; Giuglielmo Pusterla, of Milan, had at least seventeen periods of office as podestà. Some families, such as the Rossi of Parma or the Visconti of Piacenza, made of the office a family tradition. It was normal, although not essential, for a podestà to be trained in the learned law. Nevertheless, as we have seen, the podestà's liability to the losing party for giving a decision wrong in law, a liability based on incompetence or negligence, was a great encouragement to the seeking of opinions from noted jurists, and hence to the establishment of the communis opinio.

This liability was imposed on the basis of the Roman quasi-delict of the judge who makes the case his own (iudex qui litem suam facere intellegitur), although the precise meaning of the original Roman liability remains obscure. In the Italian cities there were variations in how far the judge was required to pay attention to learned opinion. In many early statutes the judge was bound to take into account any opinion given, but he was not bound to follow it. Where no municipal statute governed the

184

proceedings, this remained the general rule, with the proviso that the judge was himself entitled to seek advice. But in many cities, and particularly from the fourteenth century onwards, it was common to require him to follow any opinion he obtained, and sometimes, as in Benevento, he was required to obtain an opinion. Sometimes the obtaining of an opinion was at the discretion of the parties, but often, unless there was no serious doubt as to the point of law or the sum involved was trivial, there was no choice in the matter, despite the expense and time usually involved. Furthermore, the frequency of consultation inevitably led to a vast swelling of the legal literature; the bulk of doctrine made it unmanageable, as had been the case with Roman law before Justinian's compilation.

From the fifteenth century the system was widely extended to apply not only to the _podestà_, who usually no longer exercised any general administration but only simple jurisdiction with some police powers, but to most office holders, even those acting within their native city, who should therefore have been subject to ordinary forms of process. Inevitably judgments tended to be cautious, adhering to the letter of the _Gloss_ even when reason or changed conditions suggested that some other answer should be given. And few people were likely to act in a judicial capacity more efficiently with a permanent threat hanging over them. The system did, however, work for predictability in the law, and also enhanced the application of common rules.

As the _podestà_ took an oath to give justice according to the city's statutes, he also needed local knowledge. _Giudici dell' uso_, lawyers specializing in local or some particular area of custom, were bound to make this available to him in the earlier period. As more city statutes were put into writing or revised, _emendatores statutorum_, officers specifically

185

charged with the duty of revision in the light of felt needs and of the practice of neighbouring cities, came to the fore; thus they were another factor in the growth of the _ius commune_ as common custom, (and, because it was written custom, under the influence of the learned law). Nevertheless, particularly in the light of the 'statute theory', the doctors of civil law in the universities continued to exercise the greatest influence, even when lacking in originality; the writings of Baldus and above all Bartolus remained preeminent.

Not surprisingly in northern Italy judicial decisions were rated low and academic opinions high. But a judgment must be given by a court, and so the works on procedure of the civilians and the canonists were absorbed into court practice. The use of written pleadings developed, as did written records and written decisions. Preparatory and interlocutory stages in a process were recognized; rational rules of evidence became general. Summary proceedings for petty causes appeared in secular as well as ecclesiastical courts. However, attempts at further simplification of the complexity of procedural rules and at clearer statements of principles based on reason and good faith tended to be blocked by the continuing judicial liability for wrong judgment.

There was a limited role for appeal to a higher tribunal as a unifying factor. In the cities there was usually no appeal other than a claim against the _podestà_, although the emperor retained a theoretical supremacy of judicial as of other authority. However, as his political power waned, his superior jurisdiction might be ignored; furthermore, immunity had been purchased by many of the communes. His feudal jurisdiction survived in a limited way, providing a court for princes, or even cities, who owned no other lord and could find no other forum, as, for example, in litigation over a great fief like Montferrat. A few of the major cities had councils with judicial and sometime appellate powers, as at Milan or Venice; in Bologna and some other places the supreme court was called the Rota, on the model of the Sacred Rota at Rome. The city of Rome, the capital of the Papal States, was still relatively backward economically and culturally, and in the secular field we hear of few notable judges and not many more scholars. Nevertheless, the Church's appellate procedure which centred on Rome gave to the ecclesiastical judiciary there an active role in the creation of law, and provided an example for all Europe.

The kingdom of the two Sicilies, with its capital at Naples, was a centralized state with a hierarchy of courts, more akin to France or Spain than to the rest of Italy. Romano-canonical procedure was put into practice there by royal authority, but men continued to live by Lombard, Frankish or even vulgar Roman law. Elsewhere in Italy there was no effective ruler who could shape the development of civil procedure and civil law. Political structures, rather than litigants' needs, defined the status of the Italian courts, a fact which the men of the sixteenth century Renaissance, who reacted against Bartolism and the communis opinio, rather failed to grasp.

Although the Humanists and their new style of law were predominant in sixteenth century legal studies, they did not affect the working of the courts, which maintained the traditional blending of the Gloss, canonical procedure, general and particular custom. In the Italian cities, where this was especially true, the primacy in legal matters remained that of the learned men, who had to resolve the tension between custom and the civil law, but legal literature grew ever more complex and less innovatory. The ius commune survived as a living relic of the past into the modern world and Italian jurisprudence became relatively as backward as it had been forward. There were some Italians of the late fifteenth and early

187

sixteenth centuries - such scholars as Jason de Mayno and Philip Decio - who combined the tradition of the _ius commune_ with a degree of Humanist insight. Elsewhere the work of the Commentators was adapted to new customs, new structures, and men like Dumoulin in France and Carpzov in Saxony showed the worth of the _mos italicus_ (the Italian usage).

(iv)  German customs

After the reign of the Emperor Frederick II, Germany, like Italy, had no effective centralized authority; unlike Italy, there was no primacy of the learned men but rather the guardians of the legal order were the law-finders, the Schöffen. The movement towards compliance with the mainstream of European development became strong in the later fifteenth century. In the city court of Frankfurt-am-Main written pleadings came into use in the 1480s, mostly in cases brought to arbitration rather than to trial; in the 1490s romano-canonical procedure was in use beside the oral forms, but by 1505 the latter had disappeared. Faced with the nice distinctions and technicalities of the professional lawyers, the Schöffen, the (elected) members of the court, had to fall back on the knowledge of the city's learned clerk. They abandoned their own statements of customary practice and issued judgments which had been drafted by him in conformity with the new procedures. Frankfurt was a major city and early among first instance courts in its conversion to the new forms, but at the appellate level the princes had been taking advantage of the same movement. The learned law had sprung from a centralized Empire, and thus to adopt the new procedure tended to strengthen the princes' political authority; by offering more equitable and more subtle justice, they could strengthen their moral authority through their courts. The emperors had hastened the process with the replacement of the Reichshofgericht by the Reichskammergericht in 1495, but in the 1450s the dukes of Bavaria already had a superior court, or Hofgericht, on which doctors of law sat. There were law professors sitting on the Heidelberg Hofgericht from 1472, and doctors from Tübingen at Würtemberg from 1477. In Leipzig the Duke of Saxony's Oberhofgericht existed from 1483 in the new style, staffed by nobles, knights, and doctors of law. Thus the princes sought learned men to take over judicial functions, and professional replaced lay judges. The preference of litigants was also a factor in the growth of new procedures, which offered more subtle and rational solutions.

The major cities had been somewhat more open to legal influences from elsewhere; their Schöffen were sometimes great merchants who at least knew of other régimes. Further, these cities might themselves exercise a wide influence, for when new towns were founded on the frontier of the Wild East (or North) they might take their customs en bloc from older cities. Such daughter towns would, through their Schöffen, appeal to the mother town for advice. When the Schöffen court of a mother town replied with guidance (responsa), it can be described as an Oberhof, or appeal court. The issuing of guidance was to lead at the end of the fifteenth century to the Aktenversendung (despatch of record) to law faculties for the opinions of the professors, in an extension of private consultation. Some trace of the Law Merchant can be found in the decisions of the Schöffen, but not much; certainly there was nothing of the learned law, simply the custom of the place.

The courts spiritual naturally used canonical procedure, and it was predominantly canon rather than civil law that was taught in the German universities which began to be founded in the fourteenth century. Prague, the first within the Empire north of the Alps, was founded in 1348; it was

189

followed by Vienna in 1363, Heidelberg in 1386, and Cologne in 1388; after Tübingen's establishment in 1477 there were thirteen. Germans who had trained in the learned law practised in the ecclesiastical courts or, more frequently, served the emperor, the princes or the cities in a general administrative capacity. Although the Sachsenspiegel (Mirror of the Saxons), which we mentioned along with feudal literature, was revised and glossed in the new German universities, very little learned law penetrated Saxon custom before the later fifteenth century, and even less into the customs of other regions. The reception of Roman law into Germany was both late and sudden, and for this reason Germany had no real part in the creation of the ius commune. When the learned law was received there, it had already been modified; it was not pure Roman law that was blended with the customary laws which were codified in sixteenth century Germany. It is indicative that the first great German jurist, that is, the first notable scholar working in his native land, was Zasius (1461-1535), and he became a leader of the Humanist movement, interested in the historical Roman law, because the development of the ius commune was effectively over. It seems likely that the cultural movement we know as the Renaissance played a significant part in the speed and the thoroughness of the legal changes made in Germany at the reception.

(v)  French courts

In France the ius commune is far more apparent in the field of procedure than in the substantive law, because of the relative strength of custom, and because the French crown had good political reasons for appearing independent of the Empire and imperial jurists. In the pays de droit écrit, that is, the lands south of the Loire, Roman civilization had been deeply embedded; Roman law continued to be used there, most frequently in the form of the Lex Romana Visigothorum. The area was not, however, immune to Germanic influences; the Exceptiones legum romanarum Petri (Peter's Abridgments of Roman laws), which was produced under this title in Provence in the early twelfth century[4], explicitly took into account local custom when proffering generalizations from Roman law for modern use. The strength of customary usage is also suggested by the translation into Provençal-- as Lo Codi -- of Roger's Summa on Justinian's Code in the later twelfth century; it too mentioned local practices and made reference to a wide range of customs. There seem to have been at least three hundred identifiable jurisdictions in Provence at this period, each with its own custom. Roman law as shaped by the civilians was undoubtedly strong in the pays de droit écrit, as the flourishing law schools at Montpellier and Toulouse indicate, but Roman law was still only a subsidiary source. It was accepted as the general custom of the area, which was looked to when particular custom failed. The legists, men with legal training whose careers lay entirely in the service of the French crown, were careful to ascribe to it no more authority than that of a custom; King Louis IX stated that he was therefore not bound by it. The legists firmly maintained the doctrine that the king of France was emperor within his own realm, and this aided the introduction of the civil law; this was done, however, by royal decree, so that it was the crown which was the source of law. Philip IV, the Fair, in a royal ordinance of 1312 stressed that his kingdom was governed primarily by custom; the extensive use of Roman law was dependent

----------

4    Provence was a wider area in mediaeval than in the modern terminology, but Peter's sources were Italian and, it is now agreed, influenced by Irnerius.

on royal permission, which was normally granted because of its wide acceptance as custom.

In the pays de droit coutumier or pays de coutumes Roman law never achieved the status of a general subsidiary source. Roman terminology and concepts did, however, provide a framework within which custom could be supplemented and system imposed. It was ratio scripta, written reason, -- no more -- but by the same process as we have seen elsewhere the learned lawyers' reasonable interpretation of custom led to its modification. We have looked in some detail at the Customs of Beauvaisis; other works of the thirteenth century showing rather more civilian influence, although also primarily concerned with the law of their particular regions (Vermandois and Orléans), are Pierre de Fontaine's Conseil à un ami (Advice to a friend), and Les Livres de Jostice et de Plet (The Books of Justice and Pleading). During the later Middle Ages certain areas of law, such as obligations, about which the customs had comparatively little to say, emerged as essentially civilian; other fields too were developed with the aid of the learned law. It was possible by the sixteenth century for some jurists to hold that Roman law was the subsidiary common law of France, and that it should be recognised as such, but this was not the general opinion. In the event, the codification of the customs provided a different common law for the north, but this in its turn continued to be subject to the influence of civilian thought.

In twelfth century France innumerable private jurisdictions had replaced the Frankish community courts, the kind of court on which the royal power in England was able to build. The Capetian dynasty's struggles to become kings of, rather than merely in, France were closely linked to increasing royal control of the courts. One of their methods was the adoption of the romano-canonical procedure for use in the royal courts.

The adoption was not technically difficult because so many royal councillors and royal judges were trained in the learned law; many of them were clerics and so already accustomed to its use in some other aspect of their lives.

Philip II, Augustus, had made use of men trained in the learned law, the legists, but it was Louis IX, St. Louis, who took the first decisive step towards the adoption of the new procedure. The ordeal had fallen out of use after the Fourth Lateran Council of 1215 had forbidden clerical participation; in 1258 Louis abolished trial by battle in royal courts. He further ordained that, in order to avoid threats or improper influences, his judges should use secret examination of individual witnesses under oath. In 1278 the Parlement de Paris was established in a permanent form. Royal ordinances thereafter governed the procedure of the Parlement, although it had a subsidiary power to regulate itself, comparable to the Acts of Sederunt of the Scottish Court of Session. Royal ordinance also governed the Châtelet, the ordinary court for Paris and the surrounding area within the jurisdiction of the prévôt of Paris.

Among Louis's successors, important ordinances were issued by Philip IV and Philip V, and also Charles V, first as Dauphin and regent and then as king. In 1454 Charles VII issued the Ordinance of Montils-les-Tours. Its 125 articles treated every major point of judicial practice; they extended the new procedures to royal jurisdictions within the provinces, governed the procedure in provincial parlements, provided for summary proceedings, and dealt with details of proofs and of appeals. They were effective over a wide area since the King of France had come to rule as well as reign over most of France. (At the end of the Albigensian Crusade in 1229, the crown had acquired most of the Languedoc, although it was not until the seventeenth century that Perpignan and much of Roussillon became

French; in the fourteenth century Philip VI, of Valois, had brought Dauphiné into the royal domain, which thus at that time covered some three fifths of modern France.) The establishment of the provincial parlements followed the king's gradual recovery of the supreme jurisdictions formerly exercised by the dukes of Normandy, Burgundy, Gascony, and other magnates.

In 1360 the Languedoc was divided into three sénéchaussées, Beaucaire (south of Avignon), Carcassonne, and Toulouse, where the earliest provincial parlement was first created in 1420 and firmly established in 1443. Rouen in Normandy acquired the next Parlement, then Grenoble, Bordeaux and Dijon. It was also during the fifteenth century that further law schools were founded: Dôle in 1423, Louvain in 1426, Poitiers in 1432, Valence in 1452, Bourges in 1464, and so on. This made available sufficient trained lawyers for the multiplication of professional courts, the movement towards which was itself a major factor in the foundation of the law schools.

The core of the development in civil procedure, including the creation of appeals and their centralization on the crown lay in the Parlement of Paris which had the widest territorial jurisdiction; the provincial parlements, however, remained sovereign within their spheres. By the mid-thirteenth century some specialization of function had become normal among royal advisers, and so it was primarily, although not exclusively, those of his tenants and officers who were trained in law whom the king appointed to sit in the Parlement. In the feudal structure, appeal in our juridical sense, appeal to get a judgment reversed or amended, was not possible; one could only complain that one's lord had not done right, and accuse him of false judgment before his lord. In the Languedoc, where custom retained some Roman roots and the learned law was taught, appeal for correction of error was known and practised from the late twelfth century. In the

194

northern parts of France this form of appeal seems to have originated as special royal grants of a privilege. In 1258 Louis IX made the royal courts available to all who complained on grounds of false judgment; his Ordinance permitted the royal courts to approve or reverse the original decision, but they soon came to assert, without meeting any effective opposition, the power to modify it. The element of 'false' judgment remained, however, in that the inferior court might be subject to a fine or some other penalty.

At first it was predominantly from lesser royal courts that appeals came to the Parlement, in particular from the courts of the baillis and sénéchaux, whom Philip II had appointed to a function roughly comparable to that of the Anglo-Norman sheriff. But feudal lords learned to tolerate appeal from their courts directly to the royal courts, rather than up the feudal hierarchy to the same eventual end. A few great lords, such as the English king in his capacity as duke of Gascony, developed their own system of appeal based on Roman procedure, but the king of France had clearly become the ultimate source of justice within his kingdom.

The Parlement made some use of the group inquest (enquête par turbe) -- the institution which in Britain developed into the jury --, but the production of a suitable group required an effective central power that was by no means always available. It was simpler, as well as more in line with legal developments elsewhere, for the judges to interrogate under oath witnesses who were presented to them by the parties to a suit. In criminal cases accusations were normally matters of private initiative until the fourteenth century, when criminal investigation by a judge, acting ex officio on the canonical model and armed with powers to torture, became normal. Cases before the Parlement always began with oral pleadings, with spoken statements of claim and defence made before the Grand' Chambre, one of the three chambers into which the _Parlement_ was divided at least as early as 1296. Usually the _Grand' Chambre_ would be unable to settle the issue without investigation, and so it would order an enquiry or inquest to be made. This was done by the _Chambre des Enquêtes_, which comprised half or rather more of all the judges of the _Parlement_. Here written statements were required, repeating the claims and allegations of the oral complaint. On this basis were drawn up the articles, the summary of the evidence -- by witnesses or documents -- which each party would proffer, and the questions that each party wanted asked of the other. Objections on points of law could be raised at this stage. Thereafter commissioners, who travelled if necessary, were appointed to examine the witnesses; the commissioners would include one or more judges from the _Chambre des Enquêtes_ and might well also include other lawyers and local men of standing. The witnesses, under oath, were examined privately and separately, and their testimony written down. The whole written record was then brought back to the central court where a judge, acting as _rapporteur_, read through the whole, summarized the arguments, and recommended what facts should be found and the consequent ruling on points of law. The parties had received copies of the written statement of facts (the _procès-verbal_) and of any written evidence presented, but they had no opportunity to conduct any examination, let alone cross-examination, although a party's lawyer might appeal on the basis of this documentation.

The whole system was heavy on judicial manpower. In 1296 there were fifty-one judges of the _Parlement_ of Paris and in 1319 there were sixty-seven; from 1345 onwards there were something over eighty, as compared with the nine or so judges of the contemporary English central courts, who had juries to find their facts for them. But the procedure of the _Parlement_ was in accord with the learned law, and demanded a high level of legal skill from its practitioners; it is obvious that jurists' opinions had no significant part to play in France.

The procedure of the provincial Parlements followed that of Paris closely, and was similarly dependent on trained manpower. The Parlement of Paris also influenced other, lower, courts. In the confusion of the Hundred Years' War and its aftermath the Parlement's regulations for itself took on what was in effect some general legislative power. It issued arrêts de règlement (regulating decrees) which laid down lines of interpretation for the future, usually after consultation between the Chambers. These were not binding on other courts but inevitably they were persuasive, particularly where appeal might follow.

When appeal began to be taken direct from lesser feudal courts to the royal court, the vassals who were the judges in their lord's court might find themselves having to come to Paris to justify their verdict; they could be subject to fines if it were reversed. This was in some ways less onerous than the old liability, when they might have had to defend themselves by battle against an appeal of false judgment, but the fine might be heavy, and the proceedings both alarming and lengthy, as well as far from home. Therefore in feudal courts too the move towards specialization of function was apparent; by the sixteenth century trained lawyers had largely replaced the lord's 'men' nearly everywhere. The process was speeded up by the general growth in judicial business; when private jurisdictions had to hold courts two or three times a week, attendance was burdensome for men who were called from other duties. Lay judges retreated before the learned men, although it was not until the Revolution that feudal jurisdictions were finally swept away. The increase in litigation was  aided by the simplification of substantive law after the codification of the customs in the sixteenth century; this itself followed

197

a degree of harmonization of custom arising from single parlements deciding cases from several areas. Fundamental to the increase in both specialization and business was the romano-canonical procedure of the ius commune.


(vi) Spain during the Reconquista


During the thirteenth to fifteenth centuries, as earlier, any consideration of law in Spain must take into account not merely the existence of different principalities but also their fluid relationships and changing fortunes as the Christian forces in the peninsula steadily pushed back those of Islam. In Castile-León benefice and vassalage never completely fused to produce the fief proper; there was consequently no delegation of governmental powers through the instrumentality of the fief, and so feudal law did not develop fully. Catalonia was recovered by Louis the Pious, Charlemagne's son, less than a century after the Moslem conquest; therefore much of its history is more closely linked to the Languedoc than to the rest of Spain, although it was independent of the Frankish empire from 987. Old Castile -- New Castile is the name for the areas later reconquered -- broke away from León in the mid-tenth century, and in consequence rejected the Fuero Juzgo (Province of Judges, formerly known as the Forum Iudicum), which had been issued by the Visigothic King Ervig, since it made provision for appeal to the king (of León) as supreme judge. All available copies are said to have been ceremonially burned, and the judges were ordered, in the absence of any acceptable law book, to base their decisions on equity. In the mid-eleventh century Castile and Aragon emerged as monarchies; the former, which included Galicia and the Asturias, later reunited with León, while the latter came to include Valencia and

Catalonia.

In Castile-León the king was the fount of justice, exercising jurisdiction as the natural lord of all his subjects in the royal courts. This political strength and the existence of appeals to the king's court diminished the importance of regional customs or fueros. As early as the twelfth century the alcaldes de corte (presidents of the court) were sophisticated professional judges, while in the course of that century the Roman law of the learned men became influential. Letrados, men of law trained in the universities, were high in the royal service. The earliest students attended Bologna but in 1239 the university of Salamanca was established (as a migration from Palencia, founded in 1214); students continued, however, to study in Italy, for in 1346 a Spanish college was set up in Bologna. Ferdinand III (King of Castile 1217-52 and of León from 1230) envisaged a kingdom with a single body of law. He commissioned the translation into the vernacular of the Fuero Juzgo -- attractive as being written law --, and he granted this to each newly reconquered town as its fuero, for example, to Cordoba in 1241 or Seville in 1248; succeeding kings followed the same policy. His son, Alfonso X, the Learned (1252-84), was responsible for the publication of Las Siete Partidas, (The Seven Parts [of the Law]), an encyclopaedic and comprehensive work based chiefly on Roman law. Alfonso's tutor, Jaime de las Leyes, who wrote several books on romano-canonical procedure, seems to have been influential in its production and also in the compilation of the Fuero Real (Royal Custom), a selective code which, among other things, regulated appeal to the corte real (king's court). Like the Fuero Juzgo, the Fuero Real was issued to individual cities as their fuero, but in its case to long-established places such as Burgos and Valladolid, which lacked a clear custom of their own because in Old Castile there had been no general written law for three

199

hundred years. The _Fuero Real_ was in four books as opposed to the _Fuero Juzgo_'s twelve; there was some debt to the earlier code and also to the work of the civilians, but it was mostly a compilation of customary law.

_Las Siete Partidas_, although rearranged at various times both in Spain and in the Americas, remained the foundation of Spanish law until its supersession by the _Codigo Civil_ of 1889, and even that was not complete. It was firmly in the tradition of the received learned law, and had its own standard commentary, the _Leyes del Estilo_. The influence of the _Ultramontani_ was strong in Spain; the development of constitutional history was affected by the work of the Commentators. Many thirteenth and fourteenth century Spanish manuscripts of the _Corpus Iuris Civilis_ and of the work of the civilians have survived; the University of Salamanca had chairs of both canon and civil law.

_Las Siete Partidas_ at first met political opposition to its enforcement in areas where custom was strong. Only in 1348, by the _Ordenamiento de Alcalá_, was it promulgated as general law by Alfonso XI; it was general law, but subordinate to particular custom. The _Fuero Juzgo_ remained the custom of León, but it, like other customs, needed to be proved to a court as being still observed, whereas there was a presumption in favour of the _Fuero Real_ and _Las Siete Partidas_. The learned law of the _ius commune_ was clearly dominant in Castile-León; so much so that, to avoid confusion, in 1427 John II restricted the citation in court as authorities of canonists or civilians later than Johannes Andreae and Bartolus.

Within the territories of the Crown of Aragon the monarchy was explicitly constitutional; lordless land in Aragon, unlike Catalonia on the one hand or Castile on the other, was not automatically regarded as the crown's. As we have seen, within Valencia and Catalonia cities were influential and commercial law important. The _Consulate of the Sea_ was

200

exported from Barcelona to Castile, among many other places; it was thereafter found in force at Burgos and at Seville, and from there it was taken to the New World. Roman law had been recognized as general subsidiary law in Catalonia since 1173. The Usatges (Usages) of Barcelona were produced in the mid-twelfth century by the civilian jurists at the court of Ramón Berenguer IV; the basic texts were from feudal and customary law, with some constitutional and criminal matters, but the whole was handled in the context of the learned law. King James I of Aragon (1213-76) attracted many jurists to his court, among them Raymond of Peñaforte, compiler of Liber Extra. In 1247 an authoritative collection was made of the customs of Aragon, but they were interpreted in the light of the civil law, and in the field of procedure romano-canonical rules were specifically adopted. Peter IV's Ordinacions de Cort of 1344 among other things created a new final court of appeal under the chancellor.

In Navarre the Fuero Juzgo was accepted as the custom of the kingdom, modified after 1234, when the French acquired control, by the Fuero General, which owed much to the Glossators. Las Siete Partidas came into force there when, in the early sixteenth century, Navarre was reincorporated into Spain by Ferdinand of Aragon, who married Isabella of Castile. In the united kingdom of Spain reforms in private law were made primarily in the cortes (parliament). The Leyes de Toro of 1505, building on the Ordenanzas de Montalvo of 1485 (collecting those laws still in force which had been passed since the death of Alfonso X), dealt with sources of law and their authority, and gave due weight to the Fuero Juzgo, the Fuero Real, and Las Siete Partidas. The Leyes were confirmed by Philip II, son of Charles, and husband of Mary Tudor, and given application in the New World; they continued in force for centuries and were reissued in 1805 by Charles IV.

Just as the various city statutes in Italy needed reconciling, so did the _fueros_ of the cities and the principalities in the Iberian peninsula, and the methods used were similar in some ways. In Spain court practice played a more important part than in Italy and less than in France, while legal science was respectively less and more important than in those countries, but law in Spain, both private and public, was an undoubted example of the _ius commune._

(vii)  Scotland and the _ius commune_


Scotland too was affected by the _ius commune_, and more particularly by the romano-canonical procedure. In the twelfth and thirteenth centuries the influence of Anglo-Norman administration and legal procedures was so strong that Scotland might possibly not have developed a legal system of its own. However, the Wars of Independence, although they by no means abolished Anglo-Norman institutions, closed the way to influence from England. The most obvious external influence was that of the Church. We have records of cases heard by papal judges delegate from early in the thirteenth century; at local level, a bishop's official is recorded for the dioceses of Glasgow and of St. Andrews before the end of the twelfth century. It seems reasonable to assume that Scotland conformed in the Middle Ages to the general European pattern in ecclesiastical jurisdiction, particularly as there was no royal attempt to block (or even control) appeals to Rome. Furthermore, Scots students were attending Italian and French universities from at least the thirteenth century. In the fourteenth century law graduates seem mostly to have followed careers in the Church, but in the following century we find them busy in the courts temporal. Universities were founded at St. Andrews in 1413 and at Glasgow in 1451, with chairs in canon and civil law. In the fifteenth and sixteenth centuries, however, Scottish students preferred to resort to universities in France or Germany and, particularly after the Reformation, in the Netherlands. In 1496 an Act of the Scottish Parliament required the nobility and gentry to educate their sons in schools of art and law, so that they might have knowledge and understanding of the laws. The cultural background was thus favourable to the learned law; the reception of substantive Roman rules is harder to measure, but certainly custom was modified by learned interpretation.

In the field of procedure it is apparent that there was no deep division between the secular and the ecclesiastical courts. It has been said "there is no doubt that familiarity with the rules of an official's court procedure in the 1540s is as good an introduction as any to sixteenth century legal procedure in general"[5]. For example, procurators were much used in ecclesiastical business, and not merely as general representatives but also as advocates before a court; their employment is recorded in the early fourteenth century. The regular employment of advocates in the secular courts, which is evidenced by the early fifteenth century, was a practice alien to feudal procedure and it may well stem from ecclesiastical example. Similarly, the oath of calumny, a regular stage in canonist procedure, was enjoined upon advocates by Parliament in 1429. Lawyers in sixteenth century Scotland seem to have felt no confinement to one jurisdiction, secular or spiritual; the same man might practise before the court of the official of Lothian, the High Court of Admiralty, and the Court of Session. This versatility suggests there was little to choose

----------

5    S. Ollivant The Court of the Official (Stair Society, vol.34, Edinburgh, 1982), p.131.

between the courts in terms of practice and procedure.

Since 1424, after James I's return from exile, attempts had been made to provide Scotland with a supreme court. The _Acta_ (Proceedings) of the Lords of Council (the forerunners of the Lords of Council and Session, and in turn of the Court of Session) of the early sixteenth century[6] suggest that the model of the courts spiritual was already well established in the higher temporal courts, and the movement between jurisdictions recorded later is unlikely to have been a novelty in the early sixteenth century. The refounded Court of Session of 1532 employed romano-canonical procedure; of its original membership (fifteen judges) the Lord President and seven others were clerics. And when the religious revolution came, the bishop's officials in Lothian and Glasgow, who were lawyers first and priests second, moved naturally to head the new commissary courts of their respective jurisdictions.

Movement towards the romano-canonical procedure in the local secular courts is less clear. By the fifteenth century brieves of summons to the sheriff court had become simply written citations to appear, not pleadable forms of action. By the end of the century a version of this modern procedure, if somewhat more oral and less technical than elsewhere in Europe, had become normal in the sheriff courts. Moreover, the status of bishops and abbots as feudal magnates meant that their regality and barony courts were as important, or almost, as their courts spiritual, and it is likely that there was some harmony of procedure and personnel. In the burghs the courts recognised other jurisdictions. At Selkirk, for example, we find a party claiming under a will being sent to "ane sperituall judge", and when the assize found itself at a loss it had recourse to men of law.

------------

6    Stair Society, vols. 8 and 14.

Particularly in the cities of the east coast, where trade with France, the Low Countries and other continental regions made most impact, the *ius commune* made some penetration through the law merchant.

Some such penetration may have been merely verbal, as when one finds consuls in Edinburgh in the fifteenth century. However, Welwood's treatise on The Sea-Laws of Scotland (of 1590) assumed that disputes arising out of a voyage would be settled by a judge of the burgh to which the ship was bound, "a judge of many hundred years old in this land", who is to be identified with the Dean of Guild. The Guild Court had jurisdiction over admission to the privileges of a burgess or guild brother, over actions between merchant and merchant and between merchant and mariner, and also over the laws of neighbourhood. The Glasgow Dean of Guild Court was founded late, in 1605, but on the model of the much older Edinburgh court. "The procedure of the court was uniform, whatever the nature of the action. Actions were begun by a bill, apparently always in writing. ...The defender would then be summoned three times, lastly by the court officer, and in the event of his failing to appear, judgment would be given against him 'as confessed'. If the defender appeared, he might admit the libel, and possibly pay the sum claimed at the bar of the court; or simply deny; or plead one or more exceptions. ...Exceptions were either peremptory or dilatory. Declinatory exceptions...are not recorded. After the bill and answers a verbal debate would follow, leading to the assignment of the method of proof. Proof would be by oath, witnesses, or writs". In the course of the seventeenth century the court seems to have moved, in the case of proof by witnesses, from the mercantile custom of accepting one witness to demanding two or more, that is, corroboration, the canonist requirement for full proof. "In the case of written evidence, there were certain common law restrictions on what constituted probative writs, but in

205

merchant cases these did not apply."[7]  In most of the cases recorded the pursuer was a Glasgow merchant, but he might be a merchant from outside the burgh, or a Glasgow notary suing as the assignee of a foreign merchant. Towards the end of the seventeenth century the Court of Admiralty developed as the the principal mercantile court of Scotland, with exclusive first instance jurisdiction over maritime causes; it too had always used romano-canonical procedure.

It is impossible to read the chapter on Civil Procedure in W.A. Wilson's excellent Introductory Essays on Scots Law[8] without being struck by the resemblance between modern Scots practice and the procedure of the developed ius commune, particularly when an action goes to proof rather than to jury trial; the main difference is in the publicity of the testimony.  Also significant is a recent letter in the Journal of the Law Society of Scotland; the writer is encouraging his fellow Scots lawyers to point out to possible European clients the benefits of Scots law.  Scots has over English law such advantages as "enforcement of performance by specific implement; expedited enforcement of payment by extract-registered bond; clearly stated contracts enforceable in accordance with their terms; a coherent unitary system of law as opposed to a sprawling dichotomy of conflicting laws"[9].  The contrast with England will be apparent from the next chapter.  There the ius commune had little effect.  It did influence the civilian courts, such as the English Admiralty, but they remained peripheral to the Common Law.  As Chancery became more central to the

----------

7    A.M. Jackson Glasgow Dean of Guild Court: a History (Glasgow, 1983), p.28.

8    (2nd ed. Edinburgh, 1984).

9    J.L.S.S., Vol. 29, May 1984, p.184.

English legal system, it grew closer in its attitudes to the Common Law. The Regius Chairs of Civil Law established by Henry VIII had no effect on practice. Individuals were aware of the ius commune, but from the fourteenth century onwards the system of the Common Law survived in splendid isolation.


Further Reading:

R.C. van Caenegem  "History of European Civil Procedure" in International Encyclopaedia of Comparative Law, vol. XVI

H. Coing "The Roman law as ius commune on the Continent" 89 L.Q.R. (1973), 505

Continental Legal History Series, vol.VIII: C.Calisse  History of Italian Law (U.S.A.,1928, repr.)

J.P. Dawson  A History of Lay Judges (Harvard, 1960)
              The Oracles of the Law (Ann Arbor, 1968,)

R. Fawtier  The Capetian Kings of France (London, 1960)

R. Feenstra  Philip of Leyden (Murray Lecture, Glasgow, 1970)

E.M.Hallam  Capetian France (London, 1980)

E.N. van Kleffens  Hispanic Law until the End of the Middle Ages (Edinburgh, 1968)

W. Kunkel  "The reception of Roman law in Germany:an interpretation" in Pre-Reformation Germany ed. G.Strauss (London, 1972)

A. MacKay  Spain in the Middle Ages (London, 1977)

P. Stein  "The influence of Roman law on the law of Scotland" Jur.Rev. (1963), 205

C.C. Turpin  "The Reception of Roman law" 3 (N.S.) I.J. (1968), 162

Chapter VIII

## THE COMMON LAW OF ENGLAND

(i)  The significance of English law

English law is remarkable.  It lies outside the mainstream of European
legal development, and has been touched only lightly by juristic movements
from the continent.  Conversely, English jurisprudence probably had no
influence on European legal thinking before the eighteenth century.  So in
one sense after Bracton it is hardly part of European legal history.
However, English law absorbed the legal systems first of Wales and then of
Ireland, and it overshadows, although it has not succeeded in absorbing,
Scots law.  From the eleventh to the fourteenth centuries Anglo-Norman
institutions were a major force in the development of Scots law, and so the
two systems share some common roots.  From the Union of the Crowns in 1603
the bigger country had the power to affect the Scottish system, and this
power was enhanced after the Union of the Parliaments in 1707.  The
Industrial Revolution and the French Revolutionary and Napoleonic Wars put
Scotland firmly within England's sphere of juridical influence.  Thus the
history of English law is a part of Scotland's legal history.  Furthermore,
English law has been the only rival to the civilian systems based on Roman
law in creating a legal empire, in providing a model.  Within Europe and in
those areas colonized by Europeans one finds either a civil law or a common
law system -- or, in a few places, such as Scotland or South Africa, a
mixed system where the common law has come for political or constitutional
reasons to dominate the civilian inspiration.

There was nothing extraordinary about Anglo-Saxon customary law; it
was not particularly different from the customs of the Franks or, indeed,

the Saxons in north Germany. However, the institutions of government for the whole realm which had developed by the eleventh century were unique, if only in the extent of their development. Public law played a far more important part in England than on the continent in the formation of the legal system. Feudal law, when established in England by the Normans, was not very different from feudal law in northern France but it developed in a different way. Again, for many centuries the Church's courts administered canon law, with substance and procedure virtually universal within Christendom, and yet English law does not seem to have been much influenced. Roman law was hardly received in the twelfth and thirteenth centuries, and in the sixteenth it was definitely rejected by the legal profession, when the new kind of reception was widespread in Europe. There were indeed areas of civilian influence, for example, in the court of the Admiralty, but they were marginal; the central core of the legal system remained uniquely English.

(ii)  The making of England

The Romans abandoned Britain in the early fifth century; shortly after the middle of the century Roman-British society seems to have collapsed, but not as a result of any single invasion. The various Germanic settlements were piecemeal; indeed, in Kent the settlement seems to have been of foederati (allies), although as allies of the Romano-Britons rather than of any central Roman authority. Furthermore, the pace of the Anglo-Saxon advance was slowed by British resistance, which was led by the legendary, but not mythical, Arthur. However, during the mid years of the sixth century the advance quickened. By 613 the Anglo-Saxon conquest was virtually complete; it stretched from Kent to the Clyde, and from the Wash to the Severn.

There seems to have been some continuity of culture in Kent, because of its early settlement, observable in such institutions as gavelkind (the division of land among all the heirs), and the consolidated fields of the Kentish villages. Certainly the names themselves of Kent and Canterbury retained their Roman origins. Kent was the closest part of Britain to Gaul, where the Franks maintained some of the Roman heritage. In the north-west and in the south-west of Britain the Romano-Celtic peoples remained unconquered, although their territories were gradually encroached upon by the Anglo-Saxons during the succeeding centuries. In Wales the old ways survived, although there they had been more British than Roman anyway, and there was virtually no Anglo-Saxon presence. Christianity survived in these areas, as it did in Ireland and in Argyll.

In 597, the same year as St. Columba died on Iona, Augustine of Canterbury, sent by Gregory the Great to evangelize the heathen English, landed in Kent. The wife of Ethelbert, king of Kent, was Bertha, a Frankish princess and a Christian. Within less than a century the various Germanic kingdoms in the island had achieved a sort of unity, not only among themselves but also with their Celtic fellow Christians, in their recognition of the archbishop of Canterbury. Theodore (archbishop 668-90) established a permanent framework of diocesan goverment and held provincial synods. Thereafter English kings, like rulers elsewhere in Europe, were able to make use of trained clerics in their administration.

When King Alfred (871-99) died, although half of England was under Danish rule, the half that was English was strong and well-organized under the overlordship of Wessex, which even extended over Wales. In the face of the constant Norse attacks, royal authority was strengthened at the same time as elements akin to feudalism were grafted onto English customary law.

The king's thegns, the landed nobility, would henceforward forfeit their estates if they failed to provide due military service, and this service was in many cases to be mounted, the better to deal with raiders. No tie of blood was to excuse treason to one's lord, but failure in military aid was seen as a crime rather than as a breach of tenure; there was no concept of all land being the king's to grant -- the brute fact of conquest made this practicable under Norman William. Charters conferred not title or possession but the king's special peace; lords, whether thegns or bishops (or monasteries), might thus receive the privilege of taking fines for offences against the king's peace as well as against their own peace. In this way the personal tie, the link between land and military service, and private jurisdictions, all became part of the English social structure. But in other respects conditions were very different from those on the continent. The language of government was vernacular, Anglo-Saxon, as well as Latin. Fortified boroughs, usually with a mint and a court as well as a market, were an integral part of Alfred's centralized plan of defence, rather than being seen as the property of a lord. The crown's position was strong; the king's justice held sway over all men, and his peace ran everywhere. There was even relative uniformity of law; in broad outline the customs of Mercia and Kent became incorporated in those of Wessex, while the Danelaw was followed in eastern England.

During the tenth century the administrative system of shires extended over all England as far as the Mersey-Humber line. Within the shires the smaller unit of the hundred was formalized, a dozen or so to each shire. Linked to the hundred was the tithing system under which every free man (below the thegns) was enrolled in a group of ten, who were permanent sureties for each other's good behaviour. By the reign of Edgar (959-75) the administrative and judicial structure is clear, although there was, of course, a multiplicity of particular local customs. The shire court, presided over by the ealdorman and the bishop, met twice a year, and, under the same two men, the borough courts met three times a year -- there was normally only one borough in each shire. The hundred met every four weeks, to pursue thieves, to determine custom, to witness major transactions, and to hear the king's word. Appeal to the king's own justice was restricted to those cases where a man could not otherwise obtain redress. In the Danelaw the men of the Norse settlements acknowledged the Wessex dynasty as their overlords but kept to their own customs; there were considerable similarities and doubtless many cross-influences. The Danelaw knew more of commerce and had a uniform system of taxation and of coinage.

In the decades after the death of Edgar, Ethelred the Unready (978-1016) lost England to the Danish king Canute, or Cnut (1016-35). At his coronation in 1016 Cnut swore to observe the laws of King Edgar within the English sphere, while maintaining the separate customs of the Danelaw; his laws show that he kept his word. Edward (1042-66), known to us as the Confessor, had spent more than twenty years of exile in Normandy. Although of the line of Alfred he was accused of foreign habits, but his Chancery used Anglo-Saxon as well as Latin, and his relationship with the Church was in the old English tradition. William of Normandy came to England in 1066 not only as Edward's heir but also as the Church's champion against the forsworn Harold; he was recognized as king by the _witan_, or royal council, just fifty years after Cnut's acceptance.

(iii)   Anglo-Saxon institutions of the eleventh century


The shire courts were the major forum for administrative and judicial business. The shires were entrusted by the Wessex kings to ealdormen or earls who, together with the local bishop, each led a group of shires. The shire courts therefore dealt with ecclesiastical business as well as lay, out of step with the Hildebrandine reform movement on the continent. The earl's deputy as president of the shire was the shire reeve or sheriff; the sheriff was the king's man, and so jurisdiction in the shire was a matter for the community under the protection of the king's peace. The sheriff's tourn to take 'view of frankpledge' may in this terminology be Norman, but the actual review of the tithings to make sure that every man was adequately accounted for by his fellows seems to date from Athelstan (927-39) or Edmund (939-46). As well as being the forum to which men came twice yearly, bringing their suits, the shire court might also receive jurisdiction in cases initially brought before the king and his witan[1]; it was also the body to which, through the earl or the sheriff, the king announced any grant he had made[2].

The hundreds were closer to the primitive Germanic tradition in that all free men had suit of court there. They were meetings for all matters requiring publicity, not just for the settlement of disputes. The courts of the hundred, or of the wapentake within the Danelaw, with their four-weekly sessions, seem to go back to Edward the Elder (899-925); they were already fairly sophisticated when Edgar issued his ordinance regulating their practice. Some of the hundreds were ancient divisions, others were created in the tenth century organization, but it is as jurisdictions and as fiscal units, not as territorial areas, that they are of significance. Hundred courts were presided over in the tenth century by a royal reeve, since they were a creation of the royal administration, although they

----------

1    Harding, document no.3.

2    Harding, nos.4 and 5.

fitted well with customary usage. Naturally enough those reeves who were not already lords had a tendency to improve their status; it was also natural to put someone already a lord into such a responsible office. Hence there was some movement towards a feudal model, a tendency enhanced by frequent royal grants of hundredal jurisdiction. Grants of 'sake' (the right to hold a court) and 'soke' (the right to enforce attendance at it) were regularly made to lay and ecclesiastical magnates, particularly in the eleventh century. Grant of hundredal jurisdiction did not necessarily mean a grant covering the whole hundred; it often meant a grant of that level of jurisdiction within the lord's estates. Great sokes of several hundreds might be created, as for the monasteries of Peterborough or Bury St. Edmunds, or the right might apply to just one manor[3]. Hundred courts were particularly important because of their link with the tithing system; Athelstan prescribed summary justice for the man out of tithing or without a lord to answer for him. Ethelred laid down that at each four-weekly meeting (of the wapentake) the twelve senior thegns and the reeve were to swear that they would accuse no innocent man nor conceal any guilty man. This implies a duty to produce the guilty for judgment, and is clearly a fore-runner of the jury of presentment. Moreover, the thegns were to seize men frequently accused; this is another expression of the reliance on local knowledge and public opinion that justified compurgation.

At the lowest level of jurisdiction was the hall-moot, or future manor court, the meeting of the village at which all free men must find sureties or 'borh' in case of some misconduct which would lead to appearance before a court. In practice the tithing, which lay somewhere between the hall and the hundred, came frequently to be identified with a vill or village rather

----------

3    Harding, no.5.

214

than with a personal group. At the other end of the scale, by the eleventh century, the witan had in general ceased to act as a court; it had not, however, lost its judicial potential.

## (iv)  Procedure in shire and hundred courts

The defender in any suit, and there was as yet no clear distinction between private and criminal law, normally had the right to clear himself by oath, that is by compurgation. He summoned oath-helpers, whose number would depend on the gravity of the charge and the status of the defender, to swear that his oath of denial was pure. If the defender had been caught in the act or in suspicious circumstances or was a man who had frequently been accused or had ever been convicted of perjury, then it was the accuser's right to bring oath-helpers to join with him in swearing to the defender's guilt; the accuser had normally to take a preliminary oath that his accusation was true. If the defender managed his oath he was absolved; if he was unable to provide it, or if the accuser had the oath, he would then go to trial by ordeal. The ordeal might be of cold water, of hot water, or of hot iron[4], or, for the clergy, of consecrated bread[5]. Failure at the ordeal might result in a lesser penalty than when the culprit was caught red-handed, but it might not. There were fixed fines for many offences and in other cases there was the wergeld (or weregild). The wergeld was a sum of money calculated according to rank, and was originally the redemption price for a murder, given to avoid a blood feud; it was

----------

4    Herlihy, no.25.

5    A guilty man's mouth might well be so dry that he choked upon the bread.

extended to provide a useful valuation for other fines, for example, for adultery in the laws of Kent. Under the influence of the Church the death penalty was less common in Anglo-Saxon England than on the continent; mutilation was held to be a milder punishment, but hanging nevertheless remained quite usual. Slavery was also a customary penalty which could follow from inability to pay a fine; the kindred of the penal slave had a year in which they could redeem him, and after that year custom permitted his wife to marry again. Imprisonment was an occasional penalty, but money payments of some sort were far commoner, for reparation as well as retribution. Higher rank, while it entitled a man to higher compensation, also made him liable to higher fines. The court normally had no discretion save in its interpretation of fact, but simply published sentence according to law or custom.

A wide variety of offences were seen in terms of breaches of the peace. Every man of note had his peace; the King's peace was the greatest, but the king's cook had his peace which covered the royal kitchens and each lord had his peace and each free peasant his. Breach of the peace therefore often involved two payments, one to the actual victim and one to the owner of the peace. Breaches of a peace given by the king in person to a particular individual were reserved to the king for judgment, as were 'botlos' or uncompensatable crimes; examples of these were arson, murder by poisoning, harbouring outlaws, violent obstruction of royal messengers, and treachery to a lord. In such cases the king alone had power to pardon and restore from automatic outlawry the man who had committed them. The eleventh century is still too early for one to talk about pleas of the crown, but there was no doubt that the king's peace was specially hallowed by God and deserving of support by man.

In general the social status of women was high; royal women (and those from the old noble families which had once been royal) and abbesses are found sometimes as members of the witan. "The freedom with which women could hold and dispose of land is in striking contrast to post-Conquest conditions"[6]. Women, however, only inherited land in the absence of male heirs of the same degree; it was normal for a man's sons to divide his land equally between them. Before alienating land out of the family, and this included gifts to the Church, it was advisable to obtain the consent of one's kin, who might otherwise have a claim on it. Land thus alienated from the family, bookland, could thereafter be alienated at will. The king retained ultimate jurisdiction over bookland and hence would be heir if the land were forfeit. Under Edward the Confessor written instruments became common as giving a grant greater security.

(v)  1066

In 1066 the Normans came. William I, the Conqueror, swore at his coronation to observe the laws of England as they had been in Edward's day, but modifications, such as the general substitution of mutilation for the death penalty, were soon introduced. Slavery as such disappeared, with many slaves falling into the enlarged class of serfs, for the Normans were readier than the Anglo-Saxons to hold peasants unfree. Inevitably the attitude of a king who was, even if only temporarily, a military despot was different from that of Cnut. He could make an ab initio distribution among his followers, first of the Wessex lands of the Godwin family and later, in 1071-2 after the defeat of the earls of Mercia and Northumbria, of most of the rest of England. In this way the greater part of the country was

----------

6    D. Whitelock, pp.151-52; cf. Harding, no. 3.

divided into knights' fees, with a substantial number of manors reserved to the crown[7]. With the exception of some of the wilder parts of the north-west, he gave effect to the feudal concept that all land was held of the king. Land-holding and military service had been linked since Alfred's day, but the tie was now made systematic and almost universal.

Thus the king's court was now feudal, whereas the _witan_ had adhered to a customary tradition; however, the king's court, the _curia regis_, did retain the royal omni-competent jurisdiction of the Anglo-Saxon kings[8]. New, at least in their scale, were the honour courts, the courts of the great lords to which their tenants, the lesser lords or knights, came as suitors; these diminished the importance of the shire court. Manors, frequently being the products of the new distribution, were tidier units under the Normans; seignorial jurisdiction was that of a master, but manor courts continued to proceed by inquest in disputes about leasehold or descent. Hundred courts were very widely in private hands even before the Conquest; the process accelerated afterwards, but they continued to be centres of local knowledge[9]. Some remained as franchise jurisdictions, where being subject to the court was not dependent on being a tenant of the court's owner, but most were seignorial, where holding from a lord made a man subject to his court.

The Normans introduced trial by battle for both civil and criminal cases. It was even simpler than compurgation or the traditional ordeals,

----------

7    Tenants on royal manors had some special privileges; later we find them obtaining their own writ -- the little writ of right close -- to protect their holdings; v. Harding, p.34.

8    Harding, no. 6.

9    Harding, no. 7, third paragraph.

because there was no need to award the burden of proof to one side rather than the other. Another change made by William was his removal of clerics from the courts secular; in particular the bishop gave up his joint presidency of the shire court. Henceforward the line was drawn between spiritual and temporal causes much as in the rest of Europe, although in England as elsewhere clerics continued to serve the king in lay matters.

The Normans thus introduced some new things, in particular military feudalism with knight service and castles to overawe their surroundings, but their blending of old and new was a hopeful sign of the unity to come. This blending is well illustrated from the compilation known as Domesday Book. In the eleventh century only in England was local government sufficiently organized and central government sufficiently strong for the success of such a project. A survey was made during 1085-86 of the greater part of the realm in order to discover the annual value of all land in the kingdom, whether or not anything was owed directly to the king; it is fairly clear that the motives for the undertaking were fiscal rather than administrative. Men were sent out as commissioners to groups of counties; they made their enquiries in the shire courts. Questions were put to the sheriff, the barons and other Normans as to the greater tenements, and to the reeves, the priests and six peasants of each vill as to their knowledge of each hundred, and sometimes each village; these questions were to be answered on oath[10].

The commissioners must on occasion have decided disputes over tenure in order to make accurate returns. The sheriff was already accustomed to going on circuit (ayre in Scotland, eyre in England) to sit twice a year in each hundred of his shire to review the tithings, and so there was no

----------

10    Herlihy, no.37.

novelty in travelling judges. Some use of a sworn jury of inquest to discover the truth through local knowledge was not new to either English or French tradition; the Anglo-Saxon kings had made judicial as well as administrative use of it, regularly in criminal, occasionally in civil procedure[11].

The use of written instruments or writs to convey instructions, to make grants, and to publicize oral transactions had become regular under the Anglo-Saxons, and was readily adopted by William and his successors. Writs could be used to order a sheriff to discover something through inquiry from the men of the shire, or to command that right be done to someone by the sheriff if his lord would not, or to grant a privilege such as holding a market[12]. The use of writing was on the increase everywhere at this period, as we have seen; under Norman rule Anglo-Saxon was ousted by Latin.

William II made no mark on English legal history, save in that his brother and successor, Henry I (1100-35), was able to paint a picture of him as an unjust man, resorting to the feudal letter against the customary spirit of the law. By contrast Henry, so said Henry, would "restore to you the law of King Edward, with the reforms made to it by my father with the counsel of his barons". Henry ordered the shire and hundred courts to meet where and when they had met in Edward's time, but trial was to be by battle unless a settlement was reached.

Henry's frequent absences in Normandy led to some institutionalization of his household. The Exchequer was established for the keeping of the

----------

11    Harding, no. 7, first para.; R.C. van Caenegem, Royal Writs in England from the Conquest to Glanvill (Selden Society, vol.77, 1958-59) 69f.

12    Harding, no.7, first, second and fifth paragraphs.

royal accounts, with records (known as the Pipe Rolls) of all monies due and paid in; it also had jurisdiction in this field. It was during this period that writs issued by the royal Chancery began to take set forms. Henry was personally active in judicial business, but even so he needed deputies whom he could send where they were needed; the first predominantly judicial eyres took place in his reign. At these eyres criminals were accused under oath by a jury of presentment in the hundreds, in a manner simlar to Anglo-Saxon practice, although it was in the shire courts that the royal justices sat. As elsewhere in Europe, all feudal courts led eventually to the king, as feudal superior of every man; appeal from local courts led to the king as the source of the peace of the realm.

Around 1118 a work known as the Leges Henrici Primi (Laws of Henry I) was produced; its title is misleading in that it was a compilation of older material. Its purpose was to explain the customary and vernacular law of the local courts to the Norman sheriffs and lords in a language — Latin -- that they could understand, in order to make the administration of justice more effective. It began by remarking that the Anglo-Saxon kingdom was divided between the customs of Wessex, Mercia, and the Danelaw. It described the shires, the hundreds and the tithings, and the sheriff's tourn for view of frankpledge, and it stressed the importance of the shire courts. Seignorial courts were also mentioned, together with the duty of suit of court and the importance of the fealty of vassal to his lord. The author, although overwhelmed by the diversity of custom in his attempt to clarify the law, saw that unity lay in the king's peace; he also tried to relate the rules of law he knew to contemporary continental practice. The Normans seem to have been following a sharpened Anglo-Saxon tradition, not abrogating but up-dating old custom. In Baker's words: "The common law emerged in the twelfth century from the efficient and rapid expansion of

221

institutions which existed in an undeveloped state before 1066"[13].  It is from the reign of Henry II, the first king since the Conquest to claim to be English (however much this claim was propaganda) that one can recognize the king's courts then and thereafter playing the leading role in the creation of a single common law.

(vi)  Henry II: the eyre, the jury, and the writ

How far the reshaping of the law of England that took place under Henry II was his deliberate act is difficult to tell.  Henry after his coronation stated explicitly his intention to revive the good laws of his grandfather, Henry I.  It is certain that there were no comparable legal developments in Henry's other territories of Anjou and Aquitaine, although there were parallels in Normandy. Henry was described by contemporaries as dilatory in legal business.  Yet the royal power was such that a common law could be effective for the whole kingdom, and the old institutions provided the instruments.  The Treatise on the Laws and Customs of the Realm of England, which is commonly known as Glanvill after its supposed author, describes the remedies offered by the royal courts under Henry II; it is a work different in kind as well as in scale from the Leges Henrici Primi, and one which would have been impossible to produce in France where the king's political position was still weak outside his own domains.  As an example, in 1176 in England the royal justices were to exact an oath of fealty to the king from all men, villeins as well as free[14].

Henry's first legislation, the Constitutions of Clarendon, was issued

----------

13   J.H. Baker, p.11.

14   Harding, no. 8.

222

ten years after his accession as part of his struggle with the Church and in particular with Thomas Becket, formerly royal chancellor and then archbishop of Canterbury. Two years later in 1166 the Assize of Clarendon was enacted. ('Assize' literally means being seated, usually therefore a session of a court, and thence it was extended to cover: something roughly equivalent to an Act of Parliament; the authorization of particular judicial proceedings; the proceedings themselves; the jurors who formed an essential part of these proceedings; and, finally, the sessions of the itinerant justices who were appointed to hear such proceedings.) The Assize of Clarendon marked an innovation in the use of the eyre in that commissioners were sent out who were exclusively judicial. In each shire of the kingdom twelve 'lawful' men from each hundred and four from each township were, on oath, to present the names of those suspected of robbery or murder or theft, or of harbouring such persons, since the date of the king's accession. These suspects, of whatever status (so that serf as well as free man here became subject to royal justice), were to be arrested and put to the ordeal of water. The sheriff might receive the presentment but was to have no jurisdiction; he was simply to keep the accused safe until they could be tried before the commissioners. Nor was any other court to have jurisdiction over those accused by this sworn jury, although other criminals could be dealt with as was customary. All men, regardless of any private court they might have the right to hold, were to attend the shire court to be available to serve on a jury of presentment; no one -- and this included boroughs -- whatever jurisdiction he enjoyed was to deny the sheriff entry to enforce the frankpledges. Persons of really bad reputation, even if they succeeded in the ordeal, were outlawed and had to leave the kingdom within eight days.

The sending out of royal justices in eyre was not in itself a novelty, but the members of the royal court, the _curia regis_, who had been thus despatched had previously acted for the king in fiscal and administrative as well as judicial matters, as they did again in 1170 at the Inquest of Sheriffs or the Assize of Arms in 1181. The Assize of Clarendon was general, in that it extended to all the shires, but it was also specifically judicial, and in this it set a pattern. There was another general eyre in 1173, with itinerant justices being sent to each of six circuits. "The conduct of business at an eyre epitomised its historical role. The first part, the pleas of the crown, represents the system of itinerant government, the first stage in institutional centralisation ... The other part of the eyre's business was the common pleas, ordinary litigation between ordinary people. And since almost all our evidence comes from a time when there existed also the central court which came to be known as the Court of Common Pleas, and since that court became the ordinary forum for such litigation, it is important to emphasise that it was in the eyre that such pleas could first come to royal justice as a matter of routine. It was the central court that was at first the exceptional thing, in that cases were begun there for special reason, sometimes for special payment by a litigant unwilling to wait for the next eyre; and it always needed the special authorisation of a writ"[15].

As royal justice came to be more in demand, it was apparent that there was much that was too trivial for the solemnity of a general eyre, presided over by the greatest men in the kingdom. Elaboration of claims led to an institutionalization of the system and a division between civil and criminal causes. Eventually royal justices sat in the shires in five frequently overlapping capacities: permanently as justices of the peace;

----------

15    Milsom, pp.27-9.

as judges sent out with commissions of *oyer et terminer* (to hear and determine specific offences); or of gaol delivery (to clear the prisons in a specific shire); or of assize (to hear possessory claims); or of *nisi prius*. To explain the last, when juries needed to be summoned before the king himself or before the royal courts which came to be fixed at Westminster, they were told to come "unless before then -- *nisi prius* -- the king's justices shall have come" to the shire. Judges or commissioners were therefore sent out specifically to hear the testimony of a jury and to report back. They might be delegates without original jurisdiction in the matter or they could include one or more of the judges hearing the suit in the *curia regis*; in the former case they were often judges with other commissions to which this task was added. Unlike the *enquête* of the *Parlement* of Paris, the judges did not interrogate individual witnesses but put questions which could be simply answered by a local jury. By the fourteenth century the general eyre had disappeared, although royal judges continued to visit a county at a time, and the central courts had become permanent and professional, but in the thirteenth century the eyre dominated the administration of justice and these circuit courts remained an integral part of the legal system for eight hundred years.

The jury of presentment, or Grand Jury, the sworn jury of accusers, survived in England until 1933 and still survives in the United States. Its roots went back to the Anglo-Saxon kingdom. Such presentment or indictment was only on suspicion and so it was followed by trial. Trial by battle could not be used because the king himself was viewed as prosecutor, and compurgation gave too much scope for local pressure; Henry therefore laid down the ordeal, but when the clergy were forbidden after 1215 to take part in trial by ordeal some other method of proof became necessary. During the thirteenth century it became the custom to put the facts to

225

another jury of sworn neighbours, the petty jury. The accused must consent to this for, unlike God in the ordeal, the neighbours might be prejudiced -- the more likely since it was not until 1352 that the two criminal juries were made fully distinct. If the accused did not consent, it was laid down in 1275 that while obdurate he could be kept in prison under harsh conditions; this turned into peine forte et dure which used torture to compel his consent to a jury.

The petty jury was a thirteenth century creation, but the civil jury, like the jury of presentment, already had a long history. Athelstan had said that truthful men were to be named in each hundred to "be for witness in every suit". Nevertheless, swearing men to provide information which would settle private disputes rather than matters of public concern was a later use, perhaps first known under Edward the Confessor, perhaps not until the following century. In 1176 Henry II issued the Assize of Northampton, a revised version of the Assize of Clarendon which added arson and forgery to the pleas of the crown. However, there is a clause referring to a possible abuse by lords: "On the death of a free tenant his heirs shall have the seisin their father had on the day he died. ... And if the lord denies the heirs the seisin of the deceased, the justices of the lord king shall make enquiry through twelve lawful men as to what seisin the deceased had on the day he died and in accordance with the finding shall restore the heirs." This is the assize of mort d'ancestor which clearly makes use of the civil jury and allows common pleas, that is the suits raised between one subject and another, to be heard by the king's judges[16].

The importance of the jury in twelfth and thirteenth century England

----------

16   Harding, nos. 8 and 9.

226

led to an emphasis on the techniques of pleading and also to a growth in the substantive law. "The decision as to what were material questions of fact for the jury necessitated a decision as to what the law was. However, such questions of law were not raised after the facts had been discovered by trial, but in the course of deciding what the jury was to be asked to try"[17].

The Assize of Windsor of 1179 allowed a tenant whose title was challenged to apply to the Chancery for a writ, the writ of right, which allowed him to submit his claim to a jury of twelve knights of the shire before the justices in eyre instead of having to undertake trial by battle in the court of his lord. This procedure, before a royal not a feudal court, was itself known as the Grand Assize, in contrast to the petty assizes such as mort d'ancestor which enquired into who had last had seisin as a matter of fact rather than of right. Novel disseisin was another of the petty assizes; there continues to be argument about its relationship to the interdicts of the civil law or to the actio spolii of the canon law. It dealt with who had had seisin before a recent dispossession. The two other petty assizes were utrum, whether land was held by lay or ecclesiastical tenure (which was extended to cover similar questions, such as whether it was freehold or leasehold, and whether an heir was of age or not, etc.), and darrein presentment, or who had last exercised the right of patronage to a particular benefice; like the other two petty assizes these used a jury of twelve lawful men. A jury was also used in the investigation of encroachments upon royal property (purprestures) and at nisi prius. It was an excellent instrument in many ways for discovering local truth, but a jury was limited to its own shire and could not speak as

----------

17  Baker, p.66.

to occurrences elsewhere.  Its firm establishment as an English legal institution must be credited to Henry II.

The writ was the third element in the pattern of countrywide royal justice.  The eyre and the jury operated in the shires; the curia regis meant the king and his counsellors, including those whom he sent out as his justices in eyre, but it also had a more abstract definition as the home of the machinery necessary to co-ordinate the royal administration in the shires. although it was in theory attached to the person of the king. The Exchequer was probably the first branch of government to settle in a fixed place;  after all, the financial records of the Exchequer dealt with the mainspring of government and in troubled times were safer in some secure castle such as Winchester.  The Chancery, the writing office of the king, followed him for longer.  Writing had long been used for communication between the king and his sheriffs but under Henry we find a new kind of judicial writ.  These writs were close (sealed when folded) because they contained instructions for the sheriff's eyes only, and furthermore most of them were returnable, that is the sheriff must return the writ to the justices in eyre -- or, later, to one of the king's courts at Westminster -- with a note on it of what action he had taken in compliance with its instructions; that is why their normal ending is "and have there the parties and this writ".

So important were writs to the system of justice developed under Henry that Glanvill has been interpreted as simply a commentary upon them, although this is not a fair assessment.  When the king's command still normally meant an oral command, it could hardly be viewed as a regular stage in procedure.  "The use of writs on the other hand meant that the king's authority extended as far and as fast as his chancery officials could write them out, as aggrieved litigants could fetch and carry them, and as sheriffs and bailiffs in the localities were willing and able to enforce them."[18] The quantitative change had qualitative effects. When writs became routine -- standardized and repeatable -- they became the normal, although never the only, method of exciting justice. Glanvill knew some thirty-six original writs (initiating litigation), roughly the same number, including many with but minor variations, for process in the course of litigation, and four for ordering execution of judgment. A century later, at the end of Henry III's reign, there were some one hundred and twenty; in 1320 there were about 890, and a Register of Writs printed in London in 1531 listed about 2,500. Most of these represent trivial modifications since the creation of fresh categories of writs had been restricted by the Statute of Westminster II of 1285 which, however, allowed the clerks to draw up new writs analogous to existing ones (in consimili casu). Hence new kinds of wrongs had to look in other directions for a remedy, but the writ remained fundamental for centuries. Not until the nineteenth century were its forms of action abolished in favour of -- from 1875 -- one single original writ, and this little more than a direction to the parties to appear.

There were writs for claims to title, writs of right, as well as writs for claims to seisin, or possession, and during the thirteenth century writs were introduced for real rights. There were also writs for the personal actions such as debt and covenant. The writs for trespass became routine under Henry III. Trespass covered various delicts but always with a claim that injury had been done to the king's peace so that the matter could be brought before the royal courts. Along with the increase in writs there were developments in other aspects of procedure, such as essoins, or

----------

18    Clanchy, p.155.

229

excuses, for non-appearance. It was possible to send an attorney or procurator in one's place and this was soon encouraged, which benefited the growth of a legal profession. All writs presupposed a complaint to Chancery and so there was an increase in personnel there. Naturally it remained possible to make an oral complaint directly to the justices at the local eyre court; when this was put in writing it was known as a bill.

Many of Henry II's reforms were directed to safeguarding feudal jurisdictions and to trying to improve the working of the customary courts. In fact, these very safeguards and improvements weakened the old ways and replaced them with a dominant royal justice, but in view of the intention it is hardly surprising that the king did not concern himself much with canonist or civilian examples or comparisons. Although Glanvill's book was primarily concerned with writs dealing with common pleas it gave a reasonably coherent account of the common law of the realm. Partly because of his writing the workings of the royal courts could thereafter be equated with the _ius et consuetudo regni_, the law and custom of the kingdom. Glanvill wrote some fifty years after the appearance of Gratian's _Decretum_ and some sixty before the acceptance of the Accursian _Gloss_; he clearly knew something of the learned law. Book X in particular, which deals with contractual relationships, is influenced in arrangement, terminology and to some extent content by Justinian's _Institutes_; some knowledge is shown of romano-canonical procedure, as when the reader is assumed to know on what grounds a witness might be rejected in the courts spiritual. But the teaching of Roman law had been prohibited by King Stephen shortly after Vacarius (brought to Oxford by Theobald, archbishop of Canterbury) had published his _Liber Pauperum_; although this ban was probably soon repealed there was no lively centre of academic legal learning in England. Indeed, it was not to be very long before legal training became the prerogative of

230

the practitioners, although Englishmen in fair numbers did go abroad to study canon and also civil law. Henry's reforms were possible in the context of the lively intellectual society of the twelfth century rnaissance but they were applied to a stable, well-organized and centralized kingdom and their efficiency was such that Englishmen saw no need to acquire the new learned law. Bracton who flourished under Henry III, like Glanvill in the previous century, was influenced by Justinian's codification and saw the magnitude of the learned law (although there continues to be scholarly debate as to the depth of his knowledge) but it was already too late for the learned law to play a significant part in English legal development. Bracton marks the end of a possible line of approach, not a springboard for the future.

(vii)  **Curia regis**: the growth of the central courts

The chief innovation of the thirteenth century was the emergence of the curia regis as a professional court, or rather courts. The king's court was always supreme, and to the king's court, to his council, were summoned the wisest and most powerful men in the kingdom. The justices in eyre, when the eyre represented government itself, were normally members of the curia regis. The demand for justice stimulated by the eyres, which remained the usual forum for the ordinary man throughout the thirteenth century[19], led to an increase in the judicial business of the curia regis. The Exchequer, because of the sheer weight of its records and (one imagines) of its specie, was the first court to cease following a peripatetic king and to settle at Westminster. It continued to have a wide

----------

19    Harding, nos. 10, 12-14 and 16.

231

jurisdiction over any case where there was a revenue interest, and even in private causes, since debtors to the crown might raise actions in this court as their success was in the king's interest. Since wager of law, compurgation, was not applicable in these proceedings, it was accepted as possible to raise an action against the executor of an estate after the death of the defending party.

For tenants-in-chief, who owed suit of court to the king as their lord, and for those who wanted a remedy before the next visit of the eyre and were therefore prepared to pay for the privilege of using the king's court, it was burdensome to follow the king's person round England and Aquitaine and Normandy. Thus one of the clauses of Magna Carta, a statement of their feudal rights extorted from John by the barons in 1215, was that the common pleas should not follow the king but be heard in some certain place. After 1234 there were two sets of plea rolls, coram rege -- where the judges sat in the (theoretical) presence of the king, hence King's Bench -- and de banco -- where the judges sat on the Bench at Westminster, the Common Bench or Court of Common Pleas. Further, the chancery began to issue writs returnable to the Common Bench for actions raised in the shire courts. The King's Bench could not hear common pleas because it did not remain in a certain place; writs bringing causes before it were returnable "wherever we may then be in England". The Common Bench thus acquired an exclusive jurisdiction over causes in which the king had no kind of interest, which at this stage meant all the real actions and those personal actions which did not allege a breach of the king's peace. Because of their common origin in the curia regis, the Common Bench shared with the the King's Bench jurisdiction over pleas of the crown and cases involving trespass; however, by convention, appeals (accusations) of felony were not heard by the Common Bench after the later fourteenth century.

There were normally four or five judges of the Common Pleas, also advocates called serjeants-at-law and a staff of clerks and other assistants. It was in the 'crib' in this court that pupils stood to learn their law; it was the debates there of judges and serjeants that made up most of the content of the Year Books, which are reports -- in French, the language of the pleadings -- of selected cases before the Common Pleas or in eyre[20].

By the end of the fourteenth century the King's Bench had also settled at Westminster, usually with three judges -- the Lord Chief Justice and two puisne justices. Henceforward judicial business performed by the king in person or in his presence was described as 'before the king's council' rather than before the curia regis; it was not reckoned part of the Common Law. The King's Bench had a universal criminal jurisdiction, but after the fourteenth century it functioned as something akin to a court of appeal, except for offences committed in Middlesex, the shire in which Westminster lay. Although barred from hearing common pleas it had a civil jurisdiction, in particular over actions of trespass and also to correct errors in the Common Pleas or in the courts of record, that is, the borough and palatine courts. Since the bulk of criminal trials took place at the assizes held in the shires[21] and since debt was a matter for Common Pleas, it is not surprising that it was predominantly King's Bench which felt the loss of business during the fifteenth century to the conciliar and prerogative courts[22].

----------

20  Harding, no.20.

21  Harding, nos.21 and 23.

22  For the curious and elaborate fictions that the King's Bench adopted in order to stay competitive with the other central courts, in particular the Bill of Middlesex, see Baker, pp. 38-9.

233

When the King's Council became distinct from the King's Bench there remained people who wanted direct access to the king; the king still regarded active jurisdiction as one of his duties and prerogatives. Causes concerning the great could best be dealt with on such occasions as when the king was wearing his crown in a parliament. The first adjournment of a case to Parliament — not yet an institution but a reasonably regular and formal gathering of the magnates, lay and ecclesiastical, to hear and petition the king -- seems to date from 1236. By the later part of the century it was a normal court, at this stage not particularly different in its workings from the Parlement of Paris. Petitions, or bills, to Parliament might be made by any free man and the matter might receive judgment there, although it would more often be referred to one of the common law courts. Alternatively a bill might lead to the issuing of a general edict on the subject, and so we find early parliamentary legislation; the shape of legislative procedure, however, was only settled under the earlier Tudors. It was through its function as a court that Parliament began to deal with legal affairs and so took from the judges the sole power of technical development of the law, a position they had still enjoyed in the time of Glanvill or even Bracton.

By Bracton's time judges had already become specialists, professionals rather than general servants of the king; generality remained useful for the business of the King's Council after it separated from the curia regis. Bracton wrote his treatise On the Laws and Customs of England so that judges could follow the wise decisions of their predecessors. By the 1280s these decisions were a matter of record in the plea rolls[23] and the year books, and by the following century they were being cited as evidence of

----------

23    For an example of specimen pleadings, v. Baker, Appendix B, p.448.

law and practice - nothing peculiar to England here. Fourteenth century judges were quite clear that they were creating law as well as enforcing it, but what was persuasive was the communis opinio of the judges and serjeants in Westminster Hall, not specific previous decisions. It was not until the later sixteenth century that weight was given to particular past decisions and not until the later nineteenth century that the full doctrine of stare decisis emerged as the English aberration.

(viii)  The creation of the Common Law


The law of the Court of Common Pleas, the King's Bench and the Exchequer was by definition the common law.  Common law might be and often was used in other courts such as the Admiralty or Chancery, but the creation of common law was restricted to the three branches of the thirteenth century curia regis; in particular it was made between the thirteenth and sixteenth centuries in the Court of Common Pleas where the serjeants congregated.  As early as the fourteenth century, English law could be distinguished from that of every other country in the civilized West because its lawyers were trained purely within practice in the courts and at the Inns of Court, not at the universities.  The English legal profession refused to recognize the learned law as having any relevance to their practice.  The divergence can thus be dated, since in the twelfth century England had been unusual only in its degree of centralized and effective royal power.  The clerical servants of the king who brought about the change from the jumble of the Leges Henrici Primi to the systematization of Glanvill and, half a century later, of Bracton, would have been at home throughout western Christendom.  The teaching of civil but not municipal law in the universities was normal, and the legal professionalism which emerged during this period can readily be paralleled elswehere.

Henry de Bracton (d. 1268) was a judge of the King's Bench in the 1240s and 1250s and wrote, or at least heavily revised, the great treatise which is known by his name. Bracton made much use of the plea rolls, going back to the 1220s; he described the customary laws of England as they had recently been developed for the use of judges. Although a much more substantial work it is in the same tradition as that of Beaumanoir. There is scholarly argument about how well acquainted Bracton was with the civil law, but there is no doubt that it provided him with the concept of order, of a framework in which to handle English law.

The English legists of the later twelfth and thirteenth centuries were in perfect agreement with the notion that one must look first to one's own custom and then supplement it. William Raleigh, later bishop of Winchester, had been the champion of the traditional party in successfully opposing the introduction of legitimation by subsequent marriage into English law -- nolumus leges Angliae mutari (Statute of Merton 1236) -- although as a canon of St. Paul's in London and then treasurer and canon of Exeter cathedral before his elevation to the episcopate he must have known that canon law allowed it. But men like Raleigh and Bracton, who was archdeacon of Barnstaple and then chancellor of Exeter Cathedral, were in a somewhat invidious position as judges. As clerics they were unable to pass a death sentence, and in the thirteenth century there were repeated the decisions of the earlier clerical reform movement that clergy should not involve themselves in secular business (Extra 3,50). While clerics continued sometimes to serve the king in a judicial capacity, practice on behalf of clients other than the Church itself or the poor and unprotected was forbidden them; King's Bench was completely laicized by 1341.

236

The pleaders and attorneys (or procurators) doing regular business in the central courts came by the fourteenth century to be exclusively laymen; thus they would have had no reason to study canon law. The teaching of civil law at Oxford cannot have been strong; when Francis Accursius (son of the Glossator) was brought to England by Edward I it was to serve in the royal household, and there is no trace of his teaching before his return to Bologna. Effective royal control (combined with the geographical fact of insularity) restricted study abroad (as it could appeals to Rome) and made it less attractive. There was therefore no rival school that could offer an alternative approach in legal ideas, while law in England, as elsewhere, had become so technical that professional training was needed. Because England lay outside the spheres of canon and civil law after the clerical withdrawal from the courts, the spoken language of the courts came to be French, still the language of the upper classes, rather than Latin, the language of scholars. This further intensified the isolation of English law, although much of the written material of litigation continued to be in Latin.

At roughly the same time as Bracton's treatise there appeared a formulary of writs known as the Brevia Placitata (Pleaded Writs); other similar works of the period were Novae Narrationes (New Counts)[24] and, more restricted in scope, Placita Coronae (Pleas of the Crown)[25]. In Brevia Placitata, a conflation of writs and counts, "the writs, which in real life were always in Latin, were translated into French, the language in which

----------

24  A count was a formal statement of claim, declaring the cause of the action; it was roughly comparable to the *intentio* and *demonstratio* of the Roman formulary system.

25  Harding, no.15.

counts at any rate in the king's courts were actually spoken, the ordinary language of the upper classes. This collection was for the use, or more probably the instruction, of professional men, literate men, but men not at home in the Latin tongue and not interested in the riches to which it gave access. ... It is one of the important facts in the history of western thought (or at least of legal influence beyond Europe) that the [Brevia] was to prove fruitful, [Bracton] sterile. ... Just as the writs in Brevia Placitata show counters looking upward to learn the administrative and jurisdictional elements, so Bracton's book shows the administrator looking downward at what was happening in court. Many actual cases cited are taken from the plea rolls, mostly of the earlier thirteenth century. But the attempt is to make more than just administrative sense; it is to systematise in a substantive and not just a practical and procedural way. This is, as it were, a university law-book. When, in the half century after Bracton's death, his kind ceased to play any part in the common law and the bench came to be filled from below by counters, two qualities were lost. One was the administrative habit of seeing problems as a whole and making solutions work: the kind of man who had brought the common law into being would not have let it get into the state in which so many cases required the special treatment of the Chancellor's equitable jurisdiction. The other was a more specific quality...[Roman law] was no part of the counters' world. What centuries of development had made clear centuries earlier was to them alien learning in closed books; and they were starting again from the beginning. ... They did not see the law as a system of substantive rules at all. They saw that their ancient pattern of claim and denial had been disturbed because jurymen were fallible, and that in some circumstances the defendant must be allowed a new kind of answer. Upon the infinite details of this problem they concentrated their great abilities;

and they never looked up to consider as a whole the substantive system they did not know they were making"[26].

The young man eager for a career in law therefore came to London. He could learn the rudiments of the writ system through a little tract called the Old Natura Brevium ('Old' Nature of Writs), the basic counts from Novae Narrationes, and "a child's eye view of the feudal land law"[27] from a work known as the Old Tenures; for, before the later fifteenth century, this, with some similar works, was virtually all there was of legal literature, apart from reports in various forms, particularly the Year Books. He would also attend the courts themselves, and he would probably live with his fellows in one of the inns of chancery, as they came to be known. When or if he became a senior apprentice he would join one of the four inns (Inner and Middle Temple, Lincoln's Inn, Gray's Inn), known by Tudor times as the Inns of Court, which were established during the fourteenth century. There were lectures or 'readings' (although these seem to have been predominantly on statute), moots, and attendance in the 'crib' at Westminster Hall to hear the judges and serjeants debate the cases before them. It usually took some seven years before the student was called to the bar by the senior members of his inn as an utter or outer barrister. From this status he might achieve that of bencher, normally by being a reader and giving a course of lectures upon some selected statute. But there was at no time any coherent or programmed instruction and even this mild form of education offered by the Inns of Court disappeared in 1642 with the outbreak of the first Civil War. There was no alternative.

The senior branch of the legal profession was that of the serjeants,

----------

26   Milsom, p.41ff.

27   Baker, p.162.

for it was exclusively from among them that judges were appointed to King's Bench or Common Pleas; they emerged in the thirteenth century as advocates specializing in making counts before the Common Bench. Since such counts became the terms of the issue which would be put to trial, these were central to litigation. By the end of the century serjeants had acquired, if they did not already by definition enjoy, exclusive rights to practise before the Common Bench, the more profitable court because its site was fixed. The serjeants concentrated on elaborating their counts, which had necessarily become more complicated once the truth was not reached by an infallible, divinely backed ordeal but at the hands of the fallible but rational members of a jury. It was because the Common Law worked by producing a single issue for trial by a lay jury that the professionals could concentrate at Westminster and that their numbers were so few; there were fewer than a thousand members of the order of serjeants in all its history -- the order faded away after 1875 when the last was created; similarly, there were at any one time only seven or eight judges for the two courts of Common Pleas and King's Bench. Most serjeants who lived long enough became judges; promotion would not have been too startling a step, since it was usual for commissioners of assize to consist of a royal judge, a serjeant and a local man, and thus they would already have gained judicial experience.

The heyday of the serjeants, both in financial terms and for legal creativity, was the fourteenth and fifteenth centuries, when nearly all important civil causes were heard by the Court of Common Pleas. It was the pleadings put forward there by the serjeants and their debates with the judges, recorded in the year books and in the formularies of specimen counts, which applied the old formalities to new situations and adjusted, if hardly reformed, the law. In the Humber Ferry Case of 1348 (of which more later) trespass was the route by which contractual liability was achieved, a bizarre approach that still affects English views on contract. Their ingenuity found solutions to many problems, but they were forced into curious contortions in the process.

While the serjeants shared a collegiate life with the judges in the Serjeants' Inns, there were other practitioners at the bar, the barristers. Some would after twenty or so years themselves become serjeants, others would continue to practise before the royal courts, including those in eyre, while yet others seem to have returned to their own shires and practised in the local courts. Attorneys were procurators, whose actions in the courts bound their principals. They were clearly distinct from the serjeants at least by the early fourteenth century when the latter organized themselves into a guild. Solicitors appeared as an identifiable branch of the legal profession during the sixteenth century. Incidentally, not until the end of the seventeenth century was the independence of the judiciary finally established as a constitutional principle; furthermore, judges expected their office to be profitable, from fees, patronage,and above all from gifts from hopeful litigants.

(ix)  English civilian and prerogative courts; local courts

It was a  curious feature of the early modern English common lawyers that they tried, through statute and through pronouncements from the bench, to impose "legal restraints on the power of the Crown to erect new courts and jurisdictions, on the very power which had introduced the common law and its due process as an extraordinary alternative to regular local justice ...The notion that the king had exhausted his judicative powers by creating the common law courts was pressed to its limits by Coke CJ [Chief

Justice] when in 1608 he told James [VI &] I that he had no authority to participate in the judicial decisions of his own courts"[28]. But the king in his coronation oath swore to 'do equal right and justice', and he had a constitutional duty to furnish a remedy where the common law was deficient -- although (probably) only where it was deficient. Since the common lawyers were reluctant to recognize any deficiencies they fought against the prerogative courts, and these mostly failed to survive the struggle thus precipitated -- which seemed to the common lawyer proof enough of their wrongness[29].

In the fourteenth century, as we have seen, it was already common to petition the king for a remedy; the normal reply was to send the petitioner to the common law[30] but some bills were dealt with by the king and his Council. By the end of the century only matters of the highest importance were dealt with by the great council as a body (a body which until mid century had regularly included the judges of the King's Bench), and if bills were assented to they were then acts of parliament. Lesser matters were more often delegated to individual members of the council, such as the Chancellor or the Admiral; petitioners therefore took to addressing these officers directly in their several spheres of competence and in their several courts.

The Chancery was originally simply the royal office; someone who wished to raise an action in the royal courts had to obtain a writ from the Chancery and pay a fine for it. But if he petitioned the king because he

----------

28    Baker, p.83.

29    Treason doth never prosper!  What's the reason?

      Why, if it doth, then none dare call it treason.

30    Harding, no. 22.

was too poor to buy a writ, or because his opponent was too powerful for the sheriff to do his duty or the jurors to tell the truth, then special treatment was needed.  In hard cases the Chancellor provided a remedy other than through a writ, because he had the expertise both in framing writs and in finding other means to the same end.  By the fifteenth century the Chancery had a clerical staff of some 120, of whom the senior twelve were known by Tudor times as the Masters in Chancery.  These were usually doctors of law and able to act as the Chancellor's deputies; the chief of them was entitled Master of the Rolls, because he was responsible for the records.  Even while the common lawyers were losing all touch with the learned law, until the Reformation the Chancellor was usually a cleric -- normally a bishop or even archbishop -- and usually also a graduate in canon or in civil law.

The work of the Chancery was divided into two sides.  On the Latin side were handled the king's interests as universal feudal superior.  On the English side, where the petitions might be, and the pleadings were, in the vernacular (first French, then English), bills of complaint were received from individual petitioners.  The Chancellor treated these ad hoc. His decrees were originally made by authority of the Council or with the advice of various judges and serjeants, but from at least 1473 he was issuing them in his own name.  He was already accustomed to issuing injunctions (interdicts) to suspend a trial at common law while documents were discovered or witnesses examined; injunctions could also protect a tenant from interference until his case was decided at common law, and occasionally they came to be used to stay a common law judgment which enforced a contract formally good but brought about by fraud or with unintended evil consequences.  Sometimes the Chancellor could order specific performance of a contract, or enforce on grounds of conscience a bare pact not recognized by the Common Law. Relief was more usual than the award of damages. He also appointed commissioners to arbitrate in mercantile disputes or in cases with an international dimension.

Process in actions in Chancery was begun by subpoena which was not, like a writ, addressed to the sheriff of a specific shire but was directly binding (under penalty of a fine) on the party in whatever jurisdiction he might be. In the sixteenth century the threat of a fine was strengthened by the possibility of sequestration of the contumacious party's estate; the Chancellor could also hold men in prison for contempt of his decrees, although he had no power over life and limb. His cheap and rapid aiding, supplementing and correcting of the Common Law made the Chancellor's jurisdiction popular; while John Stafford, bishop of Bath and Wells, was Chancellor (1432-50) the annual number of petitions at least quadrupled.

This very volume of business helped to establish the Chancellor's jurisdiction on a more formal base, and it grew away from the general prerogative jurisdiction of the Council. It also came to specialize in a new area of land law, uses. A use was created when a man granted property to someone or to several people — feoffees to use — to hold in trust for himself or another — cestui que use. When the grantor or feoffor died the feoffees could, on his instructions, hand the property over to another person. In this way a feudal tenant could grant away his tenement during his life, thus avoiding the incidents of relief or wardship at his death, but at the same time he could either preserve the normal succession by letting his heir on intestacy inherit the use from him, or sidestep feudal custom by leaving the use to someone else, such as a daughter[31]. Only the grant, not the trust, was recognised by the common law, to which the cestui

-----------

31    Harding, no. 30.

que use was no more than a tenant on sufferance. Chancery, following the Church courts, established such a daughter's right in what came to be called the equitable estate; if the trustees alienated the land it was settled by 1465 that the purchaser acquired the duties of the trust. Where there was a use the legal owner had only bare title with, however, the reversion if the cestui que use died intestate and without heir. Because this conflicted with feudal rules on succession to land the common law never fully received the concept of the use into its courts, although the judges were obliged to take some account of its existence.

Chancery jurisdiction was originally based on equity and good faith, and it continued to be described as Equity even after the Chancery had become as rigid and formal as any common law court[32]. It became formal partly as a natural result of the scale of the business concerning uses and partly because the common lawyers disliked the subjective or arbitrary element in the Chancellor's judgments. During the later fifteenth and early sixteenth centuries, however, there was generally harmony between law and equity, with judges of the two benches on occasion attending Chancery to give their advice[33]. It is clear that the ordering of the Chancellor's conscience (with one or two notable exceptions, such as Cardinal Wolsey and Lord Ellesmere) was normally in accord with the common law rather than with natural or civil law, even if aspects of procedure were reminiscent of the learned law. In 1675 it could be said without any irony that a contract without consideration was binding in conscience but not in Equity. By then Chancery cases were regularly reported, and Equity had become a known body of principles from which the court would not depart for fear of

----------

32    v. Charles Dickens  Bleak House.

33    Harding, no. 29.

uncertainty.

The Court of Chivalry, the court of the Lord High Constable and Earl Marshal of England, and the Court of the Lord High Admiral of England also sprang from the general jurisdiction of the Council. Some of the matters they dealt with were outside the cognizance of the common law courts because they had occurred overseas or concerned persons not English subjects; due process in common law depended on the summoning of a jury from the shire in which the deed had been done. Fictions did occur; for example if a claimant alleged that wine had been loaded at Bordeaux in Kent and the defender denied only the substance of the claim, then a Kentish jury could be summoned. The Court of Chivalry dealt with the business side of warfare: ransoms for prisoners of war, the contracts between the captains of mercenary bands and those whom they hired, and appeals of treason or other felony committed overseas. For centuries accusations of even the most ordinary crimes in the Channel Isles or the Isle of Man could only be heard in this court. Disputes about armorial bearings were not an important part of the court's work until its revival under James VI and I; they have become the sole business of the one English court still using civilian procedure[34]. The High Court of Admiralty was much concerned with commercial affairs, for merchants could frequently find no other court willing to hear them. It also heard cases arising out of naval warfare and had a busy prize jurisdiction. It went back at least to the mid-fourteenth century and was only finally abolished in 1970; until 1875 it was a court using civil rather than common law[35]. Process could issue against ships

----------

34    *Manchester Corporation* v *Manchester Palace of Varieties Ltd.* [1955]
      P. 133.

35    Harding, no. 26.

and goods as well as persons, and it was familiar with the lex Rhodia and the customs of Oléron; its judges were frequently doctors of civil law.

The later fifteenth century was a troubled period in English political history. In 1487 a special tribunal within the king's Council was set up to deal with particular problems of law and order; its business was fairly soon absorbed into that of the Council. Since the mid-fourteenth century the Council had often met for judicial sessions in a room in the palace of Westminster known as Star Chamber, and this gave its name to the new jurisdiction[36]. From 1540 Star Chamber and the Council, now the Privy Council, were sufficiently distinct for each to have its own records and staff, but membership of the two bodies overlapped considerably. The law which Star Chamber applied was the common law but in exercising the royal prerogative it was not tied by the formalities of due process. It therefore attracted litigants by its speed, economy and efficiency. Business indeed grew too fast, particulary from men claiming they were too poor for the ordinary courts. At first a second clerk was appointed to handle such petitions, and in the 1540s this jurisdiction became that of the Court of Requests, as speedy as Star Chamber and even cheaper; it was immensely popular. Star Chamber was abolished in 1641 at the outbreak of the Civil Wars, and the Court of Requests disappeared with the disuse of the privy seal during the Wars and the Commonwealth.

The ecclesiastical courts had a wide jurisdiction in pre-Reformation England, although suits concerning advowsons (rights of presentation to benefices) were heard in the royal courts. They shared in the features common to all the western Church, such as the appointment of judges delegate with written instructions to take evidence, written

----------

36   Harding, no. 27.

interrogatories to be administered to the parties, and interdicts, ordering or prohibiting under penalty specific actions by persons subject to the court; juries did not normally feature in the Church's courts. After the English Reformation, which was doctrinally and institutionally less clear cut than elsewhere in Europe, the Corpus Iuris Canonici remained in force, except where contrary to common or statute law or to the royal prerogative. Canon law teaching was, however, suppressed at Oxford and Cambridge, which therefore continued only with the civil law.  The Court of Arches at Canterbury continued to be the normal superior court -- the archbishop of Canterbury had always exercised a more effective jurisdiction than other metropolitans; the Court of High Commission was set up to replace the supreme personal jurisdiction of the Pope. The Court of Delegates was established to hear such appeals as would previously have been heard by papal judges delegate; the new delegates included common law judges and doctors of canon or civil law.  Civilian advocates had sole audience before these ecclesiastical courts; most were members of Doctors' Commons, which had its own library as well as a social life until its dissolution in 1858.

Manorial courts often continued to flourish, although their jurisdiction was largely confined to petty larcenies, the proper cultivation of the open fields and, most significantly, the conveying of copyhold property; thus copyhold, tenure by the custom of the manor, came in the later mediaeval period to be a true property right, a tenancy at common law.  In the towns the borough courts or hustings dealt with commercial matters and the problems that arose within built-up areas as well as with local civil and petty criminal causes[37].

The shire court remained the busiest forum, although relatively little

----------

37    Harding, no. 17.

248

litigation there was before an independent court presided over by the sheriff[38]. In many civil cases the sheriff was acting as a subordinate royal judge under a writ of _justicies_, and much other business was before the justices of assize[39] or at _nisi prius_. The provision of juries was one of the main functions of the sheriff in his court; it continued to be in the shire court that solemn proclamations were made and important dealings in land witnessed, and also that coroners were elected, as were knights of the shire to Parliament.

The local jurisdiction which was increasingly important was that of justices of the peace; many borough jurisdictions fell to them in the later Middle Ages. From 1361 their office carried with it the right to try all manner of criminals, whether accused of felony or of misdemeanour (as the lesser crimes came to be named in the sixteenth century). Although the royal justices continued to visit each shire twice a year on assize to hear pleas of the crown, and in times of disquiet the King's Bench might come on circuit, the work of the quarter sessions before the justices of the peace became quantitatively the most important criminal forum, and until the eighteenth century some capital cases could be heard there. Monthly petty sessions held within districts of the shire created for this purpose, dealt with minor business and such matters as enforcing wage regulations, and also with the summary trial -- without a jury -- of such offences as drinking out of the permitted hours and eavesdropping with a view to blackmail[40]. In the fifteenth century an unfortunate side effect of the wide powers of the local gentry as justices of the peace was that

----------

38   Harding, nos. 18 and 19.

39   Harding, nos. 21 and 23.

40   Harding, no. 25.

they abused the law for their own aggrandizement[41]. The known partiality of juries in this period was an element in the popularity of the prerogative courts.

(x)  Judicial review of decisions and appeals

On the continent the establishment of royal courts was closely linked with appeal and romano-canonical procedure, but in England the strength of the royal courts was such that there was no political need for a system of appeal.  In feudal terms claims of false judgment could be made ; this was extended to cover the verdict of a civil jury in an action called 'attaint'.  This did not permit a review of the case; a motion for a new trial became a solution put forward in the later seventeenth century.  Part of the problem in England was logical; so long as the curia regis was the king's own court there was no justification for allowing appeal from the king to anyone else, and the English curia regis had a jurisdiction at first instance far greater than that of any other royal court.

There were some checking mechanisms.  Judges at nisi prius reported the jury's verdict back to the bench; the attention now given to appeals could be and was given to 'motions in banc' when, after the trial of the facts by the jury but before the judgment, further questions could be raised, originally procedural but from the sixteenth century onwards often dealing with substantive points of law.  Moreover the common law courts were reluctant to enter judgment when there was any serious difference of opinion on the bench; adjournments were preferred until a consensus should be reached, and this consensus often included the opinions of the

----------

41   Harding, no. 28.

250

serjeants. Further, errors in the record could be corrected, but not until the sixteenth century could a writ of error lead to consideration of points of substance. Courts not 'of record', such as shire and feudal courts, could be required to submit to a review by the Court of Common Pleas; from the borough and the palatine courts and from the Common Pleas itself error lay to the King's Bench; from the King's Bench, from the Exchequer and from the Latin side of Chancery error lay to the king in parliament. During the fifteenth and sixteenth centuries particularly important or difficult cases might be discussed by all the eight or nine judges of the common law, perhaps with the Chancellor, perhaps with the serjeants, either in the Exchequer Chamber or less formally at Serjeants' Inn; it is a little reminiscent of meetings of the whole Court of Session. Although they had no formal authority, the pronouncements which followed such consultations were reported as well as followed.

From the English side of Chancery there could not be error in the strict sense because there was no record. The chancellor himself or his successor might review a judgment, or a commission might be appointed to this end; not until 1675 did judicial review of Chancery proceedings fall to the House of Lords. This was a true appeal -- four centuries later than in France -- for the absence of a definitive record allowed all facts to be taken into consideration, and the absence of a jury meant that a new trial was neither possible nor necessary. The creation of a Court of Appeal in Chancery in 1851 marked the introduction of a general appellate court into the English system.

The Privy Council's prerogative power to redress grievances which could not be remedied by the common law was also more than the correction of error; but it was not part of the common law. Furthermore, the Privy Council lost its jurisdiction in 1641 when the Parliamentary party abolished the conciliar courts. For the formative period of the English common law the power of the royal courts and the importance of their procedure at first instance meant that appeal in the civilian, or the modern English, sense could not exist.

(xi)  Remedies not rights


The stress hitherto has been on the procedural nature of the common law; this is largely due to its being a system which offered remedies not rights, just like classical Roman law. The outlines of a rational system of obligations were discernible in the work of Glanvill who, like Bracton, was in the tradition of those who wrote about customary law in the light of the learned law. The total disappearance of the latter element from the common law before the fourteenth century meant that English law had to learn afresh how to move from formal **stricti iuris** contracts to ones based on good faith, that is, from the verbal and literal contracts to the real (except that these were never really understood) and consensual contracts. English lawyers had to tread this path as though for the first time, when men like Dumoulin in France or Balfour in Scotland had a body of principle and of rational discussion from which it was possible to draw when they were involved in the administration of their local law.

There were three early personal obligations enforced by writ: covenant, debt and account. Covenant, enforced by the writ **praecipe**, was formal, in that the agreement had to be contained in a written document under seal; oral agreements remained enforceable in local courts, but subject to the 40/- limit imposed there in the later thirteenth century by the Statute of Westminster II. Debt was seen not as a real contract but as unjust detention. Only much later did lawyers find an implied promise to pay when a debt arose out of a transaction such as sale or loan; the writ said flatly that the debtor owed something to the pursuer and unjustly detained it from him (so early was the English habit of seeing a wrong to be remedied rather than a right to be enforced). A comparable action, called detinue, was available to recover personal property, often where there had been a deposit or a loan; where there had been no grant to the defender by the owner it was called detinue sur trover, or simply trover. Debt was a contract entirely stricti iuris; if a debtor had paid up but had not recovered his bond nor obtained a sealed document of receipt, he had no remedy in common law against another claim — hence one cause of Chancery's jurisdiction. In a case under Henry VII payment was made but the creditor recovered the bond by force and raised his action again; he was successful, but the debtor had an action in trespass for the seizure of the bond and the damages he was awarded covered the second payment he had made. The contract of debt lacked the elements of good faith, although conditions could be endorsed on the bond. Moreover, because debt was a private matter in most cases and so unsuitable for putting to a jury, the defendant must deny it by compurgation (wager of law). One could not wage another's law and so when a debtor died his 'debts' died with him; his executors could not wage his law.

The third personal action, account, was as much proprietary as contractual and primarily applied between bailiff and lord. All three actions were effectively dead by the seventeenth century, partly because of the equitable relief offered by Chancery and partly because of developments in the common law itself which, through the development of trespass, enlarged the scope of contractual liability.

A trespass is a wrongdoing, a delict; the writ praecipe ordered someone to do something in the future but the writ for trespass ordered the defender to show why -- _ostensurus quare_ -- he had done something in the past. Any wrong which was a breach of the king's peace, actual or threatened and in the end fictitious, could be brought before the royal courts. For example, in 1317 a plaintiff bought wine from the defendants which he left with them until he could arrange delivery; his count stated that the defendants had drawn off much of the wine with force and arms, to wit with swords, bows and arrows, and had topped up the cask with salt water so that the wine was totally spoilt, to the plaintiff's great damage and against the king's peace[42]. The King's Bench fairly soon found itself prepared to entertain claims even when no force of arms was alleged. The first known case in which the royal courts used trespass to impose contractual liability is the _Humber Ferry Case_ of 1348. The plaintiff complained that the defendant, the ferryman, had undertaken to transport his mare across the Humber but had so overloaded his ferry that it sank, and the mare was drowned; King's Bench held that this was a trespass, rejecting defending counsel's plea that no action lay since there had been no covenant -- covenant would not, anyway, have compensated the plaintiff for the loss of his mare. The second such case is _Waldron_ v _Marshall_ in 1369. A horse doctor had undertaken the care of a horse which had died through his neglect; he was held liable in trespass. In these early cases there was no doubt that the defendant had undertaken to do a thing and had then done it badly; there was a positive act which could be interpreted as falling within the terms of the writ of trespass. If the defendant's fault was that he had done nothing, it was much more necessary to stress that he had undertaken to act and was therefore in breach of his duty and so had committed a trespass. Thus _assumpsit_ (he assumed [a duty]) came into

----------

42   Milsom, p.289.

being.

Assumpsit became a regular action for breach of contract during the sixteenth century. However, to ground the action it was originally necessary for there to be an element of wrongdoing, such as misfeasance or deceit, and it was not until around 1600 that this was regularly accepted as a fiction. Also it was required that the plaintiff had suffered real detriment, which was interpreted as meaning that there must have been consideration. The common lawyers' first interpretation of consideration was not far from the civilian causa, the reason why the law should hold a promise to be a serious undertaking; in the later sixteenth century consideration was established as the immediate explanation for the promise, and it must be of fitting value and not already paid over.

The next move was to bring claims for money, for debt, under assumpsit; this was finally settled in 1602 by Slade's Case, when all the common law judges, with such noted figures as Coke and Bacon as counsel, argued over a period of five years a particular claim to payment for a crop of wheat and finally came to the decision that assumpsit to pay what was due was implicit in every executory contract. This for practical purposes put an end to the wager of law (compurgation, which was eventually abolished in 1833). Further, in 1612 all the judges came to agree that assumpsit was sufficiently contractual in nature for money debts as well as others to lie against executors. In spite of its delictual youth assumpsit had come to be reckoned as a contract -- or an action for breach of contract -- although it could still be brought as an action in tort for a malfeasance. There remained technical problems in the pleadings but thereafter there was a unified law of contract. This also covered obligations quasi ex contractu where there was no prior agreement; also, where money had been paid in error there was a variant of assumpsit called indebitatus. In the seventeenth century English lawyers imported a fictional promise to pay as well as a fictional tort. This was still a society where the common law courts would not hear the evidence of the parties because their testimony would be biased; this inability to question their intentions goes some way to explain the doctrine of consideration as indicating intent. Another English aberration was to insist on a sealed document rather than on the simpler formality of writing where there was no consideration to ground an assumpsit. Lord Mansfield (1705-93) would have been quite happy to accept writing as a substitute for consideration in commercial cases, but the House of Lords held to the magic of the seal.

We may end this rapid sketch of the English lawyers' approach to obligations with a quotation. Baker could write in 1979: "Since 1833 there has been an election between trespass and case, so long as the wrong complained of is not wilful. But what is the substantive distinction, if any, between trespass and case? The election between conversion and detinue remained important until a statute of 1977 declared curtly that 'detinue is abolished'. But what exactly was thereby abolished? ...'The forms of action we have buried' said Maitland at the turn of the century, 'but they still rule us from their graves'. The passage of years seems not to have greatly diminished their influence. ... The categories of legal thought were closed in 1832."[43] Despite Bracton, despite Blackstone's timid references to Natural Law in the eighteenth century, English lawyers have looked almost exclusively to their own past, the magic of the seal and the sacred cow of the jury; their skill and ingenuity have laboriously brought them to ends they could have reached centuries earlier if they had shared in the mainstream of European legal development.

----------

43    Baker, pp. 60-1.

Further Reading:

J.H. Baker  *An Introduction to English Legal History* (2nd ed. London, 1979)

   *The Order of Serjeants at Law* (London, 1984)

M.T. Clanchy  *England and its Rulers 1066-1272* (Fontana, 1983)

A. Harding  *The Law Courts of Mediaeval England* (London, 1973)

S.F.C. Milsom  *Historical Foundations of the Common Law* (2nd ed. London, 1981)

R.C. van Caenegem  *The Birth of the English Common Law* (C.U.P., 1973)

D. Whitelock *The Beginnings of English Society (The Anglo-Saxon Period)* (Penguin, 1952)

   also

Selden Society publications (London), particularly vols. 90, 96, and 97-8.

Chapter IX

## FEUDAL SCOTLAND

(i)  Pre-feudal Scotland

By the mid eleventh century the Scottish kings ruled over an area
roughly equivalent to modern Scotland, although the Western Isles, Orkney
and Shetland were in  Scandinavian hands; the former were added to the
kingdom in the thirteenth century and the latter in the fifteenth.  The
people whom they ruled had various origins, the Picts of the North, the
Scots of Dalriada or Argyll, like Galloway not far across the sea from
Celtic Ireland, the Britons of Galloway and Strathclyde and, in the south-
east, men of Anglo-Saxon stock from what had been Northumbria north of the
river Tweed.

Comparatively little is known of the law of Scotland in the pre-feudal
era, although we may be certain that it was essentially tribal custom,
varied and largely unwritten.  The evidence  of a later period suggests
that until well into the eleventh century the laws were predominantly of
the Celtic type; we assume that customs were broadly similar to those of
Celtic Ireland, about which much more is known.

Celtic society was essentially kindred-based and the kin features
prominently in the laws and customs of Celtic Scotland.  The earliest
evidence of land law is to be found in the Book of Deer, a ninth century
manuscript from a monastery in Aberdeenshire, to which were added Gaelic
notes recording grants of land made to the monastery during the eleventh
and twelfth centuries.  These notes refer to various burdens on land. When
feudal tenure came these burdens were often turned into feudal incidents.
Of the courts of Celtic Scotland and of their procedure there is little

258

evidence. The Book of Deer makes reference to the brehon (or judge) but of his functions we know virtually nothing save that they were probably declarative, like those of the Irish brehons. Proof by compurgation was a feature of Celtic procedure generally and is likely to have been used in Scotland. There seems also to have been use of pledges or cautioners (sureties) for due appearance and the like; the Gaelic word for such a pledge is culreach and the word survived as a technical legal term -- but requiring explanation -- in the legal treatises of the feudal period.

The administration of justice in Celtic society reflects law at an early stage of development. The king's peace, together with penalties for its violation, seems to have been early recognized, but wrongs such as killing or theft were primarily a matter for the individual concerned or for his kin. The function of the court was not far from that of an arbiter, aiming to limit the extent of private vengeance; retaliation was gradually replaced by an elaborate system of pecuniary compensations with the amount payable depending on the nature of the wrong and the rank of the party wronged. Evidence of this system is to be found in an early collection known as the Laws of the Bretts and Scots. Procedure on wrong also underlines the importance of the kin in Celtic society; as well as the victim, the victim's kin was entitled to compensation.

The extent of the survival of Celtic law is obscure. In the twelfth century Anglo-Norman law was introduced into Lowland Scotland. Celtic custom stayed in use in the Highlands, as it did in Galloway, a southern province but remote and inaccessible. A statute of 1245 states that Galloway "has its own special laws" (for making criminal accusations), and as late as 1385 a plea was made for the preservation of the custom of Galloway on all points. In the Highlands the law of marriage shows the survival of Gaelic custom. The marriage customs of Gaelic society differed

259

greatly from the canon law; divorce and re-marriage were permitted, and seemingly common, while the canonical rules on the prohibited degrees were largely unknown. There is some evidence to suggest that these customs were being followed even in the seventeenth century; the Statutes of Iona of 1609, designed to regulate the Highlands, declared, among other matters, that marriages contracted for a term of years were to be illegal. Celtic law seems then to have survived until at least the close of the Middle Ages in certain parts of Scotland, but it is doubtful how far its rules made any contribution to Scots law after the time of Stair. Further research may, however, show that Celtic custom helped to mould the developing legal institutions of the modern period.

(ii)  The crown and the introduction of feudalism

In 1124 David I (d. 1153) succeeded to the throne of Scotland; it was a time when Scotland was growing in population and prosperity. The new king had lived at the English court and married an English heiress and so was familiar with the structure and institutions of the Anglo-Norman state. He took that as his model when he determined that his kingdom must be improved as part of the European-wide twelfth century renaissance. Accordingly under David and his successors the government of Scotland was remodelled on a basis similar to that of England, although in the course of time significant differences emerged. Tenure of land was gradually transformed into feudal tenure; prominent among the beneficiaries of the new feudal grants were men of Anglo-Norman origin who had come north with David or who were subsequently attracted to the opportunities which Scotland offered. The country was thus provided -- or at least the Lowlands were -- with a new style of aristocracy, but the older Celtic order was not entirely swamped by the new régime. A native lord could protect his landownership by obtaining a written title, a charter, and, as we have seen, many of the feudal incidents found in the charters are simply Celtic burdens and duties under the new French or Latin names.

Feudal law generally was the subject of chapter II. Perhaps it is worth restating that feudal and customary usage blend so well together that in many cases there is no point in distinguishing between them, but only in contrasting feudal custom with institutions derived from the civil law. 'Feudal' seems the more suitable term, however, where the language of modern law continues to speak of feus and feudal rights. In Scotland, as elsewhere, at the heart of the new structure was the fief, the lands held by a feudal tenant of his lord for a specified return. Charters recording rights in land seem to have become normal during the thirteenth century. The charter provided evidence of a tenant's right to his land and other rights as well, and sometimes also of what was due from him; it is therefore not surprising that they were carefully preserved and many still survive. The services owed by these tenants naturally varied. The classic form of Anglo-Norman feudal tenure was by the provision of one or more armed knights for so many days a year. Military tenure is found in Scotland as well as in England, but the burdens imposed in Scotland tended to be lighter; one example is the great Bruce fief of Annandale -- one of the largest in the country -- which appears to have been held for the services of only ten knights. Other forms of Scottish tenure also had their English counterparts. Lands granted to the Church were normally held in free alms, no return being required other than the saying of Masses for the grantor and his family; burgh land was held in free burgage, owing a money rent and duties within the burgh such as watch and ward. However, in Scotland subinfeudation was always possible; Scotland never knew a statutory limitation, such as the English Quia Emptores (1290).

Characteristically Scottish was the tenure known as feu-ferme. Its origins lay in the needs of the king when the old Celtic burdens were feudalized or commuted into money; in its developed form it was the heritable holding of land in return for the annual payment of a fixed sum of money, the feu-duty. Feu-ferme tenure became general as Scotland progressed towards a more money-based economy; it gave the feudal superior a guaranteed annual income and, of importance to an original grantor, its creation was normally accompanied by the payment to the lord of a substantial lump sum, the grassum. The recording of landholding in this form is found in the twelfth century and was widespread from the later Middle Ages onwards; in the century or so before the Reformation the Church set much land in feu-ferme, and in the same period the feuing of its land was a policy actively pursued by the crown. The older and more onerous feudal tenures disappeared from the fourteenth century onwards; new grants of such tenure were not made and feu-ferme tenure emerged as the normal mode of landholding in Scotland.

Feudalism also involved the dispersal of governmental powers and in particular of the administration of justice. By the thirteenth century the king was seen as the fount of all secular justice; justice was administered by others -- in feudal theory -- only to the extent that the right to do so had been delegated to them by the crown. However, the Scottish king, like other kings, could not be everywhere at once nor hope to deal with all judicial matters in person; delegation was necessary. It must also be remembered that the king's delegates -- justiciar, sheriff, chamberlain -- performed a variety of general administrative tasks as well as their judicial duties. The king had his own court, the curia regis; it was the confluence of both his administrative and judicial functions and met indifferently for both purposes. Its composition was fluid because it was composed of those from whom the king sought aid and counsel; there was no inherent distinction between the smaller group of any king's regular advisers -- the council proper -- and any larger group called by the king and meeting in parliamento. By the end of the thirteenth century the parliament sat regularly as a court of law and had become the usual forum for the dispensing of royal justice by the king in person.

The office of justice appears in Scotland under David I, as an individual to whom specific cases (criminal or civil) were remitted by the king. By 1200 these cases were so many that the jurisdiction of the justiciar (for so he is called from c. 1210) could be defined as covering serious criminal cases and important pleas concerning land. By then he was a royal officer who provided a link between central government and the localities, travelling around the country on periodic ayres. He exercised some general governmental powers as well as hearing appeals from the shrieval and baronial courts. From the treatise compiled around 1292 and known as The Scottish King's Household it appears that the justice ayres were held twice a year. The justiciars were concerned with both criminal and civil jurisdiction. In the former sphere the justiciar could hear the pleas of the crown, including murder, rape, robbery and arson, which were excluded from the jurisdiction of sheriffs and barons. His civil jurisdiction included the settlement of boundary disputes by the process of perambulation of marches and also cases raised by pleadable brieves (comparable to the English writs); brieves will be discussed shortly. The court seems to have been expected to act as a filter; The Scottish King's Household says that the justiciar was to dispense justice in such a way that "no plaints should be presented to the king save only those which, because the justices and sheriffs have failed to deal with them, cannot be remedied without the presence of the king himself." There were normally several justiciars at any one time, and Scotland was divided into regions each of which was served by one or more of them. In the later thirteenth century there were three, for Lothian, Scotia (Scotland north of the Forth) and Galloway, but after 1305 there seem normally to have been two, one north and one south of the Forth. The king's chamberlain also went on ayre to visit the royal burghs for the collection of dues, the supervision of their administration and for hearing appeals from their courts.

(iii) Sheriffs

Sheriffs and sheriffdoms were Anglo-Norman institutions, imported into Scotland from England. A sheriffdom was an administrative division of the country with at its centre (or caput) a castle, usually royal, or later a burgh which had grown up around such a castle; it was, however, some time before the whole country was thus provided. Only during the thirteenth century were sheriffdoms created in the northern and western parts of Scotland.

The sheriff was the king's officer, normally chosen from among the moderately great men of the realm. Initially there appears to have been no established practice as to the term for which the office was held, but many sheriffdoms became hereditary; this was so at the beginning of the fourteenth century in Selkirk, Kinross and Cromarty, and the process continued, despite an attempt in 1455 by parliament to forbid any future gifts of office "in fee and heritage". The sheriff was permitted to appoint deputies and this soon became common practice; as time went on the heritable sheriff-principal became mainly a figure-head, leaving most of his duties to be performed by his deputies. These duties covered a wide

264

range, administrative, judicial, financial and military, for the sheriff was the normal local agent of the crown; many acts of parliament imposed on the sheriff the task of carrying out the measures they contained.

The principal judicial function of the sheriff by 1300 was to hold the sheriff court; in effect, within each sheriffdom it was the king's baron court. By the fourteenth century there were head, or full, courts three times a year at Yule (Christmas), Pasch (Easter) and Michaelmas (29 September) and these met at the caput of the sheriffdom. The sheriff usually presided in person, and all who owed suit of court were expected to attend. Here the more important cases were dealt with; if necessary a case could be transferred to it from one of the intermediate (or lesser) sheriff courts, which could be held at other places within the sheriffdom. These intermediate courts dealt with the more routine or trivial matters; the presiding officer was usually a sheriff-depute, and not all who owed suit were called on to attend these lesser sessions. Suitors were nevertheless necessary because by custom the power of making decisions rested with them, not with the holder of the court. Suit of court was a feudal burden but in the charters a distinction seems to be drawn between attendance at head courts, which was normally an absolute duty -- although it could be performed by proxy -- and at intermediate courts, which probably required due and specific notice. Not all tenants of the crown within a sheriffdom were required to perform suit of court. Those who held their lands in blenche-ferme, that is, for a nominal return such as 'a rose in the season of roses', were generally exempt, as were church lands in free alms, and exemption could be granted by the crown as a special favour.

The sheriff had both a criminal and a civil jurisdiction, but they were subject to certain limitations. In the criminal field he was not permitted to deal with the pleas of the crown; the evidence of Quoniam

<u>Attachiamenta</u>[1] suggests that the pleadable brieves of mortancestor, dissasine and breach of the king's protection (and possibly others) could normally only be pursued before the justiciar. Certain classes of person were not justiciable in the sheriff's court, most notably burgesses in matters of burgh law and those living within a regality (where the lord's jurisdiction excluded that of the sheriff); it was also possible to obtain exemption from the jurisdiction of a particular sheriff on the grounds of 'deadly enmity and feud' where there was an existing dispute or quarrel between an individual party and the sheriff.

Nevertheless, the judicial powers of the sheriff were extensive. Provided that the culprit was caught red-handed the sheriff's criminal jurisdiction extended in practice to murder and robbery as well as to all the lesser offences. As civil judge "the sheriff could decide actions of molestation, removing, ejection, spuilzie, and personal actions of all kinds; he could authorize poindings and apprisings; before him ... brieves of inquest, terce, tutory and idiotry could be served"[2]. In other words the sheriff could hear actions dealing with such matters as dispossession and distraint of lands and goods for debt, as well as brieves relating to a widow's claim to a liferent of a share of her husband's heritable property,

----------

1    A fourteenth century treatise on procedure, which will be discussed in the next section; chapters 49-57 in the version of the text printed by the Stair Society -- Volume XI -- deal with these pleadable brieves.

2    W. Croft Dickinson <u>The Sheriff Court Book of Fife, 1515-22</u> (Scottish History Society, 3rd series, vol 12, 1928), xxxviii and App. B. Brieves of right were also important in the shrieval administration of justice; v. H.L. McQueen "The brieve of right in Scots law" 3 <u>J.L.H.</u> (1982) 52.

and to the appointment of guardians for the incapable. The sheriff also had oversight of lesser courts within the sheriffdom and it was to his court that appeals came from these inferior jurisdictions. Moreover, in theory no baron could hold a court of 'life and limb' or resort to proof by ordeal unless the sheriff or his representative was present to see that justice was done and due process observed. And it was the sheriff who arranged the holding of the justiciar's court when he came on ayre and who presented for indictment all persons charged with those crimes reserved to the crown.

(iv)  Feudal courts and burgh courts

Built into the feudal structure was the right of a lord to hold a court for his tenants; it seems possible that in Scotland this right needed to be made explicit in each lord's charter. Like the sheriff the lord normally held three head courts a year; at these the business of his free tenants was settled. His lesser courts were usually manorial courts for those who held by unfree or non-feudal tenure. The lord or his baillie presided and his feudal tenants who owed suit of court attended the head courts to deliver their verdicts. Such courts dealt with matters related to feudal holdings and similar concerns and with such crimes as assault, theft and riot, which were not reserved to the crown.

As well as holding his feudal courts a lord might exercise a franchise jurisdiction (territorial rather than tenurial), just as in England grants were made of hundredal jurisdiction. The exact limits of such a grant would be defined in a charter, but they normally included sake and soke (as in England) and also the power to hang persons living within the franchise. From the early fourteenth century such a lord is described as

267

holding of the king *in liberam baroniam* (in free barony). Grants were also made *in liberam regalitatem* (in free regality), more extensive than free barony. Such franchises have been described as amounting to petty kingdoms, for the court of the regality might exercise a jurisdiction almost equal to that of the king and include the pleas of the crown, save only treason. As a result the king's writ did not run in a regality, which had its own chancery issuing its own brieves, and neither justiciar nor sheriff had jurisdiction over the lands of the regality or its inhabitants.

Burghs were towns which had been granted the special status of burgh by charter. When they first appeared in Scotland, during the twelfth century, they were always granted their status by the crown; later we find burghs holding of other lords, lay and ecclesiastical. To encourage the growth of trade they were accorded various rights and privileges, administrative as well as judicial. By the later Middle Ages Scottish burghs were largely self-governing communities, electing their own officers and employing their own seal in matters affecting the town. From the early fourteenth century they began to acquire feu-ferme status; the community would pay to its superior a fixed annual sum in place of the various negotiable individual burdens, of which the collection and payment remained the responsibility of the burgh officers.

Each burgh had its own court to which the burgesses owed suit; this burgh jurisdiction in many matters excluded that of the sheriff. The burgh administered its own law and customs, which might differ considerably from the general law of the land; for example, tenure of burgh land did not usually include feudal casualties of ward and relief. Burghs applied the common law too, hearing cases involving, for example, brieves of right and distress. Burgh courts were also concerned with matters of trade, such as settlement of disputes between merchants, the control of markets and the enforcement of standard weights and measures. From the burgh court appeals went to the king's chamberlain, who visited the burghs on periodic ayres. The chamberlain also presided over the Court of the Four Burghs which was composed of representatives from four towns, Berwick, Edinburgh, Roxburgh and Stirling; after 1369 when Berwick and Roxburgh were occupied by the English, they were replaced by Lanark and Linlithgow. The Leges Quattuor Burgorum (Laws of the Four Burghs) is a collection of material, some probably going back to the twelfth century; much of it was derived from the customs of Newcastle and general mercantile usage. It may never have been applied directly as burgh law but provided a model for the particular customs of individual burghs. The Court of the Four Burghs heard falsing of dooms from the chamberlain's jurisdiction and also disputes between burghs; doubtful points of burgh law could be referred there for clarification. Membership of the court was gradually expanded to include representatives of most of the Scottish burghs, and during the fifteenth and sixteenth centuries it became more a convention and less a court of law. The term disappeared in the early sixteenth century and the institution was replaced in the 1550s by the Convention of Royal Burghs, which thereafter represented the interests of the burghs.

(v)  Procedure in feudal Scotland

There were considerable innovations in legal procedure in Anglo-Norman Scotland, in particular the introduction of the inquest and the writ or brieve. It seems likely that, after the initial introduction of some English usages, the two kingdoms for a time followed a course of parallel development, with Scotland's borrowings from England being selective and adapted to its needs. The inquest was originally used solely on the crown's authority and to ascertain the extent of royal rights, in much the same style as for the compilation of Domesday Book.  The judicial use of the jury of inquest remained a royal prerogative in that it needed to be granted specifically to others -- usually for a price --, although this became a matter of course as a benefit for a litigant who initiated his action by the purchase of an initial brieve or writ from the royal chancery.

The Scottish brieve of right was the equivalent of the English writ of right, being the brieve which initiated process over title to land.  The English writ was only concerned with tenants-in-chief; there was an analogous writ for land held of some lesser lord.  Scotland knew only the one form (as far as we can judge from the records) which seems to have applied to tenants-in-chief; perhaps the same procedure was used for settling other disputes as to title.  The Scottish brieve of dissasine seems to have been a more general remedy than the English novel disseisin, since it did not incorporate a fixed term for the dispossession.  Similarly the Scottish brieve of mortancestor was a broader remedy than mort d'ancestor, not being limited by a fixed term and  coming to cover a wider class of ancestor.  The differences may be due partly to the utility of specifically Scottish brieves such as perambulation, and partly to the early technical development of English law with its professional bench and bar and highly skilled chancery clerks.  Scottish judges were largely untrained laymen, and the country lacked anything approaching an established central court until the fifteenth century.  In other words, circumstances led to an increasing divergence.

Procedure by brieve remained normal throughout the Middle Ages and a number of fourteenth century registers survive.  Brieves were still important during the fifteenth century but after 1500 the system began to decline. An act of 1491 restricted the categories of brieves to those then existing; no new forms were to be introduced. About the same time the brieve was beginning to be displaced by the summons as a means of initiating judicial process. In the courts based on the king's council, which were the ancestors of the Court of Session and which had in effect given Scotland a central court by the end of the fifteenth century, the brieve was never competent as a means of initiating an action. Even in those courts where the brieve was competent, it seems gradually to have given way to the summons via the brieve of citation; that is, a brieve which was initially designed to compel the attendance of witnesses gradually acquired the more substantive function of summoning the defender to court to answer the pursuer's allegations. The advantage of the summons was that the pursuer did not need to fit his case into the formula of an existing brieve; he need only state that he had been wronged, leaving the details of his claim until a later stage. Accordingly the mediaeval pleadable brieves eventually disappeared.

(vi) Early legal literature

It is clear that from at least the thirteenth century there began to appear in most European countries writings inspired by the learned law but dealing with local customs; we find the beginnings of national legal literature. Mediaeval Scotland shared in this movement, but scholarship has done less work to reveal the Scottish details than for the treatises of England or France or Germany. The two best known of the Scottish treatises, **Regiam Majestatem** and **Quoniam Attachiamenta**, are available in modern but unsatisfactory editions, while others, such as the **Liber de Iudicibus** (**Book of Judges**), remain unedited among the manuscript sources.

Regiam Majestatem (Royal Majesty -- the opening words) is essentially
a commentary on the procedures followed in the royal courts in both civil
and criminal matters.    It is heavily based on Glanvill but nevertheless is
more than a reissue of the English book for Scottish use.   A substantial
section is direct citation, but other material from Glanvill was adapted to
take  account  of  Scottish  conditions.     There  is  also  a  significant
proportion of the text which owes nothing to Glanvill; in particular, the
first dozen or so chapters seem in essentials original.   Much of Book IV,
which deals with criminal law and procedure, appears to have been drawn
from the statutes and assizes of the Scottish kings.   At the end of Book I
and the start of Book II comes a section dealing with pacts, arbiters and
arbitration, serfs, and gifts between husband and wife; this section has a
definite romano-canonical flavour and seems to have been drawn from the
canonist Geoffrey (Goffredus) of Trano.   The evidence for the direct
influence of Roman law, the law of the Corpus Iuris Civilis, as opposed to
a debt to other works which were influenced by civilian learning, is not
strong.   The opening words may reflect Justinian's opening of Imperatoriam
Maiestatem (Imperial Majesty) for his Institutes, but it is more likely
that they simply echo Glanvill.   Again, the argument that the division into
four books is a deliberate imitation of the structure of Justinian's
Institutes is weakened by an examination of the manuscripts.   The oldest
manuscript tradition reveals a division into three not four parts; the
fourfold division may well be due to civilian influence, but an influence
exerted much later than the original composition of Regiam Majestatem.   The
date of the treatise is problematical.   The better view is in favour of the
early fourteenth century -- fairly late in the European context -- for in
1318 the Scottish parliament enacted a number of reforming statutes dealing
with procedure by brieve which seem to be reflected in the treatise's

handling of the brieve of right in a manner suggesting that the passage is an integral part of the text and not an intruding gloss.

Associated with Regiam Majestatem and sometimes overshadowed by it is the treatise known from its opening words as Quoniam Attachiamenta (Since Attachments). Along with the Regiam it is referred to in a statute of 1425 as one of "the books of law of this realm", and it was still being so described in 1566. Quoniam Attachiamenta would appear to have been compiled somewhat later than Regiam Majestatem, probably at some time in the fourteenth century. Quoniam would seem to be an exclusively Scottish work, owing no obvious debt to any English treatise. Its subject matter is procedure but, unlike Regiam, the emphasis is on procedure in the baronial courts, and this presumably accounts for the alternative title found in some manuscripts, the Leges Baronum (Laws of the Barons). The compiler of Quoniam, as of Regiam, is unknown, but seems likely to have been someone involved in the practice of the courts which he described.

During the Middle Ages Scotland was to some degree affected by the revival of Roman law on the continent, but it was some time before its doctrines began to be of direct or substantial influence. The place of Roman law in Regiam Majestatem has already been dealt with. Some of the other mediaeval law tracts show their compilers' acquaintance with Roman law. The vocabulary used is often Roman — hardly surprising since Latin was the common language — and occasionally a distinction is drawn between the Roman and Scottish uses of a term; for example, Regiam notes that in Scotland the word dos (dowry) is normally used to mean "that which a free man gives to his bride at the church on the occasion of their marriage", whereas in Roman law it signified what in Scotland was normally termed maritagium — "the portion given to the husband along with the wife". Further evidence of a knowledge of Roman law is to be found in several of the charters preserved by Scottish monasteries, in the form of renunciations of Roman remedies and of pleas in defence. Among those which have been noted are restitutio in integrum, the provisions of the Senatusconsultum Velleianum, which prohibited a married woman from standing as surety for others (including her husband), and the beneficium divisionis, which provided that when one of a number of co-sureties was sued for the whole debt he could insist on his liability being limited to his proportionate share.

(vii)  The fifteenth century

A crisis over the succession followed the death of King Alexander III in 1286, and this led to the Wars of Independence when the Scots resisted the attempts of Edward I of England to impose himself on Scotland as the feudal superior of the kingdom.  For three hundred years England was the enemy, frequently at open war, and Scotland looked to the mainland of Europe for her political allies, and also for guidance on matters of law and legal doctrine.  There appears to have been some degree of economic and administrative confusion in the aftermath of the Wars of Independence, and the machinery of justice probably did not work so well in the fourteenth as in the thirteenth century.  The many statutes of the fifteenth century enjoining the regular holding of justice-ayres would suggest that the ayres, if held at all, were becoming by then more and more irregular; the repetition hints at non-observance.  Similarly, the pressure of judicial business experienced by the crown during the fifteenth century, when steadily more litigants sought a remedy in the king's court, may suggest that local justice was not being provided or being provided in less than an impartial way.  On the other hand, the preference for royal (and for ecclesiastical) justice may be attributable to its superior quality, as it adopted romano-canonical procedure and administered an improved substantive law.

During the fifteenth century parliament began to show an interest in reform of the law, in the administration of justice and in the substantive law. For example, in the law of leases at the beginning of the fifteenth century a tenant holding under a contract of lease had a personal right only; if his landlord alienated the land, the tenant was without protection from eviction by the new owner. In 1429 a tenant was given security of tenure for one year, unless the landlord required the land for his own use. In 1450 a tenant was given security of tenure for the currency of his lease, even when ownership of the land changed hands during that period. In 1469 it was enacted that a creditor of the landlord was no longer to be permitted to recover the debt by distraint of the tenant's goods or the tenancy itself. It looks as though the men who came to parliament were consciously pursuing a policy of reform in this field.

Parliament was also concerned to settle authentic and accurate texts of the law in force -- both recent statute and the 'auld lawes', that is, the various treatises and statutes of the fourteenth century or earlier. In 1425 a parliamentary commission was appointed to "see and examine the books of law of this realm, that is to say Regiam Majestatem and Quoniam Attachiamenta, and mend the laws that need amendment". In 1469 another commission was appointed to reduce "the king's laws, Regiam Majestatem, acts, statutes and other books" which were "to be put in a volume and to be authorized and the rest to be destroyed". Nothing concrete appears to have resulted, and equally vain seem other commissions appointed during the next century. In the later 1500s various collections of post-1424 statute law were published, but it was not until 1609 that a compilation of the 'auld lawes' was published by Sir John Skene and a useful hand-book for practice was thus provided.

The fifteenth century in Scotland, as on the continent, was a period when changes were taking place not only in the substantive law but also in the structure of the courts. The king's council in parliament, when sitting as the supreme feudal court, was competent to deal with questions of fee and heritage, whereas the king's council in the narrower sense was not; it has been noted that by the end of the thirteenth century parliament sat as a court of law, and in 1399 it was enacted that the king was to hold annual parliaments "so that his subjects be served of the law". During the fourteenth century delegation from the full parliament to auditors became regular practice in dealing with judicial business which was too lengthy or too trivial for the full parliament. By 1466 (when the surviving regular and official records of parliament begin) it was normal for parliament to appoint two judicial committees of auditors, one ad iudicia contradicta (for the falsing of dooms, or challenges to the decisions of lower courts) and one ad causas et querelas (for disputes and complaints -- cases at first instance). However, the competence of these committees lasted no longer than the sitting of the parliament which appointed them.

Matters which needed judicial redress when parliament was not sitting could not be ignored, and so the king's more permanent council had to deal with them. But it was concerned with the general business of government and had neither time nor established machinery for regular judicial sittings. James I, in his personal reign (1424-37), tried to deal with the problem by sending litigants back to the ordinary courts and making the council a tribunal of last resort. The pressure, however, continued and in 1426 parliament enacted that the chamberlain (or perhaps chancellor), and with him certain discreet persons of the three estates chosen by the king were to "sit henceforth three times in the year to examine and finally determine all and sundry complaints, causes and quarrels that may be determined before the king's council". In other words, a group of men was appointed to sit -- or to hold sessions -- to dispose of judicial business on behalf of the council; its jurisdiction was not as great as that of parliament.

There were modifications to the scheme in 1439 and 1456. There were to be three groups, each consisting of nine members; each group was to sit for a month, at first in Edinburgh and thereafter wherever it seemed most expedient; the judgment of such a session was exempt from appeal to king or parliament. Parliament continued to appoint sessions during the 1460s, but thereafter we hear no more of these particular judicial bodies. The repeated statutory appointment of sessions suggests that they were not intended to be permanent institutions. Even although they exercised a very wide jurisdiction, their existence did not mean the cessation of the work of the parliamentary auditors and of the council itself.

However, the jurisdiction of the parliamentary auditors did fade away in the later fifteenth century. The committee which dealt with appeals under the feudal process of the falsing of dooms gradually became redundant, as less cumbersome procedures developed which made it simpler for an appellant to bring his case directly to the council. The jurisdiction of the committee which heard cases at first instance was replaced by that of specialist lords of council whose availability to adminster justice did not depend on the sitting of parliament. By the 1460s the practice had grown up whereby actions started before the auditors which had not been brought to a conclusion before parliament rose were transferred to the council. In the 1490s the lords of council often joined the auditors towards the end of their sessions, with the result that the

277

jurisdiction of the latter almost imperceptibly merged into that of the former. When parliament appointed auditors in 1496 it was clear that they were simply those lords of council who dealt with judicial business under another name. Although auditors continued to be appointed until 1544, it appears that their appointment was purely formal and that no judicial business was conducted before them.

The council itself never ceased to hear civil causes, and in the later fifteenth century its judicial business seems to have been increasing steadily. Under James IV (1488-1513) attempts were therefore made to improve the administration of conciliar justice. In 1491 the chancellor, along with certain lords of council, was to dispense justice at three terms in the year; in 1495 a system was established whereby the council was to hear cases in rotation, according to their place of origin. By the early sixteenth century there were clearer signs of the later division of the council into the group forming the king's secret or privy council and the group composed of the lords of council and session. There was a tendency for some members of the council to hold sessions at fixed terms in Edinburgh for the disposal of judicial business, while the king and other members of the council moved around the country, also hearing cases as required but concerned too with general administration. In 1526, after the set-backs of the politically troubled early years of James V (1513-42), certain lords of council were again appointed whose only function was to "sit continually upon the sessions", that is, to deal with judicial business; in 1528 it was laid down that members of the council not so appointed were to be excluded from these sessions. Thus the 1520s saw the emergence of a specialized group from within the council whose sole and exclusive remit was to hear and dispose of civil causes. It was this group which in 1532 was transformed into the College of Justice and whose members, as lords of council and session, formed the nucleus of the 'new' Court of Session.


Further Reading:

W. Croft Dickinson "The administration of justice in mediaeval Scotland" 34 Aberdeen.U.Rev. (1951-52), 338

Scotland from the Earliest Times to 1603 (3rd ed., revised by A.A.M. Duncan, Oxford, 1977)

W.E. Levie "Celtic tribal law and custom in Scotland" 39 Jur.Rev.(1927),191

H. McKechnie Judicial Process upon Brieves 1219-1532 (Murray Lecture, Glasgow, 1956)

J.J. Robertson "The development of the law" in Scottish Society in the Fifteenth Century, ed. J. Brown (London, 1977)

P. Stein "The source of the romano-canonical part of Regiam Majestatem" 48 Sc.H.R. (1969), 107

and Stair Society publications (Edinburgh), particularly volumes 1, 10, 11, 20 and 23.

Chapter X

## HUMANISM AND REFORMATION

(i)  An outline of the sixteenth century

The sixteenth century was marked by a ferment of ideas, religious, political, cultural and commercial.  Of considerable significance were the growth of the nation state and the consequent rivalries between nation states, and the appearance of the policy of the balance of power.  The ideal of European unity disappeared, which is why subsequent chapters will look at the development of national law within France, Germany and Scotland.  Moreover, the nation state was built up around a strong central government (save in the Netherlands) and while powerful families of course survived, the independent feudal nobility faded before the concept of national sovereignty -- although 'absolute' governments did not appear until the following century.  Italy, whose cities had been the commercial, intellectual and artistic centres of Europe, declined.  Humanism, as the new intellectual tool for legal study, was a French and not an Italian phenomenon; hence we hear of the mos gallicus (French usage) in contrast to the mos italicus (Italian usage).  Italy's decline was also linked with the shift in trading interests from the city to the state and from the Mediterranean to the wider world of the Atlantic and beyond.

The expansion of Europe was in progress.  Vasco da Gama returned from his voyage to India in 1499, and Portuguese supremacy in the Indian Ocean was soon established.  In 1492 Christopher Columbus discovered America, thinking that he had reached the Indies;  Magellan's expedition circumnavigated the globe in 1519-22.  In 1519 Cortes conquered Mexico and in 1533 Pizarro conquered Peru.  The Spaniards viewed central and southern

America as their preserve, but in 1539-43 a French expedition under De Soto explored the lower course of the Mississippi; Cartier had sailed up the St. Lawrence in 1534. English seamen searched for the North-West and North-East Passages to the East and in so doing helped bring the Russian Empire (which was under the rule of Ivan the Terrible) into the reckoning of western European states. From the East, the Moslem Ottoman Empire under Suleiman the Magnificent menaced Christendom until the failure of the siege of Vienna in 1529; it remained a serious threat until the crushing sea victory by the combined Spanish, Venetian and Papal fleets off Lepanto in 1571, six years after the Turks had failed to win Malta from the Knights of St. John.

In 1494 the French invaded Italy and for the next half century or so the French and the Spaniards fought for domination there; in the course of these wars Rome was sacked by a mutinous imperial army. Charles I of Spain, elected Emperor as Charles V in 1519, succeeded to Ferdinand and Isabella (who had united the houses of Aragon and Castile) and thus to the kingdom of Naples as well as the Spanish American empire; he also succeeded to Maximilian and Mary who had united Austria and Burgundy. He was lord of nearly all western Europe, save for the Papal States, France, and the British and Scandinavian kingdoms. Within Germany, however, Luther distracted him from other concerns.

The Lutheran Reformation can probably be said to have started with the publication in 1517 of Martin Luther's 95 theses against indulgences. A number of his points were acceptable to the reforming party within the Church but their sum led to his excommunication in 1520; this was confirmed at Worms in 1521, at Charles V's first Imperial Diet. Thereafter Luther was protected by Frederick, Elector of Saxony, not so much for his principles as because the Elector wished to remain supreme within his own territories.  Wars and compromises followed each other in rapid succession until in 1555 the Peace of Augsburg settled the religious problem for Germany on the basis of cuius regio eius religio (whoever rules, let his be the religious faith) -- orthodoxy was to be laid down by the ruler of each state.  No account was taken of imperial institutions.  This was not a triumph for toleration; each ruler could choose to stay Catholic or to become Lutheran, and his subjects must conform, although the Peace granted them the right -- for a period -- of unhindered migration if they preferred to live under the other faith.  No third possibility was envisaged; this failed to take account of the religious movements in Switzerland, which was technically within the Empire but was in practice (since the Peace of Basel in 1499) an independent federation.

Ulrich Zwingli of Zürich was a friend of Erasmus and a humane man, but he developed views on doctrine which were beyond compromise, in abolishing the Mass and holding that Christ's Real Presence was diffused among all believers in their corporate act of worship at the Communion service. Within Switzerland the Zwinglian reform movement led to a polarization of attitudes and eventually war.  Zwingli was killed in 1531 when serving as chaplain at the Battle of Kappel between Zürich and the other Swiss cantons. Thereafter each canton agreed to decide on its own faith. Zwingli's successor, Heinrich Bullinger, was a man of some influence, particularly in England but also in Geneva.

It was to an already Protestant Geneva that Calvin came in 1536. Calvin was a Frenchman who had studied law at Orléans and at Bourges; his legal training marked his subsequent thought, in particular in his stress on the ruler as sole legislator.  His studies had been Humanistic as the lucidity of his Latin (and his French) showed; in 1532 he produced an edition of Seneca's De Clementia (On Clemency).  Forced to flee from France

282

when Francis I turned to a policy of persecution, Calvin found himself in Geneva where the Zwinglian reform movement was under way, supported by Berne. After a false start, he returned in 1540 and took control. From Geneva 'pastors' were sent out, first to other parts of French-speaking Switzerland, then to France and then further afield; John Knox of Scotland was such a pastor. Refugees came to Switzerland, and Calvinist communities came to exist in France, Scotland, and the Netherlands; in France Calvinists were known as Huguenots. Luther and Calvin held very different views, and the breach between the two churches was complete from 1566, after the Confessio Helvetica (Swiss Confession).

The Catholic Reformation started simultaneously with the Protestant Reformation; materialism in high places within the Church and a decrease in vocations to the priesthood were clear signs of spiritual decline which brought forth countermeasures, in particular the foundation of the Jesuit Order in 1534, officially recognized in 1540 by Pope Paul III. Christ had told his followers to be one, and nobody who held a position of religious leadership could feel that it was right for secular governments to decide the faith of their subjects. Many therefore felt that a General Council might be able to reconcile western Christendom and, despite some papal reluctance, in 1542 a Council was called at Trent (in northern Italy) to define dogma and to promote reform within the Church. It met in several sessions between 1545 and 1563. The main outcome was much greater centralization and uniformity within the Church, and a strengthening in particular of the position of the bishops who thereafter exercised much greater authority over the clergy and the liturgy.

Francis I of France had deliberately turned to persecution to suppress the Protestants, but one of the reasons for the difficulties (difficulties which proved insuperable) in reaching reconciliation through the Council

was the continuation of the wars between France and the Empire or, after
Philip II's succession to Charles V, between France and Spain. The Peace
of Cateau-Cambrésis in 1559 finally brought these to an end, but during the
celebrations Henry II of France died from a jousting accident. His widow,
Catherine de Medici, dominated the reigns of her sons Francis II (1559-60),
Charles IX (1560-74) and Henry III (1574-89); she tried to preserve the
power of the monarchy by balancing the various factions, in particular the
Huguenots and the extreme Catholic party led by the Guise family. For
thirty years France suffered from intermittent civil war, until a rather
more stable society emerged after 1589 with the accession of Henry IV of
Navarre, who became a Catholic soon after his accession; in 1598 the Edict
of Nantes formally granted a limited religious toleration. Henry, however,
was assassinated in 1610, a year after the de facto recognition of the
independent Netherlands.

The Netherlands had long been famous as an artistic and mercantile
centre; their position as feudal inferiors of the Dukes of Burgundy brought
them under the rule first of Charles V and then of Philip II of Spain.
Philip's attempts to suppress the spread of Protestantism there led to the
wars of independence, which began in 1566. William of Orange, the greatest
landowner in the Netherlands, emerged as the Dutch leader until his
assassination in 1584. Thereafter English aid supported the Dutch cause;
the failure of the Spanish Armada in 1588 was a victory for both of them.
The death of Philip II in 1598 allowed a subsidence from open war to uneasy
peace.


(ii) Humanism and its fifteenth century origins


Humanism as a new way of thinking became widely important in the sixteenth century, particularly in the field of law. Humanism marks the change from constructing law as a supportive framework for society, as the mediaeval scholars had done, to using law as a glass through which to view society; once the development of law had reached a certain stage the Humanists could invent jurisprudence, the critical examination of different ideals of law. Humanism was not the only intellectual movement of the period relevant to the history of law; the Protestant Reformation, with which Humanism in France had some links, also brought about considerable changes in the legal institutions of those countries which it affected.

Like the Renaissance in literature and the fine arts, the roots of Humanism were firmly in the fifteenth century. Both sprang from the new interest in classical and especially Greek culture. The fall of Constantinople in 1453 led to numerous Greek scholars seeking refuge in the West and to a heightening of interest in and a search for Greek manuscripts. The Greek fragments and constitutions in the Digest and the Code were restored, and the Novels could be looked at afresh. Important technical developments assisting scholarship were the invention of printing with moveable type and improvements in the supply and quality of paper.

Humanism was a whole style of thought, in effect replacing Scholasticism as the normal method of analysis and argument, whether in the field of Biblical studies (where important figures were Valla -- to whom we shall shortly come -- and Erasmus) or Greek literature (notable were Aldus Manutius, the publisher, and Marsilio Ficini) or politics (Macchiavelli and Thomas More) or Latin philology (where Valla and perhaps Politian were the leading figures). As a tool Humanism was well adapted to these areas of study because it approached them by the study of language and the history of words. This antiquarian and philological approach is the essence of Humanism. It involved a new way of looking at law because one of its most marked characteristics was its historicism, its awareness that anachronisms existed, that evidence must be weighed critically, and that social changes were complex. This sense of history contributed to the new attitudes; so did the technological advances of the past century or so, such as the mechanical clock, small arms, the quadrant in navigation and the combination of square and lateen rig on ships. These discoveries and inventions encouraged the individual to make changes in his environment and fostered a new belief in the power of the human mind, a feeling that progress was possible by purely human means.

The Humanists did not despise the past; indeed, they were fascinated by classical antiquity which they saw as representing their ideals. However, the reverse of this fascination was a lack of sympathy with the men of the Middle Ages who had distorted the surviving classical material for expediency's sake. By the fifteenth century Scholastic thinking was very prone to the citation of vast numbers of authorities, and little else; the Humanists rejected the piling up of authorities because it tended to stifle original thought. The new emphasis on individualism and on history was linked with the growth of the vernacular, of the Italian or French or German languages, whereas Latin (like Greek) was studied more and used less. This was both an outcome of increasing nationalist feeling and a factor which enhanced it.

Humanism was a style rather than a school; it did not immediately supersede traditional methods, and this was particularly true in the field of law. In Italy its intellectual implications had for centuries very little effect on practice; in Germany too the recently 'received' Roman law took root in its glossed form  and survived as the usus modernus Pandectarum (modern application of the Pandects, or Digest). It was in France that the new Humanist influence was most strongly felt (although

286

only slowly in the courts), and it was from France that the new ideas spread within northern Europe.

The first legal Humanist to achieve prominence was Alciatus, but he had forerunners.  Indeed Petrarch (1304-74), the friend of Cinus, is often held to have been the signpost to the future.  But the story so far as law is concerned really begins with Lorenzo Valla (1405-57), a rhetorician whose philological studies led him to an investigation of Roman law (as had happened with Irnerius).  Valla stressed elegance -- lucidity -- not merely as an aesthetic ideal but as an essential ingredient of understanding. Thus the Humanist approach to Roman -- and other -- law came to be known as the Elegant Jurisprudence; the lawyers of the new style were also sometimes known as I Culti (Italian for 'the cultivated' [lawyers]), which referred to the knowledge of classical civilization which they used in interpreting Roman law.

The concept of elegance was by no means incompatible with an interest in the application of law, but Valla's approach was a deliberate attempt to set Roman law in its historical context.  He tried to uncover the words of the classical jurists whose work had been distorted by the compilers of the Digest; he rejected much that was the basis of the daily practice of the courts because it was Justinianic.  Even more strongly did he reject the bulky mediaeval commentaries on and accretions to the Corpus Iuris.  The mediaeval jurists had liked to comment on D. 50,17 de regulis iuris (On maxims of law), which could provide handy catch-phrases for practitioners; Valla, with his philological interests, set a fashion in writing on D.50,16 de verborum significatione (On the meaning of terms).  Valla's rejection of Scholasticism in favour of a strictly historical approach marked the first step in the revolution of the study of Roman law.  In particular there was a growing interest in obtaining accurate texts of the legal as well as the literary sources.  Good texts could by this period be printed, and readily disseminated; textual criticism in the modern sense began to appear.

Angelo Poliziano or Politian (1454-94) followed in this field.  He was interested in the _Paraphrasis_ of Theophilus, the earliest and much enlarged version -- in Greek -- of Justinian's _Institutes_ by one of the compilers, but his greatest fame is that he was the first man who studied the Florentine manuscript of the _Digest_ in order to correct a printed edition. Not entirely surprisingly this manuscript had been regarded as something almost sacred, kept under guard and only brought out with special ceremony; thereafter it was also viewed more literally as a historical document.

(iii)   The French Renaissance

Andrea Alciato or Alciatus (1492-1550) went in 1508 to study law at Pavia and there attended the lectures of Jason de Mayno and Philip Decio. In 1511 he moved to Bologna where five years later he took his doctorate. He learned to admire the clarity of Justinian's _Institutes_ compared with the crabbed and complex mass of glosses and commentaries adhering to the _Corpus Iuris_, and in a simple reversion to the texts he wrote _Adnotationes in Tres Libros_ (_Annotations on_ [_the Code_], _Books_ 10-12).  He returned to Milan, where he practised as an advocate and continued writing.  His writings led to his being called to a chair of civil law at the university of Avignon in 1518.  There he introduced the historical method into the teaching of law, stressing the need for reconciliation between the two disciplines of history and law.  The economy and elegance of his methods, without the customary interminable recitation of older opinions, attracted students and created the _mos gallicus_ as a way of teaching law.  The old tradition had been very much one of working with static material; in their search for the historical origins of laws the Humanists made legal study more dynamic. Pomponius' fragment on the origins of law (D. 1,2,2) made a useful starting point. Zasius, the earliest German scholar to take an interest in the Humanist approach, who was very impressed by Alciatus' work and corresponded lengthily with him, wrote on this fragment. Zasius was a professional jurist who also wrote on feudal law, but he too denounced mediaeval and Tribonianic barbarisms; he saw law as springing from custom rather than from pure reason and so he falls within the historical school of law. However, Humanist scholarship was not sufficiently advanced for either Alciatus or Zasius to take a very critical view of the Pomponius fragment.

While he was at Avignon Alciatus met Guillaume Budé or Budaeus (1467-1540). Budé came of a legal family and had been sent to Orléans to study law but, unlike Alciatus who always gave credit to Jason among his teachers (while revering Politian and Erasmus as his masters), Budé held that his teachers had given him only a distaste for the subject. Nevertheless he recognized that the most impressive monument of the Romans was their law, and he agreed with Valla's views on the need to achieve accurate texts, particularly on material held to be so near to wisdom itself. In 1508 he produced **Adnotationes ad Pandectas** (**Annotations on the Pandects**) in which he attempted to recover the original texts; this work was much plundered by Alciatus. He was also interested in such topics as the extent of Greek influence on Roman law, the social and linguistic changes which had affected the law, and the question of interpolations. The notes and commentary of Politian on the Florentine manuscript were necessarily the foundation of his method, since the Florentine itself had not yet been published; for the rest, he resorted to intelligent guesswork. He was confident, if not always right, in his emendations since he relied heavily

289

on his knowedge of classical culture, of the poets and historians, some of whom were mentioned in the _Digest_. Like Alciatus he made much use of the work of less famous predecessors, but between them they made certain of the triumph of the new ways of thought. Budé was sophisticated enough to point out that Roman historians could be wrong, and that they relied upon each other and so could perpetuate fictions. His Humanist style of thinking saw contradictions not as dissonances to be harmonized -- in the Scholastic fashion -- but as historical evidence of conflict and change; he also frequently made comparisons between ancient and modern (French) institutions and practice. He was the better able to do this because for much of his life he was in the royal service as a diplomat, as _maître des requêtes_ (dealing with the petitions of persons privileged to be exempt from suit in the ordinary courts) and as hereditary royal archivist. It was probably due to Budé, who saw Alciatus as his successor in the task of purifying the _Digest_ of its corrupt passages, that Alciatus became professor at the university of Bourges in 1528 some six years after he had returned to practice in Milan.

At Avignon Alciatus had begun his commentary _On the meaning of terms_, and he continued publishing works on a variety of topics. He also gave numerous _consilia_ or opinions of which some 800 have survived; they dealt with municipal, canon, feudal and criminal law, with wills, contracts, privileges and civil procedure. Apart from his interest in literary history he saw the importance of inscriptions as evidence of Roman life and law, so that Mommsen, the great nineteenth century legal historian, described him as having laid the foundations for the science of epigraphy. At Bourges he continued his declared policy of going back to the sources and of clarifying the texts; for the rest of the century Bourges remained the most exciting institution for legal study not only in France but in all

Europe.

In 1532 Alciatus returned to Italy; he had found the political atmosphere in France uncongenial, for he was an avowed supporter of the Empire against Gallican claims and of papal supremacy in a city where Protestant reforming ideas were freely circulating. He spent the rest of his life in Bologna, Ferrara and Pavia, but his influence and that of others among the Humanists was minimal in Italy. There the Bartolist tradition survived almost unscathed in the field of private law -- Gentili firmly held the mos italicus superior to the mos gallicus -- although attitudes to the criminal law showed some awareness of Humanism. North of the Alps, however, his inspiration was prolific. His mind was analytical rather than systematic, exploratory rather than dogmatic, looking at the Corpus Iuris in its historical setting but accepting that it had a place in modern law for its equity and technical skills.

(iv)  The Elegant Jurisprudence of Cujas, Baudouin, Hotman, Doneau

Jacques Cujas or Cuiacius (1522-90) was probably the leading figure of his generation, although both Hotman and Doneau condemned him for being too idealistic. Cujas studied law at Toulouse under Ferrier, a former pupil of Alciatus who became president of the Parlement of Paris and chancellor to the King of Navarre. Cujas began his teaching career at Toulouse, although without a chair; his deep interest in pre-Justinianic sources of law was already apparent, and he produced a book on Ulpian. He moved in 1554 to a chair at Cahors and two years later he was called to Bourges to fill the chair left vacant by Baudouin's departure to Germany for religious reasons. He was not, however, happy in Bourges and soon moved to Valence. He spent a year based in Turin during which he visited other Italian cities to see

291

their methods of teaching and to examine the manuscripts in their libraries, although he did not have sight of the Florentine. He returned to Valence and then, disturbed by the troubles consequent on the Wars of Religion, went to teach at Lyon, Bourges again, Paris, and back to Bourges.

Cujas devoted himself primarily to the exegesis of the sources; he was helped by being able to use the text of the Florentine _Digest_ which had been published in 1553. He wrote commentaries on Papinian and worked on other individual jurists such as Africanus; he also wrote on the _Pauli Sententiae_. He published editions of other western pre-Justinianic law-books, the _Consultatio veteris cuiusdam iurisconsulti_ and the _Lex Romana Burgundionum_, and began on the _Theodosian Code_. He produced an improved version of the _Institutes_ after collation of the manuscripts, restored (along with Antonio Agustín) the Greek constitutions to the _Code_, revised the _Novels_ and discovered more of the _Basilica_. He was of some note as a feudal lawyer and wrote a little on canon law, but French national law was not of intellectual interest to him in its own right, although he made some comparisons between it and other legal systems; naturally he had to take it into account when, as any law professor might, he gave consultations. He never lost touch with the need for law to be tailored to fit the exigencies of practice; he is said to have recommended that students beginning their legal studies should learn to use the _Gloss_. His published work, however, was almost entirely concerned with the historical approach to the texts. He held that commentaries were often otiose and court decisions frequently biased for expediency's sake, but that rigorous textual criticism could reveal the true basis of the law. His search for interpolations revealed such substitutions as _traditio_ (simple delivery) for _mancipatio_ (formal conveyance), already obsolete when abolished by Justinian. He did not attempt, as did some of his contemporaries, to rewrite the _Corpus Iuris_ as it should have been done -- in the eyes of the Humanists -- but he helped bring into favour the Institutes; this was to have great effect on those who tried to systematize the law in the light of Humanist (and later) learning.

François Baudouin or Balduinus (1520-73) was a disciple of Alciatus. Early in his career he practised law in Arras and wrote on the custom of Artois; in the last five years of his life he was maître des requêtes to the Duke of Anjou, the future Henry III of France. He taught canon law at Paris and then civil law at Bourges, Strasbourg, Heidelberg and Angers (as he moved from orthodoxy to Calvinism, then Lutheranism and back to a resigned Catholicism), but it was specifically as a legal historian that he was most influential. In 1545 he produced the first history of Roman legal science, not just discussing the changes within the law of antiquity but taking the story down to his own day. His most important work was his Institution of Universal History. He wrote: "I have become aware that law books are the product of history and that historical monuments evolve from the books of law."[1] He emphasised that law was of merely antiquarian interest when it pertained only to the facts of a particular time or place, but that ancient law could retain legal authority if it was still relevant to modern social facts. He spoke of the importance of legal records, equating public documents with eye-witness accounts as superior to any other written evidence; he distinguished primary from secondary sources. He was a model of the Humanist interest in legal institutions, which led to the study of the public as well as the private law of Rome. His work, however, was soon followed and somewhat overshadowed by that of Jean Bodin, who is better known for his political philosophy.

----------

1    Cited by Kelley, p.131.

293

François Hotman (1524-90) studied law at Orléans and then became an advocate and lecturer in Paris; his Calvinism led to his spending his later life in Switzerland. He took the historical Humanist approach and found that it led him to reject the Roman law in its entirety as having no legal authority in France. He saw civil and canon law as the source of the chicaneries of the law courts, and he developed a myth of the pure and simple golden age of French law before the coming of writing. He therefore approved the mandatory use of the vernacular in civil law suits, which was introduced in 1539 by Francis I. He was important, along with other Humanists such as Dumoulin and Brisson, in the development of French national law.

Hugues Doneau or Donellus (1527-91) also became a Protestant and had therefore to leave France; he taught at Heidelberg, Leiden and Altdorf (the university of the territory of Nuremburg). He had a particular interest in the systematic application of the law and was more concerned than other Humanists with the meaning of the texts in their legal context within the _Corpus Iuris_. He saw the _Corpus_ not so much as a precious fragment of antiquity suitable for historical study as a body of law which could be made the basis for a systematic modern legal régime. He was thus closer to the _mos italicus_ than were most of his contemporaries, although with no hint of being subject to the legal order of the texts. His method was to follow the order prescribed by nature; he said that he put first that which naturally came first and continued in an orderly fashion thereafter. He began his great _Commentaries on the Civil Law_ (_Commentarii iuris civilis_) with a definition of his subject matter and then proceeded in roughly the order of the _Institutes_, although with much greater elaboration. Perhaps because he was inclined to be dogmatic, he had a great influence on later writers.

(v)  The techniques of legal Humanism


An important aspect of the Humanist revolution in law was its approach
to education.  One factor which profoundly affected this was the existence
of printing and therefore the existence of relatively cheap multiple copies
of published works.  The Humanists wrote to be read privately, and in their
lecturing they could refer students to the books, whereas the Commentators
had had to rely primarily upon oral transmission of their ideas and had, so
to speak, included their footnotes in their lectures.  The availability of
printed books was another reason why the Humanists could lay less stress on
the memory work of mastering the material in the Corpus Iuris and more on
developing ideas on the nature of law and its place in society. Elegance of
expression in teacher and student was viewed as essential in aiding clarity
of thought and ease of understanding.  The Humanists looked back to a lost
work of Cicero of which only the title has survived -- De iure civili in
artem redigendo (On reducing the civil law to a practical science) -- as an
exemplar of their task.

Many followed Doneau in criticizing the order of treatment in the
Corpus Iuris; one writer said:  "Although in terms of content there is
nothing more perfect than it, in terms of arrangement of the content there
is nothing more perverse."[2] There were some Humanists, including Cujas, who
defended the traditional order of the material and explained the historical
reasons why one topic followed another; nevertheless, it was increasingly
clear that the aspect most widely accepted as requiring renewal in the
treatment of Roman law was the presentation of its content.  Many of those
who suggested improvement were in favour of the order in the Institutes,

----------

2     Hilliger in Donellus Enucleatus (1611).

that is Persons, Things and Actions; Duarenus (Douaren), to whom Stair refers (in his _Institutions_ 1,1,17), recommended starting the study of law with a thorough grounding in the _Institutes_. The Institutional order was influential with the Natural Lawyers of the seventeenth century and the codifiers of the eighteenth because it seemed rational to treat legal problems by considering first the persons involved, then the substance of the legal relationship between them, and finally the means of enforcing rights and duties.

Another attempt at a fresh start was made by the German scholar Johannes Althaus or Althusius (1557-1638) who presented the law in a series of dichotomies; for example, he divided individual things into corporeal and incorporeal, and corporeal into moveable and immoveable, and so on. At the end of each chapter he listed the Roman sources from which he had drawn his material and in the body of the work he referred to other texts and other authors. He inspired no followers, however, and was much more influential as a political theorist.

Humanism implied a great admiration for classical antiquity -- and its languages --   and also the desire to recover as much as possible of the surviving evidence for that civilization. In the legal sphere this meant recovering not only the correct text of the _Corpus Iuris_ but also all legal material that dated from before Justinian, whether in the West or the East, and also using Byzantine texts to increase knowledge of Roman law. Unfortunately some Humanists were prepared to invent sources to justify their hypotheses. Alciatus, for example, gave no provenance for the MSS he alleged he had seen; such men "carried on introducing into the classical texts, under the banner of manuscript readings, the wilful, violent and arbitrary alterations which were the product of their conjectural fantasies. In so doing they succeeded in corrupting the texts to a degree far beyond the imagination of the most wooden-headed mediaeval scribe"[3]. Others, such as Politian and Agustín, were conscientious, and so was Gregor Haloander (1501-31) who produced the first new edition of the Corpus Iuris. He did not have access to the Florentine Digest; nevertheless his suggested emendations are much cited, as are those of Cujas, in the Mommsen edition which remains the standard version of the Corpus. The Florentine was first published in 1553, but the edition of the whole Corpus of Dionysius Gothofredus or Godefroy (1549-1622) was an improvement which until the later nineteenth century provided the standard working text. Some versions were produced with the text alone, others with Gothofredus' own notes and others again with the Standard Gloss attached; the last were most useful for practitioners because of the continued importance of the Gloss in the courts. His son, Jacobus Gothofredus (1578-1652), produced a learned commentary on and a critical edition of the Theodosian Code. Modern scholars must still take into account the work of the sixteenth century French Humanists, particularly as regards the surviving pre-Justinianic sources.

A related area which the Humanists began to investigate was the problem of interpolations, alterations to the classical jurists' texts introduced by the compilers of the Corpus Iuris. Various kinds of 'interpolation' were recognized: changes in terminology and style, illogical arrangement, the abolition of previous law or the retention of anachronisms, and abridgment. Some of the criticisms addressed to Tribonian and his colleagues were on the grounds that they had not been thorough enough in their updating of the law. The Humanists assumed less

------------

3    D. J. Osler — "Graecum legitur" 2 Rechtshistorisches Journal (1983) at p. 195.

often than do most modern scholars that pre-Justinianic law was necessarily better than that of Justinian's time. Their desire to uncover the different historical layers was often linked with the historicist view, which we have seen exemplified in Hotman, that law must be relative, itself changing with changing social and economic circumstances. Others held that the confusion caused by interpolations was the root cause for what they described as the barbarous and obscure attempts at explanation of the sources by the mediaeval writers.

Whereas Hotman took the practical line that where law no longer fitted the facts it was useless, others were more concerned to enhance the practical application of the texts by interpreting them with as full a knowledge as possible of the context in which they had been written. Thus scholars like Budé saw it as an essential part of the interpreter's task to bring to bear on the texts all knowledge of classical literature and civilization; to them it was a mark of barbarous ignorance to use the texts simply as they stood. This fault, along with an utter inelegance of Latin style, the Humanists saw as the greatest failing of the mediaeval jurists. It was even worse in the case of those of their contemporaries who persisted in error when they could rejoice in the light of modern scholarship; Accursius and Bartolus must be forgiven something for being men of their time and erring out of ignorance.

The desire to apply the texts without misunderstanding was only possible after the correct text had been established and its context revealed. A few Humanists were led by their classical studies to take a disparaging view of law as compared with other preoccupations such as the pursuit of literature or the exercise of military skill; Cicero had often been very rude about lawyers -- particularly in pro Murena. Others, as we have remarked, came to see law as relative; this may be some explanation of

298

why legal Humanism flourished in France, where the balance between the sources tilted less to the Roman and more to the home-grown than in Italy. There was considerable nationalist feeling in France, in legal and ecclesiastical as well as political matters. Humanist techniques were readily applicable to the development out of -- and therefore away from -- the ius commune towards national systems of law. Although the popular image of the Humanist is of a literary figure, many of the legal Humanists were lawyers concerned with practical affairs, trying to use the lessons of history to solve current disputes. Cujas' famous reply, when asked to make a definitive statement of his position in the religious strife of the day, that there was nothing relevant in the praetor's edict ("Nihil hoc ad edictum praetoris"), was not a widely found reaction; Cujas himself had views, even if he concealed them, but most of his contemporaries were prepared to express theirs publicly, and often.

To sum up, the Humanists were an important new influence on the study of Roman law partly because they saw that the term 'law' did not necessarily mean Roman law; many challenged the authority of Roman law as the unique guide to the solution of a legal problem. At the same time they expanded knowledge of what Roman law had actually been, and by rejecting it as the sole source (almost) of legal thinking, they opened a new way to seeing in it a source of principle. The wider scope which they gave to reason as a basis for criticising authority was also important in the growth of Natural Law thinking in its particular seventeenth century manifestation. Their discussion of educational method, including the order of treatment of legal material, led to substantial changes in the form of legal instruction and to a rational shaping of national law. Their nationalist feelings led them to encourage the use of native law for its relevance, and also the use of native languages in place of Latin -- a change less happy from the point of view of communication between scholars. In all these ways they had a profound influence on succeeding generations.

## (vi)  The Reformation in Germany and Switzerland

The Reformation also  had profound effects in changing the way people thought.  In mediaeval theory Church and State had been complementary, even if in practice Pope and Emperor had frequently disagreed about the proper boundary between matters temporal and matters spiritual.  Other rulers too had within their own territories rejected the more extensive papal claims, but a widespread ecclesiastical jurisdiction, centred on the Papacy, had been universally accepted.  The Protestant Reformation changed all this. Where the authority of the Papacy had been abrogated, what was to take its place?  Where in the reformed churches did authority lie?  What was to be their relationship with the secular powers?  The answers varied between Lutheranism and Calvinism and also more locally.

In Lutheran Germany the gap created by the repudiation of Rome was largely filled by the lay powers, whether princes or cities.  In Nuremburg, for example, the Reformation was accomplished by the city council; the local magistrates introduced the necessary doctrinal changes, and the consistorial jurisdiction formerly exercised by the bishop was taken over by the council.  This was quite in accord with the thinking of Luther himself.  He disapproved of democratic church government and considered it to be the duty of the prince to oversee reform, if only because of the extensive changes required in legislation and court structures.  He did not envisage that the lay powers would inherit all the duties of the Catholic hierarchy but only the administrative and judicial functions, leaving matters of doctrine to be determined and controlled by Scripture.  Since someone had to interpret Scripture, there was a tendency for the beliefs of particular Lutheran rulers to assume a greater influence than Luther himself might have wished. The princes for their part were not reluctant to take charge of ecclesiastical affairs; quite apart from their individual religious sentiments, this was another way to consolidate their authority and possibly to enrich their treasuries from the revenues of the old Church.

In the Lutheran states secular control of the church was achieved by means of the consistory, although the establishment of a consistorial system did not always immediately follow the Reformation; in some places it was not set up until the later seventeenth century. The consistory was a church court under the control of the secular ruler. Its members -- lawyers and ministers of the church -- were appointed by the prince; it met under his presidency, or more usually that of his deputy. (In the cities the municipal authorities took the place of the prince.) The business was essentially that of the former diocesan court. Thus the Lutheran reformation did not produce a fixed frontier between church and state; men still did not make a clear distinction between the spiritual and the secular aspects of daily life. In the Lutheran states the Reformation simply transferred many of the powers of the Catholic hierarchy to the lay authorities.

Matters were different in Calvin's Geneva. Calvin pursued an altogether more theocratic line than the German reformers. Aiming to imitate the early Church, he advocated independence from the state and at the same time emphasized the divine authority of the church's ministers. He opposed the exercise of ecclesiastical power by the lay authorities, holding that the spiritual jurisdiction must be independent of the lay power and that its authority was superior. Since concern for faith and morals could legitimize the church's intervention in virtually every aspect of civic life, the city council was slow to accept the full consequences of Calvin's doctrine.  In 1541 Calvin persuaded the city of Geneva to establish a body of regulations known as the Ecclesiastical Ordinances; these outlined his scheme of church government.  In the parishes laymen were to be elected as elders, disciplinary officials whose duty it was to supervise the morals of their congregation.  The main instrument of church government was again to be the consistory; this was to comprise the pastors of the city, together with representatives of the elders and the city council.  Calvin envisaged that the consistory would act as an independent court; the city council, however, sought to limit its powers.  To the text of the Ecclesiastical Ordinances the council added a clause:  "These arrangements do not mean that the pastors have any civil jurisdiction, nor that the authority of the consistory may interfere in any way with the authority of the magistrates and the civil courts."[4]  Only in 1555 did the consistory at Geneva acquire an unfettered right of excommunication and until 1561 the council managed to maintain the symbolic presence in the consistory of a magistrate acting in his civic capacity.  The difficulty was that of determining the scope of civil jurisdiction; we find the Geneva consistory giving "its opinions on the bank rate, on the level of interest for a war loan, on exports and imports, on speeding the law courts, on the cost of living and the shortage of candles.  On the other hand the council [sometimes]... may be found supervising the clergy and performing other functions which logic would have allotted to the consistory."[5]  The dichotomy between church and city council was not absolute; if all matters

--------

4    Chadwick, p.84.

5    Chadwick, p.86.

seemed grist to the consistory's mill, the magistrates were members of the Calvinist church, perhaps even elders.

It is therefore possible to argue that the Protestant Reformation did not reject the mediaeval notion of the oneness of life; it only removed the control of Rome. As in earlier times, the problem was one of drawing a boundary between the spiritual and the secular spheres. It was in these terms that there was a problem over the control of the Reformed churches -- and of Reformed society.

(vii) The Reformation in Scotland

In 1560 the Scottish Parliament enacted that "the bishop of Rome have no jurisdiction nor authority within this realm in times coming" and that "no bishop nor other prelate of this realm use any jurisdiction in times to come by the said bishop of Rome's authority". While it was clear that papal authority was abolished for the future, the Parliament did not say what was to take its place. Nor did the Act seem to strike at the consistorial jurisdiction exercised up to then by the Scottish bishops. In the decade which followed we find a number of individuals and groups acting in a consistorial capacity and so by implication laying claim to the old jurisdiction.

The Reformation did not mean the immediate abolition of the episcopate, and the Scottish bishops therefore continued to deal with the same types of business as before in their courts. During the 1560s Archbishop Hamilton of St. Andrews dealt with matrimonial causes, as the records show; in 1566 Queen Mary formally 'restored' to him his consistorial jurisdiction. The Protestant party was indignant, not so much at his continuing to act as because he had not accepted the Reformation and might therefore seem to be still acting under the authority of the pope. The exercise of similar jurisdiction by bishops such as Alexander Gordon of Galloway and Adam Bothwell of Orkney, who had accepted the Reformation, did not lead to similar objections. Indeed, the General Assembly, the supreme court and governing body of the Church of Scotland, is found hearing appeals from their decisions without any hint that there was any doubt over their right to hear such cases.

The Court of Session also dealt with consistorial matters in the years immediately following the Reformation. Its intervention was partly due to its desire to extend its existing jurisdiction but was also a response to the prevailing uncertainty as to where such cases should be heard. Kirk Sessions, as they were established, acquired a minor moral jurisdiction over their congregations, but this was no more than a replacement for the archidiaconal courts. A scheme to establish Superintendents to inherit episcopal jurisdiction at diocesan level was abortive. The General Assembly therefore petitioned the Privy Council to resolve the issue.

In 1564 the Commissary Court of Edinburgh was created with exclusive jurisdiction throughout Scotland in causes involving benefices, marriage and status. In lesser consistorial matters, such as defamation, the confirmation of testaments, and disputes arising out of agreements fortified by oath, jurisdiction was to be exercised in local commissary courts, of which the geographical spheres approximated to those of the bishops' officials. Existing commissaries and officials seem to have been empowered to continue in office; in 1566 it was enacted that vacancies were to be filled by the Crown on recommendation from the Lords of Council and Session. Appeal from the local courts lay to Edinburgh, and thence to the Court of Session. However, the concentration, especially of marriage business, on Edinburgh was disliked by many. The Presbyterian faction was unprepared to allow the state to have jurisdiction over questions pertaining to religion; they wished the church authorities alone to deal with marriage causes, and they also resented the commissaries because they did not owe their office to the kirk. Furthermore, until 1690 when episcopacy was abolished, the bishops were intermittently given the right to appoint commissaries, which the Presbyterian faction liked no better.

The later history of the Edinburgh and local commissary courts can be briefly stated. In 1609 an Act of Parliament permitted appeal from the local commissary courts direct to the Court of Session; as a result the Edinburgh court ceased to exercise its appellate powers, although they were not formally abolished until 1830, when divorce jurisdiction too was transferred to the Court of Session. In 1823 the local commissary courts were absorbed into the appropriate sheriff courts, and in 1836 the local jurisdiction of the Edinburgh court was transferred to the Sheriff of Edinburgh.

The commissary courts had not, however, inherited all the consistorial jurisdiction of the pre-Reformation church courts. The Presbyterian Church which was ultimately established in Scotland had its own courts. At parish level the Kirk Sessions to some degree overlapped with the local commissary courts, for we find them issuing decrees of adherence (an essential preliminary for divorce on the ground of desertion) and dealing with defamation and minor assault. In addition their moral supervision allowed them to impose suitable penalties for sexual misdemeanours, blasphemy, Sabbath-breaking and the like. If their investigations brought to light matters which were in any way criminal, prosecution in the lay courts normally followed; the ultimate penalty at the disposal of the Kirk Session was excommunication. So long as excommunication was accompanied by civil penalties such as forfeiture of goods and revenues, their coercive powers

305

were significant. However, by the end of the seventeenth century the civil authorities less commonly backed ecclesiastical censure with secular sanction, and the Toleration Act of 1712 (otherwise the Scottish Episcopalians Act 1711), despite opposition, removed the power to impose civil penalties. The established church could no longer discipline non-members, and thereafter the judicial and disciplinary role of the Kirk Sessions gradually declined. Above the Kirk Sessions were the Presbytery, the Synod, and the General Assembly. These bodies were the governing organs of the Presbyterian Church and so had (and to some extent still have) a judicial function. The General Assembly heard appeals from lesser courts; it was also a tribunal where ministers of the church could themselves be tried and, if found erring, deprived of their benefices or livings.

(viii)  The survival of the canon law

The Protestant Reformation affected the jurisdiction of the Church rather than its rules. Although there were major changes in doctrine, the only really notable change in areas where the average layman might expect to find himself in an ecclesiastical court was in the law of marriage. In England in particular the institutional changes after 1534 were small -- partly in reflection of the limited doctrinal changes. The structure of the Church continued functioning almost exactly as before, although it must be remembered that in 1529 Cardinal Wolsey, the Lord Chancellor, had been condemned by the King's Bench for misuse of his authority as papal legate. The Court of High Commission was established to exercise the former supreme personal jurisdiction of the pope, particularly in criminal matters; it disappeared in the 1640s. The Court of Delegates was set up to hear those appeals which would formerly have been heard by papal judges-delegate.

306

These were prerogative not common law courts, and they were staffed by doctors of civil -- but not canon -- law.

The Catholic Reformation -- which is a better name than Counter-Reformation -- sprang from the same roots as Protestantism when, by the close of the fifteenth century, entirely loyal and orthodox men within the Church were rejecting the prevalent abuses. The effect of the Protestant Reformation was to harden attitudes on both sides, in spite of the attempts to reach an accommodation made by some leading churchmen, such as Antonio Agustín, and some rulers, such as the Emperor Charles V and Henry IV of France. One lasting result of the reform movement within the Church was the compilation of an authoritative text of canon law. In 1563 a commission was appointed to review the existing sources, whether or not they had been printed, and to produce a definitive edition, free from error and omission. The influence of the Humanist way of thinking and the echo of Justinian's instructions to the compilers of the Corpus Iuris Civilis seem both to be present. The commission worked at Rome between 1563 and 1580 and in 1582 the results of its labours, the Corpus Iuris Canonici, appeared. The new text, composed of Gratian's Decretum, the Decretals (Liber Extra) of Gregory IX, the Liber Sextus, the Clementines, the Extravagantes of John XXII and the Extravagantes Communes, was sanctioned as the official text of the recognized sources by Pope Gregory XIII; it thus became the authorized version of the law of the Church, to be used in Church courts and in the universities alike.

The Corpus Iuris Canonici formalized canon law within the Roman Catholic Church; the rules were more definite thereafter, just as authority -- of the bishops and above all of the pope -- was stricter, but the substance was much the same. The same was true generally in the Protestant states. In most of these, only that part of the existing canon

307

law which ran counter to the Reformed religion was abrogated; not until the seventeenth or eighteenth centuries had most such states built up a body of native case or statute law on wills, marriage and status. Overt secularization was also a later phenomenon.

In Scotland, for example, some forty years after the Reformation Sir Thomas Craig, the feudist and forerunner of the institutional writers, wrote: "Notwithstanding that we have thrown off the papal yoke, the authority of canon law endures ... provided always that the rule of the canon law is consistent with the principles of sound religion" (Ius Feudale, tr. Clyde, 1,3,24). More than a hundred years after the Reformation Lord Stair wrote: "And so deep hath this canon law been rooted that, even where the pope's authority is rejected, yet consideration must be had to these laws, not only as to those by which church benefices have been erected and ordered, but as likewise containing many equitable and profitable laws which, because of their weighty matter and their being once received, may more fitly be retained than rejected" (Institutions 1,1,14). The Scottish institutional writers recognized canon law, like Roman law and feudal law, as having greatly influenced the development of Scots law, and many of its principles and rules were applied as part of that law. But canon law was received for its equity and expediency; it was not in itself authoritative.

In the field of marrige, for instance, the traditional rule of the Church, based partly on Roman law, was that the only prerequisite for a valid union was the consent of the parties — parties for whom there was no impediment; the Council of Trent required that valid marriage, in all normal circumstances, must be celebrated before the parish priest of one of the parties in the presence of at least two witnesses. This was, however, subsequent to the Reformation in Scotland; in Scots law consent continued to be "the one thing sufficient and indispensable" to the valid constitution of a marriage, as Baron Hume laid down[6]. Although there was a distinction between regular and irregular or clandestine marriage, as there had been in traditional canon law, the efficacy of irregular marriage was in no doubt, until the position was somewhat modified by the Marriage (Scotland) Act of 1939 which abolished two of the forms of contracting an irregular marriage, leaving only marriage by cohabitation with habit and repute (where a man and woman hold themselves out and are generally reputed to be married) as a form recognized along with regular marriage by the secular power. The canonical rules barring marriage on grounds of consanguinity or affinity up to the fourth degree of relationship could be inconvenient; in 1554 we find Archbishop Hamilton of St. Andrews complaining to the pope of the great difficulty experienced by those of good family in finding partners who were not related to them within the forbidden degrees. The point was taken up by the Reformers, and in an Act of 1567 a less restrictive law was put in force, based on Leviticus, chapter 18. However, the canonical view of affinity as equivalent to consanguinity was retained, and only in the twentieth century were the rules concerning the former somewhat relaxed.

Some abuses that the Reformers had condemned, such as abuses of the right of sanctuary or of benefit of clergy, were suppressed by Protestant governments; however, they were also largely curtailed by the Church itself and, after the sixteenth century, governments in Catholic countries had much less hesitation in legislating on matters once falling within the

----------

6    Lectures I in Stair Society, vol.5 (1939) p.22. This is why eloping young couples from England fled to Scotland, particularly Gretna Green, to be married.

sphere of the courts spiritual. Inadvertently but undoubtedly the labours of the proponents of the Protestant and Catholic Reformations led, not to the godly rule that they had hoped for, but to the secularization of the institutions of government.


Further Reading:

O. Chadwick  The Reformation  (Penguin, 1972, repr.)

J. Durkan  "Henry Scrimgeour, Renaissance Bookman"  5(1) Ed.Bibl.Soc.Tr. (1971-4),1

M.P. Gilmore  The World of Humanism (U.S.A., 1952, repr.)

Humanists and Jurists (Harvard U.P., 1963)

H.D. Hazeltine  "The Renaissance and the Laws of Europe" in Cambridge Legal Essays (Cambridge, 1926), 139

D.R. Kelley  Foundations of Modern Historical Scholarship (Columbia U.P., 1970)

History, Law and the Human Sciences (London, 1984)

Introduction to Scottish Legal History  (Stair Society, vol.20, Edinburgh [1958]), chapters 6,7,8 and 27

P. Stein  "Elegance in Law" 77 L.Q.R. (1961), 242

F. de Zulueta Don Antonio Agustín (Murray Lecture, Glasgow, 1939)

Chapter XI

## LAW IN GERMANY

(i)   Law in Germany before the Reception

The struggle between the Papacy and the Emperor Frederick II destroyed
as events were to prove the effective power of the Empire. The later middle
ages in Germany were marked by an accelerated political fragmentation into
principalities, semi-independent states, free cities and the territories of
the lesser nobility. The imperial dignity remained elective not hereditary,
and the emperors, therefore, during their tenure of office, were more
interested in advancing their own dynastic interests than in establishing a
genuine imperial government. The _Reichstag_, or imperial diet, had no power
to enforce any acts it passed; the mediaeval _Reichshofgericht_, or imperial
court of justice, known since 1415 as the _Kammergericht_, was rendered
impotent by the widely granted privilege of exemption from its
jurisdiction. It was in the principalities that the future of effective
government lay.

The privileges of the princes largely originated in the emperors' need
to obtain support for their ambitious policies in Italy and elsewhere
beyond the German frontiers. The Emperor Frederick Barbarossa had
confirmed the status of his greater feudal magnates as a distinct, and
closed, estate of princes. Frederick II accorded to the ecclesiastical
princes extensive rights within their lands; in 1232 these rights were
extended to the lay rulers by the _statutum in favorem principum_ (statute in
favour of the princes). In 1356 the Emperor Charles IV issued the Golden
Bull, ostensibly to regulate imperial elections, in practice recognising
the _de facto_ independent authority in all matters of the seven imperial

electors[1]; these privileges were later extended to all the German princes. The grant de non appellando meant that no subject of an elector could appeal to, and the grant de non evocando meant that no such subject could be called upon to answer before, any court outside his lord's territory. Furthermore, conspiracy against an elector was to be rated as treason; the electors thus enjoyed sovereign rights.

When Charles V was elected Emperor in 1519 it seemed that he might be able to restore the imperial authority because his many other territories did not leave him dependent on the princes. However, his lands were too vast; the problems they posed were too numerous and too pressing for any one of them to be dealt with effectively. In Germany the Reformation brought about uneasy compromise. The outcome of the Peace of Augsburg in 1555 was the addition of religious division to an already divided Germany. The fundamental problem of the relations between emperor and princes was left in abeyance, and the Empire remained a loose confederation of autonomous states. Thus, although there were probably no more different customs in relation to every ten thousand people in mediaeval Germany than there were in France, these customs could not readily be collected into family groups, whereas the French crown worked steadily towards uniformity. Imperial law-making and justice hardly existed in later mediaeval Germany. Such legislation as there was dealt with the preservation of public peace and the suppression of private warfare; in the Reichshofgericht justice was available but little wanted.

----------

1    The prince-archbishops of Mainz, Trier and Cologne, the count palatine
     of the Rhine, the duke of Saxony, the margrave of Brandenburg and the
     king of Bohemia. (The duke of Bavaria became an elector after the
     acquisition of the palatinate in 1648.)

In this patchwork of localized and diverse bodies of custom, unco-ordinated by any judicial hierarchy, the court of each community developed and applied its own customary usages, without any concern for a broader systematic whole. The situation was further complicated by the fact that 'community' in this context was not necessarily geographical but covered a community of interest. Thus alongside the local territorial law, the Landrecht, there existed other bodies of law applicable on the principle of personality of law to various social groups which were united by status rather than physical proximity. The feudal law, the Lehnrecht, remained distinct from the territorial law; feudal tenants owed suit to their lords, to the extent of the latter's franchise. Similarly, unfree tenants were subject to the jurisdiction of their lord's manorial court, which applied the Dienstrecht. There had been nothing unusual about this in the thirteenth century, but only in Germany was this state of affairs permitted by default to survive unchecked into the fifteenth century.

In most jurisdictions there were Schöffen courts, courts presided over by a judge, usually the lord, but in which decisions were given by a panel of law-finders (Schöffen), laymen of the district or suitors to the court who normally enjoyed appointment for life. The law applied was usually unwritten, and the findings of the Schöffen were based on their collective memory modified by considerations of practical common sense. Their justice was thus flexible but unrelated to the growth of written law elsewhere. They had not developed skills in interpreting previously established objective criteria nor in understanding the systematic implications of each decision. The Stadtrecht (town law) worked with similar courts, although the positive law administered there was sometimes influenced by mercantile custom. Urban jurisdictions started as privileges granted by feudal lords, but the major cities acquired practical autonomy both in their courts and

313

in their right to legislate for themselves. Among the cities there was, as we have seen, more extensive grouping than in the territories of the princes and lesser lords; the existence of leagues, such as that of the Hanse in north Germany, and the development of 'daughters', taking their law from a mother city such as Magdeburg or Lübeck, led to some degree, if not of uniformity, then of compatibility of law, and written law at that.

In Germany, therefore, law was fragmented and uncoordinated, but this was not of itself discouraging for the future of the indigenous law; in France both Roman law and native customs made their own contribution to the emerging national law in the early modern period. The extent of the eventual reception of Roman law into German practice at the expense of the native Germanic law is difficult to explain — after all, in England it was the other way round. The superior attraction of written as against largely unwritten law is certainly relevant, but some written law emerged throughout all Europe in the thirteenth century, even in Germany. The most famous and influential of the privately compiled treatises which appeared in Germany was the Sachsenspiegel (Mirror of the Saxons), composed in the first half of the century by one Eike von Repgow. Eike's experience of law was as a Schöffe; his purpose was to expound the traditional law of Saxony as handed down through successive generations. The treatise therefore deals generally with Saxon law but more particularly with those areas within Saxony with which Eike was most familiar. He wrote of both territorial and feudal law, each treated separately in its own book, as was fitting for the subject matter of separate courts. Eike originally wrote in Latin, but later produced a German version of the treatise; it was subsequently translated into a number of other German dialects.

In the courts of Saxony the Sachsenspiegel soon came to be treated almost as if it were an authoritative text; like the Leges Henrici Primi in

314

England it acquired the myth of a royal and legislative origin. Throughout Saxony it provided a basis for development and gave life to the law of the whole region. During the fourteenth century it was glossed on a number of occasions, either in whole or in part, and supplements to it, especially in the form of manuals of court procedure, were produced. It provided a focus for all the courts of Saxony, so that there was a counter to legal particularism; its existence and use probably explain why Saxony was one of the areas in Germany least affected by the Reception of Roman law.

The Sachsenspiegel's influence in other parts of Germany is evidence of the widely-felt desire for written law and also for the synthesis of such law into more than localized usage. The Spiegel der deutschen Leute (or Deutschenspiegel -- Mirror of the German People) of the mid-thirteenth century relied heavily on the Sachsenspiegel; as its title suggests it attempted a synthesis of German common law, which was doomed without an effective superior court. Towards the end of the century there appeared the Kaiserliches Land-und-Lehnrecht (Imperial Territorial and Feudal Law -- also known as the Schwabenspiegel, Mirror of the Swabians) which also was heavily based on the Sachsenspiegel but again had a synthetic intention. This compilation and the Sachsenspiegel itself were revised and adapted on a number of occasions for use in particular areas.

In many parts of Germany the desire for the certainty of written law was met by the Weistum, the declaration of existing local custom, usually by means of a sworn inquest. The procedure was well suited to such matters as establishing the feudal and customary usages of a particular manorial court, and so mostly dealt with law at a very local level. It ameliorated rather than cured the problems created by the fragmentation of jurisdictions, but the Weistümer were useful if only because they were in writing. They recorded usages well enough established to have achieved the status of legal rules and gave for the future an objective statement on matters potentially productive of dispute. They remained, however, little codes of laws, not of law, unstructured and unsystematic. To blend them with the learned law, as feudal law had been and as was done with native law in France, the application of trained juristic skills was necessary, and these were never brought to bear.

In the towns too the inquest was often used in the process of reducing custom to writing; sometimes a town might order its officials to compile a law-book which would then be ratified by the oath of the citizens. When the greater cities acquired the 'elective right' to legislate for themselves they could proceed without reference to their overlord and could also introduce new custom when they codified their law. A legal literature devoted to town law appeared, comparable to that dealing with territorial and feudal law. In Saxony, perhaps because of the Sachsenspiegel, such treatises were produced early, and they also aimed at a certain generality. The Sächsische Weichbild (Saxon Precinct) and the Rechtsbuch nach Distinktionen (Lawbook according to Distinctions) were not limited to the law of one city alone but attempted to give a review of town law throughout Saxony.

As mentioned in the chapter on the ius commune, within a family of town law the court of a daughter town, faced with a new or difficult problem, might refer it to the court of the mother town where the Schöffen would hear the case sitting as an appeal court, an Oberhof. In the earlier fourteenth century it was only function which distinguished these sessions of the court from its regular sessions but, as the practice developed, it became common for the Schöffen to divide into two bodies, one dealing with local disputes, the other appellate. The business of the Oberhof was not the retrial of questions of fact but guidance on points of law. Written summaries were sent to it, and its answers were given on the assumption that the allegations were correct. Furthermore, because the duty of the Schöffen was to find the law not make it, their answers were usually terse, without a statement of how they had reasoned to their conclusions. Nevertheless, the existence of precedent books in various cities implies a concern for certainty and for a degree of systematic consistency.

Although the Oberhöfe were able to transcend merely local jurisdictions, they were not really in a position to provide for Germany the nucleus of a system of indigenous law. They were concerned only with town law and their activities had no effect upon the law administered in the territorial and feudal courts. Moreover, the very fact that families of town law crossed territorial and regional boundaries within Germany and even extended across frontiers into Polish, Swedish and other Baltic territories, meant that they would be unacceptable to princes who were trying to consolidate their rule within their own territories. Indeed, as the princes strengthened their courts they came to regard references from cities within to cities outside their lands as derogating from their authority. Accordingly they tried to limit the practice; as early as 1432 the Elector of Saxony forbade any subject to seek legal advice from outside the duchy. Similar provisions were enacted elsewhere in local as well as princely courts, but such restrictions did not become very effective or widespread until the emergence of absolutist government after the Thirty Years War (1618-48). By then the Oberhöfe were in decline both for political reasons and because of the economic devastation of the War, and the restrictions were chiefly aimed at the Aktenversendung procedure -- to which we shall shortly come. Nevertheless, the process of limitation had started in the fifteenth century and in the event made the way clearer for the reception of Roman law.

## (ii) The Reception of Roman Law

We have considered in the context of the ius commune how Roman law, as modified by the Glossators and Commentators and blended with the canon law, was absorbed into the legal systems of Europe in the later middle ages, except in England and, in a different way, in Germany. In Germany men had for centuries been studying law at university, and from the middle of the fourteenth century they had been able to do this within the Empire. But these men had gone on to serve in the government of Church or state, not to become a professional judiciary. When Roman law was finally received into the practice of the secular courts it was as a flood, overwhelming what was previously there, not the persistent trickle we find in France or the constant stream in Italy. It caused a break in the potential legal development of German common law (Gemeines Recht), and so aroused passionate responses, even into modern times. That is why, although the term is used for the adoption of Roman law by the Visigoths or the Burgundians in the fifth and sixth centuries and for the influence exercised by Roman law after the rediscovery of the Digest, the Reception refers to the authority given to Roman law by the German princes when it was accepted in its entirety as a common, if subsidiary, source of law.

To some extent there had been a much earlier reception of Roman law, in the deliberately fostered notion that the Holy Roman Empire was the continuation of the Roman Empire and that its emperors ruled in succession to those of Rome. As we saw, at Siena where Roman law was the custom of the city, Otto the Great was held to have added trial by battle to the general law in the tenth century; Otto III and Conrad II had both encouraged the concept of continuation. Frederick Barbarossa had not merely approved the revival of the study of Roman law at Bologna but had added some of his own enactments to the Novels of Justinian. In the sixteenth century the myth was created that Lothar III had prescribed the teaching and application of Roman law within the Empire at the request of Irnerius (or of the Countess Matilda of Tuscany). This theoretical reception was argued as immensely important by the proponents of the Roman as opposed to the German party when the codification of German law was under consideration, but it had no real basis in practice; the emperors in their struggles with the papacy or the princes or the king of France had sought support from the texts on the powers of the ruler, but they had shown little concern for the private law as it affected disputes between citizens. Far more important in actuality for preparing the intellectual climate were the pervasive influence of the canon law and the ecclesiastical courts and also the revival of interest in all aspects of antiquity which is associated with the Renaissance.

There were already traces of Roman law thinking in Germany. Johann von Buch's gloss on the Sachsenspiegel compared Saxon rules with those of Roman and canon law. Both the Deutschenspiegel and the Schwabenspiegel showed signs of a knowledge of Roman law on the part of their compilers, together with a willingness to make some use of it; they were in the same tradition as Beaumanoir in France or Regiam Majestatem in Scotland. In the Klagenspiegel (Mirror of Actions) of the early fifteenth century considerable use was made of Roman law; its terminology was used to describe Germanic institutions and particular attention was given to the rules of Roman procedure. Even apart from the major works on romano-canonical procedure there were manuals specifically adapted for use in Germany, such as the Speculum Abbreviatum (Mirror Abbreviated -- a fourteenth century précis of Durantis' Speculum iudiciale) or the mid-fifteenth century Vocabulary of Jodocus, which gave a simple explanation of

319

Roman and canonical terminology.

The German universities, or rather, the universities within the Empire, were originally created as centres of theological studies. The emphasis in their law schools was on canon law and on the needs of the Church; the Protestant Reformation destroyed the career prospects of many such graduates. Some of the more recent universities, such as Basel (1460) or Tübingen (1477), had chairs of Roman law from their foundation, and similar chairs came to be established at other universities, sometimes for political reasons, sometimes because of the religious troubles. Yet until the princes created the courts for their graduates to staff, the academic contribution to the application of Roman law seems more passive than active — responding to a growing preference rather than seeking to impose the learned law.

Canon law procedure had long been established in the ecclesiastical courts. This procedure relied on written pleadings and rational methods of proving disputed facts; its appellate process involved a reasoned and wide-ranging review of the issues in contrast to the 'false judgment' procedure of the essentially feudal lay courts. It required skill and learning in the framing of its processes and the disposal of its business; precision both of thought and of expression was necessary to clarify and distinguish the legal rules and concepts of which it made use. The terminology of the canonical system was, naturally, Roman and when further definition or elaboration was needed it was simple to resort to Roman doctrines. While delays might result from the attempt to balance all possible interests of the parties, the courts spiritual offered in general a more attractive justice than the less articulate or subtle Schöffen. We have seen that romano-canonical procedure began to be adopted by the princes for their superior courts in the latter half of the fifteenth century. If the preferences of litigants were leading them to the ecclesiastical courts because of the efficiency of the procedure, the princes could only recover the business they were losing by offering equally attractive justice. The increased availability of the new procedures in its turn served to confirm litigants in their preferences. Cities like Frankfurt-am-Main soon followed the example of the princes; most others took longer to respond to the pressures. Gradually, however, legally trained men serving as town clerks or civic notaries were called in as assessors or advisers to the lay tribunals, and steadily the effective power of issuing judicial decisions passed to them.

(iii)   The Reichskammergericht

Although the Reichshofgericht (and then the Kammergericht) was a court of very limited effectiveness because of the many privileges of exemption from its jurisdiction, it was nevertheless the supreme court within the Empire; it was important as a symbol or model even when it lacked the power to entertain cases or to enforce its decrees. The compiler of the Klagenspiegel, for example, lamented the troubled state of Germany and saw the remedy as lying in the provision of a certain and uniform law, adequately enforced. His concern was fairly typical, and under the Emperor Maximilian I (1493-1519) attempts were made to strengthen the imperial position. In the legal sphere the principal act to this end was the establishment in 1495 of a refurbished imperial court of justice, the Reichskammergericht.

The new court consisted of sixteen voting members under the presidency of a single director. Initially it was laid down that half of the sixteen were to be drawn from those of knightly or higher status and the remaining half from those 'learned in the laws'. In 1521 the representatives of the nobler classes were required, if possible, to have received a legal education; in 1548 legal training became a mandatory qualification for all members. In 1530 the court was divided into three divisions or senates (this number varied from time to time thereafter) in order to deal more promptly with the cases coming before the court. The sixteenth and seventeenth centuries saw further changes in the composition of the court, mainly occasioned by a considerable increase in business. The presidency was ultimately shared by four directors, and the membership of the court reached fifty in the mid-seventeenth century. It proved difficult, however, to attract suitably qualified men because the imperial treasury was constantly short of funds; the number of judges was usually below the full strength. The court's business was mainly appellate but it remained the tribunal of first instance for tenants-in-chief of the emperor.

From the beginning the Reichskammergericht was instructed to use a written procedure. This did not necessarily mean romano-canonical procedure but, in view of the composition of the court, it was the obvious way to develop. An elaborate and written mode of process, based on the ecclesiastical system, soon came into use. Further, the court was also instructed to judge in accordance with the "common law of the Empire" as well as with such "righteous, honourable and practised ordinances, statutes and customs of the principalities, seignories and courts" as might be brought before it. Here the "common law of the Empire" meant Roman law, which thus received formal recognition as, at the very least, a general subsidiary source of law. In practice the place of Roman law was more central; an imperial appellate court could not be expected to have judicial knowledge of the law and customs of each dispute's place of origin. If local law was to be taken into account, it had to be specifically drawn to

322

the attention of the court and the judges had to be satisfied that the particular provision was indeed as alleged. Roman law required no such proof; it was by definition within the knowledge of the court and so was normally applied unless displaced. Even when a local rule was established the learned judges were likely to interpret it in the light of Roman law, as had happened during previous centuries in Italy.

The **Reichskammergericht** was thus very much a court of the civil law, but it was much less effective than the **Parlement** of Paris, let alone the English central courts. It was expensive and inclined to be slow, and it lacked the power to enforce its decrees. Furthermore, as had happened with the mediaeval **Reichshofgericht**, privileges of exemption ate at its jurisdiction. The Reformation brought problems of distrust or enmity between Catholic and Protestant members of the court, as well as for parties before it. The ultimate control of the court established by the pro-imperial Catholic faction made Protestants less ready to resort to it. Then again, most of its business was of a public nature, dealing with keeping the peace and the like, and relatively little concerned the potentially receptive field of private law. Thus the immediate importance of the **Reichskammergericht** did not lie in the direct impact of its jurisprudence on German law, but in its provision of a model to the princes.

As we have seen, some appellate courts staffed by doctors of law had been established in the half-century preceding 1495 by such great princes as the dukes of Bavaria and Saxony. The era of the Reception in Germany was also the era in which the territorial rulers within Germany were trying to expand their powers and to consolidate their government; an increasing control of the administration of justice was simply one aspect of this particularist centralization. One approach was to limit resort to foreign

323

Oberhöfe or to restrict the Aktenversendung procedure; another was to set up their own appellate courts. As yet the princes as a class were not strong enough to gain control of the lesser territorial and feudal courts within their realms. The new imperial court provided a stimulus and an example. The princely high courts adopted romano-canonical procedure in both imitation of and rivalry to the Reichskammergericht. As had happened earlier and elsewhere the procedure was attractive to litigants, and the princes were usually in a position to enforce their decrees. The attraction of the new courts led to an increase in business, and this led to a need for more skilled men to staff them -- and to a closer link between the courts and the law faculties of the German universities. The superior technique and professional training of such men reinforced the Roman element in the law administered by these courts, although local custom had more weight at princely than imperial level. In Saxony in particular the tradition of the Sachsenspiegel prevented a complete romanization of the courts and the law they dispensed. The Leipzig court was certainly staffed by men trained in the learned law but they used a simpler written procedure than that of the Reichskammergericht and they had judicial knowledge of Saxon custom. In Saxony they borrowed from Roman law but they were able to blend it with indigenous law. Collections of decisions in the Saxon courts were published; for example, Benedikt Carpzov (1595-1666) in 1642 produced Responsa iuris electoralis (Answers on the Law of the Electorate). Nevertheless, at one tier below the imperial government, the princely courts of appeal were also a force for the reception of Roman law.

The influence of the Reichskammergericht became more widespread as lawyers throughout Germany came to a fuller knowledge of its proceedings; during the sixteenth century reports of the work of the court began to appear in print. The court had early realized the desirability of keeping some sort of written record of its activities, although this was as much to safeguard the position of the judges as to develop legal thinking. The court was subject to visitation by imperial commissions with power to review its decisions and, if necessary, to remove judges; the latter was a power seldom exercised, but it lent considerable weight to the commissioners' enquiries. Furthermore, in 1532 the judges were made personally liable to litigants for bad decisions, defined as arising from judicial corruption or partiality. Thus the early records were intended to protect judicial interests, not designed to publicize their decision making. Indeed, originally, like the judges of the French _Parlements_, the judges of the _Reichskammergericht_ were required to swear an oath that their reasoning, their 'mystery', should be kept secret. However, as in France, the pressures towards publication were stronger than those towards concealment.

In 1563 Joachim Mynsinger von Frundeck, a judge of the court between 1548 and 1555, published a volume of reports, entitled _Observations_. He was a doctor of law of noble birth, a former professor of Roman and canon law at Freiburg and before that a student of Zasius. He himself had participated in some of the decisions which he reported; others he took from the court's records. There was alarm that public confidence in the court might be destroyed, but his reports reflected well on proceedings there, and the volume proved very popular; it ran to twenty-one editions and was in print for a hundred and fifty years. Another former member of the court, and a graduate of Bologna, Andreas Gail, in 1578 published his own _Observations_, based on his experiences; this publication was welcomed, due to Mynsinger's work. Although the two books had the same purpose, the earlier volume was condensed and analytical, whereas Gail's was Bartolist in approach and, despite its lengthiness, it proved more popular. The publication of these and similar works did much to restore a degree of prestige to the Reichskammergericht by organising the mass of civilian learning for that court to use and others to copy. After about 1600, however, a new form of report began to appear, produced not by former judges but by lawyers practising before the court; these contained much more detail on the procedural stages of the cases reported, although many of these will have been conducted in private. Clearly, many persons had access to the official records. Moreover, after 1654 each judge in a case was required to furnish for the record a written statement of the reasons for his decision, and these too were added to the reports. The Reichskammergericht, although still slow and ineffective, "acquired a kind of leadership in the development of law through legal decision. ...the court had become a source of applied legal doctrine that was at least thought worthy of study by lawyers."[2]


(iv)   Aktenversendung and the universities


The universities played a very important part in the development of law in Germany after the Reception. In a manner similar to the obtaining of opinions from the Italian doctors, judicial consultation of the legal experts led to further interpretation of the civil law for the needs of practice. Such consultation was encouraged by an imperial statute, the Carolina, of 1532, to which we shall return. It contained in more than thirty of its clauses the instruction that in cases of doubt advice was to be sought by the courts from 'those who know the law'. The Carolina dealt

-----------

2    Dawson, Oracles, 226.

with criminal law and it did not prescribe the consultation of civilians alone, but it gave imperial sanction to the usage.

For much of the sixteenth century the consultation was of individual jurists; for example, in 1538 there was published a volume of the consilia of Zasius, although he had died three years before. There developed, however, the practice of submitting an issue for the collective response of a university law faculty, and this became the normal form. Often it resulted in the virtual abdication by the courts of their power to make decisions. Rather than deliberate an issue and seek an opinion only on the particularly thorny points, the courts began simply to send all the written documents relating to the cause to the advising law faculty. The courts which were still staffed, at least in part, by lay judges found this an attractive way round the technicalities of the romano-canonical procedure and in effect they surrendered their judicial function. The faculties which had been consulted came to send back their answer in the form of a draft decree. Of course steps to enforce decisions could only come from the courts, but their legal dealings were often limited to the 'despatching of the documents of the case' (Aktenversendung). The faculties remained in theory advisory bodies only, but their decisions were rarely questioned; if they were, the invariable course adopted by the transmitting court was to refer the matter to a different faculty. The system had various advantages. Litigants received learned and impartial justice. The ordinary courts, anxious to preserve their independence from the centralizing tendencies of the princes, were able to offer justice comparable to that of the new princely appellate courts. The faculty doctors saw the triumph of the rational learned law.

Furthermore, the law faculties were no longer simply producing graduates for legal and administrative posts and studying Roman law in academic isolation. They were using the Roman law they were working on, that is, both the historical pursuit of classical Roman law in the Humanist tradition and the accumulated interpretative knowledge of the <u>Gloss</u>, to solve actual disputes, in a sense repeating the work of the Commentators. But the new external circumstances meant that Germanic local law and custom were pushed firmly into the background, not blended in. The preponderance of Roman over Germanic solutions was encouraged by the frequency with which an advising faculty might lie in a different territory from the consulting court. Unless a local provision was convincingly argued, the faculty members would inevitably turn to the civil law in reasoning their way to a solution. A party relying on the civil law came to have a presumption in his favour and the onus was on the other party to prove that the Roman law on this point had not been received or, once received, had since been rejected. This was why the seeking of legal advice across territorial frontiers had been forbidden in Saxony as early as the fifteenth century, and in Brandenburg and a few other precociously centralized states during the sixteenth century; such measures only became widespread in the eighteenth century. The faculties themselves might sometimes consult with other faculties; faculty decisions were collected and published. In this way there was a growing body of common doctrine which transcended national boundaries within Germany. The general doctrinal approach is well described as the <u>usus</u> <u>modernus</u> <u>Pandectarum</u> (modern application of the <u>Pandects</u> -- literally the <u>Digest</u>, in practice the whole <u>Corpus</u> <u>Iuris</u> <u>Civilis</u>), although this phrase may not have been coined until the seventeenth century when Samuel Stryk (1640-1710) wrote a book with that title; however, Carpzov's <u>Jurisprudentia</u> <u>forensis</u> <u>romano-saxonica</u> (<u>Romano-</u> <u>Saxon</u> <u>Law</u> <u>as</u> <u>Applied</u> <u>in</u> <u>the</u> <u>Courts</u>) of 1638 was in the same practical tradition which the German law faculties established, the tradition of the *mos italicus.* The *usus modernus*, however, differed from the *mos italicus* in that it was inclined to give imperial authority rather than the self-evident reason of the texts as the basis for the acceptance of Roman law. In 1643, however, H. Conring (1606--81) wrote a book *De origine iuris germanici* (*On the origin of German law*) which argued that Roman law had in fact been received by a gradual process of assimilation, not by a supposed ordinance of Lothar or of any other mediaeval emperor, and that it should be applied only insofar as it had been positively accepted. This work had a fruitful future but little immediate impact. Practising lawyers continued to accept Roman law as binding and simply, as a matter of convenience, put the burden of proof on a party who wished to found his case on Germanic law.

The universities were not exclusively oriented towards Roman law; chairs of private law were until the eighteenth century concerned with the civil law, but there were also chairs of feudal law, public law, and civil procedure -- although the last remained based on the romano-canonical process. Within the teaching of the civil law the 'legal order' was no longer followed in German universities of the seventeenth century, and professors ceased to be appointed to teach the different parts of the *Corpus Iuris*. Moreover, private sessions of teaching were added to the public lectures and these could deal with any material the teacher thought appropriate. In this modern atmosphere there were complaints from students that professors neglected their teaching in order to concentrate on the more lucrative business of composing draft decrees in response to *Aktenversendungen* or else to act as judges or as members of the council of the local ruler. Another innovation in legal education was the habit of requiring a student to defend a thesis or theses as evidence of his knowledge of the sources and his ability to handle legal materials. The

thesis to be defended was a more or less controversial statement of law --
for example, that delivery is always required in order to transfer property
-- and the candidate had to produce arguments in favour of it and refute
contrary opinions. Such disputations were also collected and published,
often by the professor who had presided.

(v) The use of legislation in Germany

The sixteenth century saw a considerable enactment of imperial
legislation, but most of this had to do with public matters; hardly any of
it dealt with private law. The most important and influential of these
statutes was the <u>Constitutio criminalis Carolina</u> (Charles V's statute on
criminal law), commonly known as the <u>Carolina</u>. The <u>Carolina</u> was based on
an earlier criminal code, the <u>Bambergensis</u> of 1507, compiled for the lands
ruled by the bishop of Bamberg; this had blended existing German criminal
law with the doctrines of the Italian jurists. The <u>Carolina</u> hence
preserved the German classification of crimes but interpreted this in the
light of the learned law. It thus proceeded on the assumption that crime
was a matter of concern for the state as well as for the victim and his
family; the preservation of law and order was justification for the
imposition of punishments by the public authorities. Fault was held to be
an essential element of liability, and civilian teaching on the distinction
between <u>dolus</u> (malice or fraud) and <u>culpa</u> (fault, including negligence) was
taken up.

The <u>Carolina</u> was issued in 1532 as a comprehensive code of criminal
law and procedure to be applied throughout the Empire. This attempt at
universal application met with considerable hostility from among the German
princes; the Imperial Diet only passed the statute after it had been agreed

that its provisions would not derogate from the "ancient, just and lawful usages" of the various territories. The princes had in effect maintained their position at the expense of the emperor, and within Germany the Carolina took second place to the territorial laws. For example, in Saxony legislation was passed in the early seventeenth century requiring jurisdiction in all but the most minor of crimes to be surrendered by the lower courts to the duke's court in Leipzig. The result, as the records show, was that a huge amount of criminal business came before that court, which was thus able to mould the development of Saxon criminal law; for example, an elaborate system of safeguards for an accused person was introduced. Through the writings of Carpzov Saxon practice also influenced other German jurisdictions. Saxon decisions, together with the Carolina, provided the basis for most future thinking on criminal law throughout the whole of Germany. The Carolina was the first code of any branch of law designed to be applicable throughout the Empire; its direct influence, however, was more important in Italy than Germany.

The sixteenth century also saw many 'reformations' of the town and territorial laws, that is, a putting into writing of local customs with those modifications which were thought necessary. The cities were first in the field, with codification in Nuremburg and Worms, for example, taking place in the later fifteenth century. During the course of the following century a substantial majority of the cities and princely states had reformed their laws. This was partly in response to the romano-canonical procedures in and the recognition of Roman law by the Reichskammergericht and the princes' appellate courts; it was clearly expedient to clarify whether the rules on a particular issue were to be derived from customary or from learned law. In general clarity meant Roman clarity, partly because the men most likely to be commissioned to systematize local usage

331

in the light of the reception were those who had been trained in the learned law.

In Frankfurt, for example, the city's court received romano-canonical procedure at the close of the fifteenth century. At the time this produced a degree of confusion as the customary and the new systems for a while existed side by side. The city's court was not yet fully romanized and the lay officials who served there found considerable difficulty in understanding the technicalities of the new procedure and in dealing with the substantive Roman law that it brought in its wake. In consequence Frankfurt codified its law in 1509. The reformed law sanctioned the new procedure but attempted to make it somewhat simpler for the lay judge; the old oral procedure was thereafter limited to certain minor causes, such as small debt. The code also settled the substantive law that the city would use; the Roman did not entirely override the indigenous law, because one result of the review of the local customs was their systematization, which made them easier to blend. In general the law of persons and of succession remained rooted in custom, but in areas where there had been conflict between the two traditions Roman law was normally preferred. This is the less surprising in that the 'reformation' in Frankfurt was largely the work of the city's advocate, Schönwetter, a man trained in the learned law.

By the seventeenth century it was clear that all Germany had received Roman law, although not always to the same extent; in Saxony especially the reception was discriminating rather than general, while in some states it was thoroughgoing. As in Italy centuries earlier, the putting into writing of the local laws of the cities and territories had opened the way to civilian influence. The fact that the texts of the new codes were often terse and incomplete and that some topics might be omitted altogether -- in particular those concerned with obligations, and especially contracts --

left considerable scope for judicial interpretation. Interpretation by the appellate courts meant virtually automatic use of the learned law; interpretation by lesser courts carried a strong likelihood of reference to the learned law through **Aktenversendung.** The universities had always produced trained men, suitable for government posts; indeed, in late mediaeval and early modern Germany, to be a law graduate was the surest route to gainful and probably influential employment. After the establishment of courts with romano-canonical procedure there was great demand for trained men to staff them, which encouraged the growth of law faculties. The existence of the law faculties in itself led to a more scientific attitude to law within Germany. Over and above accepting individual doctrines of Roman law, scholars took a structured and analytical approach to the whole discipline; they distinguished between laws and law. Humanism had some impact in Germany; Zasius was much respected and Doneau, in exile from France because of his Protestantism, first found a home in Heidelberg. Nevertheless, the tradition of the universities was close to the **mos italicus**; the universities' intimate contact with the courts through their consultations meant that the purely Roman influence was strong, and thus there developed the **usus modernus Pandectarum.** In the specific field of legal education German universities were responsible for innovations which were to affect university teaching throughout the western world, but that was for the future. Meanwhile, through the Reception, with each factor -- the political ambitions of emperor and princes, the desire of litigants, the urge towards system whether in general or local legislation, the growth of professional courts, the work of the law faculties -- enhancing the effects of the others, Germany had acquired a kind of common law.

Further Reading:

Continental Legal History series,  vol.I iv;

vol.IV: R. Hübner, History of Germanic
Private Law

H. Coing "Roman law as the ius commune of the continent"  89 L.Q.R.
(1973), 505

J.P. Dawson The Oracles of the Law (Ann Arbor, 1968), ch.iii

W. Kunkel "The reception of Roman law in Germany: an interpretation" in
Pre-Reformation Germany, ed. G. Strauss (London, 1972)

P. Vinogradoff Roman Law in Mediaeval Europe (O.U.P., 1929, repr.), ch.v

Chapter XII

## THE DEVELOPMENT OF FRENCH LAW

(i)  The movement towards codification


Although the adoption of romano-canonical procedure in the Parlement
of Paris and the other parlements -- of which there were eventually twelve
in the provinces[1], each formally independent within the boundaries of its
territorial jurisdiction -- had brought about a degree of unity in the
administration of the law, the multiplicity of existing custom continued to
make for diversity.  In the Midi, the pays de droit écrit, the problem was
less acute in that Roman law was recognized as general subsidiary custom,
but in the pays de coutumes there was no such unifying factor, although the
predominant position of Paris gave its custom great influence.  In the
North customs were strictly territorial; this meant that a man might find
his status changed as he crossed into the area of some other custom, or
that a document which was valid in one region was without effect in another
through some lack of formality in its execution.  Moreover, there were no
official collections defining local custom in the North until the sixteenth
century.  There were, indeed, important unofficial compilations, such as
Beaumanoir's Coutumes de Beauvaisis or Les Livres de Jostice et de Plet
from Orléans; in Normandy the Grand Coutumier and in Brittany the Très
Ancienne Coutume had a semi-official status and could be led as proof of
custom, but these provinces were unusual.

The first serious attempt to solve the problem of status was made by

----------

1    Of these Bordeaux, Toulouse, Aix and Grenoble lay in the pays de
     droit écrit.

the Breton jurist, Bertrand d'Argentré, in the sixteenth century, in the course of his commentary on the custom of Brittany. His solution, the doctrine of **statut personnel**, was derived from the writings of the Commentators who had had to solve similar problems in connection with the different laws of the city states of northern Italy. This doctrine held that certain aspects of custom, in particular those attaching to personal status and capacity, must be viewed in relation to the person rather than the territory; a man acquired them by birth or domicile and carried them with him as he moved from region to region. This at least eased the problems of merchants and of the growing number who travelled to find employment, but it was still a long way from any concept of Frenchness.

There was also a tendency to group customs into provincial families; this was encouraged by the existence of the **parlements**, each of which had jurisdiction over a region which included many customs. As a **parlement** heard the results of various inquests into the range of local customs within its jurisdiction, it tended to assimilate comparable usages. Although its decrees concerned the present case and were not binding for the future, a consistent run of decisions would clearly be of weight in redefining custom. Local custom normally needed to be proved before the court. Some usages were held notorious, that is, so well known as not to require proof, and others would have been incorporated in a local charter or clearly been previously accepted by the court, but if there was any uncertainty a party must be prepared to lead proof of the custom on which he was relying. From the late thirteenth century onwards this was most commonly accomplished through the **turba** or group inquest. The number required to constitute a **turba** was finally fixed at ten; their verdict on whether or not an alleged usage amounted to custom had to be unanimous. A complication arose in consequence of a royal ordinance of 1499 which laid down that the verdict of a _turba_ was to rank as the equivalent of the testimony of one witness; the generally accepted canonical rule of evidence required two witnesses for full proof, and hence corroboration of the verdict came to be required. Thereafter it was necessary to put the matter to two inquests, which inevitably made the process slower and more expensive; it remained, however, the usual method of settling disputed custom until the abolition of the _turba_ in 1667, when local judges, after appropriate consultations, certified local usage.

The drawbacks of uncertainty of particular usage, doubts about the territorial extent of a custom, lack of customary law in areas such as contracts, and absence of system or principle on which to found a developed law were already recognized in the fifteenth century. To deal with these problems men such as Jean Masuer, advocate and later chancellor in the _sénéchaussée_ of Riom in the Auvergne, tried to blend together the customs of a whole province; he also linked his work with the practice of the _parlement_. Masuer's _Practica senescalliae Alverniae_ (_Practice of the Sénéchaussée of the Auvergne_) was published in mid-century; it was published bilingually and it is noticeable that the Latin editions of the work make more direct use of Roman law than do the French. In the 1540s Jean Imbert produced his _Institutionum forensium Galliae pene totius quae moribus regitur communium libri iv_ (_Four Books of Institutions of the Court Practice of Almost All Customary France_). Imbert discussed both civil and criminal procedure; he made use of many _arrêts de reglement_ (decrees -- the term covers rulings for the future as well as decisions in particular cases) of the _parlements_ as well as of Roman law in his interpretation of custom. He also wrote a book which discussed what written law was actually observed and what abrogated; this too was very popular.

The Estates-General, that is the three estates of nobility, clergy and commons, on various occasions in the sixteenth century demanded a clarification and simplification of the law. At Orléans in 1560 the Third Estate petitioned for a summary of what law was in force between the king's subjects, for the removal of what was unnecessary, and also for reforms in procedure. In 1576 at Blois there was a request for the consolidation of edicts, royal ordinances and custom by learned men and experienced persons appointed for this purpose; again, what was wanted was a compilation of those customs which were actually in force and the abrogation of others. The response was the Ordinance (Ordonnance) of Blois in which, among other matters, the king promised to codify the ordinances. We shall return to the theme of royal legislation.

(ii) The codification of the customs


The petitions of the Estates-General at Orléans and Blois were only possible because a significant codification of the customs had already taken place in the sixteenth century. In 1498 the crown had ordered that the customs and usages of the various regions in the North be codified, and official texts produced. Local assemblies, after consultation with knowledgeable parties, produced draft texts defining their region's customs; many of those immediately concerned in this work were local lawyers. Royal commissioners attended the final stages of the assemblies' meetings to approve the agreed drafts; these were then promulgated by the commissioners in the name of the king. Thus each written collection of customs amounted to a royal enactment, binding and authoritative for the future, and capable of being cited in the courts. The customs of Melun, Ponthieu and Sens were promulgated in 1506, and the Custom of Paris in 1510, a year after that of Orléans. In the 1580s revised versions of some of these codes were issued, improved after being tested by use; by then the overall work had been completed in the North. There were left in force some sixty-five separate general customs, applicable to a considerable area, but several hundred purely local customs remained as well. Some codification had also taken place in the Midi.

While the process of codification was primarily designed to provide a statement of those customs actually in force, the opportunity was also taken to reform existing law where this was thought desirable. The distinction between the two aims was not always clear because to establish the correct custom was almost the same as to choose the better one. The purpose was not in general to innovate, but the need to reduce customs to writing produced a new precision in the existing law and revealed areas where legal guidance was lacking. The form of words adopted was often affected by Roman law, and this could of itself bring about changes in institutions such as tutory or gift. Although the men chiefly concerned with the work of codification were predominantly interested in the practice of the customary courts, they were often graduates in law and not untouched by Humanist thinking. They had a sense of history and readily distinguished between ancient custom and custom to be observed in the future; in the 1530s the procedure of codification was modified to allow an official record to be kept of such innovations. The influence of the royal commissioners also sometimes worked towards a greater uniformity, tinged with the learned law, where they suggested reforms that would be acceptable on grounds of equity.

By the end of the sixteenth century the process of codification in the pays de coutumes was complete in the sense that all officially recognized customs had been reduced to writing and carried the royal authority. On the other hand, uniformity was still a long way off. On the eve of the

339

Revolution of 1789 it is easily possible to count more than three hundred customary jurisdictions. However, the compilation of settled written texts meant that for the first time the material existed for a thorough juristic treatment of the customary law. The sixteenth and earlier seventeenth centuries saw a wealth of commentary on the customs that, in effect, created a French national law, which in due course was to become fully codified.

It is significant that although such men (with whom we shall shortly deal) as Dumoulin, Coquille, Loysel and Domat were neither ignorant of nor uninfluenced by Roman law, they were not Romanists. The specifically Roman studies of the legal Humanists had little influence on French practice; in general the professors of civil law in the French universities were not in the leading rank of scholars. Furthermore, because the clearest way to fame and success lay in the service of the king, the more able or ambitious of these professors sought to enter his service, and few taught for more than a decade or so -- a pattern we observed earlier among teachers of canon law. Thus it was the advocates and judges who created French law, just as in England the bench and bar created English law, but in France these men had academic as well as practical legal training.

In the Midi Roman law retained its status as a general subsidiary source; in the North arguments based on it were frequently accepted, but on grounds of reasonableness and not authority. It had a considerable rôle to play, however, because the subject matter of the customs was restricted. Since the customs were based on feudal law or Frankish usage they dealt above all with land law, including leases, with inheritance and with family relationships, but they had little to say about obligations, whether contractual or delictual, and they were not normally concerned with criminal law or procedure; civil procedure had long been dominated by romano-canonical notions.  In the field of obligations the French jurists therefore introduced civilian ideas while, within a framework made possible by the mediaeval influence of the learned law, formally addressing themselves to the customs.  Procedure and the criminal law were spheres of interest to the crown, and royal legislation became pre-eminent there, as it did also in the field of mercantile law, as economic policy became a more central concern of government.

(iii)  Legal literature in the sixteenth and seventeenth centuries

We have remarked that the major French jurists of the sixteenth and seventeenth centuries were not academics -- although French lawyers did train for the law at universities -- but practising lawyers.  They were all, however, familiar with Roman law, on which they drew for particular solutions and comparisons.  They steadily built towards a private law common to all (northern) France, but the absence of a single central court and the persistence of local variations meant that a systematic and national French law was not achieved until the nineteenth century.

The most famous of these jurists, Charles Dumoulin, or Molinaeus, (1500-66) started his career as an advocate before the Parlement of Paris but, according to one story, a speech defect led him to consultancy and writing rather than speaking.  Dumoulin felt himself to be within the Humanist tradition, particularly the nationalist tradition of Hotman. While hardly a Protestant in doctrine, he too suffered a period of exile in consequence of his unbridled attacks on ecclesiastical jurisdictions, his rejection of papal authority within France and his opposition to the work of the Council of Trent.  In 1539 he published, as the first title of a work On fiefs, the major part of his enormously influential commentary on

341

the Custom of Paris, which he called "the chief of the customs of this realm and of all France". In this he made a vigorous attack on the feudal courts and their bad customs; strict interpretation should be used to minimize feudal rights and to stress those of the crown. In this d'Argentré opposed him, holding that feudal rights were important for the good ordering of society. Dumoulin also wrote more generally on the customs; he wanted to find a general custom common to all France which could be used in preference to Roman law as a supplementary general source, and he proposed that the Custom of Paris should be used to achieve this degree of uniformity. The reformed Custom of Paris, issued in 1580, relied heavily on Dumoulin's observations on the 1510 version; it was also in essence the law provided for the French colonies established before the Revolution. He was not concerned with the pays de droit écrit but wanted for the pays de coutumes one short, clear and equitable code; he firmly linked equity and royal power. His style was Bartolist, setting out the full arguments of various authors for and against the proposition he was maintaining, and his learning was immense; he was well acquainted with the Corpus Iuris and the work of the Glossators, Commentators and canonists. He wrote commentaries on various titles of the Corpus and also on contemporary problems of canon law. His views, however, were independent and original. He had no hesitation in rejecting doctrines he thought unsuitable to the needs of contemporary France or in adapting others in accordance with his own views. His conviction of the rightness of these views was given strength by his regular attendance at the sessions of the Parlement and his close relationships with bench and bar in Paris; conversely, the decrees of the Parlement were influenced by his published works. He more than anyone else was the creator of French law.

Guy Coquille (1523–1603) studied law at Padua and at Orléans, where he

342

also came to the practice of law; he then attended the bar in Paris and returned to Nevers as an advocate. He later became échevin and then procurator-general to the Duke of Nevers, and he was a deputy of the Third Estate at three meetings of the Estates-General, at Orléans in 1560 and at Blois in 1576-77 and 1588. He too was noted for his Gallican sympathies, but his attacks on the papal jurisdiction were more discreet than those of Dumoulin. He was interested in public law, including the popular element in the creation and acceptance of custom, and in royal legislation as well as in the customs. His major work, the **Institution au droit français** (**Institute of French Law**), was published as the possible basis for fulfilling his dream of legislative unity. For current needs he also produced a clear and simple commentary on the Custom of the Nivernois.

Antoine Loysel (or Loisel) (1536-1617) was a poet and scholar, a legal historian as well as a legal practitioner. This may partly explain why he was more willing to combine Roman with French law. He was educated at Toulouse where he studied under Cujas, whose disciple he always held himself to be, and whom he followed to Cahors, Bourges, even Paris, and Valence. In 1560 he became an advocate in Paris; some twenty years later he was for three years the King's advocate in the Protestant court permitted in Guyenne. He wrote on the Custom of Beauvais, his native town, and also on the **Parlement** of Paris, but he was most influential through his **Institutes coutumières** (**Customary Institutes**), published in 1607. His approach was brief and axiomatic, not explanatory; he saw future progress in terms of the "conformity, equity and reason of a single law, custom, and weight and measure under the king." When in 1679 the first professor of French Law was appointed in Paris, he gave lectures on Loysel's **Institutes**, which thus acquired an unofficial but significant authority as a source of law.

Under Louis XIV jurists who had the king's ear or lawyers who became royal servants had more chance of having their doctrines put into practice; we shall refer to Lamoignon and Colbert in the context of royal legislation. Natural Law was the intellectual fashion of the seventeenth century -- we shall consider it in the next chapter. Its influence is discernible in the **Institutions du droit français**, published in 1665, of Clément Fleury, who was a tutor to the royal children, and also in Domat's work; nevertheless it did not really have much impact in France until the eighteenth century. Jean Domat (1625-96) was to some extent an exception to all the jurists already mentioned. He dealt with Roman law but, like Doneau, he claimed to present it in its natural order in **Les lois civiles dans leur ordre naturel** of 1694. Although dealing with Roman law, he was working towards a new planned society; he wanted to integrate Natural Law and secular justice. He anticipated much of Montesquieu, and he is generally held to be a direct ancestor of the **Code Civil**, although his work was more widely admired than read. He was a graduate and indeed a doctor of law of Bourges, and a contemporary and close friend of his fellow citizen, the great philosopher Pascal. He spent most of his life in his native Clermont, practising at the bar there and being much involved in the affairs of the province; his interests extended to public as well as private law.

(iv)   The **parlements** and other courts

The **Parlement** of Paris had played a crucial role in the success story of the French crown; the existence by the end of the fifteenth century of a strong centralized monarchy (at least by comparison with the Empire) was very largely due to the royal control of the administration of justice. In

344

the difficulties of the Hundred Years War the Parlement had acquired a policy-making rôle; during the Wars of Religion, when the kingdom was divided and the members of the Parlement with it, it had become something of a check upon the absolute or arbitrary power of the crown. For a law to be held valid and applied it must have been registered with a parlement, most frequently the Parlement of Paris; in 1566 the right of remonstration, of telling the king to think again, was formally recognized in the Ordinance of Moulins. In 1563, indeed, Michel l'Hospital (d. 1573), the chancellor of France since 1560, rebuked the Parlement of Paris for respecting some and not other royal ordinances. Louis XI (1471-83) had made the judges of a parlement -- and some other officers -- irremovable; this together with the perquisites of office helped create from the upper levels of the legal profession the noblesse de robe to rival the old nobility. Thus the parlements were important on political and social grounds as well as for their proper judicial function.

Since the Parlement of Paris held that it was exercising by delegation the judicial powers of the crown, it felt free to depart from existing law when justice and equity demanded. The exercise of this discretion was for long shrouded in mystery owing to the scarcity of reports of decided cases prior to 1600. From early times there seems to have been a reluctance to allow the court's reasons for its decisions to be revealed; this may partly be explained by the Parlement's early rôle as the king's council when there were such awkward vassals of the French crown as the king of England, who spent much of the later Middle Ages at war with his feudal superior. The confirmation as late as 1550 of this secrecy, when it was decreed that the mystery of the court should be inviolate, was probably due to the religious tensions and conflicts of the period; certainly secrecy was not inherent in the canonical system, where it was normal to publish the evidence and the

345

full judgment. It is clear, however, that in some form adequate records were kept because the _Parlement_ was clearly concerned with consistency; as early as the later fourteenth century we know that it was prepared to consider its own prior decisions in coming to judgment.

Some reports of cases in the _Parlement_ did survive from the fourteenth century. Du Breuil, an advocate, wrote a manual on procedure which referred to numerous cases, in most of which he himself had participated; among other reporters, another advocate, Jean Le Coq, produced widely circulated notes of decisions covering fifteen years at the end of the century. In the fifteenth century there were some reported decrees from Paris which Dumoulin was able to use; for the first fifty years of the _Parlement_ at Toulouse there were digests of its sentences. In the _Parlement_ of the Dauphiné, established at Grenoble in 1451, _Decisions_ were recorded by one of the judges, Gui-Pape; since the Dauphiné lay in the _pays de droit écrit_ the arguments reflected were mainly from Roman and canon law and the learned doctors. In the second half of the sixteenth century one Jean Papon, a judge in a lower court -- a royal _bailliage_ --, published his _Arrêts Notables_ (_Notable Rulings_) which referred to decisions of all the _parlements_ and ranged over three centuries; his arrangement was by topic, rather than chronological.

The demand which Papon had done something to satisfy was even better served by the publication in 1609 -- a year after the author's death -- of the _Arrêts Notables_ of George Louet, for twenty-four years a judge of the _Parlement_ of Paris. The publication was arranged by the first or senior president of the _Parlement_ and was given formal approval by that body. The cases reported were from Louet's own experience, in particular when he had been acting as _rapporteur_ for one of the _Chambres des Enquêtes_ (of which there were by that time five). He gave the arguments (which included

346

civilian as well as customary references, and citations from Dumoulin), an outline of the facts, the decision and the reasons for that decision. In 1629 another judge of the Parlement called Bouguier published his Arrêts de la Court Decisifs (Decisive Rulings of the Court), and in 1645 a further series came from another judge, Claude Le Prestre, who quoted extensively from the private but official record kept for the court's own use.

Whether because of the secrecy rule or because the crown was again seeking to control the courts, no more case reports emerged from the bench of the Parlement of Paris until Grainville's in 1750. However, in the provincial parlements, particularly at Toulouse, some judges continued to publish decisions of their courts. The bulk, and it was a very considerable bulk, of seventeenth century reports were, however, made by practitioners at the bar. These reporters tended to concentrate on the pleadings rather than the decisions but some, like de Montholon, also reported the decrees 'in red robes'. On these occasions, after a solemn procession, the whole bar was assembled together and the judges, splendidly dressed in their red robes of office, issued decrees which were intended to instruct the legal profession on the future treatment the courts would give to the matter in question.

Despite the growing absolute power of the crown the rule-making powers of the parlements continued to be exercised freely throughout the seventeenth century. Some concerned the procedure of the parlements themselves and of the lower courts, but others dealt with matters of public order. Not surprisingly such decrees were not much concerned with the development of private law for, as in Germany, overt legislation dealt mainly with problems of law and order or with procedure, at least until Colbert's time. Thus the parlements interpreted the customs and supplemented existing law, and gave their authority to usage in disputes

347

over the law merchant.

In spite of the buying and selling of judicial office, corruption, at
least corruption as recognized by contemporaries, seems to have been rare
in the seventeenth century parlements; in the sixteenth century their
reputation had been lower when religious conflicts had confused justice.
It was largely because of the political rôle of the parlements, which led
the opposition to authoritarian government and provided a check on royal
power, that new courts were created, rather than further powers being
granted to the parlements. Francis I established prevôts des maréchaux as
officers with summary criminal powers; it was a period of harsh criminal
law. Présidiaux were set up as appellate courts from the baillis and
sénéchaussées to avoid flooding the parlements with business and to give
litigants a more convenient forum; each was based upon a strictly
geographical area with no regard to the boundaries of ancient provinces and
regions. Many litigants, however, preferred the greater security of a
judgment from a parlement, and the maximum sum over which the présidiaux
had jurisdiction meant that inflation diminished their competence. Some
attempt was made to give them an appellate jurisdiction from customary and
seignorial courts but this was resisted, by the arguments of Coquille among
others. Tribunaux consulaires were specifically commercial courts; the
first was created in 1549 for Toulouse, and L'Hospital established another
in Paris in 1563. They were courts for specific classes of person, for
négociants, marchands and navigateurs, and not for the ordinary citizen;
they were staffed by men of the merchant class and they used summary
procedure. Although the parlements disliked this further invasion of their
jurisdiction, the courts were very popular with their users; the problem
was that not enough were set up. The tribunaux survived the Revolution
without serious modification. There was an intellectual and emotional

348

argument against such special courts based on the rational desire, linked with the movement towards codification, for a single hierarchy of courts, competent to hear all kinds of suit. It was on the _parlements_ as much as any other single issue that the Revolution ultimately hinged.

(v)  Royal legislation

In the Middle Ages legislation was on the face of it a matter of declaring what was the law, of restoring good custom; this had been as true of Henry II of England as it still was for Charles VII in the Ordinance of Montils-les-Tours in the mid-fifteenth century.  But the movement towards codification of the customs, which specifically included the establishment of new practices, was echoed in the movement, seen at Orléans and Blois, towards the consolidation of the edicts and ordinances. In 1539 Francis I issued the celebrated Ordinance of Villers-Cotterêts which required the registration of gifts -- on the pattern of the later Roman law --, regulated the function of notaries, provided for registration of civil status, and substituted romano-canonical for feudal procedure in criminal trials.  In 1566 the Ordinance of Moulins substituted written proof for oral witnesses in civil procedure.

The constitutional theory of a sovereign king, developed by men like Bodin and Dumoulin, placed on the crown the duty to be active; in the seventeenth century economic planning was to appear as part of the attempt at the rational ordering of society.  The first serious step towards a code of law based on royal legislation was made by Barnabé Brisson (c.1530-91), consequent upon the Ordinance of Blois of 1577.  It was no coincidence that Guy Coquille had been a deputy at the Estates-General whose petition had led to this edict and that he also had attended the meeting in 1566 at

Orléans.  Brisson, who had already issued a popular dictionary of law,
produced a collection of all the royal ordinances then in force, arranged
on a systematic basis; it was to be known as the 'Code Henry III,
Basilica'.  It included the Ordinance of Villers-Cotterêts, which was
linked with the introduction of the official use of the French (as opposed
to the Latin) language, and the Ordinance of Moulins on the reform of
judicial procedure.  However, because it appeared just after the king's
death it was never made official; indeed, the insertion of forged
ordinances led to further confusion.  In 1614 the Estates-General (in its
last meeting before the Revolution) repeated the request for a codification
of the ordinances; the Third Estate also petitioned for the parlements to
reveal the reasoning behind judicial decrees where these depended on rules
of law or custom.  The need for the imposition of uniformity through royal
edicts became more necessary in the seventeenth century in that the
division between the pays de droit écrit and the pays de coutumes became
more marked as each became more unified within itself.

The two major legal figures of the reign of Louis XIV (1643-1715)
after his emergence from regency in 1661 were Jean Baptiste Colbert (1619-
83) and Guillaume de Lamoignon (1617-77); the one was Louis' chief minister
from 1661, the other first president of the Parlement of Paris.  Advised by
Colbert, in 1665 Louis set up a special commission, the Conseil de Justice,
composed of eminent jurists and members of the King's Council; this
excluded both the Parlement of Paris as a body and also members of the
legal profession collectively.  From the provincial parlements and from
various legal experts memoranda were requested which would detail what was
in need of reform and suggest remedies.  Maîtres des requêtes were sent out
to discuss these and to forward them to Paris.  It was a mere three months
before the publication of the Ordinance of 1667 on civil procedure that the

Parlement became involved, through its own initiative, so that the bulk of the preparatory work had already been completed; the influence of Lamoignon himself, however, was significant because the jurists on the commission knew and appreciated his outlines for a code. The Ordinance aimed to provide a complete and detailed systematic codification of this branch of the law; despite this, supplementary edicts were found to be necessary. It regulated the authority of edicts, ordinances and judicial decrees; it prescribed limits on adjournments and appeals; it abolished the enquête par turbe; it distinguished diligence -- rights of enforcement -- arising from commercial and from civil debts. In 1670, this time with the co-operation of the Parlement throughout the preparatory sessions, an Ordinance on criminal law and procedure (of which the drafting owed much to Lamoignon) was published; it defined crimes more precisely, settled criminal procedure and the spheres of the various jurisdictions, and sanctioned penalties.

Lamoignon had meditated on a reformation of the Custom of Paris as the basis of a renewed and unified French law well before Colbert's rise to power. He and the jurist Barthelémi Auzanet had circulated working papers and held discussions on the project with advocates and magistrates. Colbert, however, had the ear of the king and Lamoignon was left outside the inner circle of reformers. Indeed, many of his comments on the draft Ordinances were without effect, such as his protests at the refusal to allow accused persons legal advice. Nevertheless his book, Arrêtés ou Lois Projetées, in which he laid out his scheme for a single code based on the customary law, was immensely influential. It was much more used by jurists of the eighteenth century than was Domat's work, and in particular it was drawn on by the chancellor, Henri-François Daguesseau (1668-1751), in the composition of the mini-codes on donations (1731), wills (1735), and

351

substitutions -- entails -- (1747), which were issued as royal ordinances under Louis XV (1715-74).

Undoubtedly Colbert's inspiration lay behind the Ordinance of Commerce (or Code Marchand) of 1673; it only concerned merchants, who were still a legally identifiable class, grouped in guilds, and not ordinary citizens. Mercantile interests were widely consulted in its drafting; it was designed to free commercial law from local custom and, in thus providing a uniform law merchant within France, to diminish the length and cost of litigation. It also regulated commercial accounts and laid down rules for companies and partnerships. In 1681 the Ordinance of the Marine (Ordonnance de la Marine) was issued, dealing with admiralty jurisdiction and procedure as well as the rights of consuls in foreign countries and the duties of ships' masters. These statutes were to provide much of the material for the Code de Commerce.


Further reading:

Continental Legal History Series: vol.III   J. Brissaud History of French
       Private Law; vol.IX   J. Brissaud History of French Public Law
J.P. Dawson "The codification of the French customs" 38 Mich.L.R.
       (1940),765
       The Oracles of the Law (Ann Arbor, 1968), ch.iv
J.H. Shennan   The Parlement of Paris (London, 1968)

Chapter XIII

## THE SEVENTEENTH CENTURY

(i)  The main themes of the century


In many matters, as we have observed in both Germany and France, the
seventeenth century saw the continuation of trends established in the
sixteenth.  The conscious continuation of these trends was in itself
significant but there were new ideas as well.

From a point of view centred on Europe the world was still expanding;
journeys of exploration continued side by side with the settlement of newly
discovered areas.  Religion was still a fertile source of dispute both
within and between the states of Europe.  These nation states were
consolidating their frontiers and establishing their spheres of influence;
many political changes of this nature, such as Sweden's acquisition of
western Pomerania, Brandenburg's of Magdeburg and France's of Alsace, or
the recognition of the independence of Switzerland and the Netherlands,
resulted from the Treaty of Westphalia which, in 1648, ended the Thirty
Years War.  The Scandinavian kingdoms became more a part of the European
scene; the Holy Roman Empire was diminished and set on the path towards its
decline into the Austrian Empire.  Spain began to decline, and the
Netherlands to take a leading rôle in both economic expansion and legal
creativity.  Within states, political power was mainly in the hands of
monarchies whose pretensions to absolute authority were justified by the
writings of political theorists such as Hobbes.  Not all monarchies were
absolute and power might be shared even in those that were, but popular
democracy was still far away.  The economy was still predominantly
agricultural; land was -- as always -- important for status as well as

353

being the major source of wealth. Commerce, however, was expanding especially in the field of colonial trade; industrial production was becoming increasingly significant, along with the necessary developments in technology, although the Industrial Revolution was a century or more away. Mercantilist theory encouraged governments to intervene to protect and increase their state's share of international commerce in order to increase its wealth and power. The scientific revolution was in the offing; observation and experiment led to new understanding of the physical world.

In terms of legal history the century is remarkable for the development of a new concept of Natural Law, first by Grotius following the Christian tradition and then by the German rationalist lawyers, and for the growth of the Dutch Elegant Jurisprudence. The other new factor was that English jurisprudence began to share in the European tradition, although its own influence was not to become widespread until the later eighteenth and nineteenth centuries. We shall look at these movements in turn. It is also noteworthy that in dealing with legal thought in the seventeenth century it becomes convenient to use current jurisprudential terms.

(ii)  Natural Law as developed by Grotius

The roots of Natural Law theory (that certain legal rules are in some sense 'natural' and not purely arbitrary creations) lie in Plato and Aristotle, the great philosophers of ancient Greece. For Plato, the idea of justice was the pattern to which law ought to conform; in his thinking, however, justice was a virtue accessible only to the philosopher-kings who were to rule his ideal society and to legislate as far as possible in conformity with justice. This view, that law should conform to an ideal of justice but that knowledge of what justice demands is not granted to

354

everyone, was transmitted to the early mediaeval world by St. Augustine. Aristotle had taken a more practical approach to natural law. He made a clear distinction between morality and law, and he introduced the concepts of distributive and commutative justice. The former requires that we should give to each his due; the latter requires that we should make up inequalities brought about by our actions and give due return for what we have received. To determine what is due Aristotle relied on observation of nature, since he held that the natural world was created with a discoverable purpose; for example, observation shows that reason distinguishes men from other animals and consequently men should act rationally. Aristotle's ideas were taken up by St. Thomas Aquinas in the thirteenth century and amplified in his Summa Theologica. The Stoic philosophers, whose ideas were reflected by Cicero, had applied the idea of natural law to a wider world than Plato's city state of Athens; the world was of its nature orderly, but natural law was a moral rather than a legal order and justice a private virtue. Both Aristotle and the Stoics believed in versions of the 'social contract' as an explanation of the existence of a legal order within any particular state; the state itself was seen as formed by agreement among the members of the society constituting the state. The 'social contract' was a concept much used in political and legal theories of the seventeenth and eighteenth centuries.

Aquinas was philosophically an idealist, believing that values such as justice have a real existence; he also believed that human reason, being the creation of a rational God who is the source of natural law, could discern justice. Positive law created by human authority could and should try to conform to divine justice. In the sixteenth century Calvin held to a version of this Christian natural law tradition. He held that God has the sovereign power of making law, and that human authority has a duty to give

355

effect to God's law, which can be known partly through revelation in Scripture and partly through reason. The most influential natural law thinkers of the sixteenth century, however, were the Spanish scholars -- canonists and theologians -- whose works were among the most important of Grotius' sources. Their leading figure -- in that he was the master of several of the others -- was Francisco de Vitoria (c.1483-1546), professor at Salamanca. He departed most clearly from Aquinas' thought in being a voluntarist in the tradition of William of Ockham, the fourteenth century philosopher; that is, he held that the only ground of an obligation was an act of will of a superior directed to moving the will of an inferior. For him ius had ceased to mean what was the due, the right balance, as between the parties to any situation, and had become a right capable of exercise by the beneficiary. It was with this view of rights that he argued that the native Indians of the Americas, being peaceful possessors, must be treated as owners of their property, despite their being in mortal sin as pagans. Furthermore, since they were rational and not of unsound mind, they could not be forcibly converted to Christianity, and their refusal to be converted was not a just ground for making war on them.

Among other influential Spanish legal thinkers were Agustín, whom we have mentioned as a Humanist, and Domingo de Soto (1494-1560) who also championed the Indians and opposed the trade in slaves; he developed the notion of the ius gentium as positive law, able to bind princes -- Vitoria had held princes to be bound by their own stipulations at least --, and he wrote on the criminal law, opposing all 'purely' penal law theories which asserted that law imposed not an obligation as to conduct but simply, or purely (as in Kelsen's theory) an obligation to undergo a penalty, the performance or non-performance of the action being the condition of the penalty. Luis de Molina y Morales in the later sixteenth century discussed

356

political authority in the light of natural law; he was also the author of an authoritative treatise on the law of entail in Castile. The civilian and canonist Diego Covarruvias (1512-77) was influenced by natural law theories in his application of law to contemporary problems; he was the leading jurist who attempted to justify the Spanish conquests in the Americas. Francisco Suarez (1548-1617) continued Vitoria's interpretation of natural law, being both a voluntarist and a rationalist, and he too criticized much Spanish conduct towards the Indians, arguing for their right to life, liberty and property. Like de Soto, he wrote on the criminal law, and also on the problems of the will of the law-giver and the need to be able to depose a wicked ruler.

Another important thinker of the late sixteenth century was Althusius whom we have mentioned as a Humanist. In his _Politica_, first published in 1603, he propounded a doctrine of popular sovereignty; some of its roots lay in the Conciliar Movement of the fifteenth century but it owed more to the Calvinist view of an ideal human community. In a very different juristic tradition was Alberico Gentili, whose work we have already discussed. When Grotius appeared, his importance lay not in the novelty of any particular idea in his work but in his expansion of natural law into something separate from the civilian or canonist tradition (after him capitals are used); he laid the foundations of the Natural Law of the Enlightenment. He did not, however, use to the full the enormous potential of the new theory; in his own writings Natural Law remained essentially explanatory, providing a rational background for existing law, whereas for the German rationalists who followed him Natural Law was the justification for and guide to reform and change.

Hugo de Groot (1583-1645), better known as Grotius, studied at the University of Leiden, acquired a law degree from Orléans, engaged in practice at the bar and at the age of twenty-four was appointed Advocate-General of Holland, Zeeland and West Friesland. His religious and political views eventually brought him into conflict with the government of Holland, and he was charged with treason and with disturbing the established religion of the United Provinces; after serving nearly two years (1619-20) of a life sentence of imprisonment he escaped and left the Netherlands for France. Some ten years later he returned briefly to Holland but was forced into exile again and spent the last ten years of his life in the service of Queen Christina of Sweden. It was while in prison that he drafted the Introduction to the Jurisprudence of Holland (Inleidinge tot de Hollandsche Rechtsgeleerdheid), first published in 1631, to which we shall return later in the chapter. It was in France that he wrote his treatise, seminal for the development of Natural Law, De Jure Belli ac Pacis (On the Law of War and Peace), which built on an early work of his, De Jure Praedae (On Prize Law), and in which, so the title page says, the law of nature and of peoples and likewise the chief elements of public law are explained ("in quibus jus naturae et gentium, item juris publici praecipua explicantur").

The practical problem Grotius was trying to meet in this treatise was that of providing a law which would be binding on all nations without necessarily having its basis in any particular legal tradition. The difficulty was that there was no longer -- even in theory -- any universally accepted authority, such as pope or emperor, as a result of the Reformation and the growth of national sovereign states. Grotius tried to provide an international law by the application of Natural Law, which he based on human experience as testified by tradition. He explains his approach in an introductory chapter (Prolegomena). Warfare was prevalent -- the Thirty Years War distressed all central Europe between 1618 and 1648

358

-- and in the noise of conflict the law could not be heard, yet "among the characteristics of mankind is the craving for society, that is for a communal life not just of any sort but peaceful and ordered in accordance with reason" (para. 6). Animals instinctively seek their own good and so, although lacking intellect, do infants. "The maintenance, in a form suitable to human reason, of society is the source of that law which deserves the name, from which result abstention from what belongs to another, making restitution of anything of another's we have obtained together with its increment, the obligation to fulfil promises, reparation for loss caused by fault, and the deserved infliction of penalties among men" (para. 8). He observes that it is in the nature of man to follow, in accordance with reason, a rightly formed judgment; that his system of Natural Law is not logically dependent on the existence of God or of a god concerned with the affairs of men, although both reason and tradition, confirmed by many proofs and miracles, support Christianity. Law comes from instinct and from the will of God which we must discern by the exercise of reason. Roman law recognized the social nature of man, and Grotius cites the **Digest** as declaring that a cognatic relationship between us has been created by nature. Civil laws flow from the fact that it is of the nature of law to stand by one's agreements. "Human nature, giving us the craving to live a social life, is the mother of natural law; the mother of civil law is obligation springing from agreement and since it takes its force from natural law, nature can also be said to be a great-grandmother of this law" (para.16).

He cites approvingly Aristotle's condemnation of those who want only lawful rulers among themselves but have no care for justice among other nations. Some Christian thinkers, such as Erasmus, would solve the problem of war by forbidding all exercise of arms, but Grotius fears that this is impossible.  Books on the laws of war have been written by Vitoria and Alberico Gentili, among many others, but he proposes to improve on them. "It has been my first concern to relate the proofs of those things touching the law of nature to concepts so unquestionable that no one can deny them without doing violence to his own nature.  For the principles of that law, if you direct your attention rightly, are in themselves clear and self-evident, almost in the way of those things which we perceive with the external senses; and the senses do not err if their organs are well formed and if other necessary conditions are present" (para. 39).

For proof of this Natural Law Grotius explains that he has made use of philosophers, above all Aristotle (and also Cicero and Seneca who were much influenced by Stoicism), of historians, poets and orators, both Greek and Roman, of Scripture, of the canons of the Councils, of the Church Fathers and of the Scholastic thinkers, such as Vitoria and de Soto, also of the Roman law of the Corpus Iuris and the Theodosian Code, of the Glossators and Commentators -- he cites Accursius and Bartolus -- and of the Humanists as well as of the works of recent jurists such as Covarruvias, Bodin and Hotman.  He is not aiming to deal with the art of politics; Aristotle had seen the distinction between politics and law, although Bodin did not.

Grotius was deliberately trying to deal in abstractions and to avoid being tied to particular times or places; although inspired to write by the misery of contemporary warfare, he claimed that his theories were not related to current events.  The system he proposed could apply in any time or circumstance, and indeed his system of rules was capable of being drawn on not only in relation to disputes in international affairs but also in matters of private law.  Through Pufendorf, Christian Wolff and Thomasius his work had immense influence on the development of both private and public law, particularly in Germany; in Scotland too Stair claimed direct

360

inspiration from Grotius. His influence on these and other later writers appears both in the arrangement of materials, as in the treatment of property and obligations, and in specific rules, such as the transfer of property by consent. Accordingly, although he is most commonly known as the father of modern public international law (and he was the institutional founder of Dutch law), Grotius was also a starting point for the codifying lawyers of the Enlightenment and a support for an increasingly mercantile society, in which good order and a clearly defined system of rules of property and obligations were seen as highly desirable. He provided an overall scheme, not merely a set of rules for particular application. It is somewhat ironic that, in basing the law on the subjective rights of the members of a community, that is such rights as the right to property or to reparation for injury, his approach to the presentation of law could be taken up by the legal positivists -- a strange fate for the originator of a system of Natural Law.

(iii) The German school of Natural Lawyers

Whereas Grotius was to a large extent within the Humanist tradition, the German Natural Lawyers based, or tried to base, their approach on the scientific method of Galileo or Descartes. The method aimed at building up a system deduced logically from axioms, worked out by experiment and observation which in their turn corrected the results achieved by logic. In theory this made it possible to free Natural Law from any particular authority or presuppositions; Natural Law thereafter was based on the consideration of man as part of a natural world which followed natural laws discernible by observation and reason.

Thomas Hobbes (1588-1679), the English political theorist, was the first to apply the method in jurisprudential writing in his book De Cive (On the Citizen -- Paris, 1642) and again in his more famous work, Leviathan. He was widely read and his political philosophy was found attractive by absolute rulers and their supporters, but his general views on Natural Law were not accepted. Individual points, however, were taken over by other writers; for example, his view that a contract is a declaration of will by the parties and involves either the transfer of right by one party to another or the giving up of rights by one party in favour of another. This required that the will of a party to a contract must be expressed in such a way as to be known to the other party, and that the transfer or cession of rights must be accepted by the beneficiary in order to complete the contract. Hobbes also argued that later agreements cannot be effective against earlier ones because the right would already have been transferred; therefore the first buyer in a double sale (where the same thing is sold twice to different people) is preferred to the second.

Hobbes was an influence on Samuel Pufendorf (1632-94), who is best known for his textbook, De Jure Naturae et Gentium (On the Law of Nature and Nations -- 1672); a summary of this was published the following year under the title De Officio Hominis et Civis iuxta Legem Naturalem (On the Duty of Man and Citizen according to Natural Law). Pufendorf also made the social life of man the basis of his scheme of Natural Law but, unlike Hobbes, he argued that the natural state of man was one of peace and that the maintenance of peace was instituted and sanctioned by nature herself without any human intervention; men were therefore obliged to recognize Natural Law insofar as they were endowed with reason. He distinguished divine law, natural law and positive law, but he treated divine law, which is based on God's revelation, as being in a separate sphere from the others because it goes beyond the concerns of this life. Natural Law was law which so harmonized with the intrinsic and social nature of man that the human race could have no wholesome and peaceful social organization without it. Positive law was that law which proceeded entirely from the will of the legislator, although it should not lack reason and usefulness, at least for the particular society of men for which it had been promulgated.

Founding on the sociable nature and individual weakness of man as a species, Pufendorf worked out a general system of rules for social living in a way which Hobbes had not. Hobbes had not felt any such need, since for him the content of the law was determined by the will of the legislator, which must be accepted for the sake of peace. Pufendorf followed the method of Hobbes and of Descartes, basing his system partly on deduction and partly on observation of man's conduct. Although his conclusions were closer to those of Grotius than of Hobbes, he used different methods from Grotius. He did not rely on the examples used by Grotius to find authority for his assertions but instead used both these examples and modern authors as material for observation, and from this he justified the premises on which he worked. He set out his principles in the first two of the eight books of De Jure Naturae; thereafter he applied them to the law of obligations (especially contracts), to property, to the law of persons and to public law, which was used in the sense both of law concerning the structure of the state and also of criminal law and law relating to international transactions.

Pufendorf was greatly respected by most jurists of his day and his subsequent influence was very considerable. His first book, Elementa jurisprudentiae universalis (Elements of a universal jurisprudence -- 1660), led to his being appointed by the Elector Palatine to a chair in Law of Nature and Nations expressly created for him at Heidelberg; in this book he used the mathematical method, with axiomatic and observational deductions. While at Heidelberg he wrote a book vigorously attacking the Holy Roman Empire as then constituted, denying its descent from the ancient Roman empire and deploring the conduct of the ecclesiastical princes and of the Habsburgs. This led to his spending some years in Sweden where, after the publication of De Jure Naturae, he was appointed historiographer-royal. Shortly after the publication of De Habitu Religionis (On the Usage of Religion), which argued that the church was only a voluntary union of men, a corporation subject to the general rules affecting corporations and legally no more, he was invited to Berlin and became historiographer to the Elector of Brandenburg.

His work was influential for the structure of later codifications of law; it particularly affected the 'general part' which is commonly found at the beginning of codes and in which the principles of law are dealt with. Natural Law thinking also helped to systematize the Roman law material which was to be widely incorporated into codifications. (The work of Leibnitz (1646-1716), however -- who thought little of Pufendorf -- was also important in the movement towards radical legal reform and codification. He used a revised assembly of the Roman material; he also made clear the distinction between logical and empirical knowledge.) Pufendorf's legal theory gave a central place to contract, which he ordered into a general plan more systematically than ever before. The methods of ending obligations were also set out systematically; furthermore, obligation itself, along with succession, was seen as being a means of acquiring ownership. In the content of the rules which he sets out Pufendorf relied quite heavily on Grotius, and also on Hobbes in the case of contract, but he worked out more fully the consequences of the rules. For example, in the case of risk in sale -- which according to Roman law passed to the buyer as soon as the contract was completed even if ownership had not yet passed -- he went beyond Grotius when he argued that the passing of risk was dependent on whether the delay in delivery was necessary, on whether the seller was slow in making delivery and on whether there was any fault in the buyer; Grotius had merely said that the seller should bear the loss if ownership did not immediately pass, thus disagreeing with the Roman rule. Again, on frustration of contract Pufendorf argued that only a change of circumstances making it actually impossible to fulfil the obligation released the party under obligation.

Christian Wolff (1679-1754) was a later member of the German Natural Law school who claimed to improve on Pufendorf's analysis. He argued that detailed rules of law were not immediately deducible from nature but that they could be worked out by proceeding from those of more general application which were immediately deducible, and thus to a detailed system. He proposed a more precise specification of the Natural Law rules which were appropriate for enactment as positive law. He alleged that his system was based solely on rational arguments, but one finds within it value judgments, such as a belief in the preferability of individual to common ownership. He was of considerable importance for the eighteenth century German codifiers and for the nineteenth century Pandectists. He also influenced writers on the Gemeines Recht, the German common law, and legal education in the German universities.

Christian Thomasius (1655-1728) began as a follower of Pufendorf but moved away from the older man's ideas when he applied the logic of the rational method to remove all necessary ethical content from Natural Law. Law was for him simply a compulsory duty imposed on the individual; there were therefore no eternal natural rules of law but only rules historically variable according to time and place. His interest in the development of

German law followed naturally from this attitude, as did his interest in German language and history. His particular views were rational and humane; for example, he argued against the use of torture in obtaining evidence and against the treatment of witchcraft as a crime -- views which many states put into effect in the century of the Enlightenment.


(iv)  Dutch Elegant Jurisprudence and Dutch national law


The rise of the Dutch Elegant Jurisprudence is connected in part with the Wars of Religion in France; many of the leading Humanists were Huguenots who fled from persecution to the Netherlands or Germany. Doneau for example, left France for Geneva and was then in Heidelberg from 1573 to 1579, in Leiden 1579-87 and in Altdorf until his death in 1591. But such distinguished foreign visitors would not have been so influential if other factors favouring Humanist jurisprudence had not been present.

Towns had been important in the Netherlands from relatively early in the feudal period, and town law had close links with the general law merchant. Ecclesiastical courts had, as elsewhere in Europe, introduced romano-canonical procedure to a wide range of litigants; among the canonists the work of Johannes Andreae was particularly authoritative. There was no formal reception of Roman law but, in the fifteenth and early sixteenth centuries, there was a general acceptance of Roman law as a subsidiary source, especially in Friesland. Under Charles the Bold of Burgundy a central supreme court or Parlement had been established in 1473; this had only a brief life and not until 1504 was the court re-established to become the Great Council of Malines (also known as Mechelen). It had an appellate jurisdiction from most of the provinces making up the Netherlands, northern and southern. Of the provincial supreme courts, the

366

Court of Holland was founded in 1428 and throughout the rest of the century it increasingly came to be manned by judges trained in the learned law. Although there was no university in the northern provinces until the later sixteenth century, Louvain had been founded in 1425 and students from the Netherlands also studied law in Italy, France and Germany. In 1575 Leiden was established; other universities followed, such as Groningen in 1614, Amsterdam in 1631 and Utrecht in 1634.

During the sixteenth century there was a movement towards the collection and codification of customs within the provinces; Charles V ordered the provincial courts to undertake this work. A degree of codification was achieved in Friesland and Overijssel; Zeeland had already codified its feudal customs; Holland[1] was somewhat backward in this respect. There was also some general legislation covering all the the provinces in this period. Charles V in 1529 promulgated a general law on transfer of and charges on land, and the constitutio Carolina (described in chapter XI) was published in 1532 ; in 1570 Philip II issued an edict on criminal procedure. As a result of its wealth and of its leadership in the Wars of Independence Holland[2] emerged as the most influential of the provinces; the wide acceptance of Roman law as a subsidiary source was strengthened by its use in Holland's supreme court at The Hague which also had jurisdiction over Zeeland. Nevertheless it may be reckoned that Roman-Dutch law, as it was named by the seventeenth century jurist van Leeuwen,

----------

1     Holland, Zeeland, Friesland, Overijssel, Utrecht, Groningen and Gelderland became the United Provinces of the Northern Netherlands; the Southern Netherlands were, broadly, modern Belgium.

2     The importance of Holland is indicated by the fact that in English its name is commonly given to the whole country.

began to emerge considerably earlier.  The history of the later sixteenth and earlier seventeenth centuries not only encouraged the ever-present tendencies towards particularism but also pointed to the need for harmonization between the provinces. It is said that as late as the eighteenth century there could be doubt whether a crime should be tried by the Roman law, the Mosaic law, the constitutio Carolina or a local statute of 1342.

This was the background to the work of Grotius.  The Introduction to the Jurisprudence of Holland, first written in prison with only limited access to other literature, provided the outline of a unified legal system, built on a combination of feudal and customary with Roman and Natural law. It was thus in the same tradition as the work of Hotman and with the same purpose as that of Dumoulin and Coquille.  Grotius was already developing his theory of Natural Law, but in the Introduction he was also concerned with the growth of legal institutions and with producing solutions to particular problems.  It was with this latter intention that he dealt with the law of husband and wife, or classified delict as being directed against life, against the person, against freedom, against honour, and against property; it is also noticeable that he treated wrongs from the point of view of crime as well as delict.  He established Roman-Dutch law as a practical system open to rational juristic development; in essence this was the law taken by the Dutch to their colonies in South Africa and the Dutch East and West Indies and Guyana. In South Africa, Ceylon and Guyana, taken over by the British, it still survives.

The leading jurists who succeeded Grotius in the Netherlands continued to be inspired by the more practical aspects of Humanism and the less aggressive methods of Natural Law.  Arnold Vinnius (1588-1657), professor of law at Leiden, wrote a commentary from the viewpoint of his own time on the Institutes of Justinian which was used for centuries, also Jurisprudentia Contracta (The Law Abridged), a textbook of Roman law which drew on Doneau, and a book of Select Questions on Law which dealt with contemporary problems of private and constitutional law in a style essentially traditional but not unaffected by the latest thinking. Simon van Leeuwen (1625-82) practised law in Leiden for most of his life; the book which created the term Roman-Dutch law, Het Roomsch-Hollandsch Recht, was published in 1664, and has remained in use in South Africa as a work of authority. He naturally paid more attention to the decisions of the courts and the law of procedure than had Grotius, on whom he depended; his historical sources, however, were almost entirely Roman to the exclusion of custom. Ulrik Huber (1636-94) was professor at Franeker in Friesland and for three years a judge in the Frisian supreme court; he wrote commentaries on the Institutes and the Digest, and a treatise on Roman law as applied in Friesland. Johannes Voet (1647-1713) wrote a major commentary on the Digest, Commentarius ad Pandectas, which has had great authority in the Netherlands and South Africa and has also been much cited in Scotland -- even in this decade. Professor successively at Utrecht and Leiden, his work was in the Humanist tradition but was also affected by rationalist theory. Unlike his more 'Elegant' contemporary, Gerhardt Noodt (1647-1725), who also taught at Utrecht and Leiden, his method was to consider Roman law not as an abstract legal complex but as the product of a changing human society, but like him his teaching emphasised clarity of thought and expression.

The major figure of the early eighteenth century in Holland was Cornelius van Bynkershoek (1673-1745) who was from 1704 a member and from 1724 President of the Supreme Court of Holland, Zeeland and West Friesland. Four volumes have been published of the daily notes he made on the cases before the court, his Observationes Tumultuariae (Tumultuary Observations), but they were designed for his own use rather than for publication. He wrote on Roman and municipal law and also on public international law; he is perhaps most deserving of fame for having produced a workable solution to the problem of claims to sovereignty over the sea. Bynkershoek, following the Roman doctrine of acquisition by possession, pointed out that continuous possession of the sea was not possible and denied English claims as to the legal effect of maritime superiority; he acknowledged, however, that maritime nations might have special rights over certain parts even of the high seas, although not complete sovereignty. Effective protection, based on the force of arms, was made the criterion of sovereignty, and the marine league of some three miles, itself defined as the distance of a cannon shot, was accepted as fixing the limit of territorial waters. Bynkershoek's opinions were also influential in such areas of the law as the status of ambassadors, the taking of prizes in war, neutrality, blockade and contraband.

The Elegant Jurisprudence, the Humanist tradition, was in the seventeenth century best exemplified in the writings of the Dutch jurists, but there were Humanists elsewhere. We have already mentioned, in the context of the Humanists, the work of the two Gothofredi, Dionysius and Jacobus, who died in 1622 and 1652 respectively. Antoine Favre (1557-1624) wrote much on the civil law and also published decisions of the court of Savoy; he too was an adherent of the Humanist style. In Germany, although the usus modernus Pandectarum was dominant, there were some Humanists; J.G. Heineccius (1681-1741) was the most important of them. He was a pupil of Thomasius and, inspired by his master's ideas, wrote on Germanic law and its history; he also wrote a book entitled Syntagma Antiquitatum Romanarum Jurisprudentiam Illustrantium (Collection of Roman Antiquities Illustrating

370

Jurisprudence), which was based largely on the order of the Institutes and was a typical work of Humanist learning, and also some smaller works on Roman legal history. His elementary textbook of Roman law was much used in Scotland as well as in the Netherlands and Germany. He also wrote a manual on Natural Law which did not, as so many others had done, reject the value of the civil law; nevertheless he pointed out, for example, that the principle of reparation for wrong, commonly called Aquilian liability after the Roman lex Aquilia, was also to be found among the Turks or the Chinese, while the details of the lex had not been received[3].

(v)   English jurisprudence

The final strand in seventeenth century legal history is the appearance on the European scene of English jurisprudence. England had felt the Humanist movement in the sixteenth century but not in such a way as to affect the Common Law. In the fifteenth century two major legal works had been produced. Littleton's Tenures, first printed in 1481, was primarily concerned with feudal land law, but Littleton dealt sufficiently thoroughly with uses for the book to stay in print in student editions until the mid-nineteenth century. Fortescue's De Laudibus Legum Angliae (In Praise of the Laws of England -- c.1470) was concerned with praising the English legal system as opposed to that of France; it was important in English constitutional development but had little impact in the wider world. The most original legal work of the sixteenth century in England was Christopher St. German's Doctor and Student (published in 1523 and 1530), framed as a debate between a doctor of divinity and a student of the

---------

3    Cited by Alan Watson Legal Transplants (Edinburgh, 1974) p.80.

Common Law. At the time, it was relevant to the arguments about the extent of chancery jurisdiction and that of the ecclesiastical courts generally, but it put into popular form the natural law thinking of the canonists on the tensions between law and conscience; it remained much used as a textbook for some two centuries. It reflected European thinking but did not influence it.

A decade or so later Henry VIII, with political rather than jurisprudential motives, created Regius Chairs of Civil Law at Oxford and Cambridge; academic lawyers showed that they were well aware of intellectual movements on the continent, although practising Common Lawyers remained unmoved. William Fulbeck (1560-c.1603) wrote on the parallels between the civil, the canon and the common laws; John Cowell (1554-1611), professor of civil law at Cambridge, wrote a description of the law of England organized on the model of Justinian's Institutes. John Selden (1584-1654) was interested in legal history and, for example, proved that trial by battle had been introduced by the Normans, whereas Sir Matthew Hale (1609-76) was inclined to believe that all institutions of English law dated back to the Saxon period, if not earlier. (Hale's History of the Common Law was published posthumously in 1713.) Selden, however, did appear on the European stage when in 1618, consequent upon an international incident, he composed a reply to Grotius' Mare Liberum (The Free Sea) which had defended the freedom of the seas; Mare Clausum (The Closed Sea -- only published in 1632) was unsuccessful as an argument, but Selden's skill as a disputant was recognized by Grotius himself.

The seventeenth century conveniently marks the passage from a degree of English receptiveness towards the influence of the Humanists and the Christian natural lawyers to the recognition on the continent of some English jurists as worthy of remark. Alberico Gentili, although brought up

372

in Italy, spent the second half of his life in England and is remembered as Regius Professor at Oxford from 1587; he was widely influential, although his fame was somewhat overshadowed by that of Grotius. Richard Zouche (1590-1661), also Regius Professor at Oxford, was much read for his blending of Natural Law with a strongly Roman base in his Elementa Jurisprudentiae (Elements of Jurisprudence -- 1629), which adopted a systematic division between rights (ius) and remedies (iudicium) in a general survey of the whole field of law. He also was prominent in international law, particularly with his Jus Fetiale sive Jus inter Gentes (Ambassadorial Law or Law between Nations -- 1650). He was influenced himself by such writers as Fulbeck, Welwood and Selden as well as by Grotius. The influence he enjoyed on the continent is indicated by the frequent publication of his works; De Jure inter Gentes, for example, was printed at Leiden in 1651, at The Hague in 1659 and at Mainz in 1661, and a German translation was published in Frankfurt in 1666. Zouche invented the expressive term, law between nations, which more accurately indicated the difficulties than did the term law of nations; he also put stress on the importance of law based on agreement rather than on nature, although accepting that in international affairs the problem of enforcement diminished the force of positive law.

Another English thinker of great importance was Hobbes. As a firm believer in positive law -- law is "the command of him or them that have coercive power" -- he was the intellectual ancestor of John Austin; he was himself influenced by the thought of Sir Francis Bacon. He is best known for his political theory, supporting, in the interests of peace, the absolute power of the ruler, but he also wrote on Natural Law. He founded human society on a form of social contract, and in his system the law of nature was an ordering which restricted natural rights. "If a covenant be

373

made wherein neither of the parties perform presently but trust one another:  in the condition of mere nature, which is a condition of war of every man against every man upon any reasonable suspicion, it is void; but if there be a common power set over them both, with right and force sufficient to compel performance, it is not void" (Leviathan, I, ch. 14). He described the laws of nature as "the dictate of right reason", and gave examples such  as that one must relinquish some of one's rights, that one must perform contracts and keep trust, and, foreshadowing Bentham, that where one is in reasonable doubt one is to prefer that which promises the greater sum of good.  Hobbes also held that the degree of punishment for an offence should be related to the effect of the punishment rather than to the nature of the offence.

Natural Law in Hobbes was more a context, an explanation of origins, than a system to be applied.  This rather weak acceptance of Natural Law is also apparent in the work of Blackstone in the eighteenth century.  Both the nature and the influence of Blackstone's work are such that it is more suitably described in the context of the seventeenth than the eighteenth century. Sir William Blackstone (1723-80) was the first man to produce on the English Common Law something approaching an institutional description, in the tradition of Coquille, Grotius or Stair.  The Institutes of Edward Coke (1552-1634) may perhaps have owed their title to contemporary intellectual fashion but the content reveals only a traditional view of the Common Law. The First Institute is a commentary on Littleton, showing much learning but little system; the Second, Third and Fourth Institutes concerned the older statutes, the pleas of the Crown and the jurisdiction of the courts.  Blackstone's Commentaries on the Laws of England were based on the lectures he gave as Vinerian Professor at Oxford, where he was the first occupant of this chair (founded in 1758);  the students to whom his lectures were addressed were far more likely to become parsons or squires than lawyers since English legal education hardly existed[4] and legal training remained firmly in the hands of the profession. The move towards the teaching of municipal law in English universities was not so very much later than in other universities of Europe, but the available legal literature on the Common Law was centuries behind.

The structure of the **Commentaries** was derived eventually from the civilian division of law into that relating to persons, to things and to actions. Book I of the **Commentaries** deals with the rights of persons, Book II with rights concerning things; Book III, on private wrongs, is primarily concerned with civil procedure although there are some chapters on delict, and Book IV, on public wrongs, deals more with the substantive criminal law, perhaps on the analogy of the last title in Justinian's **Institutes**. Blackstone's structure was sufficiently logical for the work to be adapted to new conditions, as happened particularly in the United States of America. For example, the Louisiana civil code of 1808 owed a considerable debt to Blackstone in its treatment of persons, and his work was not incompatible with the earlier civilian system. At the time of the American Revolution Blackstone's **Commentaries** were already well known in America. As American legal institutions increasingly grew away from their roots in the English legal system of the colonies, they found in Blackstone an institutional base on which to found a specifically American Common Law.

----------

4.  In 1846 the House of Commons Select Committee on Legal Education reported that "no legal education, worthy of the name, of a public nature is at this moment to be had [in England]". Cited by P. Stein **Legal Evolution** (C.U.P., 1980), p.78.

Further Reading:

J.W. Cairns "Blackstone, an English Institutist: legal literature and the rise of the nation state" 4 Oxford J. Legal St. (1984), 318

A.P. D'Entrèves  Natural law (London, 1951, repr.)

R. Feenstra & C.J.D. Waal  Seventeenth Century Leyden Law Professors and their influence on the development of the civil law (Amsterdam, 1975)

J. Finnis  Natural Law and Natural Rights (O.U.P., 1980)

G. Gorla & L. Moccia "A 'revisiting' of the comparison between 'continental' law and English law" 2 J.Legal Hist. (1981), 143

Lord Lloyd  An Introduction to Jurisprudence (3rd ed. London, 1972)

K. Luig "Institutes of national law in the seventeenth and eighteenth centuries' 1972 Jur.Rev., 193

P. Stein "The attraction of the civil law in post-revolutionary America" 52 Virginia L.R. (1966) 403

C.C. Turpin "The antecedents of Roman Dutch law" 1963 Acta Juridica, 1

Chapter XIV

## THE MAKING OF SCOTS LAW

(i)   The reception of Roman law

Scots law is not, as is sometimes popularly believed, based entirely
on Roman law but the Roman system, along with feudal and canon law, was one
of the major influences of its formative years.   Much of the modern Scots
law of moveable property and contract is undoubtedly civilian, while it
still occasionally happens that argument adduced in court is backed by
direct reference to Roman law[1].   Yet important though Roman law in
its   developed mediaeval form undoubtedly was, its influence can be
exaggerated.   The use of Roman terminology does not necessarily indicate
the adoption of a Roman institution; Scots law, for example, borrowed the
Roman term 'interdict', but the remedy is a very different one in each
system.   Again, Scots law adopted the provisions of the lex Rhodia (Rhodian
Sea Law) but not so much directly from Roman law as from the general
mercantile custom of Europe.   Roman law has never been of itself
authoritative in Scotland.   Rather, as in the pays de coutumes, it was
received because of its rational system and as a source of equitable
principle when the native law was silent or obscure.   This is made plain in
the work of the early Scottish institutional writers who were the first to
reflect on the content of Scots law.   Sir Thomas Craig wrote that "we in
this kingdom are bound by the laws of the Romans insofar as they are in
harmony with the laws of nature and right reason" (Ius feudale I,2,14).

----------

1    E.g., Sloans Dairies Ltd. v Glasgow Corporation 1977 S.C. 223; 1979
     S.L.T.  17.

Lord Stair said that, although Roman law "[has] great weight with us, namely in cases where a custom is not yet formed", nevertheless it does not have "with us the authority of law; and therefore [is] only received according to [its] equity and expediency" (Institutions I,1,16).

In the Middle Ages there was not even the beginning of a true reception of Roman law. The contents of the mediaeval lawbooks were primarily feudal and customary; there was no systematic civilian influence on the substantive law or the procedures of the lay courts. Admittedly Roman law was not considered as an alien discipline but as part of the common intellectual inheritance of Europe; it was frequently used by notaries, for example, but not always with real understanding. This is definitely suggested by the evidence from charters, for the renunciations mentioned in the previous chapter on Scotland often seem to be included more to parade the learning of the scribe than to serve any real need; for example, there was little point in renouncing Hadrian's beneficium divisionis (which restricted the liability of a co-surety to his proportionate share) when it was not known in Scots law.

When Roman law first began to influence legal developments it was not directly but through canon law. The jurisdiction of the mediaeval Scottish church courts was similar to that elsewhere, but it seems that the activities of the canon lawyers were not limited to the strictly ecclesiastical sphere. Unlike England, Scotland did not have an established and powerful central court, and those who administered justice in the localities were largely untrained laymen. In contrast the Church offered justice that was both learned and sophisticated; it seems likely that many cases which in England would have gone to the secular courts were in Scotland disposed of through the courts spiritual or through the offices of an ecclesiastical arbiter. Canon lawyers formed the only established legal profession until the fifteenth or even sixteenth century.

Canon law and the ecclesiastical courts brought Roman law to Scotland in two ways. First, there is evidence of argument taken from Roman law being used as the basis of pleadings in the church courts. Examples include claims based on prescription and the use of restitutio in integrum (restoration to the original state of affairs) to set aside a sale alleged to be at an unjustly high price. The law used in the ecclesiastical courts did not necessarily affect the secular law, but litigants became accustomed to using Roman law in one forum and to the notion that it had much to offer that was profitable. Moreover, in Scotland the Church followed the general canon law more closely than, for example, it did in England; rules not given effect in England were in Scotland ultimately absorbed into the secular law, as happened with legitimation by subsequent marriage -- which the Church had taken over from Roman law.

Second, and more important, the church courts introduced romano-canonical procedure into Scotland and thus were responsible for its ultimate reception into the lay courts. Churchmen played an important part in the jurisdiction of the Council in the fifteenth century, and it seems likely that their presence resulted in the use of procedures based on those of the ecclesiastical courts. When the College of Justice was founded in 1532 the Lord President and seven of the fourteen judges were clerics, and the records show that the 'new' court from the beginning employed a procedure similar to that of the church courts.

By the later fifteenth century there were signs that Roman law was beginning to have a direct, even if generalized, influence on the law of Scotland. In 1469, for example, parliament introduced the (Roman) rule that when a child needed a tutor the nearest male agnate over the age of twenty-five was to act -- although in this context 'agnate' was used to mean any male relative and not in its specialized Roman sense of one related exclusively through the male line. But it was not until the sixteenth century that the reception proper can be said to have begun. As elsewhere in Europe the agents of the reception were those who had received a university education in law.

Scotland had no universities of her own until the fifteenth century and so Scots who wished to study law were forced to go abroad. Scottish students in substantial numbers were to be found at the universities of Italy, France, Germany and the Netherlands. Paris and Cologne were always popular, while at Orléans, famous for its law school, the Scots formed a separate student nation. Initially many of these students concentrated on canon law with a view to ecclesiastical preferment, and on their return to Scotland pursued careers in the Church and her courts, perhaps moving into the service of the crown. During the fifteenth century something of a change took place and university trained lawyers began to consider a career in the secular courts; at first their numbers seem to have been small, but they were important for the future.

In 1413 a university was founded at St. Andrews and in 1451 another at Glasgow; Aberdeen's foundation dates from 1496. From the beginning it was intended that each should offer instruction in the civil and the canon law; indeed, this was one of the purposes behind their erection. If a legal education were available in Scotland it would be easier to produce adequate numbers of legally trained men to staff the courts -- the pattern was the same as in Germany or France. Further, a statute of 1496 laid on barons and free-holders of substance the duty to ensure that their heirs attended for "three years at the schools of art and law so that they may have knowledge and understanding of the laws"; that is, all those who were expected to succeed to heritable jurisdictions were to be trained to

380

discharge their duties in a competent professional manner. However, many of the hopes placed in the new universities were frustrated, partly because of inadequate financial endowment and perhaps partly because of student preference for foreign travel. The teaching of canon law at St. Andrews seems never to have begun, and at the end of the sixteenth century it is not certain that any law at all was being taught at Glasgow. Scots students continued to go abroad in considerable numbers for their legal education, at first to France and within the Empire and, after the Reformation, to the Protestant German states and the Netherlands. Leiden was particularly attractive to foreign students, and among them was a sizeable proportion of Scots. Only during the eighteenth century did the teaching of law in Scottish universities begin to revive and the practice of seeking legal education abroad to decline, ceasing altogether after the Napoleonic Wars.

The facts of Scottish legal education had important consequences for the reception of Roman law. On the one hand, unlike the countries of the continent, Scotland did not develop in its own schools a strong tradition of civilian study. There were certainly Scottish civilians of note, but they mostly made their academic careers in Europe. Of this number were Henry Scrimgeour (1506-72), who became professor of civil law at Geneva and produced an edition of the Novels, Edward Henryson, another sixteenth century scholar, who became professor of civil law at Bourges, and William Barclay (1547-1608), professor at Angers. On the other hand, unlike the English, Scots who returned home to practise law after a legal education at a continental university were armed with a knowledge of up-to-date civilian scholarship as well as with some first-hand experience of other legal systems. Both factors had an effect on the development of Scots law. Much of the Roman law that was received was the civil law of the ius commune,

381

and in the sixteenth and seventeenth centuries this was hardly suprising. Even Germany, with its much more thorough Reception and the scholarly traditions of its universities, absorbed a Roman law that had for the most part been adapted to new circumstances. The Scots knew the Dutch civilian writers well and made much use of them, while references to the French jurists and the decisions of the French courts are to be found in Scottish works such as, for example, Spottiswoode's Practicks. Also instructive in this context is the first catalogue of the Library of the Faculty of Advocates, published in 1692; this gives a good indication of the kinds of material consulted and used by lawyers and thus helping to shape Scots law. The Library included "the Bartolists, the French customary lawyers and the Dutch civilians and customary lawyers ... the texts of the Coutumes of Paris, Bourges, Burgundy, Brittany, Troyes and Orléans, the decisions of the French parlements, and the works of Charles Dumoulin ... and of Guy Pape. ...[There were] treatises by Van Leeuwen, Matthaeus, ... Voet, Grotius, Huber, Noodt, Vinnius, and many others"[2].

The Scottish reception seems to have been accomplished largely through the practice of the courts, and in particular of the Court of Session. By the mid-fifteenth century there appears to have been a well-established, if as yet small, body of professional pleaders regularly appearing in the lay courts. The foundation of the College of Justice and the establishment on a firmer footing of the Court of Session in the following century increased the attractions of such a career; the Reformation effectively closed the door on the alternative of ecclesiastical preferment. At first it seems that Roman law was more used by advocates in the presentation of their arguments than by the judges in reaching their decisions. But the bench

----------

2    Stair Society, vol. I, 177.

was also well-disposed towards Roman law; many judges were law graduates who had started their careers at the bar. The judiciary was of course bound to administer the law of Scotland as found in the statutes of the Scottish parliament and in the various treatises devoted to the customary and feudal law. However, much of this indigenous law was uncertain; it did not exist in any authoritative form comparable to the codified customs of France. Moreover it was not a particularly mature or sophisticated law, with the exception of fields dealt with by some recent statutes. In default of other guidance the judiciary naturally turned to the _ratio scripta_ (written reason) of Roman law; one late sixteenth century Lord of Session commented: "Thus far to the laws of the realm we are restricted, if any cumbersome or troublesome cause fall out, as often chances, which can not be agreed by our country's laws, incontinently whatever is thought necessary to pacify this controversy is cited out of the Roman laws"[3].

Such ready resort to the Roman law did not please everyone. In 1609 Sir John Skene, in the preface to his edition of the 'auld lawes', complained of those who spent all their time on the study of Roman law at the expense of the laws of Scotland which, he considered, ought to have been their primary concern. Indeed, part of his purpose in producing an edition of the 'auld lawes' was probably to counter this trend and to provide for Scotland a clear and definitive statement of at least part of its native law for use in the practice of the courts. But Skene's work was not adequate for this purpose, and the reception of Roman law continued. The legal literature reflects its importance. In 1590 William Welwood, professor of civil law at St. Andrews, produced _The Sea Laws of Scotland_, perhaps the first modern treatise on an area of Scots law. Welwood's own

----------

3    Quoted by Stein, _Jur.Rev._ (1963), p.216.

sources included the law merchant and appropriate Scottish material, but his greatest debt was to Roman law. Somewhat later the institutional writers, who are considered in the next section, inevitably placed Roman law among their sources, and, particularly in the field of obligations, a great deal of what they have to say is shot through with civilian doctrines as well as with those of Natural Law.

From the beginning of the eighteenth century the direct impact of Roman law in Scotland began to decline. This was partly because by then Scots law was emerging as a coherent national system; much of what Roman law had to offer had already been absorbed, and it was more practical to refer directly to the institutional writers or to the body of case law. Moreover, after the Act of Union in 1707 English law began to influence Scots law, partly because of the appellate jurisdiction of the House of Lords and, more generally, because with the expansion of Scottish industry and trade at that period a greater interest was taken in the commercial law of England. Mercantile law there was being brilliantly developed in the judgments of Lord Mansfield; some mercantile statutes of the Parliament of Great Britain applied to both countries, and they tended to be weighted in favour of the larger country's law.

(ii) Legal literature

We shall consider reports of decisions in the Court of Session in more detail when we come to look at that court. The earliest collections or **Practicks** were compiled for private use by members of the court, not for publication; they were notes by judges (usually) of decisions they had made or witnessed. Towards the end of the sixteenth century **Practicks** of a new kind began to appear, which are sometimes known as 'digest' **Practicks**.

384

Instead of simply containing notes of decisions, they tried to offer a digest of the law, subject by subject, with all the material relevant to each topic being drawn together under the one heading -- rather similar to the English **Abridgements**. Their authors, however, drew not only on the decisions of the Court of Session but also on statute and the 'auld lawes' as found in such treatises as **Regiam Majestatem**. The first of these digest **Practicks** to be compiled was that of Sir James Balfour, completed in or shortly after 1579. Other examples include the **Major Practicks** of Sir Thomas Hope and the **Practicks** of Sir Robert Spottiswoode. They were the forerunners of the institutional works and Stair for one made much use of them in writing his **Institutions**.

While the phrase 'institutional writer' has become a term of art in modern Scots law, used to signify a small group of writers whose works -- or at least some of whose works -- are regarded as formal sources of Scots law, originally the term did no more than describe someone who wrote a particular type of book. Institutional writings were a common approach throughout Europe as the various nations began to break with the traditions of the **ius commune** and to create self-contained national legal systems. In each country the blend of indigenous law and elements taken from Roman, canon and feudal law varied, but in all we find a literature, usually in the vernacular, setting out the native law in a comprehensive and systematic way on the analogy of Justinian's **Institutes**. Often these works were intended to be used as textbooks as local and sometimes even national law began to be taught in the universities of Europe. We have mentioned Carpzov and Stryk in Germany or Coquille and Loysel in France; Blackstone in eighteenth century England was belatedly in the same tradition.

Paradoxically the first of the Scottish institutional writers, Sir Thomas Craig, owes his place in the canon to a book which was not institutional in the sense described above. Craig's reputation rests on his _Ius Feudale_ (_Feudal Law_), which was written in Latin, not English, and which dealt only with feudal law, in which context we have considered its European influence. Nor did Craig confine himself to the feudal law of Scotland; he produced what can better be described as a general work on the feudal law of the _ius commune_ with special reference to Scotland. However, it was important for the future of Scottish legal writing; its systematic approach looked forward rather than backward and placed it in a different world from the relatively crude assembly of source material found in the digest _Practicks_.

Of fundamental importance for the future of Scots law and its development as a national system was Sir James Dalrymple, Viscount Stair (1619-95). Born in Ayrshire, Stair studied and then taught in the University of Glasgow before turning to the law; in 1648 he became an advocate and in 1657 he was appointed to the bench. From 1671 until his death he was Lord President of the Court of Session, save for the years 1681-88 which he spent in exile in Holland, returning with William of Orange. Stair's contribution to Scots law lies above all in his _Institutions of the Law of Scotland_, first published in 1681. The work was a landmark. First, Stair's approach was that of the early Natural Lawyers; his primary definition of law was as "the dictate of reason" and he thought that the law of Scotland "could be no other than _aequum et bonum_ (equitable and good)". In addition, Stair held to the view -- not, he thought, shared by most lawyers -- that law "should be handled as a rational discipline, having principles whence its conclusions may be deduced". In short, Stair offered a reasoned and systematic approach to the science of law, reasoned because he took equity as his overriding principle and systematic because he attempted to expound the law in a logical and structured way.

386

Second, the **Institutions** are important as the first work of their kind to be devoted to the municipal law of Scotland. As Stair tells us, his design was to "give a description of the law and customs of Scotland, such as might not only be profitable for judges and lawyers, but might be pleasant and useful to all persons of honour and discretion". Native sources, particularly in the form of decisions of the Court of Session, have a prominent place in the exposition. The elements of the _ius commune_, Roman, canon and feudal law, are not — indeed, could not be — neglected, but "none of these have with us the authority of law", having place only where native custom was silent, and then only on the grounds of their innate equity and expediency. Stair also made use of the continental, particularly the Dutch, civilian writers. But unlike that of Craig, Stair's work was not based on the _ius commune_ with Scottish annotations but was rather an exposition of Scots law in the light of all the sources available; in particular, it was composed as a deliberate construct, designed in accordance with Natural Law principles, against which he measured Roman law (and other sources). It was an institutional work in the European sense; its appearance both marked the emergence and aided the further development of Scots law as a self-contained system of national law. It also set a pattern for the legal literature which came after it. In looking at this we shall deal first with those writers who acquired the technical status of institutional writers.

In 1684 the first edition of Sir George Mackenzie's **Institutions of the Law of Scotland** was published. This was considerably shorter than Stair's book, and it was probably designed to provide an elementary introduction to Scots law but, like Stair, Mackenzie offered a comprehensive survey of his subject. He had been a student in France before becoming an advocate in 1659; he later held the office of Lord

Advocate. As Dean of Faculty he played a leading part in the foundation (in 1682) of the Advocates' Library -- a scheme proposed by his predecessor, Sir John Dalrymple, Stair's son.

The eighteenth century saw two institutional writers of note, Andrew McDouall, Lord Bankton (1685-1760), and John Erskine (1695-1768). Bankton became an advocate in 1708 and a Lord of Session in 1755. His An Institute of the Laws of Scotland was published between 1751 and 1753; in scale it was far closer to Stair than to Mackenzie and may indeed have been intended to update the former. It was an institutional work in the general sense; it dealt with all of Scots civil law and, among other things, it was intended to protect the integrity of the Scottish legal system by comparing and contrasting it with English law. Erskine entered the Faculty of Advocates in 1719 and was professor of Scots Law at Edinburgh from 1737 to 1765. He is remembered for two books, The Principles of the Law of Scotland (1754) and An Institute of the Law of Scotland, published posthumously in 1773. The former, which is not usually counted as a formal source of law, is nevertheless an institutional work in the general sense, for it is an elementary introduction on the model of Mackenzie's, which it appears rapidly to have replaced. The Institute is a more ambitious text; its scale is similar to the works of Stair and Bankton, and so is the range of material covered and the degree of detail.

Last among the institutional writers was George Joseph Bell (1770-1843). Advocate from 1791, in 1822 he accepted the chair of Scots Law at Edinburgh; in 1829 he published his Principles of the Law of Scotland which, in the tradition of Erskine's Principles, was designed as an introductory student textbook. Of greater importance was his Commentaries on the Law of Scotland and the Principles of Mercantile Jurisprudence, which was an expanded version of his Treatise on the Law of Bankruptcy in

388

<u>Scotland</u>, first published in 1800. The <u>Commentaries</u> do, however, mark a break with the institutional tradition which had formed and developed Scots law during the seventeenth and eighteenth centuries. Bell's subject was bankruptcy and, more broadly, mercantile law; the exposition is impressive but it does not offer the breadth of coverage which was an essential characteristic of the institutional approach. Moreover, there is considerable use of and reliance on English authorities, partly because of the topic itself, partly because of the cessation of Scottish lawyers' regular contacts with the universities of the continent, and partly because in the wake of the Industrial Revolution the links between Scotland and England were inevitably closer. Perhaps Bell's work was also a sign of maturity of the legal system; the time had come when Scotland needed detailed treatises on particular aspects of the law.

These institutional writers were not the only jurists who produced works of note, even institutional ones, during these centuries; for example, there was <u>The Institutions of the Law of Scotland</u> by William Forbes (d.1745), whose other major work, <u>The Great Body of the Law of Scotland</u> (c.1720) remains unpublished. Son of a professor in Padua, he became an advocate in 1696 and in 1714 was appointed the first Regius Professor of Law at Glasgow. Forbes was responsible, as official Reporter, for the first volume of Session case reports; he also wrote treatises on various fields of law within Scotland. Another important book was the <u>Principles of Equity</u> of Henry Home, Lord Kames (1696-1782), who also published several volumes of <u>Decisions</u> of the Court of Session. Some authorities would hold that Kames is institutional (in the technical sense) and would exclude Mackenzie. In the sphere of criminal law Mackenzie's <u>The Laws and Customs of Scotland in Matters Criminal</u> (1678) and Baron Hume's <u>Commentaries on the Law of Scotland respecting Crimes</u> (1797) are generally regarded as institutional, but other works, such as those of Sir Archibald Alison (1792-1867), remain on the margin of formal acceptance. The division seems largely to be due to the practice of the nineteenth century Scottish judges; certain works passed from being frequent sources of reference to possessing a definite authority as the bench found itself increasingly reluctant to depart from the views they contained. This problem of the definition of books of authority was not unique to Scotland; it can be discerned in other European countries, such as France or the Netherlands.

(iii)   The Court of Session

In 1532 the bench of the Court of Session consisted of the Chancellor of Scotland, the Lord President of the Court, fourteen Lords Ordinary and a number of Extraordinary Lords. The size of the court is indicative of a procedure more demanding of judicial manpower than the English but less so than the French. It was envisaged that when he sat the Chancellor would preside, but in practice his attendances were infrequent with the result that the Lord President effectively became the senior judge; this position was confirmed by default when after 1707 the office of Chancellor lapsed. Initially the Lords Ordinary included both clerics and laymen. In the King's Council of the fifteenth and early sixteenth centuries it had been generally the case that those members who had received a formal legal training were clerics; the evidence of the sederunts from the pre-1532 Council suggests that such men formed the nucleus of those who sat in session to administer justice. Clerical participation in the Court of Session continued until the mid-seventeenth century; the first four Lords President were all churchmen. The Reformation had reduced the numbers, but the last churchman to hold judicial office was Archbishop Burnet of Glasgow, who was appointed an Extraordinary Lord in 1664 -- he died in 1668.

The Extraordinary Lords were crown nominees; they were entitled to sit or not as they pleased. Appointments were made on purely political grounds and many of those appointed were without any formal legal training. In 1553 when the number reached eight the Court felt moved to protest and the number was then reduced to four; in 1723 it was enacted that no further such appointments were to be made, but the last holder did not die until 1762.

Until 1808 the structure of the Court of Session remained virtually unchanged. It was essentially a unitary court, whose members gave one judgment, although up to three judges might be absent, supervising the preparatory stages of the cases coming before the court, and the junior Lord Ordinary might be sitting in the Bill Chamber, which was originally a vacation court but acquired a special jurisdiction over exceptional forms of action. Pressure of business and time-consuming reliance on written pleadings led in the nineteenth century to reforms by statute. The Court was divided into two Houses, Inner and Outer. The Inner House, whose jurisdicion was to be mainly appellate, was itself divided into the First Division headed by the Lord President and the Second Division headed by the Lord Justice-Clerk. The new Outer House consisted of a number of Lords Ordinary sitting singly to exercise a jurisdiction of first instance.

From the beginning the Court of Session had had the power to regulate its own proceedings, a power confirmed in 1540 by a statute which gave the Court the right to make such "acts, statutes and ordinances as [it] shall think expedient for ordering of process and hasty expedition of justice". This rule-making power resulted in a vast number of enactments known as

Acts of Sederunt. The power itself was akin to that of the _Parlement_ of Paris to make _arrêts de règlement_; like that _Parlement_ the Court did not always restrict itself to governing its own procedure and sometimes introduced what amounted to new rules of substantive law, for example, new rules concerning bankruptcy. By the end of the eighteenth century, however, the Court was confining its enactments to the administration of justice in the strict sense.

Initially the court conducted its business _in camera_ (secretly) but by the close of the seventeenth century this policy had been abandoned in favour of open hearings (The Court of Session Act 1693). The first reports which survive are Sinclair's _Practicks_, compiled by an early Lord President and covering the years 1540-49. Like so many others, such as Haddington's - much cited by Stair --, they have never been printed. Other examples include Maitland's _Practicks_ which dealt with the years between 1550 and 1580 and Hope's (_Major_) _Practicks_ covering the period 1608-33. _Practicks_ remained the only form of regular law reports until the early eighteenth century, when attempts were made to provide more systematic reporting, although Stair himself had published _Decisions_ to show that like cases were treated alike. In 1705 William Forbes was appointed by the Faculty of Advocates to report the decisions of the Court of Session, and with his appointment the history of the modern Scottish law reports begins. Forbes was succeeded by other Faculty reporters, but it was only in the early years of the nineteenth century that the reports began to carry the opinions of individual judges. As on the continent the bench appears to have been reluctant to allow its reasoning to be made widely known. The _Practicks_ had offered little more than terse statements of what the Court had decided, but gradually the reports became more elaborate until by the mid-nineteenth century they had substantially assumed their modern form. The aim of the earlier compilations was simply to promote consistency in judicial decision-making; there was no doctrine of precedent, in the sense of the binding force of a single decision, until in the nineteenth century something akin to the English doctrine of *stare decisis*, but considerably less rigid, was gradually absorbed into Scots law. It is difficult to account completely for this development, but it seems that the appellate jurisdiction of the House of Lords, inevitably steeped in English habits, and the creation of an appellate house within the Court of Session itself contributed; so probably did improved standards of law reporting, and it was a period when English economic strengh — with all the consequences -- was predominant.

By 1532 then the Court of Session was Scotland's supreme civil court, but its jurisdiction was for a while limited. At first it was not even quite clear that the Session had jurisdiction in matters of fee and heritage -- that is, title to land -- as these were traditionally the province of the feudal courts or the full parliament. However, whatever the position at strict law, practice (probably in the shape of the preference of litigants) rapidly proved otherwise and the Session's jurisdiction in this area expanded during the 1530s and 1540s. The principal restraints which remained lay in the existence of other courts whose jurisdiction was both specialized and exclusive. Such courts were the Commissary Courts (dealt with in the context of the Reformation), the Court of Exchequer (reconstituted in 1707) and the Teind Court (dealing with the post-Reformation fate of tithes), which survived until its absorption into the Court of Session in the nineteenth century.

The Admiralty Court also disappeared in the nineteenth century as its jurisdiction was dispersed among the Courts of Session and Justiciary and the English Court of Admiralty. Maritime matters in Scotland were

393

originally dealt with by the magistrates of the seaward burghs but, particularly where foreign merchants or questions of trading policy were involved, these matters might be of more than local concern. The Crown's interest led to the establishment towards the end of the fifteenth century of the jurisdiction of the Court of Admiralty under the High Admiral of Scotland. The court sat at Edinburgh and had competence throughout Scotland but, at least in the early years, acted through deputes sitting in the ports. It had both a civil and a criminal jurisdiction, including questions of prize, and its procedure was swift and summary -- as was characteristic of a court dealing with the law merchant and foreign litigants. Its jurisdiction was not always welcomed by other courts; comparatively their procedures were slow, and in the area of mercantile contracts in particular there was some suspicion that the Admiralty Court would attract increasingly more business away from the Session. It was unable to resist these pressures and from the eighteenth century onwards it began to decline.

Another limitation on the Court of Session appeared in the eighteenth century as a consequence of the Union of the Parliaments in 1707. Article 18 of the Treaty provided that, with the exception of revenue law and the regulation of trade, Scots law was to remain as it was, although subject to alteration by the new Parliament of Great Britain, particularly in matters of public law. The legal systems of the two countries thus remained distinct, but subject to the one legislative body. This has sometimes led to the imposition of English usages on the Scots tradition, but more significant has been the matter of appeal.

Prior to the Treaty of Union, appeal lay from the Court of Session to the Scottish parliament, but the parliament's right was challenged. In 1674 the Session's decision in Earl of Callendar v Earl of Dunfermline was

394

appealed to Parliament; this move was opposed by the court. The judges contended that they had supreme jurisdiction in civil matters in Scotland and they invoked the aid of the king, Charles II. The crown was inclined to side with the judges but support for the right of appeal came from within the College of Justice itself; a substantial number of advocates withdrew their services, thus bringing the business of the court to a virtual standstill. Then, during the political revolution of 1689, the Scottish Convention of Estates included in their Claim of Right a clause securing the right of appeal from Session to Parliament. The right of protestation thus confirmed, however, does not seem to have been much used.

Article 19 of the Treaty of Union laid down that "no causes in Scotland be cognizable by ... any ... court in Westminster Hall; and that the said courts ... shall have no power to cognosce, review, or alter the Acts or Sentences of the Judicature of Scotland or to stop the execution of the same". This left unclear the question of appeals from the Court of Session. The judicial powers of the English Parliament had been exercised by the House of Lords; absence of express provision in the Treaty meant that it was open to question whether the new parliament, acting through the Lords, was entitled to consider itself as heir to the judicial powers of the Scottish parliament and so entertain Scottish appeals. After all, the House of Lords did not sit in Westminster Hall.

Practice, if not constitutional theory, settled the matter. In 1708, shortly after the Union, the 1695 decision of the Court of Session in The Earl of Rosebery v Sir John Inglis was appealed to the Lords; the appeal was accepted, although never actually concluded. Then, in 1710, came another appeal[4]; this time it ran its course and resulted in the Lords

----------

4    Greenshield's Case (1710–11) Rob.12.

overturning the decision of the Session.  The right of appeal to  the House of Lords in civil matters was thus established.  Scottish litigants were happy to carry cases to the Lords, but the Scottish legal profession was less satisfied.  As an English court the House of Lords did not necessarily contain a Scottish judge or anyone acquainted with Scots law.  Consequently the Lords tended to think and speak in terms of English law, and on occasion gave decisions based on English rules unknown to Scots law and out of line with its principles; an English Law Lord is on record as having remarked:  "If such be the law of England, on what ground can it be argued not to be the law of Scotland?"[5] -- a splendid example of Common Law complacency, and ignorance.  However, the  contribution of the Lords has not always lain on the debit side.  Some judges there have tried to learn and apply Scots Law[6], and of course some appeals have referred to law common to both countries.  Only since 1876 has it been required that there be at least one Scottish Law Lord.

(iv)  Other courts

In mediaeval times royal justice was administered locally by the justiciars and their deputes -- and to a lesser extent by the sheriffs -- and, with the growing importance of Council and Session in the fifteenth and sixteenth centuries, this local jurisdiction became almost exclusively criminal.  In 1514 the Earl of Argyll was appointed Lord Justice-General

------------

5    Bartonshill Coal Co. v Reid (1858) 3 Macq. 266, 285 (per Lord Cranworth).

6    Wills' Trs. v Cairngorm Canoeing and Sailing School Ltd. 1976 S.C. (H.L.) 30; 1976 S.L.T. 162.

(that is, Justiciar) of Scotland, and the office remained heritably in his family until 1628. In 1524 the Lord Justice-General was instructed to remain continually at Edinburgh or with the king in order to deal with criminal business. In practice most of the work was done by his deputes; by the 1660s it was accepted that the Lord Justice-Clerk -- an officer risen to the bench from relatively humble beginnings as clerk of the court -- presided in the absence of his superior.

In the localities the ayre system had been decaying from the fifteenth century onwards; attempts then and in the following century to provide regular and efficient criminal justice other than in Edinburgh were unsuccessful. In the 1660s the inefficiencies and abuses within the system led to the appointment of a committee of investigation. The result was the creation in 1672 of a new criminal court, the High Court of Justiciary, consisting of the Lord Justice-General, the Lord Justice-Clerk and five Lords of Session. The court was based in Edinburgh, but provision was made for the holding of annual circuit courts throughout the country; in actual practice it seems that no circuits were held until the early eighteenth century. At first the position of Lord Justice-General was usually bestowed on members of the nobility, and not for their legal qualifications, until in 1830 the office was combined with the Presidency of the Court of Session; from 1887 all the judges of the Court of Session were also made Lords Commissioners of Justiciary. There was (and is) no appeal from the High Court of Justiciary to the House of Lords, although the High Court itself can also sit as a court of appeal.

In 1540 parliament enacted that the sheriff courts were to follow the same procedure as was used in the Court of Session. The act probably confirmed a change that was already taking place rather than making any positive innovation. By the mid-sixteenth century the feudal jury of

397

suitors had disappeared, save in criminal cases and in those matters which still proceeded by brieve; with the disappearance of the jury of suitors the sheriff became a judge who acted on his own initiative in place of being merely the executive president of his court. This did not necessarily improve jusice in the shrieval courts; complaints were common in the sixteenth century and later that sheriff courts were held irregularly or not at all, that the required records were not always kept and that shrieval justice was often dilatory and sometimes less than impartial. Under James VI, for example, four sheriffs were summoned to explain why, among other lapses, they had not held their head courts for fourteen years, and why known criminals within their sheriffdoms had been allowed to remain there undisturbed.

Part of the problem was lack of training. The heritable sheriff was part of a system which made no provision for enquiring into the fitness or even the willingness of such men to discharge their duties. Certainly sheriffs could appoint deputes, who could in turn appoint substitutes, and an act of 1540 specifically instructed the sheriffs to appoint "men of best fame, knowledge, understanding and experience". However, it appears that some deputes were no better qualified than their principals. Later in the seventeenth century the Privy Council tried the experiment of examining candidates for shrieval office, but this was more to discover their religious and political convictions than their legal knowledge. When after 1708 there was no longer a Scottish Privy Council, the official duty of supervising the sheriffs fell on the senators (the judges) of the College of Justice; when on circuit as Lords of Justiciary these judges invited and heard complaints against the sheriffs.

Major reform came in 1747 in the aftermath of the Jacobite risings of 1715 and 1745. In that year the Heritable Jurisdictions (Scotland) Act (technically of 1746) was passed which abolished heritable jurisdictions as from 1748, and the heritable sheriffs were replaced by advocates of at least three years standing. Under them were the sheriffs substitute; in 1825 it was enacted that they too should be advocates or solicitors of three (later five) years standing.

The importance of the franchise courts also began to diminish in the early modern period, and with the exception of the more important regalities, they gradually gave way to the Courts of Session and Justiciary. By the early seventeenth century (and earlier in the Lowlands) the baronial courts had effectively ceased to deal with anything more than minor disputes and the maintenance of 'good neighbourhood', that is, the supervision of the communal well-being, enforcing by-laws and dealing with cases relating to such matters as common pasturage, the upkeep of boundary walls and similar domestic matters. By the Heritable Jurisdictions (Scotland) Act most of the franchise courts formally lost their powers to the courts of Session, Justiciary and sheriff, as appropriate; the baron court alone survived, with a much attenuated jurisdiction.

The Privy Council, the king's inner council, existed from mediaeval times and fulfilled a variety of functions. It was the principal executive arm of the crown and, especially after the Union of the Crowns in 1603, it played a leading role in the government of Scotland. It also exercised a judicial function; although the emergence from it of the Court of Session substantially reduced the amount of business with which it had to deal, its jurisdiction did not cease. Rather, the Session was subordinate to it and subject to its supervision. The Council also exercised the equitable jurisdiction of the crown, dealing with those matters which lacked a remedy in any other forum. The Council's jurisdiction did not long survive the Union of the Parliaments. An Act of 1708 created a new Privy Council for

Great Britain, and so ended the separate existence of the Scottish body. Moreover, the new Council was to have the same powers as, and no more than, the former English Privy Council, which had lost all jurisdiction within England and Wales with the general abolition of the conciliar courts in 1641. The jurisdiction of the Scottish Council therefore disappeared; the result was that "many matters were, by the abolition of the Council, left without a remedy"[7]. No arrangements were made to confer it on other courts, and when the Court of Session stepped in by default it was only in a limited way. Kames in his _Historical Law Tracts_ urged the Session to take up the noble office of the Council, the extraordinary jurisdiction to step outside or modify strict law in the interests of justice. However, the Court of Session's exercise of this _nobile officium_ was always cautious, and gradually became restricted to established precedents or events closely analogous thereto.

(v)  The legal profession and legal education

We have sufficiently discussed the emergence of a professional judiciary. The origins of the other two branches of the profession, of advocates and solicitors, are obscure, although it is clear that they are mediaeval.

Representation in litigation was first accepted in the romano-canonical procedure of the ecclesiastical courts. Feudal mediaeval courts were generally reluctant to deal with litigants who did not plead in person, and strict rules governed the appointment of representatives.

----------

7    P.G.B. McNeill "The passing of the Scottish Privy Council" _Jur.Rev._
     (1965), 263.

Regiam Majestatem, for example, tells us that "no person should be admitted to act as attorney unless he has been so constituted by his client [who is] personally present in court". This rule survived into the sixteenth century, and is repeated by Balfour, who also adds that the powers of the representative are strictly limited and confined to the terms of the mandate given to him by his principal. Nevertheless, it is possible to trace the emergence during the fifteenth century of a small but clearly identifiable body of men practising as professional pleaders in the higher courts. The evidence is somewhat scanty but adequate for us to see the origins of what became known as the Faculty of Advocates. In 1424, for example, statutory provision was made for the appointment of a faithful and wise advocate to act for poor litigants unable to arrange their own representation; in 1455 it was laid down that all men of law who were paid to appear in court on others' behalf should wear a special dress when before parliament. The position is clearer in the sixteenth century. A decision of 1530 determined that no-one could be compelled to answer a summons without the assistance of an advocate. When the College of Justice was founded, provision was made for the licensing of ten advocates to appear before the court -- although only eight were actually appointed. At first advocates were confined to civil suits, but in 1587 they were empowered to act in criminal matters.

By the end of the sixteenth century there were about fifty advocates in practice; although it is impossible to point to the first appearance of this group as a corporate body, as opposed to a set of men with professional interests in common, it is from this time that the Faculty began to take shape. We hear of a Dean of the advocates of Session in 1582, but nothing of his powers or duties at this stage. By the middle of the next century, however, it is clear that the Lords of Session looked to the Dean for the maintenance of discipline at the bar. More telling in the evolution of the Faculty is the acquisition by the advocates of control over admission to their number. Initially scrutiny of would-be advocates lay with the judges, who seem not to have been very demanding of legal qualification. This led to complaints from the established advocates that their profession was being held in contempt; in 1610, at their suggestion, reforms were introduced. The chief article of reform was the examination of intrants -- or some of them -- by the advocates themselves; in this examination Roman law played a prominent part. It remained possible to obtain extraordinary admission by bill and thus to escape the Faculty's examinations, but in 1688 it was provided that such intrants should be examined by the judges; in 1692 the advocates acquired the right to scrutinize these men. The retention of entry by bill was probably to allow those who had had no opportunity to study Roman law to practise at the bar, for they were examined only in municipal law; nevertheless, entry by examination in civil law was always considered the more honourable. Only in 1750 did examination in Scots law become compulsory for all intrants.

We know less of representation in the lower courts. Clerical pleaders or procurators were to be found in the later mediaeval church courts of Scotland, but in the secular courts, with their lay judges and juries, litigants normally appeared in person, perhaps with the assistance of family or friends. Representation, however, was not forbidden and from the sixteenth century the practice of using procurators in the lower courts was beginning to establish itself. Often local notaries combined their forensic duties with those of procurator; by the seventeenth century such law agents become well enough established to form local professional associations, for example, the Society of Advocates in Aberdeen (at least from 1633) and the Faculty of Procurators in Glasgow (at least from 1668).

Notaries were many in mediaeval Europe and they made an important contribution to the _ius commune_. While papal or imperial licence permitted a notary to practise anywhere, it was also competent for a prince (or a city) to grant a licence valid within his jurisdiction (v. Appendix IV). An act of 1469 confirmed the Scottish king's right to create notaries and forbade imperial notaries to act within the realm without royal approval, but apostolic or imperial notaries were always much the most common. After the Reformation apostolic notaries as such had no standing and royal licence became normal. There were, however, very many notaries, not all properly qualified, and in the sixteenth century a number of statutes imposed severe penalties on the 'false notary' (one acting without licence). Attempts were also made to regulate admission; a number of statutes prescribed examination and registration of intrants. These culminated in the act of 1587 which laid down that a new register was to be drawn up, that intrants were to have a knowledge of Latin, to have served an apprenticeship, and to undergo examination before admission.

The notary was important because he provided what was in effect a register for deeds and transactions of all kinds; documents could be authenticated in his presence and a formal record of them entered in what was known as his Protocol Book. Later the practice of registering deeds in the books of a court of record made this function increasingly redundant, but the notary was also important in connection with documents concerning the completion of title to land. Particularly significant was the instrument of sasine, the notarial document formally recording the delivery of possession of land. The need for such instruments for this purpose lasted until 1858; they had, and still have, other uses.

Procurators and notaries thus practised law -- other than representation in the supreme courts -- well before the establishment of the College of Justice; from the late sixteenth century onwards there were other associations of practitioners, most notably the Writers to the Signet. The Writers to the Signet developed from the office of the King's Secretary; they were closely associated with the College of Justice because of their duty to draw up official documents and adhibit the royal signet to them. By 1594 they had formed their own society and were beginning, like the procurators, notaries and other, local, writers to act as law agents -- solicitor has come to be the more usual designation. Until the nineteenth century, however, the requirements for entry to this branch of the legal profession were not uniform. This only came to pass in 1873, and not until 1949 was the Law Society of Scotland formed to control entrance to and the conduct of the profession of solicitor.

As we have seen, the foundation of Scotland's three senior universities did not result in the growth of a strong native tradition of law-teaching and, despite attempts by James VI to establish a chair of law at Edinburgh, it was not until the eighteenth century that any real progress was made. At Edinburgh what law-teaching there was had been traditionally conducted in private by individual advocates, but during the early 1700s three chairs were founded at the university -- Public Law and the Law of Nations and Nature in 1707, Civil Law in 1709, and Scots Law in 1722. At Glasgow during the same period the teaching of law was revived; in 1714 William Forbes, to whom we have already referred, was appointed to the chair of Civil Law. Between 1761 and 1801 this chair was held by John Millar, a close friend and colleague of Adam Smith and important also in the history of sociology; Millar was also a friend of Kames, in whose house he spent two years just before passing advocate. Millar's primary duty was to teach civil law but he also offered lectures on public law, Scots law and, latterly, even English law; his reputation was immense and his gifts as a teacher attracted many students, including the future Baron Hume[8]. The increasing importance of Scots law was recognized during the nineteenth century. In 1861 a chair of Conveyancing (which in Scotland includes land-law) was established at Glasgow under the patronage of the Faculty of Procurators; the Writers to the Signet had already endowed one in Edinburgh. Thus the tradition of a university training in law was maintained by the legal profession of modern Scotland.

----------

8    The teaching had been in Latin until 1750 at Glasgow and until 1800 at Edinburgh, but legal literature was produced in English even when the writing seems to have been based on teaching, as in Erskine or Hume.


Further Reading:

J.W. Cairns "Institutional Writings in Scotland Reconsidered" 4 J. Legal Hist. (1983), 76

J. Durkan "The early Scottish notary" in The Renaissance and Reformation in Scotland. Essays in honour of G. Donaldson, ed. I.B. Cowan and D. Shaw (Edinburgh, 1983)

K. Luig "The Institutes of National Law in the seventeenth and eighteenth centuries", Jur. Rev. (1972), 193

T.B. Smith Studies Critical and Comparative (Edinburgh, 1962), especially chapters 3 and 7

P. Stein "The Influence of Roman law on the law of Scotland" Jur. Rev. (1963), 205

R. Sutherland Lord Stair and the Law of Scotland (Glasgow, 1981)

plus

Stair Society publications (Edinburgh), especially vols. 1, 20, 29 and 33

Chapter XV

## ENLIGHTENMENT AND CODIFICATION

(i)  The age of the Enlightenment


The intellectual movements of the eighteenth century are described in most European languages as being of the Enlightenment[1]. These movements which, in the field of law, were frequently directed towards reform or codification or sometimes reform by means of codification, were based on a belief in the liberating influence of reason both in intellectual life and in the organization of society; this belief itself had grown out of Natural Law. Enlightened men were inclined to be critical of received thought, but they claimed to be able to provide a rational and therefore sound treatment of all problems, social and economic, political and legal. These attitudes were to culminate in the French Revolution and in the <u>Code</u> <u>Civil</u>.

Meanwhile, changes in agricultural practices were enabling a much larger population to be supported, and the beginnings of the Industrial Revolution were becoming apparent in both England and Scotland; improvements in transport were to allow the building of large cities. These changes and an expanding commercial life were to lead in the nineteenth century to new tasks for the law. In the economic sphere Adam Smith argued for the rationality of free competition in promoting the most efficient use of resources, as against the mercantilist view that the state should intervene to protect and encourage the growth of wealth for its citizens; this laissez-faire doctrine became dominant.

----------

1    In German <u>die</u> <u>Aufklärung</u>, in Italian <u>l'Illuminismo</u>, in French <u>le</u>
     <u>siècle</u> <u>des</u> <u>lumières</u>.

Natural Law and rationalist thinking had created the Enlightenment; indeed, it was during this period that legal philosophy became a subject which could be divorced, or at least separated, from the practical needs of law because Natural Law was inevitably linked with "philosophy" in the sense of overall views of the origins and good working of human society. Not all legal ideas of the Enlightenment, however, sprang from rationalism or tended towards codification. A society which well exemplified the Enlightenment in its blending of legal and philosophic thinking, and also in its combination of those areas with history, politics and economics, was eighteenth century Scotland. Its roots lay in the Natural Law of Grotius and in the institutional approach of Stair, but it developed its own doctrines. Great names of the period are Francis Hutcheson, Lord Kames, David Hume, Adam Smith and John Millar. Hutcheson, professor of Moral Philosophy at Glasgow 1730-46, was Adam Smith's teacher as well as his predecessor; he also exercised a profound influence on the thinking of David Hume. Moreover, Hutcheson was important in that his political and legal ideas were widely disseminated in the emergent United States of America; he held liberty an indispensable pre-condition for individual happiness. Lord Kames, like John Millar, we have considered in the specifically Scottish context. David Hume (uncle of Baron Hume) was for many years Librarian of the Faculty of Advocates. His various philosophical works, especially <u>Concerning Human Understanding</u>, strongly influenced Bentham and John Stuart Mill, and also Auguste Comte. His 'sentimental', that is, psychological, approach to explaining law and society was innovatory -- and also a far cry from Natural Law thinking. He held that law was an historical phenomenon to be explained rather than a tool for reform. Adam Smith, professor of Moral Philosophy at Glasgow 1752-63, although best known for his economic theories, also held that jurisprudence, the study of law, was fundamental to any discussion of social relations. His belief in the empirical approach meant that he opposed codification as too idealistic and likely to be ineffective, if not pernicious, insofar as it tried deliberately to alter social attitudes.

(ii) Criminal law and the Enlightenment

Legal philosophy and law reform came together in an exemplary manner in the case of criminal law. As central governments had become stronger in the fifteenth and sixteenth centuries, crime had become an increasing object of their concern. Penalties had multiplied and sharpened, but crimes had diminished neither in number nor gravity; laws were constantly revised and re-enacted but the desired reform of morals was not achieved. The general tendency was towards harsh repression. Political crimes were created and punished as especially heinous; it was an age when the modern distinction between legal and moral wrongdoing was in the process of being created by the proponents of rationalism. (Just as the mediaeval world had seen no real division between the temporal and spiritual authorities, so too had men, as members of the one society, properly incurred public punishment for sin that was not seen as private.) While the commonest Christian theory of punishment held that it should aim at the correction of the criminal -- and Roman law could be cited to support this -- the weight of the Roman texts centred on deterrence, to preserve the tranquillity of the state. This was welcome to the growing number of absolute monarchies; Farinacius, an Italian jurist of the late sixteenth century, after demonstrating by citations from many authorities that the insane should be totally exempt from punishment since they were incapable of any wrongful intent, then limited his rule by declaring that in the interests of the state they could be punished.

Penalties included fines and confiscation, death, mutilation and flogging, prison and outlawry; in general torture was, as it had been in Roman law, an instrument of criminal procedure for the discovery of crime or a means of obtaining proof, not a penalty. The death penalty was widely imposed for treason, lèse-majesté, sacrilege, heresy, rebellion, homicide, robbery, and also on smugglers, forgers, false witnesses, those who broke regulations governing the food supply or public hygiene, those who committed sexual crimes (which included adultery) -- even without violence --, attempted suicides, blasphemers and many others. In England in 1776 there were reckoned to be 166 capital offences; generally there was no crime which might not be punished with death if the ruler saw fit. A deserter might have his foot amputated, a pick-pocket his hand, while a slanderer might have his tongue slit, although the two latter might get away with a flogging. Because they were designed to be deterrent, such penalties were almost invariably inflicted in public and with minatory ceremony. Criminal procedure frequently permitted secret accusation, vague suspicion was enough to ground a prosecution, informers were encouraged, and torture regularly employed to obtain a confession. These conditions did of course vary; where government was not absolute there were likely to be procedural safeguards as, for example, in England and Scotland, but grave penalties for minor offences were virtually universal.

It is hardly surprising then that men influenced by Natural Law and a belief in the power of reason should expose the defects of such practices and propose reforms. Part of the problem resulted from the continuing willingness of so many lawyers to rely on the Roman criminal law, which was much less developed than had been its private law. Natural Law had also led, as we have seen, to a recognition of the fundamental equality of men

409

as rational beings, and this attitude was bound to be opposed to the brutalization inherent in the usual punishments. Moreover, the social theories of the legal philosophers were necessarily concerned to some degree with the criminal law as the guardian of social values. They were also bound to hold that the law, being based on human nature, should be rational and the same for all. The natural behaviour of the individual should not be restricted except where harm was caused to another; crime must then be punished as a violation of the social contract. However, since a crime was defined as an act which directly injured the civil community, scope for deeming an act criminal was much reduced. Furthermore, any penalty which exceeded the level needed for the defence of civil society was unjust and indeed tyrannical. Giambattista Vico (1668-1744) held that the sanction provided by nature for wrongdoing was the remorse of a guilty conscience; since habitual depravity weakened the conscience, it could become necessary to supplement the sanction of remorse. If this stress on conscience was accepted, it was clearly wrong to punish acts which were harmful to the wrongdoer alone -- what Bentham was to call 'reflective justice'. The first duty of the legislator was to bring about amendment, the second, and only if necessary, was to safeguard society.

In France men such as Montesquieu, Voltaire and Rousseau were also including the penal law in their analyses of society, analyses undertaken in the rational philosophic mood. Cesare Bonesana, Marchese de Beccaria (1738-94), the most notable figure in penal reform, produced his ideas under their influence; on the practical side, one of his friends, Alessandro Verri, was an inspector of prisons in Milan, the capital of Austrian Italy. In 1764 Beccaria published his _Dei Delitti e delle Pene_ (_On Crimes and Punishments_). This attacked the Roman basis underlying criminal law, the contemporary approach to which had jumbled and made obscure what was already antique and alien. Beccaria accepted the theory of the social contract, and consequently the need to defend the social order thus established. He followed Vico in holding that crime only existed insofar as there was injury to some right which society was bound to defend for its own preservation, which included the rights of individual members of that society. Other acts, even if generally accepted as bad, should not be punished but left to the forum of conscience; the Church could deal with sins, but they were no concern of temporal courts and temporal penalties. The duty of the ruler was to prevent violations of the social contract; to this end he should ensure that laws were clear and simple, that all citizens had an interest in their enforcement, that all men were treated alike and that education was made widely available. Before any punishment was inflicted there must be certainty that a crime had been committed and committed by the accused. Secret accusations and the use of informers should be forbidden, and so too should the arbitrary exercise of a judge's discretion. In a trial there should be no leading questions or oaths intended to prejudice the accused; above all, torture must not be used, as it exonerated the hardy criminal and condemned the weak and innocent -- the Roman Emperors had wished to restrict its use for the same reasons (D. 48,18,1,23). Credible witnesses and sure facts must establish the crime, and punishment must be limited to what was necessary to prevent the criminal further harming his fellow-citizens. All beyond was abuse and injustice; penalties that went beyond the preservation of society's safety were of their nature unjust. Penalties therefore should not be inhumane; confiscation was unjust because it affected the victim's family and, above all, the death penalty was unjust and ineffective -- life imprisonment, being continuing and visible, was also more of a deterrent.

411

The book caused a tremendous stir, and not only in Lombardy. In 1766 it was translated into French, and there soon followed translations into other languages, including English and Spanish. It was admired by Catherine II of Russia and by Frederick the Great of Prussia; perhaps to keep him in the country, a chair in the political sciences was set up for Beccaria in Milan. In 1791 Beccaria was appointed to the commission established by the Austrian government to reform criminal and civil procedure in Lombardy but he died before this could bear fruit. Some Italian jurists opposed him vigorously, maintaining the advantages of secret justice in Venice or holding that Roman law, if purified, did provide a sound foundation for criminal procedure, but in general his ideas were rapidly accepted and sometimes rapidly put into practice. Both Catherine II and Frederick of Prussia ordered the abolition of torture within their realms. In England Bentham was much impressed with Beccaria's work, in which he saw implicit his own Utilitarian principle of the greatest happiness of the greatest number; John Howard, the notable champion of prison reform who travelled widely on the continent, must also have been acquainted with his theories.

The Grand Duke of Tuscany (the future Emperor Leopold II) in 1786 issued a code of criminal law under the influence of the reform movement. This abolished the crimes of suicide, duelling and lèse-majesté, although it retained offences against religion and morality; it also abolished the death penalty, mutilation, torture and confiscation. However, perhaps through alarm at the French Revolution, there was a reaction within a few years and the death penalty was re-introduced. In Lombardy itself the Habsburg emperor Joseph II in 1787 published a code which to some extent reformed the substantive criminal law. Further reforms, proposed by the commission of which Beccaria was a member, were frustrated by the outbreak of the French Revolution.   In France, the Declaration of the Rights of Man[2], which in 1791 preceded the first revolutionary constitution, had stated the principle that law should prohibit only actions harmful to society and should establish only those penalties strictly and clearly necessary; political factors, however, made sure that the death penalty was not abolished there.   In the Kingdom of Italy, which as created by Napoleon consisted of Romagna, Lombardy, Venetia and the Marches, the more conservative French penal code was put into effect in 1810. In 1808 in the Kingdom of Naples  were promulgated a reforming code of criminal procedure and a penal code, based in part on the work of Beccaria and his followers; in 1812 these too, however, were superseded by the French penal code.

(iii)   The codification movement


The new alliance of legal and social philosophy inevitably stimulated many projects of law reform.   Natural Law had encouraged new systems of arranging legal topics, first in treatises and then in codes.   Justinian's Institutes provided a systematic foundation but, after the seventeenth century, many jurists felt that they could improve upon Justinian's method. The Institutes remained, however, a starting point, partly because it dealt with actual law in force and Natural Law had to come to terms with the practical needs of law, and partly because, conversely, it provided an example of a coherent outline of law which nevertheless had legislative authority.   The inherent weight of legal tradition[3] also favoured the continued use of the Institutes as a model.

----------

2    Appendix V.

3    Watson The Making of the Civil Law, ch.VI.

Natural Law also led, if one accepted the logical consequence of the essential equality of man as a rational animal, to a desire to overthrow legal institutions based on privilege. Legal thinking of the new kind was therefore often characterized by the desire to abolish 'feudalism', which by this time had become a much more complex and far-reaching concept than in the days of its creation; along with feudalism were classed primogeniture, entails, the absolute power of princes, and ecclesiastical interference in secular matters. The desire of some thinkers for radical reform was eventually revolutionary; other men's views were that if the new method was to be embodied in an effective code it must be official, and that the legislator must be educated to understand his duty. In all cases there was a desire for law to be simplified and to be made easy to discover by any citizen who wished to know his rights and the limitations on them. All these factors are present to a greater or lesser extent in the codes of the eighteenth century, some of which we shall shortly describe. (There were other codes beside these four, for example, in Sweden or in some Italian states where there were civil as well as criminal codes.)

Towards the end of the century a new variant of rationalist ideas in legal philosophy appeared with Bentham. Jeremy Bentham (1748-1832) was the acknowledged founder of Utilitarianism, the philosophy which holds that the purpose of society is to arrange for the greatest happiness of the greatest number of its citizens. He graduated from Oxford and was subsequently called to the bar at Lincoln's Inn, but had no success in practice -- not that he took any serious steps to achieve it. In 1776 he published anonymously a vehement attack upon the Commentaries of Blackstone and on their author's interpretation of Natural Law. He then wrote a book on criminal law under the influence of Beccaria; this was published in French at Paris in 1811 but not in English until 1825. He was sufficiently admired in France to be created an honorary French citizen in 1792, and in 1793 he addressed to the National Convention a pamphlet advocating the abjuration of colonies. In 1789 he brought out his major published work, The Principles of Morals and Legislation, which soon appeared in French, German and Spanish editions.

Law, which Bentham saw as the command of the ruler in statute form — a positivist approach which the rationalist development of Natural Law had already reached — should be used to reinforce Utilitarian ends. Bentham was led to his position on the rôle of law partly through his utter rejection of the approach taken to law by Blackstone, and indeed all other Common Lawyers, who saw law as custom, created through its declaration by the judges, and developed only as changing needs brought particular customs to the fore or made them obsolete. In particular, Bentham favoured the abolition of the rule of evidence that an interested party was not competent to testify; he also favoured the registration of all conveyances, the paying of salaries, not fees, to court and other officials, and in general cheaper and swifter justice. He wished too to bring about the easing of the harsh penalties of the criminal law, and to relate penalties to the nature of the offence. All government and all laws were in his view to some extent evil as an infraction of the liberty of the individual, but they were necessary, particularly because fundamental improvements could not otherwise be made; he advocated universal suffrage and the secret ballot, and some of his ideas led on to protective legislation such as the Factory Acts, which will be treated in the next chapter. He firmly maintained the desirability of the codification of the law in England, to help it escape from the arbitrariness of the judiciary, to clarify what law was and to make it enforceable justly, in the sense that all men could know what its provisions were.

Bentham had considerable influence in both England and Scotland, although not so much in his lifetime. Certainly such diverse persons as Lord Brougham and Sir Henry Maine held that Bentham was the father of virtually all English legal reform in the nineteenth century; this description may give insufficient credit to the many empirical reformers of the period, but it does reflect Bentham's part in changing the climate of opinion. He numbered among his followers John Austin, professor of jurisprudence at University College, London, who had studied in Germany and had there been much impressed by the early Pandectists (to be met in chapter XVII). He developed further the concept of legal positivism, and was himself of great influence in Britain, America and Europe. Bentham was also influential abroad, particularly in France, Spain and the Spanish Americas. He seems to have invented the very term 'codification' to describe the process of issuing a code.

Codification as restatement of the law, or of custom, had been, as we have seen, a common feature of the sixteenth century, whether in France, Germany, or the Netherlands, and at this period there had been recommendations, for example by Hotman or Dumoulin, for more thoroughgoing treatment. Codification in the sense of a rationally organized statement of the whole field of law (or of all private law) was only possible after the work of the Natural Lawyers. In the seventeenth century some schemes were produced, such as the proposed code for Mecklenburg of 1658, or Christian V's Danske Lov (Danish Law) of 1683 and Norske Lov (Norwegian Law) of 1688. We have discussed the growth of institutional writings which in fact made the legislative codes possible. But in the first three codes with which we shall deal, the political factor which made them practicable was the existence of the 'benevolent despot', the absolute ruler who had accepted the new thinking of his (or her) day, at least where it did not touch his power, and who was prepared to put his ideas into practice. The French Revolution appeared to herald a radical upsetting of previously established ideas, but Napoleon's emergence led to the publication of a code which in all salient matters was the product of lawyers who had lived, worked and been generally respected under Louis XV and Louis XVI. It did, however, pay something more than lip-service to the ideals of the Revolution, and this was to affect its subsequent influence during the nineteenth century when democracy became respectable, at least in Europe, itself influenced politically by the United States of America.

(iv) Bavaria

The Bavarian Code is the first to be considered, partly because although the codification movement began to take shape elsewhere in Germany, in Prussia, it was in Bavaria that it first achieved substantial results, partly because Bavaria was one of the greater German states and partly because, as a southern state, it was subject to rather different influences from those on Prussia. Saxony was less affected by the trend towards codification because of the greater sophistication of Saxon law, traceable ultimately to the _Sachsenspiegel_ but recently developed by Carpzov and other leading figures of the _usus modernus_; there was also the strong position of the supreme court at Leipzig. In effect the Bavarian codification was the work of the Elector Max Joseph III and of Wigulãus Aloysius, Freiherr von Kreittmayr (1704-90), successively his vice-chancellor and chancellor. As a young man Max Joseph had as tutor one Ickstatt who had been a pupil of Christian Wolff; not entirely surprisingly, Max Joseph was sympathetic to Wolff's ideas, in particular, that a benevolent ruler could specify in positive law, to the common advantage of ruler and subjects, the rights and duties arising by Natural Law. Wolff's doctrines were one source of the move to codify Bavarian law, but the direct impulse to action seems to have come from the contemporary Prussian work towards the same end. In Prussia in 1746 Frederick II (1740-86), the Great, had issued his chancellor with instructions to codify the law, but the bulk of the project was postponed, first by the chancellor's death and then by the outbreak of the Seven Years War in 1756; we shall return to this later.

Max Joseph aimed at achieving a rationalized and uniform law within his territories, a law which would settle disputed points in the Gemeines Recht (the German common law). The commission which he issued to von Kreittmayr ordered him to improve the arrangement of the law, to settle controversies and to suit the law to contemporary needs. The first step was the production in 1751 of a criminal code, the Codex iuris Bavarici criminalis. This did make clear what was and what was not criminal, but it was not in the spirit of the Enlightenment: for example, witchcraft was retained as a crime, the torture of witnesses was continued and so was mutilation as a punishment. Similarly, the 1753 code of civil procedure was a reforming measure in that it introduced uniformity, but it remained based on the traditional romano-canonical forms.

In 1756 came the last part of von Kreittmayr's commission, the civil code itself, named after Max Joseph the Codex Maximilianeus Bavaricus civilis. Unlike the later codes, the Bavarian civil code did not supersede all existing law and make a completely fresh start as the foundation of a new legal order. In fact, it gave primacy among the sources of law to certain statutes, while the code itself only took second place; the Gemeines Recht was retained as a subsidiary source since Bavaria was still part of the Holy Roman Empire and had no competence to discard the common law completely. Furthermore, to a large extent the code simply restated the rules of the usus modernus Pandectarum rather than showing allegiance to any particular theory of Natural Law. The arrangement largely followed that of the Institutes. Part I dealt with the law in general, its application and interpretation and its classification; it also dealt with persons according to their status, including such matters as when a person comes into being, degrees of relationship, marriage, paternal power and serfdom. Part II dealt with the law of things, covering ownership and its acquisition, prescriptive periods, pledge, servitudes, both personal and real, and compulsory services. Part III dealt with succession, covering wills, codicils, legacies, gifts in expectation of death and trusts, and also including intestate succession. Part IV dealt with contracts and other personal obligations. It classified contracts on the Roman pattern as real, consensual, verbal, literal and innominate; there were also chapters on quasi-contract, payment and other modes of release from obligation, delicts and one on feudal law.

In spite of its widespread and heavy dependence on Roman law the code, however, did show in content and arrangement some influence of Natural Law. This influence had led to the actual planning of the enterprise, to the clarity with which the law was expressed, to the use of German for the text -- although the title was in Latin -- and to the settlement of disputed points explicitly by the light of reason. For example, I,1,6 states that the law must be made known publicly so that everyone may know and learn about it; in II,2,4 the law of nature is described as being understandable by the exercise of reason, and as allowing men to know their obligations towards God, themselves and other men, whether as fellow citizens or as individuals. In III,1,3 it is stated that all agreements are in principle enforceable. Damage done to another is said to give rise to a claim for reparation by both Natural and Roman Law, but the subtleties of the <u>lex</u> <u>Aquilia</u> on damage to property are rejected (III,16,6). Although much of the content was little more than a statement of Roman law as then accepted, it must be recalled that many Natural Lawyers accepted the rules of Roman law as rational and thus suitable for adoption into their own schemes of law.

(v)  The Prussian code

The first steps towards codification in Prussia (as the Brandenburg lands came to be best known) were taken in 1713 at the beginning of the reign of Frederick William I (1713-40). His primary aim was to simplify and unify the administration of the various disparate territories which he ruled -- the March of Brandenburg, Further Pomerania, the Duchy of Prussia, the bishoprics of Magdeburg and Halberstadt, Westphalia and the lands of the Lower Rhine. In 1714 he ordered the law faculty of Halle University to carry out a programme of rationalization of law under the leadership of Thomasius (whom he described as well known for his skill and learning). This was to settle doubtful cases, taking account of sound reason and the situation of the country. Only three months, however, were allowed for the enterprise and so its value would have been doubtful even had it been accomplished.

In 1738 Frederick William proposed a further and more extensive reform; a general law was to be published, based on the <u>usus</u> <u>modernus</u>, but also incorporating special laws which were to be gathered together separately, but under the same rubrics as in the general law; in this way both certainty and easy opportunity for reform of law could be provided. Within his territories he ended the practice of <u>Aktenversendung</u> (which was described in the chapter on Germany); he also obtained a privilege barring appeal from his courts to the imperial supreme court. He died before the proposals for a restatement of law could be carried through, but Frederick the Great picked up his father's plans and modified them, partly in the light of the doctrines of Montesquieu.

In 1746 Frederick ordered his chancellor, Samuel von Cocceji, to produce a uniform law "based purely on reason and on the constitution of the territory; [it] was to be in character German and in application general". The provisions were to include a prohibition of any commentary on the law "in order to prevent the citizens being taken in by the subtleties of professors and advocates". This uniform law was still envisaged as supplementary to the laws of the individual provinces, but their laws were to be set out in its order. Von Cocceji did produce a part of the work. In 1748 the section dealing with the law of persons was issued, and that dealing with the law of things in 1751; both were intended as drafts for a <u>Corpus</u> <u>Iuris</u> <u>Fridericiani</u> (<u>Frederick's</u> <u>Code</u> <u>of</u> <u>Law</u>) in which Roman law would be reduced to "a natural order and a correct system". The draft for the section on obligations was completed in 1753, but Cocceji's death in 1755 effectively brought this stage of the work to an end.

The project for reform of the law was taken up again in 1780 when Frederick gave fresh instructions to his chancellor, von Carmer, who had been involved in law reform in his native province of Silesia. Von Carmer was to be assisted by Carl Gottlieb Schwarz, also known as Suarez, who in fact did most of the work. In these new instructions Frederick showed his continued distrust of lawyers; he expressed his dissatisfaction with the administration of justice in Prussia and the way lawyers procrastinated. He hoped to make the whole body of advocates redundant, and thus to free

421

his subjects from a not inconsiderable burden while at the same time allowing the training of a greater number of skilled merchants, industrialists and artists, who would be of more value to the state. On a more positive note, he ordered that effect was to be given to Natural Law; the law should be expressed both clearly and simply and at the same time in a detailed and complete fashion so that all citizens might know what the law was without recourse to lawyers. The work was to be done by a legislative commission; this was to remain in being after the completion of the initial codification in order to set right any possible defects, errors or obscurities. No right of interpretation was to be allowed to judges or any other group of lawyers, or indeed to ministers of state; there was to be no expansion or restriction of the meaning of the written law. Any difficulties or deficiencies which might appear were to be reported to the legislative commission, which was to consider what was required and to report to the King for action. Frederick's ideas were clearly in accord with one aspect of the Enlightenment, the educative rôle of the benevolent ruler. Separate instructions were given for the publication of a code of civil procedure; this was completed in 1793.

The main work of codification took some time to complete. A provisional draft was published in 1784, based on the usus modernus Pandectarum and on the customary laws and the judicial decisions of the various territories under Prussian control. A revised draft was presented to Frederick shortly before his death in 1786; his comment was: "But it is very thick, and laws must be short and not wordy" -- in which he was (probably intentionally) echoing Montesquieu. Further consultations took place and further drafts were produced; most of the editorial work continued to be done by Suarez, but he had experts to assist him in the fields of criminal, commercial and maritime law. Finally Frederick William

422

II in 1794 ordered its publication as the <u>Allgemeines</u> <u>Landrecht</u> <u>für</u> <u>die</u> <u>preussischen</u> <u>Staaten</u> (<u>Universal</u> <u>Territorial</u> <u>Law</u> <u>for</u> <u>the</u> <u>Prussian</u> <u>States</u>), commmonly abbreviated to ALR.  It replaced all other laws, positive or subsidiary, whether Roman, Saxon or otherwise, which had been applied within Prussian territory; it remained in force in the lands for which it had been issued (and also in Westphalia after 1815) until it was superseded in 1900 by the civil code applying to all Germany.

The ALR covered the whole field of law, both private -- civil law in the sense inherited from the Roman sources, and also commercial law -- and public, which included constitutional and criminal law and also that relating both to the Church and to feudal privileges.  A general introduction set out the basic principles and doctrines of the law relating to legal personality; the code was then divided into two parts.  The first part dealt with law relating to the individual, the second with the individual in his social relationships, from the family through corporate bodies, local communities and the like up to the state itself.  The system went back to Christian Wolff who had taken it from Pufendorf.  Within the first part falls what may be described as the law of patrimony, although there was an introduction on general principles which defined the relationship between citizen and state, the ways in which rights came into being, were exercised, were adjusted in case of conflict, and were transferred and lost.  The first part further dealt with ownership and possession and their acquisition, retention and loss, with real and personal rights over things and with contractual obligations.  The second part dealt with marriage, parent and child, master and servant, societies and corporations (including charities), the rights and duties of peasantry, nobility and other citizens and also of soldiers and civil servants, with schools and universities and with the Church; it also covered constitutional, administrative and criminal law.

One feature of the ALR was the immense detail in which each topic was treated, far too great for a satisfactory code since it left no room for development or adjustment. In some cases it was the nature as well as the degree of detail which was unworkable; a remarkable example is the provision that a healthy mother must suckle her own child and that the father is to decide how long this is to continue before the child is weaned. The attempt to avoid leaving anything to chance was due to the influence of Wolff, while from Thomasius came the idea of a Natural Law which was nevertheless peculiar to Prussia (in the sense of local law not in conflict with Natural Law), but the ideas of Frederick himself were obviously decisive. His views were clearly reflected in the prohibition on judges applying the opinions of the learned or the decisions of other judges, which arose from his distrust of lawyers. It was his paternalism which led to the efforts in the code to regulate the conduct of the citizenry in areas which might seem to be a matter for their own personal decision. It was characteristic of his approach that the citizens were legally obliged to support the common weal, and that their individual rights might require to be sacrificed for the public good; but in such cases the state was bound to give compensation to those whose rights had been sacrificed.

Natural Law rules permeated the code. The idea was accepted that ownership could be transferred by consent; this led, for example, to the concept of a proprietorial right arising after a contract of purchase by X; even if the object of the purchase was transferred to Y, Y could not acquire a proprietorial right himself if he knew of X's right. Marriage and divorce were held to be in principle a matter of agreement between the parties, but there were requirements of form, and the existence of children

424

in a marriage prevented divorce by mutual agreement. The ALR was a product of its time, too specifically so to have the lasting influence achieved by the Austrian or French codes. It was, however, the first complete product of Natural Law attitudes -- even if adjusted to Prussian conditions -- with the logical consequence that all previous legislation was superseded and all previous jurisprudence was in principle irrelevant; these features were to be found in its successors.

(vi)  The Austrian Code

The process of codification in Austria followed a similar course to that in Prussia. It began under the Empress Maria Theresa (1740-80) when in 1753 she set up a commission to produce for the hereditary Habsburg possessions (including Austria, the Tyrol and Bohemia) a law which would be certain, which would apply equally in all the territories to all the citizens, and which would be enforced by the same procedure in all courts. However, the new law was to be based on the usus modernus, although Natural Law was to supplement and correct the predominantly Roman rules. The first draft was in German, not Latin as had been planned; it followed the order of Justinian's Institutes but was in general simply a restatement of the Gemeines Recht of the hereditary lands. It was rejected by the Empress and her Council because of its great bulk and lack of clarity but was agreed on as providing the raw material for a codification.

A new commission was set up in 1772 with instructions to make the law short and clear, to aim at simplicity and natural equity. A draft was published in 1786 by Joseph II but further work was needed; this was continued by Leopold II (1790-92) who succeeded to his brother, after having already been engaged in the work of codification in the duchy of

425

Tuscany. Under his command opinions were sought from the governments of the various provinces,from university law faculties and from commissions of the judiciary; these submissions were made public. The new draft continued, however, to be essentially a code of the usus modernus. Under Francis II (1792-1835) a legislative board was set up of which the most active member was Franz von Zeiller, a judge and professor of Natural Law at the university of Vienna. While he was aware of the recent philosophic challenges to the school of Natural Law by Kant (who interpreted rights as the area of an individual's voluntary actions which did not conflict but harmonized with the voluntary actions of others), he relied largely on that tradition and the spirit of the Enlightenment. In 1811 the Austrian Code was published as the Allgemeines Bürgerliches Gesetzbuch für die deutschen Erbländer (General Citizens' Code for the German Hereditary Territories [of the Habsburgs]), commonly known as the ABGB; it is still in force, although parts of it, especially those dealing with contracts, have undergone considerable revision.

The ABGB is confined to private law on the Institutional pattern, excluding specifically commercial law; it contains no public law because of the disparate constitutional arrangements in the various hereditary territories. The arrangement follows the typical Natural Law system with a division into three main parts: the first devoted to persons, the second to property and the third to provisions of more general application, including the constitution and alteration of rights and obligations. There is also a short introduction which deals with the application and interpretation of law. Under persons come legal personality, husband and wife, parent and child, and guardianship. Under property come both real and personal rights; real rights include possession and ownership, pledge, real and personal servitudes and succession, while both contractual and delictual obligations are included under personal rights. The third part, dealing with provisions of general application, is in later codes the "General Part" which in them normally comes at the beginning.

The content of the ABGB is neither purely Roman nor purely Natural Law but a mixture of their rules. It does not accept the Natural Law rule that consent is sufficient to transfer ownership but requires some external form of conveyance, distinguishing between title, which justifies the acquisition of ownership, and the delivery which determines the time at which ownership passes, as did Roman law. However, it excludes any future creation of customary rules other than those specifically recognized by statute, since Natural Law held that rules should be laid down and interpreted by the legislator alone; it takes a generous approach to Natural Law when the judge is told to supply deficiencies by analogy, failing which he must decide in accordance with the precepts of Natural Law. Again, every human being is said to have inborn rights which reason shows to be self-evident and which entitle him to be regarded as a person by the law; hence, slavery and serfdom are not permitted. In general the law was and is stated broadly enough to allow for its development, whether by judicial decisions or by doctrine, but specific provisions of the Code have been supplemented by later legislation. The ABGB has also been influenced by the work of the Pandectists in nineteenth century Germany and then by the German civil code; certain areas have been modified and others, such as marriage law, superseded.

The Austrian code, although accepting the doctrine of the equality of the rights of men, was little influenced by political democracy or notions of the sovereignty of the people. Its equality is, moreover, legal equality and it assumes that all citizens have roughly equal economic bargaining power in such contracts as hire and lease -- an assumption now recognized as unrealistic. However, it is comparable to the French civil code in the uncluttered expression of its provisions and in the simplicity of its style. It has not had the same influence as the French code; where German is spoken the later German civil code has carried more weight, and for political as much as legal reasons the French code was normally taken as a model for nineteenth century codifications. Nevertheless, the power of the Austrian Empire (as it became after 1804) extended the ABGB to Liechtenstein, Croatia, Slovenia, Dalmatia, the area which later became Romania and, after 1852, briefly to Hungary; thus, apart from modern Austria, it was the law in Yugoslavia, Hungary, Romania and parts of both Czechoslovakia and Poland until excluded by law based on either national or Socialist (Communist) principles.

(vii)   The Code Civil

The process of codification in France took a somewhat different course. The idea of unity went back to Dumoulin, Coquille and Loysel in the sixteenth century. It had been continued in the seventeenth by Domat, Fleury and his friend and close collaborator, Gabriel Argou[4], and Lamoignon. In the eighteenth century the most notable figures are three near contemporaries, Daguesseau (1668-1751), Louis XV's chancellor, François Bourjon (d.1751), an advocate before the Parlement of Paris, and

----------

4   Each was responsible for an Institution au droit français but the authorship was frequently confused. Argou seems to have borrowed much from his friend (who was pre-occupied with public life) but it was his book, first published in 1692, which was issued in its eleventh edition in 1787.

Robert Joseph Pothier (1699-1772) who held hereditary judicial office in
Orléans, where he also studied, was admitted to the bar and, in 1749,
became professor of French Law. Daguesseau was, as chancellor, responsible
for three codifying ordinances on gifts, wills and substitutions, which
were incorporated largely intact into the Code Civil. He was influenced
particularly by Domat but also by the Natural Lawyers including, somewhat
unusually for a Frenchman, Christian Wolff. Bourjon, to whom the compilers
of the Code acknowledged their considerable debt, was interested in the
customary law, particularly the Coutume de Paris, in which area he drew on
Dumoulin. However, he followed Domat's example in method and applied
rationalist principles to the Coutume, which he held to be as worthy as
Roman law of such treatment; in this sense he may be said to have provided
a climax to the work of Loysel. In his Le Droit commun de la France et la
Coutume de Paris réduits en principes, Bourjon drew on royal legislation,
the arrêts of the parlements, the decisions of the Châtelet (the ordinary
court for Paris and its surrounding area) and French legal literature of
all schools. His arrangement of his material may have been somewhat, if
indirectly, influenced by Natural Law through the work of Fleury and Argou,
but it also owed a debt to the approach to Roman law which took the
Institutes as the model of a systematic order.

Pothier was not a particularly original thinker but he had an immense
knowledge and tremendous organizing ability; he showed himself thoroughly
familiar with Commentators such as Bartolus, Humanists such as Cujas and Le
Douaren, and Natural Lawyers such as Vinnius -- much read in France -- and
Pufendorf. His first major work was his Pandects of Justinian in a New
Order (Paris, 1748); for this he had mastered the whole Roman law which he
then rearranged, but only within each title of the Digest. He then wrote a
treatise on the Custom of Orléans; in the general introduction to this he

laid stress on the division of the subject into persons, things and actions, very much in the Roman Institutional mould. In 1761 he published what was perhaps his most influential work, the Traité des Obligations; this was followed by a dozen or so books on specific contracts. In 1768 he published a book on marriage which was followed by various other works treating all aspects of marital relationships. In the last two years of his life he wrote on ownership and possession. Pothier's monumental energy had led him to describe minutely French law as it was in the decade or so before the outbreak of the Revolution. He did indeed do more than describe; his work gave new proportions to French law, providing it with a clear exposition of both property and obligations.

In the field of obligations it was inevitable and in the field of property likely that the superior method of Roman law, with which Pothier was so well acquainted, should dominate the lack of organization in the customs. How far Pothier deliberately chose the Roman law tradition is difficult to tell. There is no doubt, however, that his is the last expression of doctrine concerning French law before the Revolution; for that reason alone, apart fom the admiration in which he was held, it was bound to affect the compilers of the Code. Pothier seems in the mainstream of the civilian tradition, although he accepted much from the customary law. He saw Natural Law as the cause of obligations since it was Natural Law which held each man to his promise and obliged him to make good the loss incurred through his fault; this is not, however, the Natural Law as it had been developed by eighteenth century philosophers but a version much closer to the sixteenth century Spanish thinkers or to Grotius. He did, however, reject the Roman bases of the various contracts on the ground that they were all ultimately founded on agreement -- convention, as both he and Stair called it; for legal enforceability he demanded not a mere pact but that a party must promise and engage himself to the performance of his promise.

This was the state of the law at the outbreak of the Revolution in 1789, and one thing is clear:  that nothing less than a revolution would have sufficed to sweep away the traditional rights of the ancient provinces and the customs of their parlements.  Not only law reform but codification was a demand of the Constituent Assembly in 1790; the first written constitution, of September 1791, which was preceded by the Declaration of the Rights of Man, envisaged the preparation and promulgation of a civil code.  Sufficient time, however, was not allowed for any serious draft, and the legislation which was actually passed in the next decade was concerned with particular reforms.  The ancient provinces together with the bailliages and sénéchaussées were abolished; the modern departements were introduced as administrative units.  The parlements were sent on indefinite vacation -- from which they never returned.  All Frenchmen became citizens, without differentiation of status, where formerly there had been the nobility and the commoners (roturiers), and the latter had themselves been classed by legal prescription into bourgeois or serf.  All feudal burdens on land were abolished, as were all feudal privileges, such as the right of hunting over another's land and primogeniture; substitutions by means of trusts were set aside.  Civil marriage and divorce were introduced.  During the 1790s three draft codes were put forward by Cambacérès (1753-1824), but they were all rejected, usually as being insufficiently revolutionary; these outline codes were very brief because Cambacérès recognized that it would be impossible to have a code which could provide for all cases, and he also accepted that bulky laws were useless for informing the populace of their legal rights.

The actual achievement of codification only became possible after 1800

431

when Napoleon Bonaparte became First and Cambacérès Second Consul. In August 1800 a commission of four senior practitioners of law -- Tronchet, Bigot-Préameneau, Portalis and Maleville -- was appointed to produce a suitable code. Their records reveal that all these men were politically moderate, preferring Napoleon's rule to the uncertainties of Revolutionary fervour, but able to adjust to the restoration of the Bourbons in 1815. They had all studied Roman law at university in the normal way before going on to qualify for practice[5]. As their libraries reveal, all four were cultivated jurists, acquainted with Grotius, Vinnius, Pufendorf, Thomasius and Heineccius among foreign writers and with French legal literature from Domat to Pothier and Olivier. It was the authority of Napoleon himself (who admired Montesquieu's writings) which made possible the production of an enduring code, enduring because it had adequate links with the legal past; in their revolutionary zeal the Legislative Assembly had at one stage tried to give the succession always to the youngest son!

An outline of the proposed code was rapidly produced and published for comments from various courts and from the public. The commission then settled to the detailed discussions. Napoleon took a great interest in the scheme and presided over 57 of the 102 sessions which were devoted to the draft; he is recorded as having intervened frequently and effectively in the debates. Adoption in the full sense, divorce by consent, a general hypothec over the property of guardians as security for the proper performance of their duties, and unfavourable treatment of foreigners all seem due to Napoleon's own views. It was certainly because of his energy

----------

5   French and canon law were usually third year options, and French law
    was not taught in every law faculty; where it was, it was taught in
    French, not Latin, and by practitioners.

and his ambition to be remembered as much as a law-giver as a general that the code was pushed through the reluctant legislative body and issued in March 1804 as the Code Civil des Français in three books with 2281 articles. (It was re-issued as the Code Napoléon in 1807, became again the Code Civil after Napoleon's fall, was re-entitled the Code Napoléon between 1852 and 1870 under Napoleon III and after the latter's fall reverted to its present and original title.)

The arrangement of the Code Civil is firmly in the French Natural Law tradition of the previous half-century as compared with the rationalist and scientific approach of the Prussian code. The model is essentially the Institutes of Justinian, as interpreted in the light of reason. Domat had adopted this pattern in his systematization of the Corpus Iuris. Vinnius, the Humanist and moderate Natural Lawyer who was most influential in France, had earlier stayed close to it, simply dividing rights over things into either ownership and possession or obligations. This structure was used by Bourjon, whose first three books correspond closely to those of the Code, although most of the subject matter of his last three must then be distributed within the Code. His chapter on feudal law was omitted from the Code (for, after all, it had been abolished) and the general title on obligations was indebted to Pothier since Bourjon had found no such treatment in the Custom of Paris. Olivier, a professor of law and judge in the appeal court at Nîmes, was probably one of the more influential and constructive critics of the draft code after its publication for comment; his Principes de droit civil romain (1776), after a brief preliminary on the nature of law and its object, had dealt with persons, their status and capacity, with things, seen as the objects of individual rights, with obligations, both the general theory and the special contracts, and with actions. Pothier too had dealt with the last title in the Digest, (D.50,17

433

<u>de</u> <u>regulis</u> <u>iuris</u>), in a comprehensive way, dividing his treatment into a general part and then into persons, things and actions; he had stressed the same division in his introduction to the Custom of Orléans. He has frequently been described as the father of the <u>Code</u> and this is true as to content; there is relatively little in the <u>Code</u> that was not acceptable to or even drawn from Pothier. The arrangement of the <u>Code</u>, however, owes more to Bourjon. Moreover, when there was conflict between Roman and customary rules, it is clear that the compilers did not aim at producing a compromise solution but rather, in the spirit of the age, sought to take whichever was closer to reason and to the law of nature. It is probably because the <u>Code</u> <u>Civil</u> was not affected by any highly conceptualized theory of Natural Law but was simply designed to conform with the Declaration of the Rights of Man that it was found suitable in the individualistic, utilitarian, bourgeois, nineteenth century. It was also possibly advantageous that the model of the <u>Institutes</u> meant that commercial law was excluded from the <u>Code</u> <u>Civil</u>; although a commercial code was produced under Napoleon this did not attach the same emotional loyalty among Frenchmen and so it could more readily be adjusted to the new economic world.

Book I opens with six articles -- the <u>Code</u> is normally cited by article alone -- on the publication, effects and application of the law; for example, laws are not to have retrospective effect. The main part of the <u>Code</u> then begins, dealing with persons; it includes titles (subdivided into chapters) on civil rights and the formalities of status, on marriage, divorce and paternal power. Book II, that is, articles 516-710, deals with property, both moveable and immoveable, with ownership and with lesser real rights. Book III, which is more than twice as long as the other two together, deals with modes of acquisition of ownership, starting with succession and proceeding to obligations. Ownership is acquired immediately on perfection of the contract in the case of sale, without need for delivery or payment of the price (art. 1483). The law of obligations covers both the generalities applicable to obligations, and specific contracts, quasi-contract and delict; security rights and prescription also occur in Book III as does the property régime of marriage, since it is viewed as a matter of acquisition of property.

The style of the Code is very clear; the compilers sought for a simplicity of statement which would make the law accessible to everyone. At one level this was achieved; nevertheless the apparent simplicity has often led to the need for explanatory case law. For example, art. 1382 which provides that everyone is obliged to make reparation of the damage caused by his fault[6] has given rise to an enormous quantity of case law on the law of reparation[7]. The Code itself has been much amended and supplemented by later legislation, as is inevitably necessary with all codes, but it has never been subject to a full revision, despite discussion.

The Code Civil dealt only with that part of private law which was considered in Justinian's Institutes, excluding the final titles on procedure and the criminal law. The Code de Procédure Civile came into effect on 1 January 1807; it dealt with procedure before the courts, execution of judgment, and also with the formalities necessary for proving and giving effect to wills, and with arbitration. It embodied such revolutionary ideas as the freedom of the parties to determine the scope of

----------

6    Tout fait quelconque de l'homme, qui cause à autrui un dommage, oblige celui par la faute duquel il est arrivé, à le réparer.

7    v. F.H. Lawson and B.S. Markesinis, Tortious Liability for Unintentional Harm in the Common Law and the Civil Law (C.U.P., 1982).

the case, the right of immediate access by the parties to the judge, oral pleading and an independent judiciary. The Code de Commerce came into force the following year; its four books dealt with commerce in general, with maritime law, with bankruptcy and with mercantile jurisdiction. It drew heavily on the royal ordinances which had been the work of Colbert, the Code Marchand of 1673 and the Ordonnance de la Marine of 1681. It defined the status of merchant and dealt, for example, with the duty to keep books, with companies and partnerships and with bills of exchange. It did not innovate, but produced a clear and rational statement of the existing law merchant. The Code d'Instruction Criminelle or code of criminal procedure and the Code Pénal both came into force on 1 January, 1811; the Code Pénal was a revision of an earlier code of 1791, dealing with serious crimes and dominated by the idea that both crimes and penalties should be precisely defined by law without room for any judicial discretion. The code promulgated in 1810 was rather more flexible but retained the principle that crimes and punishments must be clearly defined in advance; its penalties however, were severe as well as inflexible.

The influence of the Code Civil and of the accompanying codes was enormous. This was partly due to its introduction into much of Europe as a consequence of Napoleon's conquests and partly to its use in the French colonial empire. It was also widely imitated or borrowed, because of its quality as a piece of legislation, because it was accessible and because it expressed more generally, and therefore more attractively than its rivals, the ideals of the codification movement which continued in civil law countries throughout the nineteenth century. It was imposed on Belgium and the Netherlands, on those Italian states which fell to the French, on Baden and the Rhineland. Belgium kept it (as did the Rhineland until 1900); the Dutch code of 1838 drew much from it; the Italian codification movement, which was finally successful after the creation of a united Italy, was based on it. In Egypt, Syria and the Lebanon, in Algeria, Tunisia and Morocco, and in Indo-China it was the law of the colonial settlers and affected, profoundly in most cases, the law that followed the end of colonialism. In Louisiana and Quebec the direct impact was of the French law of Pothier's time, but the **Code Civil** had indirect influence. In Spain and the Spanish Americas, in Portugal and most of the Portuguese colonies and in the Balkans the **Code Civil** was admired and largely absorbed. Its dominance has lessened in this century for ideological or political reasons, and because some countries, like Brazil or Turkey, preferred to take the more modern German or Swiss code as a model, while others, like Italy and the Netherlands, have felt the need to produce a new code. Napoleon, however, was right to think he had produced an enduring monument.

Further Reading:

A.J. MacLean "Jeremy Bentham and the Scottish legal system" Jur.Rev. (1979) 21

J. Maillet, "The historical significance of the French codifications" 44 Tul.L.R. (1970), 681

A. Watson, The Making of the Civil Law (Harvard U.P., 1981)

K. Zweigert & H. Kötz (tr. T. Weir), An Introduction to Comparative Law (Amsterdam–Oxford, 1977)

Chapter XVI

## NEW TRENDS IN LAW 1815-1914

(i)  Public law and liberal democracy


While the economic consequences of the Industrial Revolution -- which
we are to take in a wide sense, to include the growth in population, the
invention of mechanized transport and developments in medicine and public
hygiene as well as the more strictly commercial and manufacturing changes
-- were predominant, both in the daily lives of ordinary men and in the
growth of new or changed areas of law, this Revolution also affected
political society, which itself was undergoing changes.

Nationalism as such  was not a new factor in Europe; it went back to
the sixteenth century at least.  Nationalism in the nineteenth century,
however, was something new.  It was often based on a common language and it
arose out of the ashes of institutions which could be traced back to the
beginnings of mediaeval Europe.  The most important of these was the Holy
Roman Empire, of which the death under Napoleon was recognized by the
Treaty of Vienna in 1815, when Europe tried to settle down after the French
Revolution and the Napoleonic Wars.  It was also in this period that the
greater part of the present map of Western Europe was defined, although in
the eastern parts, where the Austrian Empire lingered as part-heir to the
old Empire, significant changes were to follow at Versailles from the next
great attempt at a peace settlement after the First World War.  The
unification of Italy and of Germany are important parts of nineteenth
century political history. A major consequence in both cases was the
movement towards producing a unified law that would replace the legal
systems of all the smaller states which were being absorbed into the new

nations. We shall follow the history of these national codifications in the next chapter, but legal thinking was everywhere affected. The idea of the nationhood of a people, bound together by ties of race, language and culture, found its clearest expression in Savigny's theory of the origin and development of law, and in the work of those members of the Historical School who attempted to shed light upon Germany's legal past. But it was not only in Germany and Italy but also in the Netherlands and Switzerland, and to a lesser degree in other countries, that codification was seen as part of a wider process aimed at creating a sense of national identity and, where necessary, providing new national institutions.

Another aspect of nationalism in the nineteenth century was the growth of an active citizenship. Political theories were based on liberal reform or radical democracy; the latter was not to have much practical effect until the twentieth century. The new concept of citizenship was inspired by the creation of the United States of America and by the enduring consequences of the French Revolution. The notion was generally accepted that all men should have equal citizenship before the law, although this was not yet applied to a share in governmental powers. Explicitly in the United States, but to the same effect elsewhere, the idea was accepted that if the new large states were to have a soul they must bind individuals into a patriotic union: if men were required to participate in the common cause, they must be able to feel that this was in their own interests. Universal adult male suffrage was not by any means immediately achieved in most nations of Europe but such ideas were ripe for consideration. The economic changes, of course, also played a part in the growth of active citizenship; it was not so much that there was a new middle class, but that the existing prosperous middle class grew to huge proportions, and this inevitably upset the balance of internal power.

Although the Congress of Vienna tried in general to restore hereditary and absolutist monarchy, the new political factors which we have mentioned and the new spread of economic power made the consent, if not yet the participation, of the governed inevitable. Nineteenth century liberalism, to put it simply, aimed at extending the politically privileged classes to include professional and commercial men; it favoured constitutional monarchy and a parliament in which property, and not people as such, was represented. Democracy was a more radical idea, locating sovereignty in the whole body of the people; because of the excesses of the French Revolution it was widely feared for a long time, a fear enhanced by the events of 1848, the year in which the Communist Manifesto was issued. 1848 is sometimes known as the Year of Revolutions; in that year there were liberal or radical uprisings in France, Italy, Austria, Hungary, Prussia, Ireland and Romania and unrest was felt in many other countries such as Switzerland, Denmark and England. Democracy entailed equal civil and political rights; it meant universal suffrage and, in contrast to liberalism, held that the elected representative assembly should be guided by the will of the electorate.

For the legal historian the influence of liberalism and of democracy is apparent in the public law concerning parliamentary representation and the franchise. The processes of change naturally varied from country to country; moreover, the boundary between liberal and democratic motives for reform was seldom clear. Nevertheless, all the various states of western Europe experienced and responded to the same pressures. By the mid 1870s both France and Switzerland had adopted universal male suffrage. In 1907 Finland and Norway extended the vote to all adults, male and female. After 1871 the _Reichstag_ — the representative assembly of the German Empire — was elected by universal male suffrage using a secret ballot but Prussia retained a three-class franchise; the reality of power, however, remained with the Emperor and with his chancellor. In Italy universal male suffrage was achieved early in the twentieth century. In Belgium the right to vote remained based on a property qualification until 1893, and even after that date the claims of property continued to be favoured, in that those who satisfied a prescribed qualification enjoyed a plurality of votes.

The electoral law of Great Britain also underwent a series of alterations during the nineteenth and twentieth centuries. In the early years of the nineteenth century, largely as a result of the Industrial Revolution, it became clear that the existing allocation of parliamentary seats throughout the country was out of step with the demographic changes that were taking place. Many of the new and expanding industrial towns were without any representation, while others (some of which, like the notorious Old Sarum, had virtually ceased to exist) were grossly over-represented. The new balance of economic strength also led to a shift away from the idea that parliament should represent landed property.

The first steps in the direction of parliamentary reform were the Reform Acts of 1832, extending the franchise[1]. The English Act granted the vote to the occupier of every house with an annual rental value of £10 or more in the boroughs and to leaseholders with property worth £50 in the shires; this measure increased the electorate from some 435,000 to over 650,000, but some men lost their votes. The Act also gave parliamentary representation for the first time to forty-three boroughs, including Manchester and Birmingham, while fifty-six lost all representation. The Scottish Act similarly gave the vote to the occupiers of premises with an

----------

1    More properly, the Representation of the People and Representation of the People (Scotland) Acts, 2 & 3 Will.4, cc.45 and 65.

annual value of £10 or more in the burghs -- moreover, election was to be directly by the voters and not indirectly through the burgh councils -- and to leaseholders in the shires with property of £10 or £50 worth, depending on the length of lease. It too revised representation in the shires, and revised and added to burgh representation. The Scottish Act raised the number of voters from about 4,500 to some 65,000 -- a huge leap. The Acts failed, however, to introduce the secret ballot, with the result that undue influence at elections remained a problem[2]. The secret ballot was introduced by the Ballot Act of 1872 by which time the Reform Acts of 1867 and 1868[3] had roughly doubled the electorate, granting the vote to all ratepayers. The Reform Act of 1884[4] brought some five million voters onto the electoral rolls, approximately one sixth of the population; only in 1918 was universal suffrage introduced, and it was not for another ten years that women acquired the same voting rights as men. Furthermore, the relative constitutional positions of Lords and Commons shifted in the decade before the 1914-18 War, culminating in the Parliament Act of 1911, which laid down that bills certified as money bills by the Speaker of the Commons could not be touched by the Lords, that other bills passed by the Commons in three successive sessions should become law two years after their introduction despite the Lords' rejection, and that the life of a parliament should be reduced from seven to five years.

----------

2    See Charles Dickens   The Pickwick Papers, ch.xiii.

3    Representation of the People Act, 30 & 31 Vict., c.102 and Representation of the People (Scotland) Act, 31 & 32 Vict. c.48.

4    The Representation of the People Act, 48 & 49 Vict., c.3 marked the introduction of a uniform system of eligibility in the United Kingdom; it was complemented by the Redistribution of Seats Act of 1885.

## (ii)   The organization of business


The Industrial Revolution slowly but fundamentally altered the economic base  of Europe.   Before 1800 most European manufacturing industry had been very local; it depended on workers who laboured individually or in small groups with the aid of simple tools and unsophisticated machinery. With unimportant exceptions, any power other than that of men and animals was that of wind or water.   The refinement of the steam engine and its application to industrial machinery changed all this.   The new machinery was expensive, requiring a considerable initial capital outlay.   It therefore made economic sense to concentrate manufacturing industry and the necessary workers.   The result was that mass-production and the factory began to replace small-scale domestic production; this was achieved first in the textile, pottery and iron industries.   The advent of more sophisticated steam-powered industrial plant in its turn stimulated the production of coal to run it, and iron and steel from which to make it.

The revolution in industry was accompanied by a revolution in transport.   Communications had indeed been improving during the eighteenth century with the development of better techniques of road building and with the construction of canal networks which could provide a cheap and relatively efficient means of transport.   The real change, however, was brought about by the use of the steam engine in locomotives and the creation of the railways.   In 1830 there were only two public railway lines in Europe, the English Stockton-Darlington and Liverpool-Manchester lines, but by 1840 there were some 1800 miles of track in Europe; by 1870 there were approximately 65,000 track miles.   Journeys which had taken days could now be accomplished in a matter of hours, and goods could be transported more speedily and more efficiently than ever before.   This was clearly a major factor in the growth of the urban population. Prior to 1800 the population of Europe seems to have been around 180 million following a long, slow climb; by 1900 the figure had more than doubled to something like 400 million. The factors behind this increase remain somewhat obscure -- although less so than in the eleventh century; improved agricultural techniques and the ability to transport fresh food into large cities were certainly important, but so were the absence of serious epidemics and improvements in medical science.

The Industrial Revolution affected the organization of business in two ways. First, the advent of mass-production and the large industrial complex meant that those industries involved were now organized on a larger scale than ever before. In the second place, new ways of financing industry were needed. While any business needs steady capital investment if it is to succeed and create further wealth, the nature of these changes was such as to require financing on a scale which it was increasingly beyond the capacity of one individual or family to provide. Public funding thus became widely necessary; that is, contributions were needed from members of the public with capital to invest, who would take shares in an industrial concern and in return receive a proportionate share of the profits. This posed problems for, as had been the case with the compagnia, the purchase of a share was in law the purchase of a share in the ownership of the firm; as well as carrying an entitlement to a share of the profits, it also rendered the investor liable -- potentially without limit -- to contribute to any losses incurred. The eighteenth century had seen the bursting of many 'bubbles', as speculative ventures were called; this had rendered investors more cautious and indeed brought the very concept of the joint stock organization into disrepute. In the early nineteenth century the risks involved in investment were often found unacceptably high. When a firm was small enough for all who contributed funds and took profits to be actively involved in its management, or at least to have an effective voice in determining company policy, the liability of co-owners was not unreasonable. When, however, large enterprises emerged with which the individual investor had no real contact, but only a certificate evidencing his fractional share in its ownership, the investment of even a few pounds (or other currency) carried with it, in the event of the company's bankruptcy, a liability quite beyond the investor's control and potentially far exceeding the amount invested. The problem was economic, in that capital investment was needed and had to be made attractive, and legal, in that a device must be found to make safe investment practicable. The solution lay in the intelligent development of the joint stock company and in the concept of limited liability. We shall look at the developments in commercial law in Britain and France.

The joint stock company is an incorporated body, a legal person in its own right, distinct from its shareholders and directors. This eases the path for those having commercial dealings with it; unlike an unincorporated body such as a partnership (put on a sound statutory footing in the Partnership Act of 1890), a company does not need to be reconstituted every time its membership changes. Moreover, it can sue and be sued in its own name -- unlike a partnership in England. The participation of all its members is not required to validate conveyances of property and the like; usually it is sufficient for such purposes for the company seal to be adhibited, together with the signature of a stated number of its directors. Then too, the liability of shareholders in a joint stock company is usually limited, which solves the problems we have mentioned concerning investment. Further, the shares in such a company are usually transferable, which facilitates the movement of capital and attracts the individual investor.

Its advantages for the running of business on a large scale are considerable.

The development of the joint stock company in Britain was a slow process and not without opposition. Prior to the nineteenth century, incorporation was a privilege rather than a right, and it was granted only by royal charter or private act of parliament, for example, to the East India Company (1600) or the Bank of England (1694) or, in 1766, to the Grand Trunk (or Trent and Mersey) Canal Company. The Bank of Scotland was incorporated in 1695 by an Act of the Scots Parliament; the British Linen Company seems to have been operating as a joint stock company well before it received Letters Patent in 1746, which were replaced by a royal charter in 1819 when its business had become clearly that of a bank. Judging from the remarks of both Adam Smith and George Joseph Bell, it seems likely that by the eighteenth century in Scots common law limited liability was already treated as characteristic of a joint stock company.

As business developed the need for incorporation became seen as more a matter of course; at the same time a simpler process was clearly becoming increasingly desirable. In 1841 a parliamentary committee was appointed to "inquire into the state of the laws respecting joint stock companies, with a view to the greater security of the public". The result of this inquiry was the companies legislation of 1844 and 1845. An act of 1844, applying in the case of Scottish companies only to those having an office or place of business in some other part of the United Kindom, created an office for the registration of joint stock companies; it also laid down regulations for such companies' formation, including the duty to provide information about the company's promoters and about the nature of the intended business. Further acts of the same year dealt with the liquidation of English and Irish companies. In 1845 separate Companies Clauses

Consolidation Acts for Scotland and England and Ireland eased further the process of registration by setting out standard provisions which individual companies, if they were "undertakings of a public nature", were permitted to adopt by reference. The combined effect of this and other legislation was, as the remit of the 1841 committee had instructed, to provide for the greater security of the investing public, and to establish the Registrars of Companies as watchdogs. The principal drawback was that there was no general provision for limited liability.

In 1852 a mercantile law commission was appointed to investigate the consequences of limited liability and whether such an alteration of the law would be of general benefit to trade. The majority on the commission were against change, but it was admitted that in very large undertakings, such as railway and shipping companies, or in very humble ones, such as washhouses and reading rooms, the proposed reform might be advantageous. In spite of the majority view, in 1855 parliament passed for England the Limited Liability Act which limited the liability of shareholders to the amount of their unpaid share capital, provided that the company had the word 'Limited' after its name and that at the registration of the company this intention had been stated. This Act was replaced a year later by a more comprehensive measure, the Joint Stock Companies Act, which applied to the whole United Kingdom but provided separate Registrars for England, Scotland and Ireland. Then in 1862 the Companies Act consolidated all previous legislation and established the company in its modern form.

As an indication of the pace of development, for much of the eighteenth century the principal English work on commercial law was Beawes' Lex Mercatoria Rediviva (Law Merchant Renovated), published in 1758, and still including descriptions of the chief commodities of various countries and of the weights and measures to be found in different parts of Europe,

447

as well as matters of legal interest. Only in the last years of the century did published books show a clear division between commercial law and the practice and theory of trade; Park on <u>Marine Insurance</u> was published in 1787 and Bayley on <u>Bills of Exchange</u> in 1789 and in the 1840s the American jurist Joseph Story wrote on <u>Partnership, Bills of Exchange</u> and <u>Promissory Notes</u>. Bell's <u>Treatise</u> and <u>Commentaries</u> show by contrast a much readier access to commercial aspects of the common law of Scotland, where Welwood had written on maritime law in the sixteenth century. Stair, Bankton and Erskine, who had dealt with the law coherently and systematically in their institutional writings, had provided the fundamental material needed by the student of mercantile law.

By the beginning of the nineteenth century the concept of the <u>société en commandite</u> had been developed in France. This had its origins in the mediaeval <u>commenda</u>. Such a <u>société</u> retained the unlimited liability of those actively involved in running the business, but it limited the liability of the individual whose only connection with the firm was an investment of capital to the amount of that investment. It is essentially a limited partnership, and is usually restricted in size. During the course of the century there appeared the <u>société anonyme</u>, a form of company in which all the shareholders enjoy limited liability. Before 1867 such a company could only be created by government licence, but a law of that year laid down the fundamental rules concerning the formation and running of public companies. There are legally prescribed formalities for registration, designed to protect the interests of shareholders, before entry on the national Commercial Register. The law of 1867 also laid down the obligations of directors to shareholders and provided safeguards for the company's creditors. From the nature of the business, such transactions are regulated in French law by the <u>Code de Commerce</u> rather than the civil law.

## (iii)   The regulation of employment

The industrialization of Europe brought with it changes in the nature
and conditions of employment.   Much of the new industrial machinery could
be operated by unskilled or semi-skilled labour, displacing the craftsman.
The increase in population meant that there was a ready pool of such
labour.   Moreover, the late eighteenth and early nineteenth centuries were
the age of individualism and laissez-faire.   The attitudes implicit in
these theories discounted the value of protecting the weak and relied on
market forces to settle relationships; nor did they encourage interference
by the state in the life or business interests of the individual.   Further,
the scale of the new industries meant that there was a marked remoteness in
many cases between employer and employee.   Competition demanded that
production costs be kept as low as possible; there was nothing to prevent
an employer from paying only starvation wages, nor from employing women and
children in preference to more costly adult male labour.   While the
nineteenth century capitalist entrepreneur by no means always corresponded
to his caricature, grinding the faces of the poor, there was no general
concern on the part of employers for the conditions in which their
employees worked.

However, as the century passed, the conditions of 'the labouring
classes' began to attract the attention of humanitarians, but because of
widespread non-interventionist attitudes even among those of a liberal
persuasion it was not easy to get governments to act.   The pressure to do
something came first not from the established political parties but from
concerned individuals and groups, such as -- in Britain -- Lord Shaftesbury

(the seventh earl) and the Benthamites. Legislation was forthcoming to deal with the worst of the abuses, and so the foundations of modern labour law were laid.

In August 1834 all slaves within the British Empire became free, and in the previous year the first Factory Act to set up an inspectorate was passed. This Act covered the textile industry and forbade absolutely the employment of children under nine and night-work for all under eighteen; a nine-hour day was laid down for those under thirteen and a twelve hour day for those between fourteen and eighteen. In spite of the salaried inspectors, its enforcement was probably not very effective. Another Act tried to stop the oppression of chimney sweeps' boys[5] and another to check the old abuse of paying wages in 'truck', that is, in goods necessarily acquired from premises owned by the employer or in tokens only exchangeable at his shop.

In 1842 there appeared the disturbing Report on the Employment of Children in Mines which gave a shocking picture of life underground, recording that the conditions experienced there anticipated "the period of old age, decrepitude and death". The result was the Coal Mines Act of the same year; the employment underground of boys below ten and of women was forbidden altogether and, again, inspectors were to be appointed to enforce this. The Factory Act of 1844 fixed a maximum working day of six and a half hours for children under thirteen and of twelve hours for women; further, machinery was to be fenced. In 1847 Lord Shaftesbury — and the unions — finally succeeded in having the ten-hour day and the six-day week recognized by the law. The Factory Act of 1874 assumed the fifty-six hour week; the Employers and Workmen Act of 1875 gave the Sheriff Court (County

----------

5    v. Charles Kingsley The Water Babies.

450

Courts and courts of summary jurisdiction in England) cognizance of claims by employees against their employers as well as vice versa. A Public Health Act of the same year created a sanitary authority in every English district; a similarly named Scottish Act of 1867 had made provision for local authorities to put into force measures safeguarding the public health. There had been some earlier legislation in this field in both countries, for example, the Nuisances Removal Act of 1848, but it was only in the later part of the century that advantage could be taken of the developments in medical and engineering science. These and other legislative acts did much to ameliorate conditions of employment in industry and the life of the urban poor. Adequate enforcement, however, remained a huge problem and the related problems of unemployment, loss of earnings through illness and the like were left untouched.

These problems were tackled by the Liberal government which came to power in 1905. Economic and political factors weighed in favour of reform and the Elementary Education Acts of 1876 and 1902 had laid a foundation of universal education in England; in Scotland the Education (Scotland) Act of 1872 had extended earlier legislation already providing such measures. In 1908 non-contributory old-age pensions were introduced and an eight-hour day for miners; in 1909 came labour exchanges and minimum wage rates in some industries. The National Health Insurance Act of 1911, borrowed from a German example, laid down that all manual workers (further defined by maximum earnings) between the ages of sixteen and seventy were to share in a compulsory national insurance scheme, to which contributions would be made by the state, the employers and the workers; its benefits were to be administered either by approved societies (friendly or assurance societies and the trade unions) or by the Post Office. Thus there was protection from the consequences of unemployment or absence from work through illness,

451

and also provision of medical assistance; from this Act, indeed, dates the framework of a national health service. But child labour in industry was not prohibited until after the 1914-18 War.

Legislation of a similar kind was passed during the nineteenth century in many other of the industrialized countries of Europe. In Prussia the employment of children was limited in 1839 and 1853, and in the latter year a factory inspectorate was introduced. After the establishment of the German Empire, centred on Prussia, in 1871, the twelve-hour working day became the legally permitted maximum. Legislation between 1883 and 1889 introduced and extended a general contributory insurance scheme against sickness and accidents at work; provision was also made for financial support in old age. Germany was in general ahead of her neighbours in this field; although the government's motive was to take the sting out of labour agitation, German workers were better protected against the hazards of industrial society than those of any other nation before the Great War.

In France too there was some legislation in this sphere. It tended to lag a little behind, probably because French industrialization was a somewhat slower process than that of Britain and Germany. Legislation governing conditions of work and the length of the working day was passed during the 1890s; in 1900 a maximum working day of ten hours was introduced, and in 1906 a six-day working week. In Austria a factory inspectorate and also national insurance against sickness and accident were introduced during the 1890s. An Austrian industrial code of 1907 consolidated and improved on earlier regulations concerning the employment of children, the length of the working day and safety at work. By the outbreak of the First World War practically all the countries of Europe had found solutions -- if only partial -- to some, at least, of the problems produced by the industrialization of society.

452

(iv)   Trade unions


The nineteenth century also witnessed the rise of the modern trade union movement.  The concentration of workers in larger units than ever before provided a new kind of opportunity for associations; the stimulus came from the conditions in which they worked.  This development of organized labour was something of which the law in all European countries had to take account, but this was done reluctantly.  Quite apart from the vested interests of those represented in even the more liberal governments, there was among all governments (as there had been in ancient Rome) an ingrained suspicion of associations of any kind.  Whatever its origin or apparent purpose, an association could too easily be turned to political ends.  At best this represented a threat to law and order (as with the Chartist movement in Britain), at worst it raised the spectre of incipient revolution (as among the United Irishmen).  Furthermore, the nascent labour movement found its ideological backing in the writings of the early socialists who attacked the whole capitalist system.  Louis Blanc, who knew and influenced Karl Marx, believed that the capitalist system was esentially evil because it was based on competition.  Competition divided rather than united the working class, as its members competed for employment; it even prejudiced the small manufacturer in that he had to compete for markets against the already advantaged entrepreneur.  The solution advocated by Blanc was the elimination of private enterprise and its replacement with state-financed and state-run industries.  Similarly, Karl Marx's doctrine of the class struggle laid stress on the enslavement of the proletariat -- "physically broken, spiritually bestialized" -- and approved revolution as a means of attaining a just society.  It is hardly surprising that the legal recognition of trade unionism had to evolve from an attitude of outright hostility to a gradual and usually grudging acceptance of such organizations.

In France the _Code Civil_ rejected the concept of organized labour. In 1791 associations both of workers and of employers had been declared illegal; the _Code_ reiterated this, forbidding the formation of groups of twenty or more people and outlawing both striking and picketing. It also provided that in any dispute between employer and employee over pay the final decision lay with the former; this remained a legal requirement until the reign of Napoleon III. The dangers of organized labour were made clear in 1831 when the silk-workers of Lyon, in an attempt to secure a minimum wage, revolted and seized control of the city; order was only restored by the intervention of the army. As a result, a law of 1834 closed a loophole by banning associations even of less than twenty persons when they were linked with a larger body. However, in 1839 the print-workers of Paris, without any overt interference from the government, formed a union for the purpose of collective bargaining; in the years following other groups of workers formed similar organizations. By the 1850s it was apparent that the total repression of organized labour and its demands was politically -- and economically -- unacceptable. Under Napoleon III conciliation boards, composed of employers and workers, were re-established as a procedure for dealing with industrial disputes. In 1864 the _Code_'s prohibition of strikes was repealed; labour associations became legal, and they obtained specific recognition in a law of 1884.

In Germany unions of skilled workers became widely established during the nineteenth century, although they only received legal recognition in 1869. In 1878, however, Bismarck, the German chancellor, obtained the passage of a series of repressive laws as part of a more general campaign against German socialism. Among other things, these laws forbade meetings by any unauthorized labour organizations and gave the government power to suppress such unions. This legislation remained in force until 1890, when the German trade unions finally won full legal recognition.

The British trade union movement also experienced a gradual recognition of its existence and its rights against a background of general suspicion and of some hostility from the courts. The Combination Act of 1800 (itself a replacement for the Act of 1799) made it illegal for men to form combinations to negotiate wages or working conditions or even to arrange preliminary meetings to this end. Also, any attempt to persuade others not to work for a master was an offence. The crime of conspiracy in this context was abolished by the Combination Act of 1824 which, however, forbade intimidation and acts of violence as breaches of the perfect liberty which ought to be allowed to parties to any contract. In 1825 another Combination Act repealed that of the previous year; it permitted associations which aimed at improving wages or conditions of work, provided that violence and intimidation were not used to advance these objectives, but incidentally revived the crime of conspiracy. With a limited right to collective bargaining thus established, the British trade union movement expanded and even began to attract a degree of public sympathy. Nevertheless, the attitude of the judiciary towards organized labour was slow to change, and the inclination of the bench was to interpret the rights of the unions in as strict and limiting a way as possible -- perhaps as derogating from the principle of free competition. For example, in 1834 a group of agricultural labourers from Tolpuddle, Dorset, were sentenced to seven years' transportation on the grounds that they had administered an illegal oath to the members of their association, although its aims were to further their interests by peaceful negotiation.

In 1867 a royal commission was appointed to inquire into the unions and their activities. Its report was favourable and resulted in the Trade Union Act and the Criminal Law Amendment Act of 1871. The combined effect of these statutes was to establish that the activities of a union would not be held unlawful, and so in breach of the criminal law, merely because they tended to restrain trade, unless they were accompanied by aggravating factors such as violence or intimidation. In effect, the right to take action in support of legitimate claims had been acknowledged. Moreover, unions had acquired a degree of protection for their funds; a registered trade union was permitted to vest its property in trustees who had powers of administration. Further legislation in 1875 (the Conspiracy and Protection of Property Act) established the right of peaceful picketing. Boycotting was held not to amount to intimidation in Curran v Treleaven ([1891] 2 QB 545) but the courts found no difficulty in condemning trade unionists on the grounds that they were 'besetting' a place of work, and not just 'attending' to give information (Lyons & Sons v Wilkins [1899] 1 Ch. 255).

The courts continued to give a restrictive interpretation to the rights laid down in the statutes. There was also an increase in the use of civil actions for damages by those whose business interests had suffered as a result of union activities. These civil actions were at first raised against individual union members, but in 1901 there came the decision in Taff Vale Railway Co. v The Amalgamated Society of Railway Servants ([1901] A.C. 426). The House of Lords decided that a registered trade union could be sued in its registered name (for a strike which it had not authorized); this overturned the previous assumption of immunity and threatened the effective existence of the unions. A union could now be sued and its funds attached whenever the activities of its members caused loss to any person. The Trade Disputes Act of 1906 reversed the decision in Taff Vale and cut

456

away the grounds on which the courts had previously entertained civil actions against unions or their members. It lifted from the unions all liability to actions for conspiracy for acts done in furtherance of a trade dispute, and it re-defined peaceful picketing, specifically allowing the peaceful communication of information and the peaceful persuasion of others to refrain from work, even if this induced the breach of a contract of employment.

A further challenge to the unions came with the case of <u>Osborne</u> v <u>The Amalgamated Society of Railway Servants</u> ([1910] A.C. 87 ), when the House of Lords decided that the unions were not entitled to levy from their members a contribution for political purposes. Public opinion and the majority in Parliament however, supported unions, their aims and methods. The Trade Union Act of 1913 permitted the political levy, although it made provision for those who wished to 'contract out' of payment. The Act made clear that a union, provided that its objectives were those defined in the Act, could pursue aims and use methods of any lawful kind. It confirmed the 1906 Act's ruling that "An act done in pursuance of an agreement by two or more persons shall, if done in contemplation or furtherance of a trade dispute, not be actionable, unless the act, if done without any such agreement or combination, would be actionable".

After the First World War a period of poor labour relations led to the General Strike of 3 May to 12 May, 1926. This was a failure, and it led to the Trade Disputes and Trade Unions Act of 1927. The chief feature of this measure was the requirement that individual union members 'contract in' to payment of the political levy. It was repealed by the Labour government of 1945 and not restored by the Conservatives in 1951. Nevertheless, the courts have continued to interpret strictly legislation concerning organized labour.

## (v) Harmonization of laws

The increased commercial intercourse between the countries of Europe consequent upon the Industrial Revolution and the new speed with which goods could be moved from place to place brought their own problems. There were many economic benefits, but the divergencies of law among the nations were highlighted as never before. Accordingly, from the middle of the nineteenth century onwards attempts were made to harmonize at least the commercial aspects of the various legal régimes. Both the concept of harmonization and discussions on particular problems were promoted by several governments and by such interested bodies as the Association for the Reform and Codification of the Law of Nations. Success, when it came, was reached by a variety of routes. Sometimes harmonization was achieved by incorporation into national legislation of the terms of a previously agreed convention. Sometimes voluntary agreement without the backing of legislation was found sufficient, as with the York-Antwerp rules, which will shortly be described. On other occasions harmonization was attained by the development of uniform rules in areas where there had been conflicts of law, or by the international recognition of institutions such as the International Postal Union and their regulations.

Commercial law, as well as being the field most affected by the new pressures, was also that in which the resolution of the problems was least difficult. The commercial law of all the European states had to a varying degree a common foundation in the mediaeval law merchant and there were no major local idiosyncracies -- even in England, after Lord Mansfield had done his work. There was therefore less nationalistic opposition to foreign influences and the adoption of foreign rules. As examples of these trends we can look briefly at the maritime law of general average (previously discussed in the chapter on the Law Merchant), the law of railway freights, and at the law of negotiable instruments.

Maritime law displayed a general similarity in principle, but much variation in detail. Attempts were made, by means of international conferences and discussions, to promote uniformity. In 1876, for example, the Bremen meeting of the Association for the Reform and Codification of the Law of Nations appointed a committee to look into the law of general average. At its Antwerp meeting in the following year the Association produced a set of regulations, known as the York-Antwerp Rules. These were based on the regulations drawn up in 1864 at an earlier international conference at York, held under the auspices of the British National Association for the Promotion of Social Science, but as amended in 1877 by resolution of the Antwerp conference. The York-Antwerp rules went a long way towards achieving an assimilation of the law of general average; despite some opposition from Lloyd's of London, they found general favour in the maritime world. These rules were nowhere given statutory force, although they did help to shape later Belgian, Spanish and Italian legislation on the subject, and also the Marine Insurance Act of 1906 in Britain. The implementation of their provisions, and of later modifications, rested solely on voluntary agreement and commercial practice; for example, it was agreed by most of the maritime trading nations that the rules would be adopted into the terms of all bills of lading and contracts of marine insurance as from 1 January, 1879.

Unlike carriage by sea, railway freight was a new mode of transport. As we have mentioned, the railway network grew enormously after the middle of the century and travel became both reliable and reasonably speedy. In the course of a single journey and in a comparatively short space of time, goods might well cross several frontiers. It was therefore clearly desirable to have a uniform set of rules governing disputes over carriage by rail rather than to leave their resolution to the chance application of the law of one particular country, whether the country of origin or that where some accident occurred. The impetus for assimilation came from Switzerland, since her small size and position at the heart of Europe inevitably meant that many international consignments passed through her territory. In 1874 the Swiss government issued a set of draft proposals to the governments of all countries having direct railway links with Switzerland. These were then discussed and amended as appropriate at a number of international conferences. The result was the Berne Convention of 1886 by which the participating states agreed to accept into their systems a uniform set of rules to govern the international carriage of railway freight through their respective territories.

Negotiable instruments had, like general average, a long history. The reasons for attempting harmonization in this field were also obvious. During its lifetime a negotiable instrument (of which the bill of exchange is typical) might well travel through a number of countries. Although there was an underlying similarity of principle in the treatment of this area of law throughout Europe, based again on the law merchant, there was much variation in detail. Prior to 1857 in Germany, for example, there were some sixty different sets of statutory rules governing bills of exchange. In that year the Diet of the German Confederation passed the Bills of Exchange Act, which was then given legislative force in all the member states of the Confederation.

A wider approach to international harmonization was taken in the later nineteenth century. The subject of bills of exchange was taken up in the 1870s by the Association for the Reform and Codification of the Law of Nations. It appointed a committee of experts who, between 1876 and 1878, produced what are known as the Bremen Rules, a body of proposals (largely based on Germanic law) which was designed to regulate the international use of bills of exchange. The proposals were readily taken up by the Scandinavian countries and formed the basis of new legislation there. They were also taken into account in both Italy and the Netherlands during the compilation of their commercial codes. In France their reception was less cordial; since they were based principally on Germanic law they were not readily accepted into the French legal system. Cheques, however, had been introduced into France in 1865 in imitation of British practice. In Britain itself a Bills of Exchange Act of 1882, covering Scotland as well as England, had codified a limited area of law; business interests favoured further codification and a wider degree of harmonization, but the government was not enthusiastic.

Various other associations and interested bodies continued to promote assimilation in the field of negotiable instruments, calling further conferences and producing further draft proposals. At the Hague Conference of 1910, at which thirty-five countries were represented, a set of draft regulations was produced which was submitted to the governments of the member states for consideration. The Conference reassembled in 1912 and amendments were made in the light of criticisms received; nevertheless, disagreement remained on some matters -- particularly those on which there was a marked divergence between French and German law. Further, it was thought best to postpone detailed discussions on the assimilation of the law of cheques until a later meeting. It also became apparent at an early stage that neither Britain nor the United States would associate itself with any agreement reached. The Conference did, however, produce a convention for the unification of the law of bills of exchange which the participating states undertook to observe as their national law; departure

461

from the terms of the convention was restricted to where it was in those terms specifically allowed. A greater degree of uniformity on both bills of exchange and cheques came at the Geneva Convention of 1930 and 1931.

The close relationship of law with matters of economic and social policy was not precisely new to the nineteenth century; what was novel was the degree to which law became used as an instrument of policy, and also the extent to which state intervention in the lives of citizens became normal. We shall glance very briefly in chaper XVIII at the institutions of the mid-twentieth century, including the welfare state, which clearly have their roots in this period of change brought on by the industrialization of western society.

Further Reading:

Continental Legal History Series, vol. XI: The Progress of Continental Law in the Nineteenth Century

J. Roberton Christie "Joint stock enterprise in Scotland before the Companies Acts (1909-10)" 21 Jur.Rev. (1909-10), 128

H.R. Hahlo "Early progenitors of the modern company" Jur.Rev. (1982), 139

N.Horn & J.Kocka (eds.) Law and the Formation of the Big Enterprises in the Nineteenth and early Twentieth Centuries (Holland,1979)

B.C. Hunt The Development of the Business Corporation in England (U.S.A., 1936)

A.H. Manchester Modern Legal History (London, 1980)

P.L.Payne Entrepreneurship in the Nineteenth Century (London, 1974)

H. Pelling A History of British Trade Unionism (2nd ed., Penguin, 1976)

G.R.Rubin & D.Sugarman (eds.) Law, Economy and Society (London, 1984)

D. Thomson Europe since Napoleon (2nd ed.,Penguin, 1966, repr.)

Chapter XVII

## CODIFICATION IN GERMANY AND ELSEWHERE

(i)  Codification in Italy

Codification was both a consequence of and a factor in the unification
of Germany and of Italy in the nineteenth century.  Italy's codes owed much
to the French codification, and therefore they will be described before we
turn to the nineteenth-century intellectual movements in Germany, from
whose fruitful conflict there emerged the German civil code, the BGB
(Bürgerliches Gesetzbuch).  Italy's debt was more directly to the past.

The chapter on Enlightenment and Codification mentioned that some
Italian states issued codes of various sorts in the eighteenth century.
For example, by 1790 Venice had produced codes of criminal, feudal and
maritime law.  Under Napoleon the Code Civil was gradually extended
throughout the peninsula as the various states fell to France; in this way
Italy experienced a brief spell of legal unity for the first time since the
Gothic invasions.  The defeat of Napoleon saw a return to the earlier
political fragmentation of Italy, but many rulers wished to maintain the
legal benefits of the French occupation.  Moreover, the Code Civil had
introduced irreversibly the concept of the equal rights of man before the
law.

Over the next half century we must look again at separate developments
in the individual states.  By the time unification was achieved most
Italian states had achieved systematic, codified statements of their law;
to these codes French law had made a significant contribution.  The code
promulgated in 1819 for the Kingdom of Naples and Sicily was modelled
fairly closely on the French codes; it was divided into five books,

covering the fields of civil and criminal law, civil procedure, criminal procedure and commercial law. It did, however, contain a number of reactionary elements, such as restoring the religious effects of marriage -- among them, indissolubility -- to the secular law, and including ecclesiastical offences along with lay crimes. In the Papal States the codes of civil procedure (1817) and of commerce (1821) were little more than copies of their French equivalents, but the codes of criminal law and procedure which were issued in the 1830s were untouched by any spirit of Enlightenment. In Modena the resumption of independence meant a return to previous law, but the process of reform was at work and resulted in 1852 in codes of civil law and civil procedure and in 1855 in a criminal code. Parma preserved the Code Civil until the work of a commission for reform of the law produced in 1820 a civil code and a code of civil procedure; the civil code was a blend of French style and enlightened current thinking on local law. Codes of criminal law and procedure followed. In Lombardy and Venice, which had been returned to the rule of the Austrian emperors, the Austrian Code of 1811 was put into force, although the French commercial code was retained with some modifications. The reactionary Austrian criminal code of 1804 was only replaced by a more liberal work in 1852.

It was, however, what happened in the Kingdom of Sardinia -- which included Genoa and Piedmont and came to centre on the latter -- that was most significant for the future of Italian law since unification (save for Rome itself) was finally achieved in 1861 under the leadership of Victor Emmanuel II of Piedmont. In the years immediately following the defeat of Napoleon the old law had been restored but, under Charles Albert (1831-49), a comprehensive codification was planned which owed much to the French model. Five codes were produced -- a civil code (1837), a criminal code (1839), a commercial code (1842) and codes of criminal and civil procedure

464

(1848 and 1854). For political reasons these codes were inevitably the most influential in the production of a law for all Italy. Meanwhile, in some territories, such as Modena and Parma, the Piedmontese civil and commercial codes were introduced; Piedmontese criminal law was made applicable in northern Italy. The commissions which were to produce the new Italian codes actually began their work in 1860. In 1865 were issued a Codice Civile, a commercial code (replaced in 1882 and abolished as a separate field of law in 1942), and codes of civil and criminal procedure. There were greater difficulties in reconciling different penal traditions, and it was only in 1890 that a criminal code was promulgated. The commissioners who worked on this great project were influenced not only by the Natural Law tradition which was an element in the French codes but also by the thinking of the Historical School, of which the leading scholars were to be found in the German states; to their thought we shall now turn.

(ii)  The German Historical School

The general principles of the Historical School were not new; indeed, they bear marked similarities to many of the notions put forward by the Humanists. Essentially, its followers maintained that law evolved and was continually modified by conditions of time and place. What made their thinking important in European jurisprudence was its rejection of the schematic, universal approach of the Natural Lawyers who had dominated the previous two centuries. The men of the Historical School were interested in legal history in order that contemporary law could be firmly rooted in its historical past. Natural Law thinkers in Germany such as Thomasius and Wolff had argued that the principles of Natural Law could only be discovered by rational deduction from the nature of man. Their theories

465

had been extremely abstract; the study of what was actually followed as law in any particular society was of less importance to men like Wolff than the logic of the system. This extreme approach was not adopted universally by Natural Lawyers -- we have seen a much more comparatist method in France, for example -- but it had been predominant in much of Germany. The other main reason for support for the historical approach was political, and again in contrast with that of the Natural Lawyers. They had been inclined to support absolute rulers who would impose on their subjects the law which jurists and rulers knew was good; furthermore, in this kind of Natural Law theory any controversy or doubt must be settled by reference to the ruler as law-giver and final arbiter on the dictates of reason. In a more liberal society such reliance on a single source of authority was not generally acceptable. There were other factors which explain the jurisprudential importance of the Historical School. There was an increasing interest, admittedly often antiquarian, in the study of history; we have mentioned the origins of historical sociology in the work of men like John Millar. This was linked with the developing organization of universities, particularly in Germany, as centres of study in the arts as well as the sciences, but Montesquieu in France and Edmund Burke in Britain had already fervently held that a people's past was ··itally important in determining its future. Among lawyers concerned with the practice of the law it was widely, if not always explicitly, recognized that law must be in sympathy with the spirit of the people for whom it was framed, and that penal sanctions could only work where the law was habitually and willingly obeyed. Then, too, there was widespread nationalist feeling in Germany; more people than ever before were interested in what made them different from the French or the English. This nationalism was associated with the Romantic Movement in Germany but also with law as the spirit of the people.

The name most closely associated with the Historical School is that of Friedrich Carl von Savigny (1779-1861) but, naturally, he built on the work of his predecessors and in particular that of Gustav Hugo (1764-1844) who was appointed to a chair at Göttingen in 1792. Hugo was a Roman lawyer but one, like the Humanists, who believed that the internal development of Roman law must be studied against the background of its social context. He was particularly influenced by his reading of the chapter sketching the history of law in Gibbon's Decline and Fall of the Roman Empire (published 1776-88). Hugo shared Gibbon's admiration for the lawyers of the classical period and their creative role; this was reflected in his opposition to codification which he saw as stifling the creativity of judge and jurist.

Savigny was instrumental in the founding of the university of Berlin, where he held a chair from 1810 to 1842; he came of a landed family and was for many years a member of the Prussian Staatsrat (the legislative body) and for some seven years Prussian minister for legislation. In 1803 he produced his first major work, Das Recht des Besitzes (The Law of Possession). The treatise made a considerable impact; it drew from the Roman sources the Roman principles of possession but it also aimed to show how these principles had been modified during the Middle Ages and that the original Roman principles were superior to the civilians' modifications. His next major work was his Geschichte des römischen Rechts im Mittelalter (History of Roman Law in the Middle Ages), which is still worth consulting. In 1815 he was instrumental in founding a periodical called the Zeitschrift für Geschichtliche Rechtswissenschaft (The Journal of Historical Legal Science), and this marks a convenient point for the coming into existence of the Historical School -- using capitals.

When those German states which had been subject to French rule during the Napoleonic Wars regained their independence, the Code Civil was in general rejected along with most other reminders of French domination, although the Landrecht of Baden, for example, was little more than a translation of the Code Civil. There was hot debate on whether the gap should be filled by new local codes or whether there should be a return to the Gemeines Recht (common law) which was based on modified Roman law. Anton F.J. Thibaut, a professor at Heidelberg, published a pamphlet calling for a general civil code for all Germany to replace the existing divisive chaos of contradictory provisions, which was impossible even for lawyers to know thoroughly. The Roman law of the Corpus Iuris he held to be inadequate for the modern world; further, it was obscure and ill-arranged. What was needed was a simple code in German, which would make the law accessible to all; this would be a symbol of unity and the first step towards unification.

Savigny responded in 1815 with a pamphlet which conceded the ills and the need for a remedy, but argued that codification was not the right remedy, certainly not at that particular time. Rather, jurists should examine what was good and what was bad in the German legal tradition and develop the law accordingly. A code was not a suitable tool for development because it was by nature static and, even if a code were one day to be desirable, it must be built on a sound historical undertanding of Germany's legal past and no proper study of this had yet been attempted. Law, like language, was largely a product of unconscious growth, reflecting the spirit of the people or Volksgeist -- a term coined by Puchta, although the concept is largely due to Montesquieu. A nation's law was the product of its Volksgeist and reflected the different influences which composed its history. Lawyers might have a special task in the development of the law and in giving it the necessary technical expression, but their work must go with, not against, the grain of the Volksgeist. This last point explained

468

why Savigny held, contrary to the Natural Lawyers, that no system of law could be of universal application. Finally, Savigny argued, the only suitable time for the preparation of a code was when a nation had reached maturity, and then it would be superfluous. His opposition to the project undoubtedly played a large part in postponing codification for Germany as a whole.

Savigny as a Romanist argued that the great age of Roman law was the classical period, and that this greatness was due to the work of the jurists. However, Roman law had undoubtedly been extensively received in Germany during the sixteenth century and developed as the basis of the Gemeines Recht, and this Roman law was that of Justinian. While Roman law could hardly be described as the product of the German Volksgeist, Savigny argued that in the period of the Reception the lawyers, as the trained representatives of the people, had fulfilled a need of the Volksgeist when they received Roman law; the Roman law of the mos italicus had thus become part of German law and the German legal tradition. Roman law still had much to offer, if only in the application of the principles of classical law; further development of German law should be founded on the Roman law of the great age. Later accretions to the classical law could be discarded if they were not worthy of use in the creation of an improved modern system; it was one of the tasks of historical legal science to determine what was and what was not of value in the legal tradition. Savigny did not, indeed, reject specifically Germanic law as unworthy of study; one of the achievements of the Historical School was to make German law a discipline in its own right and the basis for further scientific development. The first comprehensive account of the development of Germanic law, based on original sources, was Karl Friedrich Eichhorn's Deutsche Staats-und-Rechtsgeschichte (German Constitutional and Legal

History, published 1808-23).

Savigny intended that Roman and Germanic law together should provide the foundations of a new German legal science, but to some younger, Germanist members of the school, Savigny and his Romanist followers were champions of Roman law at the expense of the native tradition. By the middle of the century a split had developed between the Romanists and Germanists. Some of the latter argued that the Reception had been nothing short of a national disaster, others merely that it had been unnecessary; Otto von Gierke (1841-1921), for example, in his Genossenschaftsrecht (Law of Associations), held that a satisfactory system of partnership and company law could be built on the customs of the Germanic guilds without any recourse to Roman doctrines.

Nevertheless, the work of the Romanists and the Germanists represents two sides of the same coin; both engaged in an historical investigation of the evolution of law in order to advance the law in nineteenth century Germany. The Germanists were breaking new ground. The Romanists were bringing new techniques of scholarship to bear on their study of sources which were for the most part well known; some new sources, however, were revealed. In 1816 Niebuhr discovered the Veronese palimpsest of Gaius' Institutes and thus brought to light the only largely complete classical work to survive untouched by Justinian's compilers; other pre-Justinianic fragments of legal writings were also found during this period, such as the Vatican Fragments. Bluhme's investigations resulted in his generally accepted theory of how the Digest had been compiled by three committees, each going through a different block of material.

Later in the century, when the eventual production of a code had become a certainty, Romanists were freed from the need always to think in terms of Roman law as a system for current application. In the later years of the century Lenel's Edictum Perpetuum and Palingenesia Iuris Civilis were published; in the former he reconstructed the Edict of the Urban Praetor, in the latter he re-assembled the writings of the individual classical jurists, which the compilers had scattered in their arrangement by subject, so that, for example, one may read what survives of Ulpian's 31st book On the Praetor's Edict and then go on to the 32nd - a Roman book was about the length of a short modern chapter. Other works appearing in this period which are still fundamental to scholarship were C.G. Bruns' collection of sources other than the legal literature, and Theodor Mommsen's surveys of Roman public and Roman criminal law, his (by now standard) edition of the Digest, and his foundation of the great collection known as the Corpus Inscriptionum Latinarum in which are edited and arranged by geographical source all surviving inscriptions in the Latin of antiquity.

Savigny's position was outstanding, but he had his critics. Hugo thought his theory of the Volksgeist too abstract and out of step with a reliance on empirically ascertainable historical fact. German commercial lawyers were satisfied with the Roman law developed by the Commentators as relevant to their needs; they did not want to regress to doctrines taken from the less developed classical Roman law. Rudolph von Jhering (1818-92) was also a Romanist; his thinking about legal evolution, as expressed in Der Geist des römischen Rechts (The Spirit of Roman Law), differed from Savigny's in stressing the similarities between legal systems. He was not prepared to accept the strongly nationalistic approach of the Historical School, but thought that the ability to borrow wisely was one of the glories of a legal system. The comparative method of studying other systems as well as one's own enabled the absorption of those foreign doctrines and institutions which were most profitable.

471

## (iii)  The Pandectists

The Pandectists originated as an off-shoot of the Historical School, and their main concern was the scientific application of the Roman texts. Like the Historical School, their methods prompted discussion and imitation throughout Europe -- including England -- and also in America.  The Pandectists took their name from the <u>Pandects</u> (i.e. <u>Digest</u>) of Justinian and their scholarship was essentially concerned with the systematization of Roman law for contemporary use, with the emphasis on the jurists of the classical age.

The Pandectists were to some extent influenced by the Natural Lawyers, back to Pufendorf, in that they aspired to a rigidly schematic approach. They too tried to create an interlocking system of legal rules and concepts, from which solutions to new legal problems could logically be drawn; this was undoubtedly due to the particular influence of Wolff.  Like the Natural Lawyers the Pandectists were influenced by the natural scientists of their time; they aimed to identify a new kind of truth, the positive or scientific truth, by observation and experiment.  They were thus legal positivists in that they expounded the principles of observed law as something without any logical link to moral justice.  Once data had been collected, analysis could determine what was cause and what effect; classification and definition were also essential parts of the scientific method.  It was possible, if not common, for a Pandectist to compare the discovery of legal principles with the analytic methods of chemistry.

The school was founded by Georg Friedrich Puchta (1798-1846), a pupil of Savigny who succeeded his master in the Berlin chair in 1842.  Puchta himself was indebted to Savigny, particularly for the latter's theory of the jurist as representative of the <u>Volksgeist</u>, and in his turn he influenced his master. Puchta believed that the jurist, as representative of the people, was responsible for both the theory and the practice of the law and must use his skills to express rules and concepts hidden from the untrained mind. This special position meant that the rules elucidated by the jurist should *ipso facto* have the force of law -- legal science therefore joined custom and legislation as a source of law. Moreover, it was the jurist's duty to guide both legislator and people and guard the law from any rash or ignorant interference. The jurist must also place legal rules in their systematic context, recognizing their effect upon one another, and acknowledging their lines of derivation so that each rule could be traced back to its underlying principle; thus he could demonstrate the internal harmony of the legal system. This method, which is known as Begriffsjurisprudenz (Jurisprudence of Concepts), aimed at creating a hierarchy from the very concept of law itself down to each particular rule, the validity of an individual rule being dependent on its logical place in this hierarchical pyramid.

The construction of such a systematic hierarchy of concepts clearly demanded definition of all the concepts involved. As time went by, these definitions tended to become more and more abstract and to lead their framers into language more familiar to legal philosophers than to practitioners. For example, a legal right was defined as "a power of volition", a legal act as "a definition of will", while the protection of peaceful possession was justified on the grounds that "the law respects the realized will".

Savigny, under the influence of Puchta, moved in his later years more strongly towards the systematic and away from the empirical in his study of Roman law. Even in his treatise on possession, some of his deductions had had more in common with mathematical formulas than with the social

473

realities of Roman law. His (unfinished) System des heutigen römischen Rechts (System of Modern Roman Law) well typifies Pandectist legal science (Pandektenrecht). The material was to be arranged under obligations, property, family law, and succession, with further sub-headings as appropriate. Certain basic concepts which applied throughout the system, such as status and juristic personality, he treated separately in the General Part with which he opened. He followed the same method within his treatment of obligations, explaining the generally applicable concepts before dealing with particular fields and their rules. The other major work of the Pandectists was Windscheid's Lehrbuch der Pandekten (Textbook on the Pandects, first published in 1862) which went through seven editions in the author's lifetime and became the standard manual of the school. It was arranged according to the system outlined by Savigny. Unlike that of most of his fellows, Windscheid's work was of use to practitioners because he made frequent reference to court decisions.

Although the Pandectists became as rigidly schematic as any of the more extreme Natural Lawyers, their roots in the Historical School meant that they preferred the Roman law of the classical period to Justinianic law, let alone the modifications of the mediaeval civilians. This caused a degree of conflict with the majority of lawyers actually practising law, who adhered to the Gemeines Recht in the tradition of the usus modernus Pandectarum. Of the supporters of the latter approach, Bruns, for example, in his treatise on possession examined both the original Roman law and its evolution and the changes the concepts and rules had undergone since the twelfth century. He justified these changes on the grounds of their expediency and thus implicitly approved their continued application.

The Pandectists were a strong force in German legal thinking in the nineteenth century. Greater systematization than the Gemeines Recht offered was certainly desirable for the exposition of the law, whether to students or to the public, and also for its application. Again, although the Pandectists claimed to be politically neutral and concerned only with private law, their values were those of the prosperous middle class which believed in the theory of laissez-faire; they stressed freedom of contract and the protection of private property -- as indeed the Romans had. Finally, Pandectist legal science was attractive because it represented unity and not diversity; it offered a common juristic culture which took no account of regional variations, and it was therefore of appeal to the forces of nationalism. Their Romanism, however, was disliked, particularly by the Germanists of the Historical School. Many others, like Jhering, came to find their methods far too abstract and doctrinaire, and quite neglectful of the realities of social life.

In his **Geist des römischen Rechts** Jhering moved away from Pandectist legal science and attempted to provide a sociological explanation for the evolution of the rules of Roman law. He laid the foundations of what was to become known as the Jurisprudence of Interests: that is, the approach which argues that the duty of a judge, especially when faced with a doubtful decision on a matter for which there is no explicit legislative provision, is to settle the case according to that estimate of the correct balance between the competing interests of the parties concerned which was to be found in the work of the legislator. The judge is not free to follow his discretion but must always look within the written law for this balance; nevertheless, he should concern himself with the legislator's social aims rather than with the ordering of concepts. Jhering stressed that legal science was concerned with social relations in general and business purposes in particular, and that the ideas of justice, law and the state were interdependent. There could be no clear and permanent line

475

drawn between private and public law since the state must be interested in
the pursuit of activities desirable for the community.  Historical
evolution and present needs defined justice for the particular place and
time.  Legal concepts had no meaning apart from the activities of human
life.

(iv)  The BGB and its background

Even after the creation of the German Empire in 1871, Germany remained
a legally divided country.  The states of which the new Empire was composed
still retained a measure of autonomy, and the creation did not immediately
affect the legal systems of its members.  These legal systems continued to
be various blends of codified law -- Saxony acquired a code as late as 1863
--, Gemeines Recht and local custom, although Schleswig-Holstein was under
Danish law while much of the Rhineland  adhered to the Code Civil.  There
was also variation among the states over which of the three elements took
precedence.  Under the North German Confederation, created in 1866 as a
step towards unification, the Reichstag and Bundesrat (lower and upper
houses of a federal governing body,  under the King of Prussia) were
established; they made possible direct federal legislation in the specific
areas of criminal and commercial law.  In 1869 a supreme federal court was
set up with jurisdiction in these two fields; in 1877 this court was re-
established at Leipzig with no restrictions on its jurisdiction.  Since
1873 legislation too had been competent in any area of civil law.  From
1877 therefore there was the machinery for a unified German law.

In the previous chapter the process of harmonization, especially in
the field of commercial law, was described.  In 1861 the German Commercial
Code was issued.  This was introduced by local legislation into the various

476

member states of the North German Confederation in the following years. In 1871 it was re-issued as an imperial law. This Code expanded the scope of commercial law beyond that of the French code; in the latter, a matter was commercial only if both the parties could be described as merchants, but in the German code it was the commercial nature of the transaction which was stressed, even if only one party was engaged in pursuing his business. When the Commercial Code was revised and re-issued in 1897 it reverted to the more usual narrower sphere, limiting its authority to cases where the transactions involved business interests on both sides; this was possible because the Civil Code had already been passed as statute -- although it was not yet in force.

In 1871 there was enacted an imperial German Penal Code, which largely repeated the penal code of the North German Confederation, itself based on the Prussian penal code of 1851. However, it was Prussia which had opposed a scheme, known as the Dresden Draft, put forward in 1865 in an attempt to reach uniformity in the law of obligations. There was no government inspired attempt to unify the civil law until after the extension in 1873 of the imperial legislature's powers. The following year a single clause statute authorized the codification of German civil law and a commission was appointed to consider ways and means. The recommendations of this commission, although not given binding force, were followed in substance by the commission which was then appointed to produce a draft code.

The drafting commission consisted of eleven men under the chairmanship of the president of the imperial commercial court; it included Bernhard Windscheid, the Pandectist, who left the commission before the work was completed, but who, nevertheless, had a very considerable influence on the final draft. The commission included other academics and also practitioners as well as officials regularly employed in the drafting of legislation. At the outset it was agreed to omit commercial law and certain aspects of land law from the code. After thirteen years of work a draft was completed in 1887 and published the next year, together with explanatory notes, to receive comments and criticisms.

Much comment was received, and a considerable proportion was unfavourable. Only one critic objected to codification in principle, and he was a member of the imperial supreme court, but there were two main lines of attack adopted by others. Some thought that the draft was excessively reliant on Roman as opposed to German law. To some extent, this was only to be expected, in view of the membership of the commission which included Windscheid and others trained in Pandectist legal science; both the structure and the substance of the draft revealed the Pandectist approach. Others criticized both the language and the matter of the draft as too abstract and doctrinaire; insofar as one purpose of a code was to make the law readily known, it was a failure. As one wit remarked: "Before it can be understood, it must be translated into German."

A second drafting commission was appointed in 1890, but with the task of working on a revision of the original in the light of the comments received. This was a larger commission, and it included, as well as a range of lawyers, interested parties such as commercial experts, landowners, economists and representatives of other special interests. This commission kept consultations going while it worked, and it made some effort to simplify the condensed language of the code. The revised draft was finished in 1895 and was approved by the imperial council with relatively few amendments; it was given statutory force in 1896 with effect from 1 January, 1900. A supplementary codifying statute on international private law was issued at the same time. The new civil code (the BGB) and the commercial code were comprehensive within the fields they covered, but

478

other areas of the law were left to be dealt with by separate legislation; for example, insurance and copyright.

The BGB is divided into five books, but the articles are consecutive throughout. The first book contains the General Part; it covers persons -- both natural and juristic --, the definition of things, the classification of legal acts, prescriptive periods and so on. The second book deals with obligations, with the creation and discharge of voluntary obligations, with the individual contracts and delicts. The third book is on things, dealing with possession, then ownership of immoveable and moveable property, with servitudes and real security. The fourth book is on family law, which includes marriage, other relationships within the family and tutelage. The fifth book deals with succession, starting with the concept of hereditary succession and then going on to the rights of heirs, rules concerning wills, settlements and technical details of proof in connection with inheritance.

In its final form the BGB still owes a considerable debt to Roman law but it also takes account of German tradition. The arrangement conforms to the Pandectist system but the substance within each section is based on predominantly Roman or German rules according to the particular history of the relevant branch of law. The Roman contribution is dominant in the field of obligations, while in family law and succession the bulk of the material comes from the German tradition. Moreover, the opportunity was taken in producing the BGB to reform various areas of law; the law of husband and wife was brought up to date, for example. The language remains technical, rigorously consistent and not easy for a layman to use. Ready comprehension of the law is further hampered by the need to read different parts of the Code in the light of each other in order to obtain a complete picture. For example, to settle a problem on sale, the judge might well have to look first to the General Part, then to the generalities about obligations, thence to the general law of contract and finally to the particular rules affecting the specific contract of sale; cross-reference to the commercial code may become necessary.

Despite these drawbacks the BGB has had considerable influence outside Germany. In Greece the Pandectist approach dominated academic law and when a Greek Civil Code was finally produced in 1946 its structure and content both owed much to the German model. The Austrian code was revised in the early twentieth century in the light of what the BGB had to say about obligations. In Switzerland and in Hungary it was influential; with the exception of family law and succession it was the basis of the Japanese Civil Code of 1898, and it was noted in China. Brazil too preferred the BGB to the Code Civil as the main source for its codification. In Britain it was the German experience as much as the process of harmonization in the commercial field which aroused in many a desire for at least limited codification. Such views did not in general owe much to the radical proposals of Bentham or Austin but rather aimed at revising and consolidating, as in the Sale of Goods Act 1893. This approach was similar to that most commonly taken in the U.S.A., but there were some such as Maine and Stephen who, after experience in codifying the Common Law for Indian use, saw the benefits of a more fundamental undertaking.

(v)  The French reaction to codification


French legal thought in the nineteenth century, while in some ways parallel to that in Germany, is most obviously different in that the Germans were working towards --or against-- codification while the French were trying to come to terms with their existing codes, particularly the

<u>Code</u> <u>Civil</u>. It had been a deliberate aim of the Revolution to subordinate the judges to 'the legislator' and to abolish their law-making powers. Distrust of the judiciary and of judicial discretion had been marked in the reformers as well as the radicals; it was therefore not surprising that it was given effect in the <u>Code</u> <u>Civil</u>. It lay behind the requirement that judges should cite the articles of the <u>Code</u> on which they relied and explain their reasoning rather than rely on their own intrinsic authority; this requirement led to the extremely terse style adopted by the judges of all courts for their decisions, since too much explanation gives more room for argument. Thus the main problem that faced French lawyers was that legislation was in their theory the only source of law, and yet the law must be applied and understood.

The strong feeling which had imbued the <u>Code</u> that judges should limit themselves to the administration of its provisions and not usurp the place of the legislator was expressed in article 5, which forbids any judicial pronouncement on a matter before the court by way of a general disposition having effect for the future. This became a fundamental tenet of French legal thought. How far it could be enforced in actuality was a problem ignored by the legislature. Academic lawyers held grimly to the theory and proceeded therefore to elaborate on the actual contents of the <u>Code</u> in an attempt to provide the judges with something to administer in every conceivable situation. The judges themselves observed the forms but soon, inevitably, began to interpret, and the accumulated effect of their decisions is what is meant by the French term <u>jurisprudence</u> -- as opposed to the <u>doctrine</u> of the academic lawyers. Nevertheless, even the <u>Cour</u> <u>de</u> <u>Cassation</u>, the supreme court administering the <u>Code</u> <u>Civil</u> (in contrast to the <u>Conseil</u> <u>d'État</u> which is the supreme tribunal in matters of public law), has been carefully restricted so that it should not to appear to make law.

Decisions appealed to it may be quashed (cassé) but they are then sent to a second lower court, equivalent to the first, for a fresh trial.  Only since 1837, and then only when all the chambers of the court sit together, has the Cour de Cassation been able to give a final decision, and the effect of this is, supposedly, restricted to the case before the court.  However, although the theory of the subordination of the judiciary means that there can be no doctrine of precedent, there has been a natural tendency in the courts towards consistency, aided by the reports of decided cases.

Every judgment must by law be constructed from the main relevant facts and the statutory provisions which apply to them in a series of logical steps leading inexorably to the conclusion of the particular issue; this is described as a jugement motivé.  To avoid any appearance of discretionary interpretation such judgments are laconic.  The case report may give the arguments of the advocates in some detail but the stated reasoning of the judges remains terse.  However, such reports -- the most notable surviving series are those of Dalloz and Sirey -- have traditionally been accompanied by analytical notes and comments which can reveal the influence of sources older than the Code or of previous decisions of the court.  These comments can be collected into répertoires or encyclopaedias, commonly arranged by topic, which fill the silences in the judicial decrees.  The tradition of producing such works was established early, despite Napoleon's dislike of legal commentaries.  Merlin, procureur-général[1] of the Cour de Cassation,

----------

1   The responsibility of the procureur-général was and is to state to the
    court a reasoned and objective view of the law, with proposals for the
    action to be taken on the appeal before it; a similar function is
    performed by the advocates-general of the Court of Justice of the
    European Communities.

was immensely learned in the old law and well placed to analyse the decisions of the new régime; the ample material he provided in his books during the 1810s and the 1820s was in itself an encouragement to the Cour de Cassation to supplement what was lacking in the Code. Partly through his influence and partly through that of Savigny and the Historical School many lawyers became involved during the earlier years of the century in the effort to describe the working law of France and to classify and analyse its development. The German scholars were interested in the Code Civil both as a product of legal science and as the law in force in the German Rhineland until the coming of the BGB. During the 1840s, however, academic interest in répertoires and case law waned, and the field was almost wholly occupied by practitioners. Their work was sufficiently thorough and critical for the courts to be secure in developing a jurisprudence constante which, in some areas, has achieved major changes in the law. For example, articles 1119 and 1121 forbid entering into a stipulation on behalf of another, except in very narrowly defined circumstances; because these rules are most inconvenient in the context of life assurance -- an institution which had not been imagined by the drafters of the Code -- the courts have in effect put them into abeyance[2]. In connection with gifts the courts have also departed from the obvious meaning of the Code and have introduced new rules[3]. The means by which the courts achieved these changes have often been tortuous, but this has been because of the deliberate constraints on judicial power established by the framers of the Code. For practitioners, coming to terms with the Code meant accepting a

----------

2    C.K. Allen, Law in the Making (7th ed., Oxford, 1964), p.182.

3    J.P. Dawson, Gifts and Promises (Yale, 1980) gives a good picture of
     the different treatment of the topic in the French and German systems.

gap between theory and practice; the restrictive theory is impossible to apply, but practical interpretation must always be achieved by using some provision of the Code, however pervertedly.

French academic lawyers played a small part compared with their German colleagues in the development of their legal régime, and their status was much lower. They had a bad start; as a direct consequence of the Revolution the law schools were defunct by 1793 and they were actually abolished in 1795. They were revived in 1804 by Napoleon but with the specific intention that their professors should be obedient exponents of the Code and nothing more. Even when men of more originality came to be appointed their focus was on the Code Civil and the other codes. Although some jurists in the 1820s were influenced by the Historical School, the dominant approach from the 1830s on was analytical and dogmatic, following the lead of Jean Proudhon, who held a chair of law at Dijon.

For decades the great majority of academic lawyers concentrated on the texts of the codes and their interpretation, and on the relationships between the individual provisions and their possible interpretation. They assumed that legislation was the only source of law, that the coverage of the codes (and of the laws passed in the new fields of law which appeared during the nineteenth century) was complete and that there were no inconsistencies and contradictions. Careful analysis, they thought, could fill every apparent gap in the provisions of the law and supply an answer to any conceivable legal problem. Like the Pandectists, whom they much admired, they built up a structure based on logical deduction, but it was sterile because it ignored what was happening in the courts. Moreover, Pandectist legal science, because of its wider range of materials, had more hope of covering all possibilities than the French. French jurists restricted themselves almost entirely to the codes, occasionally looking back behind them to Pothier, but recognizing virtually no other source, while the Pandectists, although they concentrated on the classical Roman law, did acknowledge its Justinianic and mediaeval developments as well as the fact of the Reception, even if they tried to minimize the importance of these aspects of the law.

For half a century an immensely learned and ingenious flood of literature was produced in France, of considerable value as far as it went but not fertile in new ideas. The exponents of doctrine despised the exponents of jurisprudence and their scorn was returned; it was only towards the end of the century that they began to see how their skills and their subject matter could be complementary. Some academic journals began to take notice of judicial decisions; analytical notes in the case reports came to be written by academics. The natural exhaustion of the restrictive approach to the codes meant that the leading intellectual figures in the 1890s readily took a more historical or sociological approach to the study of law, including the study of its application. The distinguished Romanist Esmein remarked that jurisprudence, "just as much as the Code itself, must be studied directly and scientifically". An exponent of the historical approach appeared at the end of the century who did much to reconcile the theory of the supremacy of the Code and of the inability of judges to make law with the reality of practice; this was François Gény.

Gény raised the question of whether a merely logical interpretation of the Code was desirable, or even possible. He held in his Méthode d'interprétation et sources en droit privé positif (1899) that it was necessary to investigate the realities of social life; from such researches he added  custom, judicial authority and juristic tradition to the effective sources of law, looking to the Volksgeist of French law, and 'free scientific research', which must take into account concepts like

485

equity -- hitherto rigorously rejected -- the public order and interest, and the just balance between conflicting private interests. While defining the function of judicial decisions as 'propelling' the formation of custom, he held that the operation of the courts was to look at the interests of the parties, "estimate their respective force, weigh them in the scales of justice so as to give preponderance to the most important of them, tested by some social standard, and finally bring about an equilibrium". If the judge had no other guidance, he should apply the same principles as would a legislator. Gény's theories were not new, even in France, but the way he put them forward made a great impact. Because he still could not openly acknowledge explicit judicial rule-making, he had to complicate his discussion of custom with problems considered long before by the Commentators, such as: Who are the necessary users of a custom? How can one tell if they do consent to the formation of a custom? Are they 'represented' by jurists and judges? It was, however, on foundations laid by Gény that Planiol could say: "Jurisprudence is a customary law of recent creation."

In his other major work, Science et technique en droit privé positif (1914-24), Gény developed the more sociological aspects of his legal philosophy. He was part of the same intellectual movement as was expressed in Germany by the Freirechtsschule (Free Law School). This movement opposed legal positivism and the Jurisprudence of Concepts and looked to men like Jhering who had advocated the Jurisprudence of Interests. (In some cases the doctrine that the judge should be quite free to choose his interpretation of the most suitable rule led to a cavalier disregard for statute and considerable unpredictability in the application of law, but mostly it was enlivening.) Gény defined Natural Law as the limits within which any legal system must work. There are four premises, le donné réel, le donné historique, le donné rationnel and le donné idéal. Le donné réel covers physical and psychological facts, such as sex, or climate or religious traditions; le donné historique covers the historical facts and traditions which mould le donné réel; le donné rationnel (which includes much of the classic doctrine of Natural Law) states such things as the sanctity of human life, the right to property, the inviolability of the person and freedom of thought; le donné idéal describes how society understands the facts and how it wishes changes to take place. Thus to apply Gény's terms to marriage, its first basis is the sexual instinct of man and woman, its second the historical institution in any society, the third the need for a relatively permanent -- although not necessarily monogamous -- relationship for the secure life of the family, and the fourth comprises current ideas in any society on the proper relations between husband and wife, even if not yet embodied in the law. Gény provided a realistic foundation for the continuing relationship between jurisprudence and doctrine and in this way his work was immensely valuable, even if his more purely philosophical notions were not able to withstand much criticism.


(vi)   The Swiss Code


In 1815 Switzerland was still a loose confederation of twenty-two virtually independent cantons; in 1848 the modern federal state was created, with a federal legislature whose powers were extended in 1874 and 1898 by constitutional amendments. In 1874 the private law of the several cantons ranged from being essentially that of the Code Civil in the French speaking cantons, being based on the Austrian code, as in Berne and Lucerne, or even largely original, as in Zürich where, however, Pandectist influence was apparent. After 1874 the legislature was competent to issue general legislation in the fields of personal status and obligations as well as certain aspects of commercial law; this led to a Code of Obligations, promulgated in 1881, which drew from the German Commercial Code and the discarded Dresden Draft. After 1898 the legislature had an unrestricted competence in all aspects of civil and criminal (but not public) law. Eugen Huber, a professor at Berne, had already been asked to prepare the draft of a civil code and this was published for comment in 1900. A commission of jurists and other experts was then appointed to amend the draft in the light of the criticisms. The final draft was submitted to select committees of both houses of the Swiss legislature in 1904; in 1907 it was enacted, with effect from 1 January 1912 as the Schweizerisches Zivilgesetzbuch (ZGB - Swiss Civil Code); the old Code of Obligations was revised and attached as, in effect, a fifth book.

The Swiss Code begins with a preliminary title on general matters and then has four books dealing respectively with persons, family law, succession and property; then there is the book on obligations. While the book on obligations is very clearly indebted to Pandectist thinking in its method, proceeding from the general to the particular, those who framed it did not allow system to dominate at the expense of clarity and accessibility. Nor was the rest of the Swiss Code framed in highly technical language. As with the Code Civil, it was deliberately kept as simple as possible in style so that it would be comprehensible to the intelligent layman as well as the lawyer. Furthermore, it is in the French tradition in that it does not purport to provide a complete and detailed statement of the law from which the solution to every legal problem may be deduced. (This interpretation of the Code was adopted only by Proudhon and his followers; the framers of the Code had consciously argued that a code

488

could do no more than lay down general principles for guiding future legal developments.) Instead it offers a statement of general principle, deliberately leaving scope for further development by judicial interpretation, as is expressly ordained in art. 1 of the ZGB. Certain areas of commercial law which were in a state of flux at the time of the promulgation of the Swiss Code, such as insurance and copyright, were left to be dealt with by future legislation -- which could also be adapted to the harmonization process within European legal systems.

In spite of both German and French influences the Swiss Code is a distinctively Swiss product, firmly rooted in the existing cantonal law. The blending of disparate influences in the legal code was a reflection of the similar political, linguistic and cultural blending in the Confederation itself. This sympathetic relation to juridical history owed much to Huber, the drafter of the Code. Before starting on the work of preparing a draft, he had established himself as an authority on Swiss law and produced the fundamental System und Geschichte des schweizerischen Privatrechts (System and History of Swiss Private Law). This book has much in common with the work of men such as Dumoulin in the aftermath of the codification of the French customs, for it is a comprehensive and comparative account of the customary laws of the cantons. Huber describes both differences and similarities and, on the basis of common underlying jurisprudential principles, attempts to distil a common customary law for Switzerland, using the knowledge and techniques developed by civilians and by Natural Lawyers to produce a balanced portrait.

Like the Code Civil and the BGB, the Swiss Code has been of influence beyond its own frontiers. It was much admired in Germany, where some even favoured its adoption. It influenced French juristic thinking, in particular in the French law of adoption of 1927. In 1926 it was imported virtually without alteration into Turkey when Kemal Ataturk decided on enforcing immediate westernization. It was also an influence in the production of the Polish, Russian, Czech and Hungarian codes.


Further Reading:

Continental Legal History Series, vol. XI: The Progress of Continental Law in the Nineteenth Century.

M. Berger "Codification" in Perspectives in Jurisprudence, ed. E.M.M. Attwooll (Glasgow, 1977)

F. Dahn "The new code for the German Empire" Jur.Rev. (1890), 15.

J.P. Dawson The Oracles of the Law (Ann Arbor, 1968), ch. vi.

W. Friedmann Legal Theory (5th ed., London, 1967).

H. Kantorowicz "Savigny and the Historical School of Law" 53 L.Q.R (1937), 326.

Lord Lloyd An Introduction to Jurisprudence (3rd ed., London, 1972)

P. Stein Legal Evolution (C.U.P. 1980).

I. Williams The Sources of Law in the Swiss Civil Code (O.U.P., 1923).

Chapter XVIII

## AN OUTLINE SKETCH OF THE TWENTIETH CENTURY

Although, as was explained in the Introduction, there are good reasons for bringing the main part of this book to a close with the First World War, it has not escaped the authors' notice that some seventy years have elapsed since then. Much, indeed most, legal development in the twentieth century has been only a progression along lines laid down in the nineteenth, but in some cases a quantitative has led to a qualitative change. Codification is not a spent force; Turkey's deliberate and complete adoption of the Swiss code has drawn it within the ambit of western Europe. Italy and the Netherlands have produced new codes; Quebec produced a revised draft code in 1977 which is now in force. Liberal democracy seems to have survived, despite the Italian and German interludes under Mussolini and Hitler. The undoing of overseas colonialism which has marked the years since the Second World War has sprung partly from the nature of the democratic ideal and partly from the pressures of socialism. The rise of Russia, the Union of Soviet Socialist Republics, to the status of a super-power has created new political pressures within and outwith Europe; in particular, Germany is divided into the Federal Republic (BRD) and the Democratic Republic (DDR) and Poland, Czechoslovakia and Hungary, like East Germany, have been to some extent cut off from their legal roots in the West.

The creation of the concept of Socialist Law, in line with Marxist-Leninist doctrine which has the ultimate aim of the withering away of law and of the state itself, has been a new feature. In a way it is closer to the ideas of those oriental societies which hold that law is only a poor substitute for reconciliation. In practice, however, until the time is

491

ripe for the withering away, Socialist doctrine holds that the necessary equality of man can only be achieved at the expense of liberty and the welfare of the community as a whole is deliberately given priority over the happiness of the individual. Socialist law does not assume private property, immoveable or moveable, as the norm but thinks in terms of the means of production and of goods for consumption; only in the latter can there be private property. The scope of private law as the western tradition understands it is therefore very much restricted; it is also subordinate by its nature to law as an instrument of policy. The divisions of law, like legal terminology, have to a large extent remained the product of a legal science constructed on the basis of Roman law in the European universities; in particular, the Austrian code and Pandectist thinking have been influential. The ideological purpose of Socialist law, however, means that judges are the elected representatives of the sovereign people and that they apply a law which is defined as an instrument of policy and has a very limited function as a restraint upon the executive. Because of this nature of law there can be no valid legal developments other than those which result from the will of the legislators; furthermore, the duty of academic lawyers is not to criticize but to clarify and to convince their audience of the wisdom and the justice of Socialist law. In those Socialist countries which are in the mainstream of European history, as opposed to the Balkans which were within the Ottoman Empire, there is a clearer recognition than in Russia that Socialism itself is rooted in the European tradition, and that Socialist law can be interpreted as improving on rather than as necessarily being in conflict with western law.

The liberal democracies have tried to solve the problems of inequality not by socialism but by the introduction of the welfare state, in which no citizen should ever lack the necessities of life: food and clothing, shelter, medical care, and support in old age or disability; its roots lie in the nineteenth century, although the plant has grown enormously. The welfare state inevitably leads to many more points of contact between the state and the citizen, a contact which is enhanced by the much greater proportion of the population in the employment of the state (no matter whether the actual government is of the left or the right). The increase in the scale and complexity of taxation is one legal consequence of the welfare state and of state intervention. Another is the perceived need to defend the individual against the tyranny of the state; this has led to the growth of administrative law. In Britain, for example, tribunals have come into existence to provide non-technical remedies for such ills as unfair dismissal or excessive rents and, in some countries, parliamentary, local and other commissioners (the ombudsmen) have been created to deal with failings in officialdom. The European Convention of Human Rights has attempted to lay down a standard to which each nation should conform, enforceable at the European Court of Human Rights in Strasbourg.

It is not only human rights for which there is an international court. The scale of industrialized militancy revealed by the First World War led to the creation of the League of Nations, and in 1926 Unidroit was founded to encourage the further harmonization of laws within Europe. After the Second World War the League of Nations was replaced by the United Nations, whose forum is the International Court of Justice at The Hague. More relevant to our theme, the European Communities were created, above all in order to reconcile France and Germany but also to provide an economic, political and cultural counter to the super-powers of Russia and the United States. The Court of Justice of the European Communities sits in Luxembourg and, in dealing with the cases which come before it, tries to manage, as do the other European institutions (such as the Council of

Europe), the problems arising from economic inter-dependence and national rivalry. The process of harmonization of law continues. For example, the June 1984 issue of the *Information Bulletin on Legal Activities* of the Council of Europe (vol.18, p.4) records that Portugal has signed without reservation the agreement which allows the free temporary import of medical materials for use on free loan for diagnosis or treatment in hospitals and other medical institutions. In the same issue (pp.20-1) the member states, using committees of experts, were noted as considering the problem of identity documents and movement of nomads and as drafting a convention on the protection of vertebrate animals used for experimental and other scientific purposes; the Committee for Equality between Men and Women was also in session, discussing the rôle of the media as agents of social change, and employment policy and advertising.

A few completely new fields of law have emerged in recent decades. Perhaps the most talked of has been the growth of the concept of discrimination, whether on grounds of race, colour, sex or religion, and the attempt to counter this by positive discrimination, affirmative action; both sides of this coin have been fruitful of litigation. The change in the legal balance between the sexes in the last century has undoubtedly been radical. This could not have happened without the industrialization and technological advances which have made possible women's liberation from domestic drudgery and perpetual child-bearing, but it also springs from the ideological and cultural changes foreshadowed in the Declaration of the Rights of Man. For example, in England there were no female legal practitioners until after the Sex Disqualification (Removal) Act of 1919; the English Court of Appeal had previously held that a woman was in the Common Law under a general disability by reason of her sex. In the 1920s the League of Nations was working towards the abolition of child marriages;

one consequence was the general lifting of the age of consent for marriage or for sexual relations to sixteen years. In 1971 "the German Constitutional Court refused to apply certain rules of German private international law because, in their reference to the national law of the husband, they violated the principle of equality between the sexes" given force by article 117 of the Fundamental Law[1]. Another aspect of the law of persons which has seen significant changes has been the move to put bastards on the same legal footing as their legitimate siblings. In the issue of the **Information Bulletin** already cited it is recorded that in Greece: "The distinction between legitimate and illegitimate children is abolished. Children born out of wedlock are assimilated to those born within a marriage, so long as their paternity has been recognized" (p.25). In the United Kingdom: "The [English] Law Commission has published a paper in which it recommends the abolition of all legal disadvantages of illegitimacy so far as they affect the illegitimate child" (p.28).

The newest field of law, however, arises from the technological revolution, in particular that part of it brought about by the computer and the micro-chip. Scientific changes have been immense; in the last half-century, physics has split the atom, biology has made possible surrogate motherhood, chemistry has created wonder drugs carrying unforeseeable risks, but nevertheless weapons of war, sources of energy, problems of identifying parentage and hidden poisons have long been with us. The electronic revolution, however, is posing genuinely new problems for lawyers. "One recent introduction, now available, is called 'electronic mail'. A letter can be typed at a terminal in Edinburgh and received at a terminal in London, the central processing unit connecting the terminals

----------

1    David and Brierley, p.138.

being situated in London, Paris or Washington. The text can be stored in any of these places. In none of them will there be any inspectable document unless somebody chooses to print out the text. The stored text, wherever it is, consists of nothing more than charged particles, susceptible all the time to interference and manipulation. ... One important question therefore is: what are the consequences for the law of contract? Has a contract been concluded when the letter of acceptance has been transmitted by electronic mail but has not been seen by anybody at the receiving end other than the computer? Is a printout of what is _now_ in the computer -- which is, as I say, susceptible to interference and manipulation -- sufficient evidence that the contract was made? And where was it made -- in Edinburgh or London, where the sending and receiving terminals are, or in Washington (in a different time zone) where the text is processed and stored? And how is a court to verify, by any normal process to which we are accustomed, whether, when and where a contract has been made?"[2]

There are, of course, many other legal issues which, while not being new, have come to the fore in recent times. Partly as a consequence of former colonialism, partly because of new wealth based on oil, people following Islamic and other legal régimes have become involved in Western legal systems, and the clash of cultures in a pluralistic society is not always easy to resolve. On the intellectual side there has been a revival of natural law in reaction to legal positivism and the 'pure' theory of law. In jurisprudence generally American thinking has been of great influence in Europe, both through the legal science of academics and

----------

2    D.A.O. Edward "A little cloud like a man's hand" 30 _J.L.S.S._ (1985), 10.

through the deliberations of the courts.   The Commonwealth, moreover, has enriched the Common Law tradition. American, English and civilian lines of legal thought have been following similar paths because of the many common political, social and economic factors.   Economic changes in particular have had legal consequences; the existence of state enterprise and of multinational corporations needs to be reconciled with the human scale  of values.   Above all, our interdependence within the nation, within Europe, within the world, has become more obvious and more urgently in need of recognition.

Further Reading:

R. David and J. Brierley  Major Legal Systems in the World Today   (2nd ed. London, 1978)

W. Friedmann  Legal Theory (5th ed. London, 1967)

D. Lasok and J.W. Bridge Introduction to the Law and Institutions of the European Communities (3rd ed. London, 1982)

A.D. Lindsay  The Modern Democratic State (O.U.P., 1943, repr.)

Lord Lloyd  An Introduction to Jurisprudence (3rd ed. London, 1972)

A.H. Manchester  Modern Legal History (London, 1980)

D. Thomson  Europe since Napoleon (2nd ed. Penguin, 1966, repr.)

A general point worth noting is that, although the Glossators and the Commentators knew Justinian's divisions into books, titles, and fragments or laws, and also dealt separately with individual sentences, they did not refer to them in the modern style by number.  For us C. 8,55,8 seems easily the simplest form of reference, but the mediaeval jurists referred to Code de revocandis donationibus -- the rubric of the title --, law Si umquam -- the opening words of the particular constitution.  Similarly when Azo referred to D. 9,2,27,3 he said "ff (=Digest) ad legem Aquiliam, law si servus, paragraph Iulianus".  Later scholars, right up to this century, often used the order l.8 C. de rev.don. (8,55), or l.27,3 D. ad l.Aquil. (9,2).  Where no part of the Corpus is specified the Digest should be understood.

Similarly, the mediaeval division of the Corpus was different from Justinian's or our own (different even from Justinian's division into sections for teaching purposes in constitutio Omnem).  As the mediaeval lawyers reckoned it, it was made up of the Old Digest (Digestum Vetus), i.e. D. 1,1 to D. 24,2; the Infortiatum, i.e. D. 24,3 - 38,17; the New Digest (Digestum Novum), i.e. D. 39,1 to the end; the Code, meaning Books 1 - 9 thereof; and the Volumen, which comprised the Institutes, the Tres Libri (or last three books of the Code), the Authenticum (one version of Justinian's Novels), the Books of the Feus, and the Extravagantes, other legislation of the Holy Roman Emperors, including the terms of the Peace of Constance of 1183.  This division of the Digest is slightly baffling, but may have been made for ease of handling the actual manuscripts and also as a convenient division for teaching purposes, or even because of the order in which the MSS came to light.  Further, the mediaeval writers generally knew no Greek and so the many passages in that language were often omitted or sometimes translated.


(a) A Gloss of Irnerius on the rubric to D. 1,1 - On justice and law (printed in P. Vinogradoff, Roman Law in Mediaeval Europe, 1968, p.148).

While equity and law deal with the same matters, yet they differ.  For it is a property of equity simply to lay down what is lawful.  But it is the property of law to lay down the same thing by an act of will, namely vested with some form of authority.  On account of the fallen nature of mankind this may differ very much from equity, partly by containing less than equity would demand, partly by laying down more than ought to be laid down. Equity and law also differ from each other in many ways, and the interpretation of any discrepancy with a view to making general law is a matter reserved to rulers alone.

(b) A Gloss from the Standard Gloss of Accursius on C. 8,55(56),8 – On the revocation of gifts.

If at any time a patron, having no children, shall have gifted to his freedmen his whole property or any part thereof, and afterwards shall have had children, all that he gifted shall revert, to remain within the power and disposal of the donor. Gloss on all: No; it seems to be a share of the property only, as in C. 3,29,5 which is a conflicting text. Solution: this is a special case when there is a gift to freedmen; it is otherwise if the gift is to another class of person. Perhaps it is better to say that C. 3,29,5 applies when he had given to other children, who should not be deprived of the whole property; this text applies where the gift is to a stranger. For I would give the same decision if he made the gift to any class of stranger, because it is improbable that he would prefer succession by an outsider to succession by his own children. See also C. 6,42,30. Gloss on revert: Ipso iure, and so he has the kind of action a man uses to recover what is his own.

(c) A Distinction of Irnerius quoted by Roffredus, on the topic of locatio conductio -- leasing and hiring (printed in F.C. von Savigny, Geschichte des römischen Rechts (2nd edn., 1850) vol. IV, App.II, p.469).

Sometimes one lets one's property, sometimes one's services, sometimes one's property and services. When someone lets his property and the hirer is unable to use the thing which he has hired, either by reason of the acts of the landlord or by some accidental occurrence affecting him, then the landlord is liable to an action on the lease. But in the former case, namely when it is because of his act, the landlord is liable for damages, which includes gains lost, or for any penalty which he promised, provided that the tenant has paid his rent and cultivated the property as he ought and not misused the thing which he has hired. See C. 4,65,3 & 15; D. 19,2,15 & 54 & 33 & 24. In the second case, namely where it was by accident, the action lies for a proportionate remission of rent or for the return of the rent, e.g. if a house or land is destroyed by earthquake. See D. 19,2,9 & 15 & 19 & 30. If, however, it was by the act of the tenant or by an accidental occurrence affecting him that he was prevented from using the thing hired, then he is required to pay the whole rent. See D. 19,2,61. Where, however, someone lets his services or his property and services, and it is not by his act that he is prevented from rendering these services but it is by the act of the hirer, even if the hirer is prevented from claiming the services by some accidental happening, the one who lets his services will recover the fee for the whole time, as for example in the case of someone who undertook to transport slaves. See D. 50,13,1; D. 19,2,19, & 38 & 33; D. 14,2,10. If, however, it was through the act of the one letting his services that he was unable to provide those services, or if he was prevented by an accidental happening affecting him, in the first case he is liable for damages and for the restoration of the fee, even for the period during which he rendered the services. See C. 4,65,14; D. 19,2,13,4; C. 4,6,11.

(d)    From Azo's Summa Codicis on C. 8,53 On gift.
[ (i)    What a gift is.    (ii)    Gift is derived from the giving of a gift.
(iii)    The kinds of gifts.]

(i) Let us see then what a gift is. Gift is a pure liberality which is conferred without any legal compulsion (cf. D.39,5,29; D. 50,17,82), whether the compulsion be from civil law or from natural law. But I do not mean that the mere existence of an obligation by civil law which is unenforceable because there is a defence to the claim makes a gift impossible, for such an obligation gives no right of retention, but this is not so in the case of a natural obligation (cf. D. 13,5,1 & 3; D. 39,5,19). It is called pure because there is no gift when something is done out of necessity (cf. D. 34,4,18). Nevertheless, in these cases one sometimes speaks improperly of a gift, that is, a giving which is irrevocable (cf. D. 9,2,27).

(ii) The derivation of the name. It is, as it were, a giving of a gift (cf. D. 39,6,35), but one must note that, unless there is the intention to transfer ownership, the ownership does not pass (D. 39,5,9; D. 6,2,13). It is not necessary, however, that there should be a transfer of ownership in order to constitute a gift.

(iii) What are the kinds of gifts? One is simple, another is where there is a *causa* -- specific grounds. It is simple when the donor does not wish what he has given, or what he has promised to give, to be returned to him in any circumstances, and this applies whether the gift is unconditional or postponed or conditional. A gift is for a *causa* when it is given in order that something be done or be not done, and I hold that there fall into this class *donationes propter nuptias* (gifts on account of marriage) or *mortis causa* (in expectation of death) and dowry. But it may be otherwise in the case of an engagement gift, because that is made unconditionally and is a simple gift although there is a tacit condition in it by force of law (see D. 39,5,1 & 19; *Inst.* 2,7*pr.* & 2).

(e) Cinus' Commentary on C. 8,56,8 -- the same passage as in (b).

Note that a gift made to freedmen of all one's property, or of part thereof, is revoked if children are born afterwards. And there are two reasons for this: One is because a freedman must act dutifully towards his patron (see D. 37,14,17). The second reason is that it is improbable etc. [i.e. that a person would prefer an outsider to his own progeny], as can be argued from C. 6,42,30. But a question is raised with regard to the present text: what if the gift has been made to an outsider? The same rule seems to apply, as can be argued from the said C. 6,42,30. But on this branch of the discussion you should take the view which I have set out fully in my commentary on C. 3,29,1 (on invalid gifts). The text we are here dealing with leads to the following question: A certain man legitimated his natural son because he had no legitimate children; he afterwards had legitimate children. Will the legitimation be revoked? It seems from what we are saying that it will, but appears in fact that it will not, see D. 43,19,2; C. 5,27,10.

(f) *Quaestio* with solution attributed to Bulgarus (printed in E. Genzmer, "Die Justinianische Kodifikation und die Glossatoren"- Atti Congr.int.dir.rom. Bologna, 1934, vol. I, 347-430).

The following is the statement of the facts in this affair, arising between Stichus and Titius: Stichus theftuously took away a horse of Titius, which he afterwards returned to a slave of Titius, unknown to Titius. The horse then perished in the hands of the slave (through accident) before it had come to his master.

*Pro*: Stichus says that he is released by the death of the horse after

501

returning the horse, for when he returned it to the slave he is regarded as having returned it to the slave's master, since what is acquired by a slave is acquired for the master. Therefore possession is regarded as having returned to the master and the horse is capable of being usucaped [which a stolen object could not be], in as much as the vice of the thing has been purged.

Contra: Titius says that the horse is not regarded as having returned to his power, even if it was returned to the slave, because someone who pays to someone other than the person to whom he owes does not release himself.

Solution: Bulgarus said that the thief was still liable for the value of the horse under an action called the condictio furtiva, and cited D. 41,3,4,7.


(g) Dialogue between doctor and student from the Quaestiones de iuris subtilitatibus (ed. G. Zanetti (1958), p.18), dealing with the interpretation of laws, and constitutions.

Student: Interpretation involving a decision between law and equity and also all interpretation of statute is a matter for the emperor alone. However, against this it is said (in D. 1,3,12 and C. 1,14,1) that a judge may interpret laws, namely, by applying them to similar cases. Others also may interpret the law in teaching or in disputation. Custom also is said (in D. 1,3,37) to be an interpreter of laws.

Doctor: There is a form of interpretation which, although it is rightly called interpretation, has no necessary force, e.g. an interpretation by disputants or teachers. There is another form of interpretation which has necessary force, but only in relation to a particular case, for the interpretation of a judge is binding in the matter which he decides, but other judges are not to give judgment in accordance with this as precedent. For any interpretation which is to have general force is a matter for the emperor alone. That interpretation which is accepted by the force of custom is of the same kind, but with this restriction, that an interpretation arising from an error is not to be sustained.


(h) Hugolinus' Dissensiones Dominorum (ed. G. Hänel (1834), repr.) p.330),, para. 91, on C. 3,1,8.

Whether unwritten equity should be preferred to the strict letter of the law?

There is disagreement on this text: "It is established that in all matters arguments of justice and equity are superior to those of strict law". There are some who say that where it speaks of justice, this means as laid down by law and not justice as understood by someone from his own talents; for they prefer the strict law, as in Nov. 18,8. The other view is that in all matters justice, whether written or not, is to be preferred to strict law, since, even if it is not written, it ought to be pursued as a good, as in D. 1,3,32 & 33 and C. 1,14,1.

(a) A <u>Quaestio</u> of Jacques de Révigny on <u>Inst</u>. 4,6,13 (ed. R. Feenstra, <u>Studi Senesi</u> 84 (1972), 379 = <u>Fata Iuris Romani</u>, 298). The Roman law on <u>emphyteusis</u>, the hereditary and alienable perpetual lease of state land, is here applied by analogy to tenure in feudal law.

A vassal cannot alienate his feu against the will of his feudal superior, on the argument of C. 4,66,3. But I ask: If the superior will not consent to the alienation, and does not himself wish to buy, can the vassal sell after he has once asked the superior and the superior wishes neither to buy nor to consent to the alienation. It appears that the answer is yes -- an <u>emphyteuta</u> (hereditary tenant) can, see C. 4,66,3. Therefore the same applies in the case of a vassal on the argument of D. 45,1,122. In this question the doctors admit as a matter of equity that a vassal can alienate in favour of someone like himself, so that the position of his superior is not prejudiced. For example, suppose the vassal is a knight, and he has alienated in favour of a knight, but not in favour of a cleric nor in mortmain, on the argument of C. 4,66,3 and on the argument that one may proceed from one case to another similar case, as in D. 45,2,5, I say that I see no reason why it can be alienated against the wishes of the superior, and that the case of the <u>emphyteuta</u> is not the same, because he holds by virtue of a contract and the superior receives money from him and it does not matter from whom he receives the money.

In this context the following question arises. A certain person is a count in the kingdom of France; he rebels against the king; he wishes to gather an army against his superior, the king; he orders all his vassals to help him. The question is whether they ought to help him against his superior. Supposing the answer is no; if they in fact obey him are they excused because they are following his orders? To the first question the answer indeed is that they ought not to obey him; in the oath of fealty the person of the superior is excepted. In the oath of fealty illicit acts are not covered, because an oath simply given does not extend to illicit acts. A man who rebels against his superior acts in breach of the law, see D. 12,6,6 and D. 42,8,12. And that they offend against the <u>lex Julia maiestatis</u> (the statute on treason) is proved by the argument that the king is an emperor because he does not recognize any superior. I, however, say that this is an act against the emperor, not, as they say, because the king is emperor, but because the act is committed against a magistrate of the emperor, see D. 48,4,1, because France and Spain were at one time part of the Empire, see C. 1,27,2, and therefore will always be so, as I have shewn elsewhere from C. 7,39,6. So far as the second question is concerned, it would seem that the order of their superior would excuse his vassals, on the argument of D. 3,2,6. But the orders of a master do not excuse in the case of atrocious acts. This is an atrocious act, namely offending against the statute on treason. It follows that the orders given do not excuse, see D. 50,17,157.

(b) Commentary of Pierre de Belleperche on C. 1,1,1 -- Cunctos populos -- (ed. E.M. Meijers, Etudes d'Histoire du Droit III (1959) 141ff.) which reads: "We wish all peoples whom the sovereign power of our clemency rules to follow the religious belief ... that there is one Deity of Father, Son, and Holy Spirit." The Accursian Gloss already made the point on this text that legislation, any legislation, applies only to the subjects of the legislator.

The present fragment is used as a basis for questions. If it were at the end of the book, it would not have led to a single question, but because it is the first fragment it is given special attention. The modern writers put it as an actual case. There is a statute in a city that if someone draws his sword [within the city] he is to lose his hand. Suppose that some stranger from another city draws his sword, is he affected by the statute? The Doctors say that this fragment is an argument that he is not affected, because the emperor's order is binding only on the emperor's subjects. Therefore, a fortiori a statute of a city will not be binding on strangers. This is the first line of argument, and to support it there are D. 2,1,20 and D. 42,5,12,1 [which both talk about the limits of a judge's jurisdiction]. What, then, are we to say? The modern doctors distinguish as follows -- [a] the matter which falls under the statute is a wrong quite apart from the statute, or [b] it is not a wrong apart from the statute. [a] If it is a wrong quite apart from the statute, e.g. drawing a sword for the purpose of murder is a wrong quite apart from the statute (as in C. 9,16,7), then strangers from another city are bound by this statute. ... [b] Or the matter on which the statute was passed would not be a wrong in the absence of a statute, e.g. there is a statute that anyone who crosses the bridge into the city after a certain hour should pay a fine, then if a stranger crosses the bridge after the certain hour he is not liable to the statutory penalty. This is what the old doctors say.

Some newer writings [of Jacques de Révigny] make a fuller distinction, and it is a good one. If you ask whether a stranger is bound by a statute of a city it is important [a] whether the matter is a wrong quite apart from the statue, or [b] the matter would not be a wrong apart from the statute, and [c] the matter on which the statute was passed relates to the public interest, e.g. one must not sell dead fish [which might go off in the days before refrigeration] under penalty of a fine; in this case the statute will bind strangers, on the argument of D. 1,12,1,11 & 12 [which say that the Prefect of the City is responsible for keeping order at the public games and for the control of the meat market], or [d] that the matter does not affect the public interest, e.g. where no one must cross the bridge after the curfew bell under penalty of a fine, and then the statute will not bind a stranger. I accept this distinction.

However, there is one point on which I am in doubt. The doctors say that if there is a statute on a matter which would in any case amount to a wrong, for example, drawing a sword with intention to kill, then if a stranger draws his sword he, in effect, chooses to be tried in this jurisdiction. But I think there is a doubt whether he chooses this jurisdiction in the sense that he will be subject to the relevant punishment laid down in the [Roman] law or will be subject to the penalty laid down in the city's statute. It may be that the penalty in the law is not as great as the penalty in the statute. I accept that he is liable to a penalty, but I wonder whether he can be punished with the [harsher] penalty of the statute. On this point I think it should probably be said that if some stranger has committed a wrong here, and thus becomes liable here, he is not only liable to be punished with the penalty in the law but with the penalty in the statute, and the modern authors though this but did not venture to say so.

My argument is this: the texts say that where someone proposes to commit one delict and commits a greater delict -- which he did not realise he was committing -- he is punished in accordance with the delict which he committed, and his intentions are not taken into account. Now the person who draws his sword ought to know that he is committing a wrong, and although he did not think he would be punished with so great a penalty nevertheless he will be punished according to the statute. In favour of this solution I cite: Someone thought that he was stealing from me a block of brass and so should not be punished beyond double the value of the brass in an action for theft, but the block was of gold and he is therefore liable to double the value of the gold. The text (D. 47,2,21,2) says that, insofar as he intended to commit a delict, he will be punished to the extent to which he in fact committed a delict.

Moreover, I am moved by other arguments in this direction. You must know that, just as someone in effect chooses the jurisdiction by committing a wrong, so he does by entering into a contract (as stated in D. 5,1,19). From this I argue: as the text says that if a stranger makes a contract here he chooses the jurisdiction here, not only in so far as he is bound by any penalty in the [Roman] law but also in accordance with the statutes and customs of the place, therefore it will be the same in the case before us, namely that a wrongdoer is punished not only by the penalty of the law but according to the statutes and customs of the place. A further argument may be adduced from D. 21,2,6, which holds that a seller of land must guarantee the buyer against eviction from that land in accordance with the custom of the region. This is what I think should be said on the present matter.

The commentary then goes on to discuss other questions, such as what law applies where a citizen of Orléans sues a Parisian in Chartres; the rule is that matters of procedure are ruled by the customs of Chartres but matters of substance by the customs of the place where the contract was made. Again, if a will in England requires ten witnesses and a will in Orléans requires seven, and a testator who has property both in England and Orléans leaves a will with seven witnesses, then, if English law specifically requires ten witnesses for the will to be valid, the heir will get only the property in Orléans. Pierre rejects the view taken by some that the will made in Orléans can in no circumstances affect the devolution of property in England; he would allow such a will to carry the property in England if there be no specific prohibition in English law depriving it of effect.

Gratian's Decretum, Causa 29, quaestio 2, printed in Corpus Iuris Canonici, ed. E. Friedberg (Leipzig 1879-81, repr.).


First Part [by Gratian himself]:

A second question concerning status is put: can a woman put away a man she had thought free if, after [marriage], she found he was a slave? From many arguments it seems that it can be proved that a woman is not allowed to divorce a slave. For in Christ Jesus there is neither Jew nor Greek, there is neither bond nor free [Gal. 3,28], therefore neither is there in marriage of Christians. For each is ruled by the same law, in the faith of Christ. For the apostle said at large to all: "Who wishes to marry, let him marry in the Lord"; and again: "A woman is at liberty to marry whom she will, only in the Lord" [1 Cor. 7,39]. He did not command that a freeborn woman marry a freeborn man, or a slave a slave, but each may marry as she wishes, but only in the Lord.

c.1 - A slave is allowed to marry (Pope Julius, 337-52).

For all of us there is one Father in Heaven, and each of us, rich or poor, free or slave, shall, on equal footing, render account of our souls to Him. We cannot, therefore, doubt that all men, of whatever condition, have only one law before God. But if all have only the one law, therefore, just as a free man cannot be put aside, nor can a slave, once married, be put aside thereafter.

c.2 - A man may not put away a slave girl he has taken to wife (Pope Zacharias, 741-52).

If a free man shall take a slave girl to wife, he has no power to put her away, provided they were married with the consent of both parties, except for fornication; but there shall be one law hereafter in all matters, for both men and women.

c.3 - Marriage between patron and freedwoman is held legitimate (Pope Julius).

If someone shall have given his slave girl her freedom and joined her to himself in marriage, certain persons have doubted whether this is lawful marriage (nuptiae legitimae) or not. But we, settling this ancient uncertainty, hold that such marriage is lawful. For if all marriage springs from intention [ -- affectio maritalis, the freely consenting intention to be married, which had been all that was required to constitute a marriage under Roman law (D. 23,2,1) -- ], and if there is no possibility of something impious or contrary to law in such a union, what would lead us to prohibit the aforesaid nuptials?

Second Part [Gratian]:

To these it can be replied: it is not denied that a freeborn woman can marry a slave, but the point is, what if she does not know his servile status? Can she be free to put him aside when his servility is made known? For the apostle [Paul] and Pope Julius are to be understood as speaking to those whose status was known to each other. But the man's status was not known to the woman; she is not, therefore, by the aforesaid authorities bound to remain with him, but is shown to be free to stay or to put him aside.

c.4 -On him who marries a slave girl, thinking her free (canon 6 of the Council at Verberie[1] at which King Pippin was present, 753).

If a free man should take another's slave girl to wife, thinking that she is free, and if she is afterwards found to be servile, he should redeem her from slavery if he can; if he cannot release her, he may take another wife, if he wishes. But if he knew she was a slave girl and yet commended her, he shall hold her as his lawful wife. Similarly, a free woman ought to behave in the same way with a man who is another's slave.

c.5 - A woman may not put aside a man she married knowing he was a slave (c. 8 of the same Council).

If a freeborn woman marries a slave, knowing that he is a slave, she must keep him, because we all have one Father in Heaven. The law is the same for men and women.

c.6 - There is no valid putting away on the grounds of servile status if there is subsequently a successful claim to liberty (Pope Gregory I, 590-604).

[This is a judgment given in 596 on a particular case where a man had discarded his wife; she proved herself free; he must therefore take her back.]

dictum post c.6 [Gratian].

When it is said [in c.5] 'knowing him to be a slave', it is implied that if she had not known that he was a slave, she is not bound to stay with him.

----------

1    In the modern French departement of Oise.

Because, therefore, she was deceived both as to his person and as to his status she is not bound to stay with a man by whose deceit she was misled. If, however, she took him when he was a free man  and he, to provide grounds for divorce, becomes the slave of a third  party, he cannot put her away, nor can she be reduced to servile status because of the marriage tie. c.7 - Having changed his status by fraud, a man cannot divorce her whom he took when he was free (at the Council of Tribur[2], 895).

To this synod was brought a case in which a free man married a free woman and, after the birth of children to them, as an occasion of divorce made himself slave to a third party; it was asked whether she must abide with him? and, if she does, whether she too should become servile according to secular law?  Judgment was given that she ought in no way to cease to be his wife, but neither, because of the law of Christ, ought she to be reduced to servile status, provided that he had not made himself a slave with the consent of the wife, who herself had married a free husband.

dictum post c.7 [Gratian].

It is also asked, if the slave of one person marries the slave girl of another, whether there may be marriage between them?

c.8 - Masters may not on their own authority undo the legitimate marriages of their slaves (as was laid down at the Council of Chalons-sur-Saône, 813).

It is told us that certain persons, presuming on their right of ownership, are parting lawfully wedded slaves, not heeding the evangelist:  "What God hath joined together, let not man put asunder" [Matt. 19,6].  Whence it seems to us that the marriage of slaves may not be dissolved, even if they have different masters, but let them serve their masters while remaining in the one marriage.  And this is to be observed where the union was legal and permitted by the masters.

----------

2    Not very far from Koblenz.

## APPENDIX IV

Bartolus, in his commentary on cunctos populos -- the same title as was the subject of Pierre de Belleperche in Appendix II(b) -- at one point discusses the position of notaries; here local legislation or custom is distinguished from general law, that is, matters pertaining to imperial (or papal) jurisdiction. The translation is that of J.A. Clarence Smith in 14 American Journal of Legal History (1970), at page 247.

My seventh point concerns permissive local legislation; and in this connection there are two matters to be examined, namely, whether the act permitted may be performed outside the territory of the permitting authority, and again, if it is performed in that place or in a permitted place, whether it has any effect outside the teritory. We shall deal with the two side by side.

Sometimes then local legislation grants and permits something which in nature could be within no one's power, but only by franchise particularly granted, and in matters to which it extends. For instance, under a city's legislation someone is appointed notary: may he draw up deeds outside the territory of that city? This is a point discussed by Speculator. In my own view he may not draw up deeds outside the territory; and the rule is the same for similar matters which may be peformed only within the territory.

For acts of non-contentious jurisdiction, under power granted by authorities inferior to the Emperor, may not be performed outside the territory. D. 50.16.2: "Every provincial governor has jurisdiction immediately on leaving the capital, but only in non-contentious, not in contentious, proceedings"; which is a leading authority on this point. Sextus 2,2,1,4: "Nor should they send their clerks into the dioceses of their suffragans for contracts to be entered into or acknowledged before them, nor compel the subjects of the same suffragans to submit their differences to them for decision on such an occasion" (Pope Innocent IV on the limits of an archbishop's jurisdiction) is also helpful, and is cited by Speculator as illustrative.

But in my view deeds drawn up by such a notary within the territory should have full faith and credit anywhere outside the territory. So also an emancipation before the authority having jurisdiction by the law of any

511

one borough is treated everywhere as confirmed — C. 8,48,1:  "If a law of
the borough [municipium] in which your father emancipated you gave power to
the co-mayors [duumviri] to allow even outsiders to emancipate their
children, then your father's proceedings must be treated as confirmed"; and
for this reason, that it goes more to the formalities than to the dealing
itself, as we shall see below.

It was important that the status of notaries was clear because, as we have
seen their forms and styles were in use throughout Europe, and were one of
the unifying factors in the ius commune.  There were also a great many of
them; in thirteenth century Bologna there are said to have been some 2,000,
and in Padua 600.

The French <u>Declaration</u> <u>des</u> <u>droits</u> <u>de</u> <u>l'homme</u> <u>et</u> <u>du</u> <u>citoyen</u>, issued in 1789, confirmed in the preambles to the French constitutions of 1946 and 1958. The translation is by Ian Brownlie, <u>Basic</u> <u>Documents</u> <u>on</u> <u>Human</u> <u>Rights</u> (Oxford, 1971), p.8.

<u>Article</u> 1: Men are born and remain free and equal in respect of rights. Social distinctions shall be based solely upon public utility.

<u>Article</u> 2: The purpose of all civil associations is the preservation of the natural and imprescriptible rights of man. These rights are liberty, property and resistance to oppression.

<u>Article</u> 3: The nation is essentially the source of all sovereignty, nor shall any body of men or any individual exercise authority which is not expressly derived from it.

<u>Article</u> 4: Liberty consists in the power of doing whatever does not injure another. Accordingly the exercise of the natural rights of every man has not other limits than those which are necessary to secure to every other man the free exercise of the same rights; and these limits are determinable only by the law.

<u>Article</u> 5: The law ought to prohibit only actions hurtful to society. What is not prohibited by the law should not be hindered; nor should any one be compelled to do that which the law does not require.

<u>Article</u> 6: The law is an expression of the common will. All citizens have a right to concur, either personally or by their representation in its formation. It should be the same for all, whether it protects or punishes; and all being equal in its sight, are equally eligible to all honours, places and employments, according to their different abilities, without any other distinction than that of their virtues and talents.

<u>Article</u> 7: No one shall be accused, arrested or imprisoned, save in the cases determined by law, and according to the forms which it has prescribed. All who solicit, promote, execute, or cause to be executed, arbitrary orders, ought to be punished, and every citizen summoned or apprehended by virtue of the law, ought immediately to obey, and becomes culpable if he resists.

<u>Article</u> 8: The law should impose only such penalties as are absolutely and evidently necesary; and no one ought to be punished but by virtue of a law

promulgated before the offence, and legally applied.

Article 9: Every man being counted innocent until he has been convicted, whenever his arrest becomes indispensable, all vigour more than is necesary to secure his person ought to be provided against by law.

Article 10: No man is to be interfered with because of his opinions, not even because of religious opinions, provided his avowal of them does not disturb public order as established by law.

Article 11: The unrestrained communication of thoughts or opinions being one of the most precious rights of man, every citizen may speak write and publish freely, provided he be responsible for the abuse of this liberty, in the cases determined by law.

Article 12: A public force being necessary to give security to the rights of men and of citizens, that force is instituted for the benefit of the community, and not for the particular benefit of the person to whom it is entrusted.

Article 13: A common contribution  being necessary for the support of the public force, and for defraying the other expenses of government, it should be divided equally among the members of the community, according to their abilities.

Article 14: Every citizen has a right, either of himself or his representative, to a free voice in determining the necessity of public contributions, the appropriation of them, and their amount, mode of assessment, and duration.

Article 15: The community has the right to demand of all its agents an account of their conducts.

Article 16: Every community in which a security of rights and a separation of powers is not provided for needs a consitution.

Article 17: The right to property being inviolable and secure, no one shall be deprived of it, except in cases of evident public necessity, legally ascertained, and on condition of a previous just indemnity.

# SELECT BIBLIOGRAPHY

The suggestions for further reading at the end of each chapter were limited to works in English and to those adopting a relatively straightforward approach to the relevant topic; they are not listed again here. In this Bibliography we mention, without restriction of language, standard works of reference, fundamental monographs and also the more recent treatments of particular fields. We include the principal works to which we have had recourse. We are conscious of the extent of the specialized literature on the topics we have merely outlined; our debt is sometimes direct, at others it explains the shading of the picture. The extent of our obligation will be evident; we gratefully acknowledge it.

An indispensable bibliographical tool is the:
Handbuch der Quellen und Literatur der Neueren Europäischen Privatrechtsgeschichte (Munich, 1973-  ), published by the Max-Planck-Institut für Europäische Rechtsgeschichte in Frankfurt-am-Main. The Institute also publishes Ius Commune, a journal of European legal history, with its supplementary Sonderhefte which contain texts, monographs or collections of studies.

Among other major tools of research are:
Bibliography on Foreign and Comparative Law, ed. C. Szladits (U.S.A., 1955
   - )
Dictionnaire de droit canonique, ed. R. Naz (Paris, 1935-65)
Handwörterbuch zur Deutschen Rechtsgeschichte, ed. A. Erler and E. Kaufmann
   (Berlin, 1971-  )
Histoire du droit et des institutions de l'église en occident, ed. G. le
   Bras and J. Gaudemet (Paris, 1955-  )
Introduction bibliographique à l'histoire du droit et à l'ethnologie
   juridique, ed. J. Gilissen (Brussels, 1963-  )
Ius Romanum Medii Aevi (= IRMAE) (Milan, 1961-  )
Repertorium bibliographicum Institutorum et Sodalitatum iuris historiae
   (Leiden, 1969), with Supplement, 1969-74 (Leiden, 1975)

These in turn give further information about bibliographies of the law and legal history of individual countries, which themselves may list works relevant to the full European picture. Historical bibliographies also have entries on legal history and law.

515

Up to date information is given in the relevant sections of indexes to
legal literature, such as:

Index to Foreign Legal Periodicals (London, 1960-  )

Index to Legal Periodical Literature (USA, 1888-1924; 1933-  )

Index to Legal Periodicals (USA, 1908-  )

and in the bibliographies, bibliographical notes and similar material in
the relevant specialized periodicals themselves, such as:

American Journal of Legal History (Am.J.Legal Hist.)

Annali di Storia del Diritto (ASD)

Journal of Legal History (J.Legal Hist.)

Law and History Journal (L. & Hist. J.)

Revue historique de droit français et étranger (R.H.D.)

Rivista italiana di storia del diritto (R.I.S.D.)

Studia et documenta historiae et iuris (S.D.H.I.)

Tijdschrift voor Rechtsgeschiedenis (T.v.R.)

Zeitschrift für neuere Rechtsgeschichte

Zeitschrift der Savigny-Stiftung für Rechtsgeschichte - Germanistische,
    Kanonistische, Romanistische Abteilungen (Z.S.S. - Germ.,Kan.,Rom.).

    Other journals of interest to the legal historian include:

Acta Juridica (A.J.)

American Journal of Comparative Law (Am.J.Comp.L.)

Cambridge Law Journal (C.L.J.)

Harvard Law Review (H.L.R.)

Irish Jurist (I.J.)

Juridical Review (Jur.Rev.)

Law Quarterly Review (L.Q.R.)

Michigan Law Review (Mich.L.R.)

Oxford Journal of Legal Studies (Ox.J.Legal St.)

Seminar

Tulane Law Review (Tul.L.R.)

Virginia Law Review (Virg.L.R.).

    Other series of studies and periodical literature dealing with themes
in legal history are:

Atti del convegno internazionale di Studi Accursiani, Bologna 1963, ed. G.
    Rossi (Milan, 1968)

Atti del terzo congresso internazionale delle Società Italiana di Storia
    del Diritto -- La formazione storica del diritto moderno in Europa

(Florence, 1977)

Quaderni Fiorentini per la storia del pensiero giuridico moderno

Recueil de la Societé Jean Bodin pour l'histoire comparative des
   institutions.


Then there are accounts of the legal history of individual European
countries, many of which relate their history to its European background.
Examples are:

Besta, E. and Giudice, P. del  Storia del diritto italiano (Milan, 1923-27,
   repr.)

Blécourt, A.S. de  Kort Begrip van het oud-vaderlandsch Burgerlijk Recht
   (6th ed., H.F.W.D. Fischer, Groningen, 1950)

Coing, H.  Epochen der Rechtsgeschichte in Deutschland (2nd ed., Munich,
   1971)

Hahlo, H.R. and Kahn, E.  The South African Legal System and its Background
   (South Africa, 1968)

Holdsworth, W.S.  History of English Law — 16 vols., various editions

Ourliac, P. and Malafosse, J. de  Histoire du droit privé (Paris, 1968-71)

Plucknett, T.F.T.  A Concise History of the Common Law (5th ed., London,
   1956)

Viollet, P.  Histoire du droit civil français (3rd ed., Paris, 1905)

Wesenberg, G.  Neuere Deutsche Privatrechtsgeschichte (3rd ed., G. Wesener,
   Lahr, 1976) — this has a particularly good basic bibliography

Wieacker, F.  Privatrechtsgeschichte der Neuzeit (2nd ed., Göttingen, 1967)


There are various wide-ranging treatments of European law and legal
themes.  The Continental Legal History Series, of which some volumes have
been mentioned in the Further Reading, had much the same aim as our present
work, but it is based on the viewpoints and the researches of more than
half a century ago and was compiled by persons of very varying expertise.
Of particular interest because of their stance are:

Cannata, C.A.  Lineamenti di storia della giurisprudenza europea (2nd ed.,
   Turin, 1976)

Gilissen, J.  Introduction historique au droit (Brussels, 1979)

Lawson, F.H.  A Common Lawyer Looks at the Civil Law (Ann Arbor, 1953)
            Selected Essays (New York & Oxford, 1977)

Lombardi, G.  Saggio sul diritto giurisprudenziale (Milan, 1967)

Merryman, J.H.  The Civil Law Tradition (Stanford, 1969)

Stein, P.  Legal Institutions (London, 1984)

Watson, A.  Legal Transplants (Edinburgh, 1974)

The Nature of Law (Edinburgh, 1977)

The Evolution of Law (Johns Hopkins, 1985)


Finally we suggest some books -- not individual articles; they will be found in the journals listed -- to supplement the Further Reading, arranged in chronological groups.

**For the early mediaeval and feudal periods:**

Kern, F.  Kingship and Law (tr. S.B. Chrimes, OUP, 1939)

King, P.D.  Law and Society in the Visigothic Kingdom (CUP, 1972)

Pocock, J.G.A.  The Ancient Constitution and the Feudal Law (CUP, 1957)

Pollock, F. and Maitland, F.W.  The History of English Law before the time of Edward I (2nd ed., S.F.C. Milsom, CUP, 1968)

**For the mediaeval period generally:**

Berman, H.J.  Law and Revolution (Harvard, 1983)

Calasso, F.  Medio Evo del Diritto -- Le Fonti (Milan, 1954)

Clanchy, M.T.  From Memory to Written Record (London, 1979)

Feenstra, R.  Fata Iuris Romani (Leiden, 1974)

Gouron, A.  La science du droit dans le Midi de la France au moyen age (London, 1984 -- reprinted articles, 1963-79)

Kantorowicz, H.  Rechtshistorische Studien (ed. H. Coing & G. Irnmal, Karlsruhe, 1970)

and Buckland, W.W.  Studies in the Glossators of the Roman Law (CUP, 1938, repr. with additions by P. Weimer).

Knowles, D.  The Evolution of Mediaeval Thought (London, 1962)

Koschaker, P.  Europa und das römische Recht (4th ed., Munich, 1966)

Meijers, E.M.  Études d'histoire du droit (ed. R. Feenstra & H.F.W.D. Fischer, Leiden, 1956-73)

Savigny, F.C. von  Geschichte des römischen Rechts im Mittelalter (2nd ed., Heidelberg, 1834-51)

Ullmann, W.  Law and Politics in the Middle Ages (CUP, 1975)

**On notaries:**

Abbondanza, R., ed.  Il notariato a Perugia (Rome, 1973)

Barraclough, G.  Public Notaries and the Papal Curia (London, 1934)

Cheney, C.R.  Notaries Public in England (OUP, 1972)

Costamagna, G.  Il notario a Genova tra prestigio e potere (Rome, 1970)

Petrucci, A.  Notarii: Documenti per la storia del notariato italiano (Milan, 1958)

**On canon law and ecclesiastical history:**

Bras, G. le  L'age classique 1140-1378 (Paris, 1965)

Gaudemet, J.  Le gouvernement de l'Église à l'époque classique: le gouvernement local (Paris, 1979)

Helmholz, R.H.  Marriage Litigation in Mediaeval England (CUP, 1974)

Jullien, A.  Juges et avocats des tribunaux de l'Église (Paris, 1970)

Kuttner, S.  The History of Ideas and Doctrines of Canon Law in the Middle Ages

Mediaeval Councils, Decretals and Collections of Canon Law

Gratian and the Schools of Law, 1140-1234 (all reprinted articles, London, 1980, 1980, 1983)

Tierney, G.  Church Law and Constitutional Thought (London, 1979)

Tillman, H.  Pope Innocent III (London, 1980)

Ullmann, W.  The Growth of Papal Government in the Middle Ages (3rd ed., London, 1970)

**On the Law Merchant the basic monograph remains:**

Goldschmidt, L.  Handbuch des Handelsrechts (Stuttgart, various eds., 1868-91); also worth consultation are:

Jados, S.S., tr.  Consulate of the Sea and Related Documents (Alabama, 1975)

Lopez, R.S.  The Commercial Revolution of the Middle Ages 950-1350 (USA, 1971)

and Raymond, I.W.  Mediaeval Trade in the Mediterranean World (London, 1955)

Roover. R. de  Money, Banking and Credit in Mediaeval Bruges (USA, 1948)

"The organization of trade" in Cambridge Economic History vol.III (CUP, 1963)

**On the Renaissance and its aftermath:**

Franklin, J.H.  Jean Bodin and the Sixteenth Century Revolution in the Methodology of Law and History (New York & London, 1963)

Kelley, D.R.  History, Law and the Human Sciences (London, 1984)

Kisch, G. Studien zur humanistischen Jurisprudenz (Berlin, 1972)

McNeil, D.O.  Guillaume Budé and Humanism in the reign of Francis I (Geneva, 1975)

Maffei, D.  Gli inizi dell' Umanesimo giuridico (Milan, 1968)

Mortari, V.P.  Diritto romano e diritto nazionale in Francia nel secolo xvi (Milan, 1962)

**On the seventeenth and eighteenth centuries:**

Arnaud, A.J.  Les origines doctrinales du Code Civil français (Paris, 1969)

Carey, J.S.  Judicial Reform in France before the Revolution of 1789 (Harvard, 1981)

Kupiszewski, H. and Wolodkiewicz, W., eds.  Le droit romain et sa reception en Europe (Warsaw, 1978)

Prest, W., ed.  Lawyers in Early Modern Europe and America (London, 1981)

Thieme, H.  Das Naturrecht und die europäische Privatrechtsgeschichte (2nd ed., Basel, 1954)

Vanderlinden, J.  Le concept de code en Europe occidentale (Brussels, 1967)

**On the nineteenth and twentieth centuries:**

Atiyah, P.S.  The Rise and Fall of Freedom of Contract (OUP, 1979)

Coing, H. and Wilhelm, W., eds.  Wissenschaft und Kodifikation des Privatrechts im 19ten Jahrhundert (Frankfurt, 1974- )

Dicey, A.V.  Law and Public Opinion in England (2nd ed., London, 1914)

Rotondi, M. ed.  La science du droit au cours du dernier siècle (Padua, 1976)

Schwartz, B., ed.  The Code Napoléon and the Common Law World (USA, 1956)

Schwarz, A.B.  Rechtsgeschichte und Gegenwart (ed. H. Thieme and F. Wieacker, Karlsruhe, 1960)

Villey, M.  La formation de la pensée juridique moderne (Paris, 1980)


There are some books which trace specifically Roman rules or institutions into the modern world; for example, in English are:

Buckland, W.W. and MacNair, A.  Roman Law and Common Law (CUP, 1965)

Gordon, W.M.  Studies in the Transfer of Property by Traditio (Aberdeen, 1970)

Jolowicz, H.F.  Roman Foundations of Modern Law (OUP, 1957)

Lawson, F.H. and Markesinis, B.S.  Tortious Liability for Unintentional Harm in the Common Law and the Civil Law (CUP, 1982)

Stein, P.  Regulae Iuris (Edinburgh, 1966)


Finally, for the history of Scots law we recommend:

Barrow, G.W.S.  The Kingdom of the Scots (London, 1973)

          The Anglo-Norman Era in Scottish History (O.U.P., 1980)

Burleigh, J.H.S.  A Church History of Scotland (OUP, 1960)

Cowan, I.B.  The Scottish Reformation (London, 1982)

Dickinson, W. Croft  The Sheriff Court Book of Fife 1513-22 (Sc. Hist.Soc., 1928)

The Court Book of the Barony of Carnwath (Sc. Hist. Soc., 1937)

Early Records of the Burgh of Aberdeen (Sc. Hist. Soc., 1957)

Donaldson, G.  The Scottish Reformation (CUP, 1960)

Scotland:  James V to James VII (Edinburgh, 1971)

Duncan, A.M.M.  Scotland:  The Making of the Kingdom (Edinburgh, 1975)

Ferguson, W.  Scotland: 1689 to the Present (Edinburgh, 1968, repr.)

Hannay, R.K.  The College of Justice (Edinburgh, 1933)

Jackson, A.M.  Glasgow Dean of Guild Court (Glasgow, 1983)

Nicholson, R.  Scotland: The Later Middle Ages (Edinburgh, 1974)

Sanderson, M.H.B.  Scottish Rural Society in the Sixteenth Century (Edinburgh, 1982)

Smith, T.B.  Scotland: The Development of its Laws and Constitution (London, 1962)

Walker, D.M.  Scottish Legal System (5th ed., Edinburgh, 1981)

The Scottish Jurists (Edinburgh, 1985)

Webster, B.  Scotland from the Eleventh Century to 1603 (CUP, 1975)

Whetstone, A.E.  Scottish County Government in the Eighteenth and Nineteenth Century (Edinburgh, 1981)

Wilson, W.A. Introductory Essays on Scots Law (2nd ed., Edinburgh, 1984)

Wormald, J., gen.ed.  The New History of Scotland (8 vols. by various authors, London, 1981-84)

and many articles from the Juridical Review (Edinburgh, 1888-  ).

The Stair Society's publications also are devoted to the history of Scots law.  Vol.1 (1936) surveys the sources and literature of Scots law; it is brought up to date by W.J. Windram and H.L. McQueen "The sources and literature of Scots law:  a select critical bibliography, 1936-82" 4 J.Legal Hist. (1983), 1 (repr. in New Perspectives in Scottish Legal History, ed. A. Kiralfy and H.L. McQueen, London, 1984).  Also of use as an introduction to Scottish legal history is vol. 20 (1958).

# INDEX

The Index is designed to be used in conjunction with the Contents. For example, French customs are given the fullest treatment in chapter XII, but the pages relevant to France in chapters VII and XV should also be consulted; in the Index a semi-colon divides the different chapters in the list of references to custom.

There are too few cases and statutes for separate tables, and so both are listed in their alphabetical place, e.g. Taff Vale under T.

Rulers are listed before other men - in the order: Popes, Emperors, Kings and other rulers. P. = Pope, Byz E = Byzantine Emperor, HRE = Holy Roman Emperor, K = King, Q = Queen. Like rulers, mediaeval men are normally to be found under their first names. Dates, especially mediaeval ones, may be approximate.

Within a major heading it is the keywords which provide the alphabetical order.

Because chapter XVIII is only a coda to the work, its contents have not been included in the Index.

Amsterdam  367

Ancona  157

Andreae, Johannes  see Johannes Andreae

Andreas (Andrew) de Barulo (d. after 1291) 116

Angers  293; 381

Anglo-Normans in Scotland  202; 208; 259,260,264,269

Anglo-Saxons  17,20; 46; 153; 208,209-17,218,220,221; 372
  language  46; 211,212,220

Anjou  222

Anselm, (archbishop of Canterbury, 1093-1109)  42

Antonio (Mincucci) de Pratovecchio (c.1380-1468)  66; 136

Antwerp  154,173,176

apparatus  77,79,80,83,84,85,86; 134

appeal  63,64; 127,142,143,144,149; 186,187,194,195,196,197; 221,250-52;
  316,322,324; 348; 366; 394,395,396

Aquinas, St. Thomas  106; 181; 355,356

Aquitaine  29,32; 222

Arabs  see also Moslems  19,24,32

Aragon  159; 198,200,201

archdeacons  143,146

Arches, Court of (the)  142; 248

Argentré, Bernard d' (1519-90)  336,342

Argou, Gabriel (1640-1703)  428,429

Aristotle (384-322 B.C.)  42; 75; 106; 354,355,359,360

Arras  293

arrêts de règlement  197; 337; 392; 429

Ars notariatus  89

Artois, Custom of  293

Assembly, General, of the Church of Scotland  see General Assembly

assize defined  223
  Grand  227
  petty  225,226

Association for the Reform and Codification of the Law of Nations
  458,459,460

assumpsit (indebitatus)  254,255,256

Athelstan of Wessex and England (927-39)  213,214,226

Attila and the Huns  10

attorneys (in England) 241

aubaine = *ius albanagii* 171

auditors, papal, etc. 135,143,148

        parliamentary, in Scotland 276,277,278

Augsburg, 173

        peace of (1555) 282; 312

Augustine, St, archbishop of Canterbury (597-604) 210

Augustine, St, (354-430) bishop of Hippo 8,16; 106; 137; 355

'Auld Lawes' 275-6; 383,385

Austin, John (1790-1859) 373; 416; 480

Austrasia 23

Austria 25 see also Bavaria

     Austrian Empire 410,412,425-28; 438,452; 464 see also ABGB

*authenticae* 82

*Authenticum* see *Novels* of Justinian

Auvergne 337

Auzanet, Barthelémy (1591-1673) 351

average, general see general average

Avignon 136; 164; 288,289

ayre 219; 263,264,267,269,274; 397

Azo (c.1150-1230) 75,79,80,84,85,89,90,92,94,95,97,98; 130,131,134;

    *Summa Codicis* of 89,90,94; App.I(d)


Bacon, Sir Francis (1561-1626) 255; 373

Baden 468

*baillis* & *bailliages* 195; 346,348; 431

Balduini (Baldwin), Jacobus (James) de see James

Baldinus, Franciscus see Baudouin, François

Baldus de Ubaldis (1327-1400) 66; 113,117; 135,136; 186

Balfour, Sir James (c.1525-83) 252; 385,401

Balkans 157; 437

ballot, secret 415,442

     Ballot Act 1872 (c. 33) 442

Baltic 161; 317

Bamberg & *Bambergensis* 330

banking 171,172; 446

Bankton, Lord (Andrew McDouall, c.1685-1760) 388; 448

Barbarossa  see Frederick I, HRE

Barcelona  25,29; 158,159; 201

Barclay, William  (1547-1608)  381

Bardi  172,173

Bari  156, 157

barony & baron court  263,267,268,273; 399

barristers  239,241

Bartolist  183,187; 291; 325; 342; 382  see also mos italicus

Bartolus de Sassoferrato (1314-57)  105,110,111,112,113,119,120; 186,200;
    298; 360; 429; App.IV

Bartonshill Coal Co. v Reid, ((1858) 3 Macq. 266)  396

Basel (Basle)  167; 320

    Peace of (1499)  282

Basil I, Byz E (867-86)  41

Basilica (c.888)  41; 292

Bassianus, Johannes (John)  see John

battle, trial by  20,21; 47,62; 193,197; 218,220,225; 372

Baudouin (Balduinus) François (1520-73)  291,293

Bavaria, duchy of  189; 323; 417-20  see also Codex Maximilianeus
    bavaricus civilis

    Bavarians and Law of the Bavarians in the Dark Ages  12,23,24,25,27,
    29,34

Beaumanoir, Phillipe de (c.1250-96)  67,68,69; 236; 319; 335  see also
    Beauvaisis

Beauvaisis, Customs of Clermont in (c.1283)  67,68,69; 192; 335

Beawes, Wyndham (fl 1775)  447

Beccaria, Cesare Bonesana, Marchese de (1738-94)  410,411,412,413,414

Begriffsjurisprudenz (Jurisprudence of Concepts)  473,486

Belgium  367; 436; 441,459  see also Flanders, Low Countries

Bell, George Joseph (1770-1843)  388,389; 446,448

Belleperche (Bellapertica), Pierre (Petrus) de  see Pierre

Benedict, St. (c.480-47)  15

benefit of clergy  309

Benevento  22,25; 98; 185

        Beneventanus  see Peter; Roffredus

Bentham, Jeremy (1748-1832)  407,410,412,414,415,416; 480

    Benthamites  450

Bouguier, Jean (fl 1629)   347

Bourges   194; 282,290,291,292,293; 344; 381,382

Bourjon, François (d.1751)   428,429,433,434

Bracton (Bratton), Henry de (d.1268)   208,231,234,235,236,237,238,252,256

Brandenburg   328; 353,364; 420   see also Prussia

Brazil   437; 480

brehons   259

Bremen   167

    Rules   461

Brescia   164

Breuil, Guillaume du (fl 1330)   346

*Brevia Placitata*   237,238

*Breviarium* of Bernard of Pavia   131,132

brieves   204; 263,266,269,270,271,272; 398

Brisson (Brissonius), Barnabé (c.1530-91)   294; 349,350

Britain, Great   441,442,445-48,450-52,455-57,461; 472,480

British National Association for the Promotion of Social Science   459

Brittany   25,27; 160; 335,336; 382

brocards   78,89,94; 134

Brougham, Lord (1778-1868)   416

Bruges (Brugge)   163,167,173

Bruns, C.G. (1816-80)   471,474

bubbles   444

Buch, Johann von   see Johann

Budé (Budaeus), Guillaume (1467-1540) 289,290,298

Bulgarus (d.1166)   74,80,84,89,90,91,93,94,95,96,97; 130; App.I(f)

Bull, Golden of 1356   311

Bullinger, Heinrich (1504-75)   282

*Bundesrat*   476

Burchardt (c.965-1025), bishop of Worms   124,125

burgage tenure   60,61; 261,268

burghs (inc. English boroughs)   60; 161-65; 204,205; 211,212; 266,268,269;
    442   see also cities
      courts   162-65; 233,248,249; 268-69; 394   see also Law Merchant
      Four Burghs   269

Burgos   199

Burgundians under Gundobad, etc. & *Lex Romana Burgundionum* 12,17,18,23,27,

29; 292; 318

Burgundy, duchy of 194; 284; 366

Burke, Edmund (1729)-97) 466

Buttrigarius, Jacobus (James) de  see James

Bynkershoek, Cornelius van (1673-1743) 369,370

Byzantine Empire 5,13,14,17,22,24,28,40,41; 155,156,157


Cahors 31; 171; 291; 343

Calabria 17,28,35,41; 157

Calixtus II, P. (1119-24) 38

calumny, oath of 203

Calvin, Jean (1509-64) 282,283,301,302; 355,356-7

Calvinism 300,302; 357

Cambacérès, J-J. Regis de (1753-1824) 431, 432

Cambridge 207; 248; 372

canon law 77,98; 101,104,115,117,120; V passim; 181,183,189,203;231,237,
248; 290,292,293,294,306-09; 318,319,320; 342; 360; 377,378,379,380

procedure  see procedure, canonical; see also church courts

canonist defined 66  see also Decretist, Decretalist

canons defined 8; 122

Canossa (1077) 38

Canterbury 42; 142; 210,248  see also Arches, Court of

Canute (Cnut), K of Denmark & England (1016-35) 212,217

Capet, Hugh, K of France (987-96) & Capetian dynasty 28,29; 63; 192

capitularies 25

Forged 31

of Quierzy 52

Carmer, C. von (1721-1801) 421

Carolina = constitutio criminalis Carolina (1532) 326,330,331; 367

Carolingian Franks 19,22,23-8,29,33,34; 45,54,55; 153

Carpzov, Benedikt (1595-1666) 188; 324,328,331; 385; 417

cartularies 41

Casale Monferrato 116

cases  see individual names

reports of  see reports

Cassation, Cour de 481,482,483

Castile, New and Old 198,199,200,201; 357

Castile-León  198,199,200

castles  219  see also feudalism

casualties  see feudal obligations

casus  88,90; 110

Catalonia  25,27,32; 198,199,200,201

        Catalan language  160

Cateau-Cambrésis, Treaty of (1559)  284

cathedral chapter  143

Catherine II, E. of Russia (1762-96)  412

Catherine de Medici (1519-89), Q of France  284

Catholic Church  122  see also Orthodox

        Roman  122; 283  see also Protestantism

causa  130,151,152

Celestine I, P. (422-32)  8,9

Celtic peoples and customs  258-60,261

Ceylon  368

Chalcedon, General Council of (451)  9,10,15

chamberlain, king's (in Scotland)  262,264,276

Chambres of the Parlement of Paris (which see)  195,196

Champagne, fairs of  166,167

chancellor and chancery in England  168; 206; 212,221,228,230,235,238, 242-46,251,253; 306

        in Scotland  276,278; 390

Charlemagne, K of the Franks (768-814) & E. (800-14)  22,23,25,26,30; 56,64

Charles IV, HRE (1347-78)  311

Charles V, HRE (1519-58) = Charles I of Spain  281,307; 312,330; 367

Charles V, K of France (1364-80)  193

Charles VII, K of France (1422-61)  193; 349

Charles IV, K of Spain (1788-1808)  201

Charles Albert of Piedmont (1831-49)  464

Charles of Anjou, K of Naples (1266-85)  102,104

Charles the Fat (881-87)  26

Charles Martel of the Franks (Mayor 719-41)  19,23

Charles (Karolus) de Tocco (early 13c)  64; 97

charters, Merovingian and Carolingian  31,32,33  see also capitularies

        feudal  46,47;261

Châtelet  193; 429

children at work  see employment law

China  480

Chivalry, Court of  246

Christian V, K of Denmark (1670-99)  416

Christianity, introduction of  7; 124

          survival in Britain  17; 210

Christina, Q of Sweden (1632-54)  358

Church  7,20; 122 and V passim

    courts  123; 189,202,203; 209; 247,248; 307; 320; 366; 378,379,400,402

    Doctors of the  8

    Early  7-10,14,15,36

    Roman Catholic as compared to Reformed  307,310

Cicero (106-43 B.C.)  1,42; 295,299; 355,360

Cinus (Cynus, Cino) Sinibaldus of Pistoia (1270-1336)  105,107,108,110,111;
    287; App.I(c)

cities (as self-governing bodies)  21,29,31,35,39,41; 45,60,61,66; 72,87,
    94,95;102.107,111; 153,161-65; 189,200,201; 313,314,316,331; 336; 366
    see also burghs, Stadtrecht

citizenship (inc. suffrage)  415; 431; 439,440

civil law  64; 73,98; 116; 181,183,203; 208,231,235,237; 289,293,294; 329;
    381; 430  see also learned law

      civilian defined  65,66

civil service, professional  55,61,62,63

Civil Wars, English  239,247; 400

Clarendon, Assize of (1166)  223,224,226

Clement V, P. (1305-14) = Bertrand de Got  104; 133

Clementines (Clementinae) (1317)  133,135; 307  see also decretals

Clermont in Beauvaisis see Beauvaisis

Clermont [Ferrand]  344

Clovis, K of Franks (baptized 496, d.511)  11,14,23

Cnut  see Canute

Coal Mines Act 1842 (Mines and Collieries Act, c. 99)  450

Cocceji, Samuel von (1679-1755)  421; 476

Code (of Justinian, cited as C.)  4,5,13,33,40,41; 72,80,82,89,96; 132;
    191; 285,292

    (C. 1,1,1  112; App.II(b); App.IV.
        3,1,8  App.I(h)

commenda  174; 448

commenta  88,90; 110; App.I(e); App.II(b)

Commentators  85,95; IV passim; 182,188,200; 295; 318,328; 336,342; 360; 471

commercial law  120; 154; 244; 423,426,434,436; 458-62; 464,471,476,480
  see also codes, commercial; Law Merchant; trade

commissaries  144

commissary courts (in Scotland)  204; 304,305; 393

Common Law of England  207; 208 and VIII passim, esp. 235-42; 371,372,374,
  375; 384,388,390; 445,448; 480

common pleas  see pleas, common

Common Pleas, Court of (also Common Bench)  118; 224,232,233,235,240,251

Commons, House of (in British Parliament)  442

communis opinio  115,118; 184,187; 235

Communist Manifesto (1848)  440

Como  116

compagnia  173,174; 444

company law  172; 444-47; 470
        Companies Acts 1844  (Joint Stock Companies Acts, c. 110  England
    and Wales, c. 111  Scotland)  446
        Companies Act 1862 (c. 89)  447
        Companies Clauses Consolidation Acts 1845  (c.16  England and
    Wales, c. 17  Scotland)  447
            see also joint stock companies; limited liability;
            partnership

compilationes antiquae  131,132

compurgation  21; 47; 149; 170; 215,218,225,232,253,255; 259

Comte, Auguste (1798-1857)  407

Conciliar Movement  136; 357

Concordia discordantium canonum  see Decretum, Gratian's

Conrad II, HRE (1024-39)  35; 53,64; 318

Conring, Herman (1606-81)  329

Conseil à un ami  192

Conseil d'État  481

Conseil de Justice  350

consideration  255,256

consilia  88,89,94; 107,113,114,115,118; 136; 184,185; 290,292; 326,327

consistory courts  301,302

Consolato del Mar (Consulate of the Sea)  158,159,160,161; 200

Conspiracy and Protection of Property Act 1875 (c. 86)  456

Constance, Council of (1413-17)  136

       Peace of (1183)  66; 158,162; 184

Constantine, Roman E (306-37)  6,7,31

       Donation of  31; 124,126

Constantinople  3,7,41; 157; 285

       General Council of (381)  8

constitutio Antoniniana (212)  5,6

constitutum possessorium  87

Consuetudines feudales  see Libri Feudorum

consuls  158; 183,184

Consultatio veteris cuiusdam iurisconsulti  292

contracts, iuris gentium  155,177

      law of  176,177; 252; 337; 379; 479-80  see also insurance;
  negotiable instruments

contraria  78,81,82

Convention of Royal Burghs  269

copyhold  248

copyright  479,489

Coquille, Guy de (1523-1603)  340,342,348,349; 368,374; 385; 428

Cordoba  199

Corpus Iuris Canonici  133; 248; 307

Corpus Iuris Civilis  3-5,40,41,42; 64,66; 72,73,75,76,85,86; 100,107; 132;
  200; 328,329; 342; 360; 433; 468; 498  see also Roman law,
  institutions of
  subject of Glossators, Commentators, Humanists, whom also see

cortes  201

Council, King's (English)  168; 233,234,242,243,247,251,252; 400

        (Scottish)  262,276,277,278; 390

    Lords of (Scottish)  203; 277,278; 396

    Privy (Scottish)  278; 304; 398,399,400

Councils, General of the Church  8  and see Chalcedon, Constance,
  Constantinople, Ephesus, Lateran I, Lateran II, Lateran III, Lateran
  IV, Lyon I, Lyon II, Nicaea, Trent, Vienne
      provincial  9,14,15

count (= Frankish royal officer)  56

count (= pleading)  237,238,240

Counter-Reformation  see Reformation, Catholic

court  see modifying term; e.g. Court of Session  see Session

    Court of Session Act 1693 (c.42)  392

Covarruvias, Diego (1512-77)  357,360

covenant  229,252

Cowell, John (1554-1611)  372

Craig, Sir Thomas (1538-1608)  70; 308; 377,386,387

Cremona  90

criminal law  101,110,120; 195; 249; 290; 330,331,341,351; 356; 396,397,398;
    408-13,415,418,423; 464,465,476,477

        Criminal Law Amendment Act 1871 (c. 32)  456

Crusades  138; 157

Cujas (Cuiacius), Jacques (1522-90)  291-93,295,297,299; 343; 429

curia [= court] papal  30,41; 95; 135,143

         regis (in England)  218,224,225,228,231-35,250

Curran v Treleaven ([1891] 2 QB 545)  456

custom as law  6,20; 45,46,47,58,66,67,68,69,70; 104,115,116; 124; 153,176,
        177; 179,180,187,191,192,200; 208,210,221; 258-60,271; 293;
        312,313,315,322,328,332; 335-38,340,341,342,343; 368,378,
        382; 415,416; 434; 476,489

    collected and codified  192,197; 312,331; 338-41,342,349; 367; 489

Czechoslovakia  428; 490


Daguesseau, Henri François (1668-1751)  351; 428,429

Dalrymple, James  see Stair, Lord

Damme  160

Danelaw  28; 210,211,212,213,221

Dante  111; 126

darrein presentment  227  see also assizes, petty

Dauphiné  194; 346

David I, K. of Scotland (1124-53)  260,263

Dean of Guild Court  163; 205

deans of Christianity/rural deans  144  see also diocesan organization

death penalty  216,217; 409,411,412,413  see also criminal law

debt, action of  229,233,252,253,255

Decio, Philip (1454-1536)  118; 188; 288

Declaration of the Rights of Man  413,431,434;  App. V

échevins 56; 214 see also scabini, Schöffen

Ecloga 40

Edgar of Wessex and England (959-75) 211,212,213

Edinburgh 205; 277,278; 304,305; 388,394,397,404,405

Edmund of Wessex and England (939-46) 213

education 30,31,42 see also universities; trivium and quadrivium

       Education (Scotland) Act 1872 (c. 62) 451

       Elementary Education Acts 1876; 1902 (c. 79; c. 42) 451

       legal 13; 74,77-9,80,96-9; 107-09; 116; 235,237,239; 295,299;
          329,330,333; 341; 365,375; 380,381,400-05; 432

Edward I, K of England (1272-1307) 104; 237; 274

Edward, the Confessor, of Wessex and England (1042-66) 212,217,220,226

Edward, the Elder, of Wessex and England (899-925) 213

Egypt 437

Eichhorn, Karl Friedrich (1786-1854) 469

Eike von Repgow (c.1180-1233) 67; 314

electors of the Holy Roman Empire 311,312

Elegant Jurisprudence 287,295; 354,366-71 see also Humanists

embassies 183; 370,373

emendatores statutorum 185

Empire see Austrian; Byzantine; German; Holy Roman; Ottoman; Roman

employment law 449-52

       Employers and Workmen Act 1875 (c. 90) 451

England 17,28,38; 46,63,66; 97; 104; 123,139; 154,159,164,168;
   202,206,207; VIII passim; 274; 282,284,306; 314,318,323; 345; 370;
   378, 378,379,384,389,393; 409,412,415,416; 458; 472

   English jurisprudence 354,371-75 see also Common Law

      language 243 see also Anglo-Saxon

Enlightenment, The 357,361,365; 406-13,418,422,426; 464

enquête par turbe (= turba) 195

Enquêtes, Chambre des see Parlement of Paris

Ephesus, General Council of (431) 8

episcopacy 303,305

Epitome Juliani see Novels of Justinian

Epitome of St.Gall 12

equity, in English law 245

      opposed to strict law 94

Erasmus, Desiderius (1466-1536)  282,285,289; 359

Erskine, John (1695-1768)  388,405; 448

Ervig, K of the Visigoths (680-87)  18; 198

escheats  see feudal obligations

Esmein, A. (1848-1913)  485

Estates-General (États-Généraux of France) 337,338,343,350

Estilo, Leyes del  200

Ethelbert of Kent (560-616)  210

Ethelred, the Unready, of Wessex and England (978-1016)  212,214

Euric, Code of  11,12,18

examinations  98; 402,403

Exarchate  see Ravenna

Exceptiones legum romanarum Petri  191

Exchequer, and Court of the (English)  220,228,231,232,235,251

(Scottish)  393

excommunication  146,147; 305    see also penances

expansion of Europe overseas  175; 280,281; 353

Expositio ad librum papiensem  40  and see Liber papiensis

Extra, Liber Extra (1234)  132,133,134,135,136; 307    see also decretals

Extravagantes communes  133; 307

Extravagantes of John XXII  133; 307

eyres (= ayres)  219,221,223,224,225,228,230,231,232,233


Faber, A.  see Favre

Factory Acts 415;  1833 (Labour of Children etc. in Factories Act, c.103); 1844 (Factories Act, c. 15); 1874 (c. 44)  450

Faculty of Advocates  see advocates

Faculty of Procurators in Glasgow  402,405

faenus nauticum  155,156,161

fairs and their courts  164,165-71

'families' of town law  189; 314,317

Farinacius, Prosper (1554-1616)  408

Fathers of the Church  8; 360

Favre (Faber), Antoine (1557-1624)  370

fealty  46,48-50  and see feudal obligations

Ferdinand of Aragon (1479-1516) & Isabella of Castile (d.1504)  201; 281

Ferdinand III of Castile-León (1217/30-52)  199

Ferrara  112; 291

Ferrier, Arnaud (1508-85)  291

feu  see feudal institutions

feu-ferme  262,268

feudal courts and procedure  46,47,48,4953,54,55,56,57,58,63,64,65;  148;
     183,184,186,194,197,204;  209,218,221,230,250;262,267,268,269,271;
     316,329;  342;  397,398,399,400
          feudists  61,65,66
          institutions46,47,48,50,51,52,53,54,55,57,62; 217-19; 260,261,265;
     340; 368; 414,431
          law  II passim;  89,95;  101,110,115,120;  140,148;  153,166;  198;
     209,254;  289,290,292,308;  316,329;  340;  377,378,386
          literature  39; 64-70
          obligations  46,48-50,51,52,53,54,57,63; 198; 222

feudalism defined  44,58-61
          formalized  61-4
          origins  22,32,33,34,37;  44,45;  210,211
          see also De Feudis; Ius Feudale; Libri Feudorum

fief  see feudal institutions

Fieschi (Fliscus), Sinibald de  see Innocent IV, P.

fines  216; 409

Finland  440

Flanders  62; 160,169  see also Belgium, Low Countries

Fleury, Claude (1640-1723)  344; 428,429

Florence  136; 162,163,164,167,172,173

Florentine MS of the Digest  72; 288,289,292,297

Forbes, William (d.1745)  389,392,404

formularies  89,94

Fortescue, Sir John (c.1394-c.1476)  371

Forum Iudicum (= Fuero Juzgo) (681)  18,32; 198

Four Burghs  269  i.e. (Berwick) Edinburgh, Lanark, Linlithgow, (Roxburgh)
     Stirling

Four Doctors, the  ( Bulgarus, Hugh, James, Martin)  80,92,94,96

France  17,18,24,27,28,32;  56,63,68;  95;  106; 130,135,139;  153,158,159,
     164,171,176; 180,187,190-98; 222,251; 280,281,282,283,284,286,288-94;
     299; 312,314,316,318; XII passim; 353,358,366,367; 380,381,382,390;
     410,413,414,415,416,428-37; 440,448,452,454,461; 463,466,480-87,489

God, Peace of and Truce of  35; 137

Godefroy   see Gothofredus

Goffredus  see Geoffrey

Golden Bull of 1356   311

good faith  see *bona fides*

Gosians  93,97  and see Martin Gosia

Gothofredus (Godefroy), Dionysius (Denis) (1549-1622)  297

                  Jacobus (Jacques) (1587-1652)  297

Göttingen  467

Grainville, C.J. de Lespine de (d.1754)  347

*Grand Coutumier*  335   see also Normandy

Gratian (fl.1140)  86,91,94; 122,126,127,129,133,150; 230

Greece  285; 480

    Greek language  6,7; 285,292

*Greenshield's Case* (1710-11 Rob.12)  395

Gregory I, the Great, P. (590-64)  15-17; 132; 210

Gregory VII (Hildebrand) P. (1073-85) 36,37,38; 127

Gregory IX, P. (1227-41)  103; 127,132,134; 307

Gregory XIII, P. (1572-85) 307

Grenoble (in Dauphiné), *parlement* of  118; 194; 335,346

Gretna Green  309

Groningen  367

Grotius (de Groot), Hugo (1583-1645)  183; 354,356,357-61,363,364,365,368,
    369,372,373,374; 382; 407,430,432

Gui-Pape (d.1477)  346; 382

Guido  see Guy

Guild, Court of Dean of  see Dean of Guild Court

guilds  153,158,161-65,168; 470  see also *collegia*

Guillaume (Guillelmus) de Cunh (Cugno, Cuneo, Cuniho)  (d.1336)  103,106

Guillelmus Durantis (Durandus) (1237-96)  see Speculator

Gundobad of the Burgundians, *Code* of  12,17,18,23,27,29

Guy (Guido) of Como (de Cunis) (d.c.1265)  103,104

Guy (Guido) de Suzaria (Suzzara) (d.1293)  101,102

Guyana  368


*Habita, authentica*  96

Habsburg dynasty  364; 425,426

Haddington, Lord (Thomas Hamilton, 1563-1637)   392

Hadrian (Adrian) I, P. (727-95)   25

Hadrian IV, P. (1154-59)   181

_Hadriana_   26; 124

Hague, The   367

        Conference of 1910/12   461

Hale, Sir Matthew (1609-76)   372

Halle   420

hall-moot   214   see also manor

Haloander, Gregor (1501-31)   297

Hamburg   161,167

Hanseatic League   161,167;   314

harmonization of laws   458-62; 489

Heidelberg   189,190; 293,294; 333; 363,366; 468

Heineccius, J.G. (1681-1741)   370; 432

Henry III, HRE (1039-56)   35,40; 124

Henry IV, HRE (1056-1106)   36,37,38

Henry V, HRE (1106-25)   38

Henry I, K of England (1100-35)   220,221,222   and see _Leges Henrici Primi_

Henry II, K of England (1154-89)   222-31; 349

Henry III, K of England (1216-72)   229,231

Henry VIII, K of England (1509-47)   207; 372

Henry III, K of France (1574-89)   350

Henry IV , K of France (1589-1610)   284,307

Henry the Fowler, D of Saxony (919-36)   34

Henry the Lion, D of Saxony & of Bavaria (1142/56-80)   167

Henry de Bracton (d.1268)   see Bracton

Henry of Susa (de Segusio) (1200-71)   see Hostiensis

Henryson, Edward (1510-90)   381

Heritable Jurisdictions (Scotland) Act 1746 (c. 43)   398,399

High Commission, Court of   248; 306

Highlands, Scottish   259,260,264

Hildebrand   see Pope Gregory VII

_Hispana_   15,26

Hispanus   see Laurentius

Historical School   439; 465-71,472,474,483,484

historicism   285,286,288,290,292,293,297,298; 339; 466

Hobbes, Thomas (1588-1679)   361,362,363,364,373,374

indebitatus assumpsit  256

India  480

Indians  see Amerindians or India

Indies  see  East, West Indies

Indo-China  437

Industrial Revolution  389; 406; 438,441,443,444,449,458

injunctions  243

Inleidinge tot de Hollandsche Rechtsgeleerdheid  358,368

Innocent III, P. (1198-1216)  127,130,131

Innocent IV (Sinibald de Fieschi), P. (1243-54)  98; 127,134,135,139,140,
    141

Inns of Chancery  239
    of Court  235,239

inquest  269,270

Institutes (or Institutions) of Justinian (cited as Inst.)  4,5,13,40,41;
    67; 72,80,85; 230; 272; 288,292,293,296; 369,372; 385; 413,419,425,
    429,433,434,435
    (Inst. 2,1,12    93
        4.6.13     App. II(a) )

Institutes coutumières  343

Institution au droit français  343

'institutional writers' in Scotland  384,385-90

Institutions of the Law of Scotland  386,387

instruments, negotiable  153,172; 459,460,461,462

insurance  161,175,176; 479,489

international private law  110,112,113,120

interpolations  292,297,298

introductiones titulorum  80,81,88,90

Investiture Contest  36-39; 125

Ireland  208,210

Irnerius (Guarnerius) (c.1055-1130)  71,72,74,75,80,82,96; 127; 191; 287;
    319; App. I(a)(c)

Isabella, Q of Castile (1474-1504)  201; 281  see also Ferdinand

Islam  23; 198  and see Moslems

Italy  3,5,14,16,17,19,21,27,29,35,40,41; 63; 86,88; 100; 153,155,156,158,
        159,176; 180,183-88; 280,281,286,291; 318,326,331,332; 336; 367;
        380; 413,436,437; 438,439,441,459,461; 463-65

Italian language  22; 157,158,160; 286

       national law  412,413; 463-65

ius  see also *jus*

ius albanagii  (aubaine)  171

ius commune  70; 107,110,116,117,118,120; 123,134,152; 177; VII *passim*;
    299; 318; 381,382,386,387,403

Jus Fetiale  373

ius gentium  155

ius proprium  179

Ivo of Chartres (d.1116)  37; 125,128


Jacques de Révigny  (de Ravanis, Raveniaco) (d.1296)  66; 103,104,105,106;
    139; App.II(a)

Jacobus = James, or Giacomo, Jacopo, Jacques

James I, K of Aragon (1213-76)  201

James I, K of Scotland (1406-37)  204; 276

James IV, K of Scotland (1488-1513)  278

James V, K of Scotland (1513-42)  278

James VI, K of Scotland (1567-1625)  398,404

James (of the Four Doctors) (d.1178)  80

James de Ardizzone (earlier 13c)  65

James de Arena (d. after 1296)  101,102,111

James Balduini (d.1235)  74,84,95,97,98; 103; 134

James de Belvisio (1270-1335)  66; 110

James Buttrigarius (d.1348)  111

Japan  480

Jason de Mayno (1435-1519)  113,118; 188; 288,289

Jean le Coq (late 14c)  346

Jean Masuer (d.1450)  337

Jean de Monchy (Monciaco) (later 13c)  104

Jerusalemm  138

jettison  see general average

Jhering (Ihering), Rudolph von (1818-92)  471,475,486

Jodocus (mid 15c)  319

Johann von Buch (fl.1325-35)  319

Johannes = John, or Giovanni, Jean, Johann

Johannes Andreae (1275-1348)  135,136; 200; 366

549

Romana Visigothorum  12,13,18,32,39; 191

Leyes del Estilo  200
    de Toro  201

Libellus disputatorius  94

Liber Extra  see Extra

Liber de iudicibus  271

Liber Iudiciorum = Forum Iudicum  18

Liber papiensis  39,40; 64

Liber Pauperum  97; 230

Liber Sextus  see Sext(us)

liberalism  439,440; 466

Libri Feudorum (Books of the Feus,  also Usus Feudorum or Consuetudines
    feudales)  65,66; 107,110

libri legales  66

Liechtenstein  428

Liège  167

limited liability  445,447,448
    Limited Liability Act 1855 (c. 133)  447

Lincoln, diocese of 141-48

Linlithgow  269

Littleton, Sir Thomas (1402-81)  371,374

Liutprand of the Lombards (712-44)  20,21,23

Livres de Jostice et Plet  192; 335

Lo Codi  97; 191

Loire, river  45,46

Lombarda (= lex Langobardica)  40; 64; 97; 116

Lombards and their law  14,16,17,18,19-23,24,25,29,40,41; 73; 102,116; 187

London  61; 163,168,176; 416

Lord President  see Session, Court of

Lords of Council and Session  118; 204; 277,278,279; 304; 390,391,396
    and see Session, Court of

Lords, House of (in British Parliament)  251,256; 384,393,395,396,397; 442

Lothar III, HRE (1125-37)  319,329

Lothar of Cremona (early 13c)  95

Lothian  204; 264

Louet, Georges (d.1608)  346

Louis IX, K of France (1226-70)  95; 191,193,195

Louis XI, K of France (1461–83) 345

Louis XIV, K of France (1643–1715) 344,350

Louis XV, K of France (1715–74) 352; 417,428

Louis XVI, K of France (1774–93) 417

Louisiana 375; 437

Louvain 194; 367

Low Countries 160; 204  and see Belgium, Burgundy, Flanders, Netherlands

Loysel (Loisel), Antoine (1536–1617) 340,343; 385; 428,429

Lübeck 161,167; 314

Lucas de Penna (c.1320–90) 102,116

Lucerne (Luzern) 487

Luther, Martin (1483–1546) 281,283,300,301

     Lutheranism 300,301

Lyon 166,167; 292

    General Council of I (1245) 132

                      II (1274) 132

Lyons & Sons v Wilkins ([1899] 1 Ch. 255) 456


McDouall, Andrew   see Bankton, Lord

Mackenzie, Sir George (1636–91) 387,388,389

Magdeburg 314

Magna Carta 232

Magyars 26,27,28,34

Maine, Sir Henry (1822–88) 416; 480

Mainz (Mayence) 167; 373

Maitland, F.W. (1850–1906) 256

Maitland, Sir Richard (1496–1586) 392

Malines (Mechelen) 366

mallus 56

Manchester 441

        Manchester Corporation v Manchester Palace of Varieties ([1955]
        P. 133) 246

manors, manorial courts 45,59; 214,218,248

Mansfield, Lord (William Muray, 1705–93) 256; 384; 458

Mantua 95,97; 102

Maria Theresa, HRE (1740–80) 425

maritime law 155,156–61; 352; 383,394; 458,459

Marine Insurance Act 1906 (c. 41)   459

market overt   176

marriage law   150; 259,260; 303,304,305,306,308,309; 379; 424,427,431; 464, 487

Martin (Martinus) Gosia (d.1160)   80,89,90,91,93,95

Marx, Karl (1818-83)   453

Mary, Q of Scotland (1542-67)   303

'master' as title   71   see also quadrivium

Masuer, Jean   see Jean

Matilda, countess of Tuscany (1069-1115)   38; 71,74; 319

Maximilian I, HRE (1508-19)   321

Max Joseph III, Elector of Bavaria (1745-77)   417,418

Mechelen   see Malines

Mecklenburg   416

medicine and public health   438,444,451

Mediterranean   17; 156; 280

mercantilism   349,354; 406

Mercia   211,221

Merlin, Philippe Antoine (1754-1838)   483

Merovingian Franks   14,16,17,23,33; 54,56; 166

Merton, Statute of (1236)   236

Messina   163

Middlesex, Bill of   233

Midi   29,32; 193,194,198; 335,339,340   see also pays de droit écrit

Milan   9; 65; 163; 187; 288,290; 412

Mill, John Stuart (1806-73)   407

Millar, John (1735-1801)   404,405; 407; 466

ministeriales   59

Modena   65; 97; 102; 135; 464,465

Molina y Morales, Luis de (late 16c)   356

Molinaeus   see Dumoulin

Mommsen, Theodor (1817-1903)   290,297; 471

monasticism   15,27,30; 143

Montalvo, Alfonso Diaz de, Ordenanzas of (also known as Ordenamiento Real, Ordenanzas Reales de Castile)   201

Montesquieu, Charles Louis, Baron de (1689-1755)   344; 410,421,422,432; 466,468

Montholon, Jacques de (1560-1622) 347

Montils les Tours, Ordinances of (1454) 193; 349

Montpellier 42; 95,97; 191

Morocco 437

mortancestor (in England mort d'ancestor) 226,227; 266,270 see also
    assizes, petty

mos gallicus 280,288,291 see also Elegant Jurisprudence; Humanism
    italicus 188; 280,291,294; 329,333; 469 see also Bartolism

Moslems 19,26,27,28,35; 156,157; 198; 281

'motions in banc' 250

Moulins, Ordinance of (1566) 345,349,350

Munich (München) 167

mutilation (as criminal penalty) 216,217; 409,412,418

Mynsinger see Frundeck


Nantes 167

    Edict of (1598) 284

Naples 22; 64,66; 98; 102,110,116; 156,163; 187 and see Sicilies, Kingdom
    of the Two

Napoleon Bonaparte (1769-1821) 413,417,432,433,436,437; 438; 463,464,482,
    484

Napoleon III, E of France (1852-70) 454

Napoleonic Wars 381; 438; 467

National Health Insurance Act 1911 (c. 55) 451

nationalism 280,286,299; 358; 438,439; 466,475 and see French, German,
    Italian, Scots Law

Natura Brevium 239

Natural Law and Lawyers 122,141; 182; 256; 296,299; 344; 354-66,368,371,
    372,373; 384,386,387; 406,407,409,413,414,415,416,418,419,420,422,424,
    425,426,427,429,430,433,434; 465,466,469,472,474,486,487,489

nautae caupones stabularii 156

Navarre 201

negotiable instruments 153,172; 459,460,461,462

Netherlands 160,176; 280,283,284; 353,358,366-70,371,373; 380,381; 416,
    436,437; 439,461 and see also Burgundy; Holland

Neustria 23

Nevers 343


554

New World   see Americas, Spanish etc.;   United States of America

Newcastle  269

Nicaea, General Council of (325)  7,8

Nicholas (Nicolaus) Tedeschi (Tudeschi, Tudisco; abbas Siculus) (1389-1445)
     see Panormitanus

Niebuhr, B.G.  (1776-1831)  470

nisi prius  225,227,250

nobile officium  400

noblesse de robe  345

Noodt, Gerhard (1647-1725)  369; 382

Normandy  27,28; 49,52,53; 160; 194; 222; 335

Normans in England  46; 209,217-22

          in Normandy   see Normandy

          in Scotland   see Anglo-Normans

          in Sicily and Calabria  28,41; 157

Norsemen   see Vikings; see also Danelaw; Normans

North German Confederation   see German Confederation, North

Northampton, Assize of (1176)  226

Norway 416; 440

notabilia  78,83,89,93; 134

notaries  22,32,41; 89; 148; 163,177; 182; 349; 378,402,403,404; App.IV

Novae Narrationes  237,239

novel disseisin  151; 227   see also assizes, petty

Novels of Justinian  4,13,40,41; 65,66; 80,82; 285,292; 318
     (Nov.105    118 )

          of Holy Roman Emperors    82

Nuremburg (Nürnburg)  167; 300; 331


oaths, oath-helpers   see compurgation

Oberhof (pl. Oberhöfe)  316,317,324

Obertus de Orto (mid 12c)  64,65

Odofredus (d.1265)  78,84,97,98; 101

official (e.g., bishop's official)  104; 144; 202,203,204; 304

Old Sarum  441

Old Tenures  239

Oléron, Rôles de  160

Olivier, J. de D. (1753-1823)  432,433

opinions    see consilia

oppositiones  109

ordeal, trial by  18,21; 47,62; 193; 215,218,225,226

Ordenamiento of Alcalá  200

Ordenanzas of Montalvo  201   and see Montalvo

Ordinacions de Cort  201

Ordinances (French ) of 1258   195

       Blois  338,349

       Montils les Tours  349

       Moulins  345,349,350

       Villers-Cotterêts  349,350

       1667 on civil procedure  350,351

       1670 on criminal law and procedure  351

       1673 (Code Marchand)  352

       1681 (Ordonnance de la Marine)  352; 436

ordo maris  158

Ordonnances, French royal  429   and see legislation; Ordinances

Orléans   31; 102,103,104,105; 133; 192; 282,289,294;  335,338,342,349;
  357; 380,382; 429,434

Orthodox Church  24; 122

Osborne v Amalgamated Society of Railway Servants ([1910] A.C. 87)   457

Ostrogoths  3,10,16,19

Otto I, the Great, HRE (962-73)  28,34,35; 64; 184; 318

Otto III, HRE (983-1002)  318

Ottoman Empire  281

outlawry  216; 409

Overijssel  367

Oxford  97; 146; 183; 207; 230,237,248; 372,373,374

over et terminer  225


Padua  66; 97; 101,102,111,112,118; 133,136; 342

paleae  129

Palermo  163

Pandectists  365; 416,427; 472-76,478,479,480,484,485,487,488

  Pandektenrecht  474

Panormitanus (Nicholas Tedeschi, 1389-1445)  136

Papacy  8,9,10,16,17,20,22,24,27,28,30,31,35,36-39,41; 122,125,126,127,129,

142,143; 164; 291,300,303,307; 311

see also curia, papal

Papal States   114; 464

Pape, Guy   see Gui-Pape

papiensis = of Pavia,   see Bernard; Liber

Papon, Jean (1505-90)   346

Paris   97; 103,104; 134; 163,167; 292,293,294; 335,338,342,343,348,351; 380,382; 429,433

   Custom of  335,338,342,351

   Parlement of 167;  193,194,195,196,197;  225,234;  291;  323,325;  335,341, 342,343,344,345,346,347,348,350,351;  392

parlements  118;  193,194,197,198;  325;  335,336,337,344-49,350;  382;  429,431

   see Paris and also Bordeaux, Dijon, Grenoble, Rouen, Toulouse; see
   also  arrêts de règlement

Parliament, British  384,394   see Commons, House of; Lords, House of

            English  234,251

            Scottish  263,272,275,276,277,278;  379,380,383,393,394,395

       Parliament Act 1911 (c. 13)   442

Parma  97; 136; 464,465

Partidas, Las Siete  199,200,201

partnership, law of  172; 445   see also commenda; compagnia

       Partnership Act 1890 (c. 39)   445

Pascal, Blaise (1623-62)  344

Paschal II, P. (1099-1118)  38

Passagieri, Rolandino   see Rolandino

Patriarchates  (Alexandria, Antioch, Constantinople, Jerusalem, Rome)  9

Paucapalea (mid 12c)  129

Paul III, P. (1534-49)  283

Paul (Roman jurist, fl.200) and Pauli Sententiae  6,11; 292

Paul the Deacon (d.c.797)  31

Pavia  21,22,25,34,39,40,42; 64,65; 73,96; 113,118; 161; 183; 288,291

pays de droit coutumier, pays de coutumes  45,46,67;  192;  335,338-40,342, 350; 377

   de droit écrit  46; 106; 190; 335,339,342,346,350  see also Midi

Peace of God  35; 137 and see Truce

peace, the king's  153,166; 211,213,216,221,254  see also kingship

peine forte et dure  see torture

Peñaforte, Raymond de   see Raymond

penances and ecclesiastical penalties   146,147,148

Penitentials   16,26; 124

Pepo (fl.1076)   72

Perugia   40; 66; 110,111,113; 183

Peruzzi   173

Peter IV, K of Aragon (1336-87)   201

Peter Abelard (d.1142)   91,94,96; 125

Peter de Benevento (early 13c)   131

Peter Damian (1007-72) 39

Peter Lombard (1110-60)   127

Petrarch (1304-74)   111; 287

Petrus (=Peter) Jacobus (early 14c)   182

Philip II, Augustus, K of France (1180-1233)   164; 193,195

Philip IV, the Fair, K of France (1285-1314)   191,193

Philip VI, of Valois, K of France (1328-50)   194

Philip II, K of Spain (1556-98)   201; 284; 367

Philip Decio (1454-1536)   118; 188; 288

Philippe de Beaumanoir (c.1250-96)   see Beaumanoir

philology   285,287,288,289,292,298

Piacenza   97

piepowder courts   166   and see fairs and fair courts

Piedmont   464,465

Pierre d'Auxonne (fl.1250-70)   104

Pierre de Belleperche (Petrus de Bellapertica) (d.1308)   103,105,107,111;
    App.II(b)

Pierre de Fontaine  (fl.1250s)   192

Pillius de Medicina (d.1210)   65; 74,90,94,95,97

Pippin II (of Heristal) of the Franks (Mayor 680-714)   23

Pippin III, the Short, of the Franks (Mayor 741-51, K 751-68)   22,24; 45
        Donation of 24,25

piracy   182

Pisa   28; 111,116,118; 157,158,162

Pistoia   41; 102

Placentinus (d.1192)   65; 74,95,97

Placita Coronae   237

Plato (429-347 B.C.)   354

'red robes', decrees in  347

Soto, Domingo de (1494-1560)  356,357,360

South Africa 208; 368,369

Spain  11,14,15,17,18,19,32; 123; 158; 180,198-202; 281,284; 353; 416,437;
459

Spanish language  199

Speculator (William Durantis) (1237-96)  101,114; 135,139; 182; 319

Speculum Abbreviatum  319

Spiegel der deutschen Leute = Deutschenspiegel  315

Spottiswoode, Sir Robert (1596-1646)  382,385

Stadtrecht  29; 313,316

Stair, Lord (James Dalrymple, 1619-95)  296,308; 360,374; 378,385,386,387,
388,392; 407,430

staple courts  168

Star Chamber  247

'statut personnel'  336

'statute theory'  116,117,118;  186

statutes   parliamentary legislation   see under title of Act
specifically of the Italian cities  115,116; 202

Stephen III, P. (752-57)  24

Stephen of Tournai (Tornacensis) (d.1203)  130,137,138

Stephen, Sir James Fitzjames (1829-94)  480

Stirling  269

Stoicism  355,360

Story, Joseph (1779-1845)  448

Strasbourg  293

Stryk, Samuel (1640-1710)  328; 385

studium generale  98

style books  41,89

Suarez, Francisco (1548-1617)  357

Suarez = Schwarz, Carl Gottlieb (1746-98)  421,422

subinfeudation  see feudal institutions

subpoena  244

suffrage  415; 439,440,441,442  see also citizenship

suit of court  48,49,57     and see feudal courts and procedure

Summa Codicis of Azo  75

Summa de legibus  49

summae  88,89,90,97; 130,134

trade unions  450,453-57
        Trade Union Act 1871 (c. 31)  456    Trade Union Act 1913 (c. 30)  457
        Trades Disputes Act 1906 (c. 47)    457    Trades Disputes and Trade
        Unions Act 1927 (c. 22)  457
Trani  156,157
transport  156; 406; 438,443  see also railways
Trent, Council of (1545-63)  122,135; 283,308
Très Ancienne Coutume  335,336  see also Brittany
trespass  229,232,233,241,253,254,256
trial  see battle; compurgation; ordeal;  see also jury; procedure
tribunaux consulaires  348
trivium  42; 75
trover  253
Troyes  167 (Grands Jours of); 382
Truce of God  35; 137  and see Peace
Tübingen  189; 320
Tunisia  437
turba  195; 336,337,351  see also enquête par turbe
Turin  292
Turks, Turkey  157; 281; 437; 489
Tuscany  412  see also Leopold; Matilda


Ugo = Hugh
Ulpian (d.223) and his Regulae  2,6; 291
Ultramontani  100,103-07,111; 200
Union, Act of, 1707 (10 Anne, c.7 & c. 11)  and Treaty of  202; 384,394,395
United States of America  375; 407,416,417; 439,461; 472,480
universities  42; 68,69,70; 103,104; 163; 181,186,189; 202,203; 235; 307;
        320,326-30;
        See also Aberdeen, Altdorf, Amsterdam, Angers, Avignon, Basel, Berlin,
        Berne, Bologna, Bourges, Cahors, Cambridge, Cologne, Dijon, Dôle,
        Edinburgh, Ferrara, Florence, Franeker, Freiburg, Glasgow, Göttingen,
        Groningen, Halle, Heidelberg, Leiden, London (U.C.L.), Louvain, Lyon,
        Mantua, Milan, Modena, Montpellier, Naples, Orléans, Oxford, Padua,
        Paris, Parma, Pavia, Perugia, Piacenza, Pisa, Pistoia, Poitiers,
        Prague, Reggio, Rome, St. Andrews, Salamanca, Salerno, Siena,
        Strasbourg, Toulouse, Tübingen, Turin, Utrecht, Valence, Vercelli,

Vicenza, Vienna

Visigoths 10,11,12,14,17,18,19,32; 198; 318 see also Spain

Vitoria, Francisco de (c.1483-1546) 356,357,360

Vocabulary (Vocabularium) of Jodocus 319

Voet, Johannes (1647-1713) 369; 382

Volksgeist 85; 468,469,471,472

Voltaire, François Arouet de (1694-1778) 410

von see principal element


Walcausus (fl.993) 40

Waldon v Marshall (1369) 254

Wales 208,210

wapentake 213,214

war 'just' 49 footnote ; 137-41

    laws of 183; 360,370

    private 47,61

Wars of Independence (Dutch) 284; 367

               (Scottish) 202; 274

    of Religion (French) 284,292; 345; 366

Waterrecht 161

Weistum (pl. Weistümer) 315,316

Welwood, William (d.1622) 205; 373; 383; 448

wergild 20; 215

Wessex 210,211,221

West Indies 368

Westminster 231,233,239,240

       Statute of Westminster II (1285) 229,252

Westphalia, Treaty of (1648) 353

William I, the Conqueror, K of England (1066-87) 212,217,219

William (Guillelmus) Durantis = Speculator (1237-96) 101,114; 135,139;

    182; 319

William of Longchamps (d.1197) 135

William Raleigh (d.1250) 123; 236

Wills' Trs. v Cairngorm Canoeing and Sailing School Ltd. (1976 S.C.(H.L.)

    30) 396

Windscheid, Bernhard (1817-92) 474,477,478

Windsor, Assize of of (1179) 227

Wisby 161 see also Waterrecht